The
SHADOW
LAND

Center Point
Large Print

This Large Print Book carries the Seal of Approval of N.A.V.H.

The
SHADOW
LAND

Elizabeth
Kostova

CENTER POINT LARGE PRINT
THORNDIKE, MAINE

This Center Point Large Print edition is published
in the year 2017 by arrangement with Ballantine Books,
an imprint of Random House,
a division of Penguin Random House LLC.

Epigraph from *Antigone* translated by Robert Fagles (1982)

The text of this Large Print edition is unabridged.
In other aspects, this book may vary
from the original edition.
Printed in the United States of America
on permanent paper.
Set in 16-point Times New Roman type.

ISBN: 978-1-68324-397-7

Library of Congress Cataloging-in-Publication Data

Names: Kostova, Elizabeth, author.
Title: The shadow land / Elizabeth Kostova.
Description: Center Point Large Print edition. | Thorndike, Maine :
Center Point Large Print, 2017.
Identifiers: LCCN 2017008765 | ISBN 9781683243977
    (hardcover : alk. paper)
Subjects: LCSH: Americans—Bulgaria—Fiction. | Large type books. |
BISAC: FICTION / Literary. | FICTION / Suspense. | FICTION /
Psychological. | GSAFD: Suspense fiction. | Mystery fiction.
Classification: LCC PS3611.O74927 S53 2017b | DDC 813/.6—dc23
LC record available at https://lccn.loc.gov/2017008765

за Георги
ноември 1989
с обич

for Georgi
November 1989
with love

Do as you like,
whatever suits you best—
I will bury him myself.

—SOPHOCLES, *Antigone*

This book is a train with many cars, the old kind, moving clumsily along a track at night. One car contains a small supply of coal, which spills out into the passageway when an internal door is opened. You have to step over piles of slippery black grit to get through the corridor. Another car contains grain, shipped for export. One car is full of musicians and instruments and cheap overnight bags, nearly half an orchestra sitting according to their friendships and rivalries in the seats of the second-class compartments. Another car contains bad dreams. The final train car has no seats but instead is full of sleeping men, who lie crushed together on their coats in the dark.

The door to that one has been nailed shut from the outside.

BOOK
I

One

Sofia, the year 2008. The month of May, impeccable spring weather, and the goddess Capitalism sitting on her long-since-tawdry throne. On the top step outside Hotel Forest hovered a young woman, more a girl than a woman, and more a foreigner—which she also was—than anything else. The hotel looked out over NDK, the former communist regime's palace of culture, a giant concrete blossom now patrolled by teenagers; sunlight falling across the plaza glinted off their spiky heads. Alexandra Boyd, exhausted from an endless plane ride, stood watching the Bulgarian kids on their skateboards and trying to tuck her long straight hair behind one ear. To her right rose apartment buildings of ochre and gray stucco, as well as more recent glass-and-steel construction and a billboard that showed a woman in a bikini whose breasts surged out toward a bottle of vodka. Stately trees bloomed near the billboard, white and magenta—horse chestnuts, which Alexandra had seen during a trip to France in college, her only other time on the European continent. Her eyes were gritty, her scalp grimed with the sweat of travel. She needed to eat, shower, sleep—yes, sleep, after the final flight from Amsterdam, that jerking awake every few minutes into self-exile across an ocean. She glanced down at her feet to make sure they were still there. Except for a pair of bright red sneakers, her clothes were simple—thin blouse, blue jeans, a sweater tied around her waist —so that she felt dowdy next to the tailored skirts and stilettos that made their way past her. On her left wrist, she wore a wide black bracelet; in her ears, spears of obsidian. She gripped the handles of a rolling suitcase and a dark satchel containing a guidebook, a dictionary, extra clothes. Over her shoulder she carried a computer bag and her loose multicolored purse with a notebook and a paperback of Emily Dickinson at the very bottom.

From her plane window, Alexandra had seen a city cradled in mountains and flanked by towering apartment buildings like tombstones. Stepping off the plane with her new camera in her hand, she'd breathed unfamiliar air—coal and diesel and then a gust that smelled of plowed earth. She had walked across the tarmac and onto the airport bus, observed shiny new customs booths and their taciturn officials, the exotic stamp in her passport. Her taxi had looped around the edges of Sofia and into the heart of the city—a longer route than necessary, she now suspected—brushing past outdoor café tables and lampposts that bore political placards or signs for sex shops. From the taxi window, she'd photographed ancient Fords and Opels, new Audis with tinted gangster windows, large slow buses, and trolleys like clanking Megalosauruses that threw sparks from their iron rails. To her amazement, she'd seen that the center of the city was paved with yellow cobblestones.

But the driver had somehow misunderstood her request and dropped her here, at Hotel Forest, not at the hostel she'd booked weeks earlier. Alexandra hadn't understood the situation, either, until he was gone and she had mounted the steps of the hotel to get a closer look. Now she was alone, more thoroughly than she had ever been in her twenty-six years. In the middle of the city, in the middle of a history about which she had no real idea, among people who went purposefully up and down the steps of the hotel, she stood wondering whether to descend and try to get another taxi. She doubted she could afford the glass and cement monolith that loomed at her back, with its tinted windows, its crow-like clients in dark suits hustling in and out or smoking on the steps. One thing seemed certain: she was in the wrong place.

Alexandra might have stood this way long minutes more, but suddenly the doors slid open just behind her and she turned to see three people coming out of the hotel. One of them was a white-haired man in a wheelchair clutching several travel bags against his suit jacket. A tall middle-aged man held onto the chair with one hand and a cell phone with the other; he was speaking with someone. Beside him stood their companion, an old woman with one hand on the tall man's elbow and a purse dangling from her wrist, bowlegged beneath her black dress. Her hair was auburn, with streaks of gray that radiated from a painfully bare parting. The middle-aged man finished his call and hung up. The old lady looked up at him and he bent over to tell her something.

Alexandra moved aside and watched them struggle across the hotel landing to the top of the steps and felt, as she often did, a stab of compassion for other people's fates. There was no way for them to descend, no ramp or wheelchair access, as there would have been at home. But the dark-haired tall man appeared to be magically strong; he bent and lifted the older man out of the chair, taking his luggage along. And the woman seemed to come alive inside her empty gaze, long enough to fold the chair with a few practiced motions and carry it slowly down the steps—she, too, was stronger than she looked.

Alexandra picked up her own satchels and suitcase and followed them, feeling that their sense of purpose might propel her forward. At the bottom of the steps, the tall man put the old man back into the wheelchair. They all rested a moment, Alexandra standing almost next to them

16

at the edge of the taxi lane. She saw that the tall man was dressed in a black vest and an immaculate white shirt, too warm and formal for the day. His trousers were also too shiny, his black shoes too highly polished. His thick dark hair, with its sheen of silver, was brushed firmly back from his forehead. A strong profile. Up close he looked younger than she'd first thought him. He was frowning, his face flushed, glance sharp. It was hard for her to tell whether he was nearer to thirty-eight or fifty-five. She realized through her fatigue that he might be one of the handsomest men she'd ever observed, broad-shouldered and dignified under his somehow out-of-date clothes, his nose long and elegant, the cheekbones flowing up toward narrow bright eyes when he turned slightly in her direction. Fine grooves radiated from the edges of his mouth, as if he had a different face that he reserved for smiling. She saw that he was too old for her after all. His hand hung at his side, only a few feet from one of hers. She felt an actual twinge of desire, and took a step away.

Now the tall man went over to the window of the nearest taxi and plunged into some sort of negotiation; the taxi driver's voice rose in protest; Alexandra wondered if she might learn something from all this. While she was watching, she had a moment of vertigo, so that the traffic receded to an uncomfortable buzz in her ears and then returned louder—jet lag. The tall man could not seem to come to an agreement with the driver, even when the old woman leaned in and added indignant words of her own. The driver waved a dismissive hand and rolled up his window.

The tall man picked up their luggage again, three or four nylon and canvas bags, and stepped to another taxi, even nearer to where Alexandra stood. She resolved not to try the first driver herself. Then the tall man abruptly concluded his bargaining and opened the back door of this acceptable new cab. He set their luggage down on the sidewalk and helped the crooked figure out of the wheelchair and into the back seat.

Alexandra wouldn't have moved toward them again if the old woman hadn't suddenly stumbled, trying to get into the taxi beside the old man. Alexandra reached out and caught the woman's upper arm in a firm sudden grip she hadn't known herself capable of. Through the black fabric of the sleeve, she could feel a bone, surprisingly light and warm. The woman turned to stare at her, then righted herself and said something in Bulgarian, and the tall man looked fully around at Alexandra for the first time. Maybe he wasn't really handsome, she thought; it was just that his eyes were remarkable—larger than they'd seemed from the side, the irises amber when the sunlight touched them. He and the old lady both smiled at her; he helped his mother carefully into the seat of the taxi, reaching back with his other hand for their bags. It was as if he knew Alexandra would come to their rescue again. And she did, catching the smaller bags up in a tangle and passing them to him. He seemed to be in a hurry now. She kept a grip on her own heavy satchel and laptop, and especially on her purse, just in case.

He straightened up and glanced down at the bags she had handed to him. Then he looked at her again.

"Thank you very much," he said to her in heavily accented English—was it so obvious that she was a foreigner?

"Can I help you?" she asked, and felt foolish.

"You already helped me," he said. Now his face was sad, the momentary smile gone. "Are you in Bulgaria for a vacation?"

"No," she said. "To teach. Are you visiting Sofia from somewhere else?" After she said this, she realized it might not sound complimentary. It was true that he and his elderly parents did not look cosmopolitan in this setting. But he was the first person she had really spoken to in almost two days, and she didn't want to stop, although the old man and the old woman were waiting for him in the cab.

He shook his head. She had read in her guide-book that Bulgarians traditionally nodded to mean "no" and shook their heads to mean "yes," but that not everyone did this anymore. She wondered which category the tall man fell into.

"Our plan—it was to go to Velin Monastery," he said. He glanced behind him, as if expecting to see someone else. "It is very pretty and famous. You must visit it."

She liked his voice. "Yes, I'll try to do that," she said.

He did smile then—slightly, without activating all the grooves. He smelled of soap, and of clean wool. He started to turn away, but paused. "Do you like Bulgaria? People say that it is the place where anything will happen. *Can* happen," he corrected himself.

Alexandra hadn't been even in Sofia long enough to know what she thought of the country.

"It's beautiful," she said finally, and saying this reminded her of the mountains she had seen as she flew in. "Really beautiful," she added with more conviction.

He inclined his head to one side, seemed to bow a little—polite people, Bulgarians—and turned toward the cab.

"May I take your picture?" she said quickly. "Would you mind? You're the first people I've talked with here." She wanted a photograph of him—the most interesting face she'd ever seen, and now would never see again.

The tall man bent obligingly close to the open cab door, although he looked anxious. She had the impression that he was in a hurry. But the old woman leaned out toward Alexandra with a smile of her own: dentures, too white and regular. The old man did not turn; he sat gazing ahead in the back seat of the taxi. Alexandra pulled her camera out of her purse and took a swift shot. She wondered if she should offer to send the picture to them, later, but she wasn't sure that elderly people in this country—or a formal-looking middle-aged man—passed photos around on email, especially with strangers.

"Thank you," she said. "*Mersi.*" That was the simple Bulgarian version of thanks; she couldn't bring herself to attempt the longer, infinitely harder word she'd tried to memorize. The tall man stared at her for a moment, and she thought his face was even sadder. He raised a hand to her and shut his old people quickly into the cab. Then he swung down into the front seat beside the driver. Their conversation had taken only a couple of minutes, but a taxi somewhere along the line had lost patience and was honking. The driver of the little family took off with a rush of tires and moved into the river of traffic, vanishing at once.

Two

But now what should she do? The driver in the next cab had noticed her, apparently; he rolled down the window and looked out with an alertness that she thought might get her to her hostel at last.

"Taxi?" he called. She noted his fair face and wide-set eyes, the first blue eyes she remembered seeing since she'd arrived in Sofia. He had straight light hair that fell in a bowl cut over his forehead, as if he had swapped himself with one of the early Beatles. When she showed him her slip of paper, an address she had written out in Cyrillic letters, he nodded at once and held up his fingers to demonstrate the right amount of *leva*. An honest guy, and apparently he meant "yes" by a nod. He hopped out, took her big suitcase, and put it in the trunk.

Alexandra got quickly into the back of the taxi. He didn't speak to her further, although his face looked pleasant in the mirror; apparently he already knew enough about her to satisfy him. She set her bags on the seat beside her and leaned back at last. The driver pulled out into traffic and around the corner so that suddenly they became part of Sofia. She could see tall straight poplars next to the street, people walking fast in their dark clothes or blue jeans, teenagers in vivid T-shirts with English words on them, the shine of litter and broken glass along a muddy gutter, as if this were both a city and a kind of dilapidated countryside. It was another world, but she realized now that she would manage here—especially after a few hours in a quiet room where she could lock the door and go to sleep.

Exactly at that moment she noticed the tall man's satchel, or was it the old man's, resting on the seat beside her, pressed against her own bags, all the straps dropping over her knee together. The sight of it went through her like a whisper of voltage—plain black canvas, long black handles, the upper side closed with a black zipper. She touched it. No, it was not one of hers. It was similar to her smaller bag; but it was his, theirs, and they had disappeared into the city.

She touched the bag. There was no marking on the canvas, on the handles or sides. After another breath she unzipped it and looked for an internal label. She could feel something angular, something hard wrapped in black velvet. When she couldn't find any identification on the inside, she dug around for a moment and unwrapped the top of the object.

It was a box made of wood—ornate carving around the upper edge, the rest beautifully polished —and here at last was a label, or rather a thin wooden plaque with Cyrillic lettering chiseled onto it. Two words, one longer than the other: Стоян Лазаров. She felt the taxi turn a corner. Because there was no other information, she sounded the words out very slowly, using the alphabet she had tried to memorize. *Stoyan Lazarov*. No dates. The ending of the second word made her think, from other passages in her guidebook, that it must be a last name. Alexandra searched numbly in the bag, but there seemed to be nothing else. Without really wanting to, she raised the hinged lid of the box. Inside sat a clear plastic sack, sealed. It was full of ashes—dark gray, pale gray, rougher white particles among them. She touched the outside of the plastic with a fingertip; in a more normal situation, the movement of her hand would have looked like reverence, and in fact she could feel the reverence even under her terrible consternation.

Alexandra glanced all around, ahead and behind, at the blurred city. She had no idea what to do. Jack would have known, if he'd lived to his almost twenty-eight years now. This was when one needed a brother. They might have been traveling together across Europe, slinging backpacks on side by side.

She reached over the seat and shook the driver by his bony shoulder—shook him hard.

"Stop!" she said. "Please, stop!" Then she began to cry.

Three

My brother and I were raised in a small city in the Blue Ridge Mountains. My mother taught history at a local college, and my father taught English at a local high school. They decided early in their married life to go back to the land, and for much of my childhood we lived in a very old farmhouse out in the country. Our lives there, in the 1990s, were remarkably like the lives people might have lived on that spot a century before. The house had a porch across the front and around two sides, its floorboards painted gray. One board creaked just in front of the door, like a doorbell; Jack, who was two years older than I, always tried to make that board speak. The house had a real and unusual doorbell as well, a brass key you turned in the doorframe, which made a powerful friendly ringing throughout two floors. The field that sloped away south from the yard was an orchard, or the ruins of one—gnarled, nearly human trees, their trunks split by winter storms, slippery apples attracting yellow jackets underfoot.

Inside the house, high-ceilinged plain rooms were filled with our hand-me-down furniture. I've never stopped missing that place, its currant patch and rhubarb beds, its ancient irises with flat bulbs branching as big as my wrist, and the tall grass Jack and I could lie in without being seen—or seeing much, except the blue outlines of mountains. The back parlor had a full-bellied Franklin stove my father fed with apple-wood and oak all winter. He and my mother read to us next to the stove when their truck couldn't get up or down the mountain in the snow.

In fact, because it was a long drive to the homes of any of the friends Jack and I made in our rural elementary school, we were often isolated on that hill, talking, cooking, perfecting our Chinese checkers strategy, playing my father's record collection of great European symphony orchestras, exploring the mountainside. Have you ever seen an LP, a black vinyl disk on which a needle drops into grooves, adding a scratchy sound here and there to the music? And there were several books in the living room bookcase that we particularly loved. One was a giant dictionary, which we used for a game of reading obscure words out loudand making each other guess their meanings. Another was a book of Rembrandt's self-portraits, his face getting older and more knowing—but not exactly wiser—as you turned the pages.

The book that most fascinated us, however, was an atlas of Eastern Europe. I don't know why it was on our shelves, and I forgot until too late to ask our mother or father; probably it had turned up on some giveaway table at the college. We quizzed each other on the names of countries and regions no one we knew had ever seen and whose borders changed depending on the dates printed at the tops of the pages. Jack would cover a place name or even close the book and say, "Okay, the small pink one in the middle of the page, 1850. Five points." Whichever of us got more than fifty points first had to make cookies for the other, although I usually ended up tending the oven while Jack wandered off to kill wasps or dig a hole to pee into under the porch. Each of us had a favorite country—mine was Yugoslavia after World War I, magically solidified into a neat yellow mass from the little patches of different colors on the previous page. Jack liked best the countries that lay in a ring around the Black Sea—in theory, at least, you could go from one to another by boat, which he said he planned to do someday. Bulgaria, pale green, was his favorite; if I could name all the countries that bordered it, he gave me an extra ten points.

We read to ourselves, too, Narnia and Middle-earth, Arthur Conan Doyle, and the piles of *National Geographic* in the back room where the stove was. I devoured some girl books Jack disdained, like Nancy Drew. My parents listened to the radio instead of watching television, and the branch library dominated our lives until a friend from school took Jack and later both of us to an arcade full of wondrous games—and we gradually realized that the computers in the math room at school had other possible uses. I liked the games less than Jack did, and craved the arcade less, which was my first sense of losing my bond with my brother.

Jack and I tormented each other, like most siblings; he bullied me sometimes and I told on him. But we were inseparable in our isolation, fond and resourceful. We grew up able to pitch a tent, build a campfire, whistle through a blade of grass, scramble safely over icy rocks, and follow water downhill to a settlement if we got lost. We could read aloud with expression, although Jack often balked at this task. We knew how to clean out the chicken house, make popovers in our mother's ceramic cups, and dig potatoes. I learned to knit and to mend my clothes. I mended Jack's as well, since he was never interested; his ran mostly to rents in the knees, for which I devised patches in sedate dark colors. We could play any-where we wanted, except near the houses at the foot of the road, with their creekside trash dumps and big chained-up dogs. "Good fences make good neighbors," said my father, who always touched his cap to them on their porches as we drove by.

All of this should have been happy, and for me it frequently was because I loved our house on the hill and I had my brother for company. By one of those strange chemistries of family life, however,

Jack seemed from earliest childhood unable to get along with our parents, and his discontent with them extended to whatever they proposed or provided. By the time he was seven or eight, he was as apt to destroy something as to do what he was asked: when we weeded the garden, he pulled out half a row of carrots instead of thinning them, and I knew it was on purpose. If we had to clean the eternal chicken shed, I worked hard; I loved the groaning sound the hens made in the corners on a hot afternoon, the discovery of new eggs, my father's praise for a job well done. Jack varied the chore by breaking a hole or two in the bottom of the walls, which let in foxes and touched off a bloodbath a few nights after. Jack wrote "the hell with everybuddy" using a charred stick on the wall above his bed. When he burned down a tree in the orchard one afternoon and the fire almost spread to the house, our father grounded him for a week—not that there was much to ground him from—and our mother took time away from her office hours at the college to talk about him with the elementary school counselor.

Middle school was worse. Jack smoked at the bus stop until another boy told on him, and I found myself mending dime-sized burn holes in his jeans instead of rents from the blackberry briars. He cut off the top of his red curls and shaved off both his eyebrows and then explained to our father that it was part of the thrift they were forever extolling (our mother had always trimmed our hair for us with special scissors). The next year, he told our parents he would run away, seriously, he would, if they didn't take him to town once a week to hang out with "the guys"—other scrawny seventh-graders with their own bad haircuts. Our father invited him to fulfill his threat, but our mother reluctantly drove him down the mountain on Saturdays, saying that we were growing up and needed social life, and taking me with her to get an ice-cream soda. I lived in fear that there would be a fight, an even worse one, between Jack and our parents. But to me Jack was mostly affectionate and even confiding. When he told me that he and the guys occasionally shoplifted cheap pocketknives or packages of beef jerky, I kept his secret—that seemed a small price to pay, especially since he brought me gifts of candy and comic books, which he always said he'd bought with his allowance.

We lived out in the country until Jack was going into ninth grade and I was starting seventh, and then our parents sold the house and bought an apartment in the newly revitalized downtown in Greenhill, where they couldn't grow vegetables but we could walk to the best public schools in the city. Once we moved into town, my brother and I led more separate lives; I was at the middle school, a stable full of terrifyingly well-groomed girls and mysterious boys, and Jack began to run track and play basketball for the high school teams and to hang out with wholesome-looking athletic new friends. Our mother and father were clearly relieved—he seemed too busy now to get into much trouble, and the early morning practices sent him straight to bed in the evening, exhausted. That first year in the city went well; so did the beginning of the second. But I missed him, as I missed our mountain house; I felt that Jack had slipped away while I wasn't looking. He was nicer to me than he'd been when we were children, but more distant. My happiest times with him were when he dropped by my cramped bedroom in the evening, often while I was doing homework.

"Oh, that kind of equation," he would say. "I remember those. Need some help?" Or he would come in suddenly, his hair wet from the shower, and sit on the edge of my bed with a grunt. "Wiped out. Extra practice today." Those moments were never long enough, because sooner than later he would knuckle the top of my head and depart to do his own homework or phone a girlfriend.

I think our parents mainly accepted this rift as the growth of a young man upward and outward, away from family; but to balance it they insisted on retaining a few rituals from our old life, foremost among them the hike we took together about once a month. We usually waited for the right weather—some sunny, clear weekend morning when the high mountains showed vividly, whatever season it was. On those days, we would be returned as a group to the experience of looking out over range on range, the blue folds beyond.

That was how we lost him.

Four

When Alexandra opened the urn, she began to cry not because she was afraid of human remains but because it was just too much, the last straw. She was in a strange country, she was exhausted, her plans had already gone awry, and in the dramatic way of the young she felt herself in the grip of something larger—destiny, or some plot that could as easily be evil as good.

She had to shake the driver's shoulder and cry out "Stop!" a couple of times before he turned to look at her, scanned her stricken face, and pulled rapidly through the Sofia traffic to a side street. A couple of kittens and a mangy cat scattered as the taxi halted at the curb; Alexandra saw they had been eating something bloody there. The area was shaded by big trees that she couldn't have known yet were *lipa*—lindens, with their masses of upside-down greenish blooms. This street was weirdly quiet after the big boulevard and the hotel. Alexandra waited, trying to stifle her sobs, while the driver put the car in park and left the engine running.

"Is there a problem?" he said. She wondered how he knew such clear English, and why he hadn't used it earlier.

"Please," she said. "I'm sorry—I'm sorry, but I have somebody else's luggage here."

It was too fast for him, apparently, or her voice was shaking too much. He frowned at her. "What? Are you okay?"

"Yes, but I have somebody's bag."

"Somebody?" he said. He craned over the back of the seat. She pointed, wordless now, and patted the object.

"This is not yours?" He looked hard at her, rather than at the bag—could that be a Bulgarian characteristic, the business of checking a person's face for clues before getting into the situation itself? The tall man had done that with her, too, but perhaps it was because she was a foreigner.

Next he got out of the driver's seat and came around to her door. He opened it and leaned in to examine the pile of luggage. "Whose bag?" he said.

She looked at him harder, too, because he was so close to her. In that moment, she saw him for the first time not in his commercial function, her ride to a hostel, but as a person, a man not much older than she—maybe twenty-nine, or at most in his early thirties. She saw again that he had a square pale face and that his light hair fell forward to obscure it when he bent over. His eyes were indeed blue, true blue, not blue-green. He was not large, and there was a grace to his movements, his thin hands.

"I don't understand," he said. "How did this happen?"

"I took it from the man on the steps at the hotel, those old people. The tall man and the old man in the wheelchair, and an old woman." She tried to speak distinctly.

"You stole their bag?" He shot her a look, more of surprise than disapproval. She understood that he had seen the old people, too, as they made their painful way out of the hotel.

"No." She felt tears prick again. "I took it by accident when I helped them get into their taxi. But I think it is—look."

She opened the lid of the urn and showed him the plastic sack inside. He leaned in closer—she felt she must be thoroughly puzzling him now—and touched it, as she had. He frowned. She watched his fingers searching for a sign from the box, as hers had, exploring the outside of the polished wood. He peeled back the velvet bag and this time she saw that the carved border was a wreath of leaves, with the head of an animal on each side. He found the name before she could show it to him, and read it aloud.

"I think this is a person," he said. "It was a person—a man."

"I know," she said, remembering the figure in the wheelchair. The image made her face feel weak. Maybe the old man had lost his other son? Or his brother?

"Do you understand? This is the body of someone," the taxi driver repeated.

"I *know*," she said. "Not the body, the *ashes*."

"Yes, ash." His voice was sharp. "In Bulgarian, we call it *prah*. Dust." The word had a guttural sound. "Maybe you have to give it back to them quickly."

"Of course I have to," she almost wailed. "But I don't know who they are or where they went. I think I should go to the police." She pictured the police searching a computer system, finding this man's name, taking the urn into respectful custody, telling her they would return it to its owners. Perhaps they would give her an address and she would take it to them herself. Then she imagined facing the people whose treasure she had kept. Her throat closed—they must be looking all over Sofia for her. But she had found her cab after they'd left in theirs; would they have seen yet that the bag was gone? Surely they would have noticed at once.

"No—actually, we have to go back to the hotel," she amended. "I think they might return to the hotel to look for me."

"That is a good idea," he said. His English sounded warmed up now, more flexible, although his face was wary. His accent was hard to place—British, almost cockney. "Come on. We'll go right away." In the midst of her misery, she liked the way his thin, nicely shaped lips found the words. His front teeth were a little crooked, with a dark spot of decay on one of them, like a freckle. His cheekbones looked like exactly that—bones, wide and tight—and she noted again how the skin on his face was milky smooth except for a con-stellation of pale brown moles near one corner of his mouth. He closed the lid of the urn with care, settling the canvas over it. Then he got back into the driver's seat and put the car into gear before she could thank him.

Five

Windy Rock Trail was one of the most beautiful hikes in the North Carolina Blue Ridge. No doubt it still is. I haven't been on that trail since 2007, when I revisited it, painfully, with my mother.

In fact, Windy Rock was a family favorite, but Jack woke up in a bad mood that October morning —I never quite knew why. I speculated to myself for years afterward that it could have been because the previous day had been his sixteenth birthday. With that date had come a driver's license, which my father had taken him to get, but of necessity no car. My parents had agreed that they could afford to put a few hundred dollars toward a car for him, not more, and that he could use his first teenage jobs to earn one. He had saved up a little, but not enough, by then, to buy a car they deemed safe.

Perhaps that was the immediate cause of friction between my father and Jack, or perhaps he simply resented not having wheels once the magic day had come and gone. He stumbled in, groggy and sullen, for our pre-hike breakfast, and I knew better than to speak to him. As we were putting on our boots and jackets, he made a half-hearted try at getting out of the excursion. My mother must have looked sad, or my father simply glanced his way, questioning and stern, because Jack desisted at once.

He was silent during the drive up the Blue Ridge Parkway to our trailhead. To keep my mind off his unexpected mood I looked out the window at the autumn foliage, which was dying away into brown and faded-gold poplars, and at the startling red berries of the mountain ash, set among gray branches. It was a brilliantly clear day, and I could see wave on wave of mountains—I puzzled, as I had throughout my childhood, over their being universally blue in the distance when they were sometimes so colorful in the foreground. When I first saw mountain ranges in the Balkans, twelve years later, I felt a pang of strangeness and then a pang of recognition: those mountains rose in peaks instead of falling softly back on themselves, and their slopes were a forbidding dark green and black, scarred with rock. But like my mountains at home, they were magnificently there, uncaring, solid, comforting.

My father parked at the trailhead and we climbed out and put on our daypacks, Jack tightening his boots one at a time on the back bumper of the car, his face dark. I loved the way he looked like himself but newly adult—his height, to which I wasn't yet accustomed, his broadened shoulders and the powerful build of his legs under khaki cargo pants, the big leather boot with striped laces he set firmly on the bumper. He glanced up then and gave me the last smile that ever passed between us, I think, and nodded for me to go ahead of him—it was our family's custom to let my father hike first, my mother behind him, then me. Since he'd grown big and competent, Jack brought up the rear. If anything chased us up the trail, it would have Jack to contend with first, which worried me for his sake, and pleased me for my own.

Partway along the first ridge, he called out, "Just a minute," and I turned to see him retying one of his boots on the outcropping of rock there. I stood nearby, watching in silence, and after a moment he muttered grouchily that he hadn't wanted to come anyway.

"I've got a lot of other stuff to do today." He was

yanking on the lace while I studied his tanned profile, so like our father's. He seemed angry even at his boots. "Don't you ever get tired of clambering up a mountain just because Mom and Dad say it's time, right now, no matter what?"

"But we've always hiked," I said clumsily. "I kind of like it."

"Well, they're forgetting I'm a little old to be ordered around. I mean, here we are again, in the middle of nowhere." He had finished with his shoelace and now he waved one hand out toward the view, the open sweep of mountains and sky. I loved that view.

Then I said what I shouldn't have. I suddenly resented his spoiling his one day with us. I hated his rudeness to our misguided but (after all) well-meaning parents, his previous desertions, his inability to simply enjoy being with me for a change, when friends and girls and basketball took all the rest of his attention.

"Well," I said angrily, "why don't you just get lost, if you're going to be such a jackass about everything?"

He looked at me with disbelief in his face—how I loved that face, even when I'd sparked it to fury, and how I still do. Then he told me two things. First, to go to fucking hell. Second, that he might fucking do that himself.

Those were his words, and I will not put them in quotation marks, and they were the last ones we knew him ever to say to anyone. I was fighting tears—both of regret at my own meanness and of keen hurt. I turned my back and strode ahead, falling into a desperate rhythm, ignoring the silence I was rapidly leaving behind. There was no sound of his step; I told myself it served him right if I ditched him for a while. I crossed a stream, or rather the stream crossed our trail and I had to pick my way from stone to stone in the noisy water. After a few minutes I could see my parents ahead of me, hiking quietly along, and I followed them.

Jack had not caught up with us when we stopped for a water break at the first big view. It was an enormous panorama of mountains, surges of them, cresting on the horizon in smoky blue. The valley lay four thousand feet below, just beyond the wine-colored leaves of the huckleberry bushes that lined our path. My mother smiled encouragingly at me and glanced around for my brother, and then we all sat down and stretched our legs and waited for a few minutes.

"Was Jack behind you?" my father asked, after a while. I explained that he'd stopped to tighten his bootlaces but added nothing about our argument. "Well, he'll catch up," my father said. My mother must have shown some vague sign of unease, because my father added, "He's a big boy."

We walked on, but more slowly. I wondered if

my parents knew how angry he'd been about having to come out today, then allowed my mind to wander to other things: the new haircut I wanted to get, just like that of two girls in my social studies class, and then the story we were reading for Language Arts on Monday. It was a retelling of "Little Red Riding Hood," with teenaged characters, and I wasn't sure it worked that well. I thought of writing another version, to see if I could do it better. I watched the swing of my worn hiking boots, which had once been Jack's (my mother had assured me they were "unisex," and as long as I didn't have to wear them to school, I could accept that).

At the next overlook we stopped and my mother suggested that we get out our lunch a little early and sit there to eat it until Jack caught up. My father agreed and slipped his full daypack off his shoulders. My mother found a flat area near the trail and I helped her spread the small plaid cloth she always brought for our picnics. She had packed my favorite deviled eggs and slices of my father's good homemade bread, and there was a bottle of sparkling lemonade for each of us, a treat in our thrifty household. She set Jack's bottle next to the rocks, ready for him. My father saw no reason to wait, so we began our lunch. But the bread tasted dry in my mouth, as if I were already chewing the words I'd said to my brother in anger, and I saw that my mother was looking back down the trail every few minutes. None of us had cell phones yet—they were rather new to our world then—although the remaining three of us got them a few years later.

Finally my father touched her shoulder. "Don't worry, Clarice," he said. "Jack's a very experienced hiker. He probably needed a little time to himself. He's growing up."

"I know he's growing up." She sounded almost irritable, a rare tone for her.

"Well, would you like me to walk a little way back and give him a wave?" My father collected the remains of our picnic, not leaving even a crumb for the wild birds: pack it in, pack it out.

"Yes, could you do that?" My mother smiled, as if this was a mere bit of trouble we ought to go to. "We can wait here for you two."

My father was gone about thirty minutes, and he returned alone, with a shadow of displeasure on his face.

"I walked all the way back to the big bend," he said. "I even shouted for him for a while, but he didn't answer. I'm afraid he may have gone to the car by himself." I knew that edge in his voice: it meant Jack had broken the rules of outdoorsmanship and would be in trouble for it later. I also knew that Jack had a driver's license now—and a key to our car, which had been my father's concession for his birthday.

"We didn't hear you calling," my mother said

doubtfully. "You couldn't have been calling very loud."

"It was loud enough." My father sat down for a moment. "How about if you go on slowly and enjoy the views, and I'll go to the car." *If it's there,* he didn't add. "If I haven't returned with him in an hour, head back this way and we'll just all wait at the parking lot." *And even if the car's there, Jack will have consequences.*

I could see that my mother didn't want to hike on without knowing where Jack was; years later, I realized that she must have felt that if she did, it might make everything come out right, or at least make everything seem normal for a little while longer. I realized this after I became a mother myself—the feeble bargains we strike with risk, with our own fears.

My father loped back down the trail and my mother and I headed out slowly, keeping his pack with us because it had extra water bottles in it. We were soon just two women feeling small under a big sky; the trail opened into meadows, crossing a natural bald I'd always particularly liked because it was dotted with the ruins of trees, weather-beaten and silver. My mother consulted her watch from time to time, and at last she told me in a reluctant voice that we would have to turn around.

Six

As her driver turned back toward the hotel, Alexandra saw that the street where they'd parked was a short one, lined with fraying apartment buildings, laundry hung on balconies. She could look around again a little, now that he was helping her. The beauty of the city lay in its trees: heavy canopies tasseled in those yellowish blooms like thousands of insects with folded wings, sunlight threading through them to dapple the parked cars. She saw a long-haired man with a backpack strolling past under the trees, brushing his teeth. At one door on street level, a woman in a tan and blue dress stood fitting a key into the lock, plastic shopping bags heavy over her arm. Two old men in suits wandered by, carefully navigating the treacherous sidewalk. Alexandra wondered why they did not fix the sidewalks in such a beautiful place. The two men gestured to each other, deep in discussion. Everyone seemed more alive here than she normally thought people were, or perhaps they just waved their hands around more, or she was just so much more tired than usual that she herself was partly dead. She held the stranger's bag on her lap, her arms around it, not wanting to leave it on the seat beside her like something ordinary. At least she could hold it until she gave it back, although the urn's smooth heaviness through the canvas made her feel queasy.

A moment later they were in the flow of the big boulevard again. Alexandra's driver pulled in to the hotel taxi line and jumped out. Alexandra got out more slowly, leaving her bags on the seat but staying close. The driver ran up the steps. She felt grateful for his energy on her behalf; he was thin and moved strongly, dressed in blue jeans and a black T-shirt, black tennis shoes, brushing his hair out of his eyes as he ran. He disappeared through the glass doors at the top.

But when he came out again, minutes later, his face was empty. He stopped to question a few of the people on the landing, others on the steps. Then he came back to the taxi line and stood in front of her.

"I'm sorry," he said. "I asked every person there, and some clerks do remember the family with the wheelchair." He said it "clarks," like an Englishman. "Those people are not here now. They had coffee with a man at the restaurant before they went away. They did not take a room. One of the clerks said that the younger man was in a bad argument with the man they were drinking coffee with, a journalist—I mean, the man they met there was a journalist well known at the hotel. The journalist went away, angry, through the back door, and then the tall man and the old people left through the front door." He made a couple of vivid gestures, his hands pointing opposite directions.

And then, Alexandra thought, she had spoken with them at the foot of the front steps.

The driver behind them was beginning to tap his horn. Alexandra's driver got into his taxi, and she climbed reluctantly back in, too. He started the engine and pulled out of line, then stopped again at the curb.

"What do you want to do now?" he said. She detected wariness in his voice and body—as if he thought he might not like her answer—but also curiosity.

"I think I have to go to the police station and show them this," Alexandra said. "Could you take me there?"

He was silent for a moment. "Okay," he said at last. "Just to tell you first, the police are not always very helpful here, unless they are getting money from you for going too fast or talking on your mobile phone while you drive. Then they are very efficient." His face had darkened to a scowl. "But I can take you to a station if you would like. That is probably the right thing. Maybe they can discover some information about this name on the box, but I will be surprised if they do very much."

In the heart of the old city, he stopped half a block from a concrete building with glass doors. "That is the nearest police," he said, pointing discreetly. "Probably they will want to see your passport at the entrance."

"Would you be able to help me just explain to them? They might not speak English."

He shook his head. "Please excuse me if I do not come inside. I would like to help you, but—" Then he seemed to find his own lack of gallantry unforgivable. He turned and met her eye. "I have been in trouble with the police recently, you see, so this is not my favorite place."

Alexandra's heart sank under the weight of the surreal. Two hours in Bulgaria, and she had already fallen in with the wrong people, in addition to receiving the burden of the bag in her lap. She could imagine what her parents would have said, even if Jack might have understood. But it had simply happened.

Her taxi driver seemed to expect a response. She said, "So you—what did you—?"

"I'm not a *criminal,*" he said, and his chin jutted forward. "Please do not think I am a criminal. I was arrested in a demonstration last month. It was just an eco-demonstration, but we did not go with them quietly. There was a little madness and they made an example of me, so I was in jail for three days."

She softened. "What were you demonstrating about?"

"The government is reopening some mines in the northwest of the country—these mines were closed for many years because they were not safe for the miners and because they let a terrible poison into one of our biggest rivers, which many towns use. The government thinks everyone has forgotten, and some businessmen think this, too. But we know that they only want to open them without fixing anything, and to make money from them again. You see."

He snorted. "The police told me I might go to a real prison the next time, and they told this to some other people who were arrested." Then he was silent for a moment. "I have several reasons to not like them very much."

"Well," said Alexandra, relieved. She'd been in a demonstration or two herself, in college, against wars. "I understand why you wouldn't want to go in there again."

He rubbed his jaw. "There are a few decent chaps in the police, but also some who still think that you can beat up people, even in a democracy."

She nodded. "I know." Although she had only the vaguest idea. "All right. Or—wait—" She paused. "What did you call this, again—the ashes?"

"*Prah*," he said patiently.

She repeated it. "Also, I don't know how to get to my hostel, but I'm sure I can figure that out if you have other work to do. Would you rather I paid you now?"

He waved away any consideration of money. "Later. You are already very tired, and I have your suitcase in the boot," he said, as if he were her father, or at least her elder. Then he shook his head. "It's okay. I'm not going to steal it."

"I believe you," said Alexandra. She found that she did.

"Meet me just here. It will take you more than half an hour to see someone inside, but I will get the newspapers."

Seven

The return on any trail always seems to take half the time of walking out it, whether it's a downhill retracing or not, and this time we were mostly going down. We moved swiftly, and as we went I couldn't help glancing over the most dramatic edges of the mountainside, where it ended in that sheer drop to the valley below. I felt sure my mother, behind me, was doing the same. When we reached the parking lot, my father was there, leaning against our car with his arms crossed. He didn't say anything until we came close, and then he sounded grim. "I've spent an hour and a half looking for him and shouting up and down. If this is his idea of a joke, or a rebellion, it's one too many."

"You don't think anything's happened, do you?" my mother said, and her voice quavered. When we found Jack, there would be a scene, and if we didn't find him, or at least didn't find him for hours—that was unthinkable.

"Of course not," snapped my father. "But we'll have to talk seriously about this. It's not funny to scare people."

"I don't think he intended to scare us this much," I said in what I knew was a small voice.

They suddenly seemed to remember that I'd seen him last.

"Honey," my father said, "did Jack mention he was going off the trail, or back to the car, when you were with him?"

"No," I said, miserably, "but he was in a pretty bad mood." I was having trouble swallowing. "Actually, we had an argument."

"What kind of an argument?" My mother looked surprised, and it was true that Jack and I rarely fought anymore.

"Well, he didn't want to go on the hike—you know—and he got angry and said we were spending our day in the middle of nowhere. Then when I told him to stop talking like that, he said something rude and I walked away and left him there."

"That's all?" My father shook his head, as if none of this was helpful.

"Yes," I said, because I couldn't bring myself to tell the rest. I'd left out the part about how I'd told Jack to get lost. Above all, I'd left out the part about how he'd said he might just do that.

"Do you think he could have gotten ahead of us, and maybe is still waiting out there?" My mother seemed almost pleased at this thought, although it wasn't the first time they'd considered it.

"Impossible." My father kicked the curb of the parking lot. "We were right on the trail the whole time. We would have seen him pass us."

"Well, we've got to wait here for a while," she said, and we did. We leaned against the car, we sat on the low wall at the edge of the lot, we walked around on the grass verge. This all seemed to last for hours, but I believe that after only another forty-five minutes my father drove to the lodge nearby and made a call. Even before he'd returned, three rangers arrived in different cars and began to question my mother and to scour the area; we could see them moving off the trail at various points to search in the woods. They carried walkie-talkies that fuzzed audibly on and off among the trees. They brought us reports of nothing.

"This happens pretty often with teenagers," one ranger told my mother. My father stood with his arm around her shoulders now. "They get riled, go off. He'll be back up here sooner or later, hungry and mad, or repenting, or he'll come out on the Parkway a little farther down. We had one kid hitchhike from Pisgah all the way home to Boone the other day, scared his poor folks half to death. But teenagers are like that."

51

Had Jack really become "like that"? I wondered. He was rebellious, but never stupid. I'd grown up roaming the woods and fields with him at our old house, and I thought he never would have been such a moron as to walk to another county just to show us. The Jack I knew would have stayed and argued about everything, even if he sometimes threatened to run away. Even, I told myself around the cold lump in my throat, when other people taunted him to get lost. Did growing up change people that much?

Despite the ranger's assurances, Jack didn't reappear that afternoon. By dinnertime I was as angry at him as my parents were, although I could no longer tell whether the pain in my middle was rage or fear or—my new companion—guilt. He didn't appear at home that evening, after one of the Forest Service cars took me and my mother back to town to see if he'd arrived there alone and to call around asking all his friends if they'd seen him, leaving my father up on the Parkway to continue the search. He had not shown up in any of these places—or anywhere else—by early morning, when my mother's face was stark in the light from the apartment windows and my father came home looking not much better. Watching them, I knew I couldn't tell them the rest of my conversation with Jack. Besides, it would make no difference in the search—the rangers were looking everywhere, anyway. If they didn't find him, knowing about our conversation would only multiply my parents' pain a hundredfold. And they might blame me, although not as much as I blamed myself.

In fact, Jack didn't appear to any of the teams that went out from the Forest Service and the sheriff's department, or to their genius dogs, or to any of the volunteers who soon joined us. He didn't turn up safely downstream—as we'd been taught from earliest childhood to do if we ever got lost—in any of the valleys of the National Forest or the tiny towns just outside it. He didn't come walking into the Cradle of Forestry museum or a store on the main street of Brevard.

We waited at home, or drove up the Parkway again, now randomly. But Jack didn't show up Monday morning for his biology class at school or Monday afternoon for the basketball practice he never skipped even if he had the flu. He wasn't found, weeks later, sulky but triumphant, at some friend's house in West Greenhill or in a grocery store in Tennessee or on a Greyhound heading west. No one recognized him in New Mexico or Oregon or southern Alaska from the "lost child" (although my father had insisted that he was growing up) campaign coordinated by my parents with the aid of every available authority. He never appeared on a boat to Russia or Honduras or Brindisi. And, perhaps mercifully—yes, I still think mercifully—his beautiful, young, strong body was never discovered broken at the foot of any Blue Ridge precipice.

At first I'd stayed silent because they might find him. Later, I didn't tell anyone about what he had said to me because they hadn't found him. The National Forest was enormous, as the rangers reminded us every day, and it was not unheard of for the person (they called him "the person" now) to die without being found, although some "people" were found years after. In addition to the cliffs above the forests, there were deep crevasses of rock; there were swift cold rivers that hurled themselves over waterfalls and vanished into caves underground. And when we held our memorial for him at last, more than a year later, there was no one to bury. My parents and I had only our tears and the emptiness of a field near our old house in the mountains, the too-young friends in awkward best clothes, the helpless relatives standing around us. That night, I dreamed of a black bear running over the long spines of the Blue Ridge, always far ahead of me and then passing out of sight.

For a long time, I still believed that Jack would never, ever have done anything to harm himself; he was too thoroughly bound to life, to the ordinary pleasures of the basketball under his hand, too temperamentally in favor of staying alive and losing his virginity. I knew it the way I knew that I would myself live to be very old. If he'd fallen, it was the slip of a moment, an error in the midst of irritation, a mistake in his footing. I knew also that even if he could leave our parents, temporarily, he would never have left me, not before it was time. He would have come back to us, dirty and defiant. But perhaps I'd tempted him to the edge of some danger. In time I came to doubt my very belief in his love of life. Whenever I looked at my parents or glimpsed any of Jack's friends, I wondered if I should have said something more and then remembered I had vowed to spare them further pain.

He was simply gone, and he took all our peace with him.

Eight

Alexandra slid out of the back seat, her purse over one shoulder and the bag with the urn balanced in her arms. She made her way along the block and then up four concrete steps. In the lobby of the building, she found two guards sitting inside a glass cubicle, with a nicked wooden desk next to them and a counter around the outside. One of them was pouring hot water from an electric kettle into a cup. The other, who was younger, opened his window and looked her over with little visible interest.

"*Dobur den*," she said, and it tasted odd in her mouth. "Do you speak English?"

He shrugged toward his colleague, who had turned from the tea to look at her.

"No," said the tea guard.

"A little," said the younger one, as if he had suddenly remembered this.

"I'm an American—teacher—visiting Bulgaria. I arrived in Sofia this morning and I accidentally picked up someone else's luggage." She tried to stand very straight as she produced her passport. "I would like to find that person and return it to him."

The younger policeman took her passport and propped it open, then scratched the back of his neck. He wore a blue uniform shirt so carefully pressed that it made his bulky trunk look like a mannequin's. "Probably you must ask at Sofia Airport. We cannot help with luggage here."

She set the bag between her feet, squeezing it with her anklebones; she didn't like to put it on the floor, but it grew heavy so quickly. "It isn't airport luggage. I mean, I met this person at a hotel and accidentally kept one of his bags."·

"At a hotel?" Suspicion or perhaps contempt flickered over his clean-shaven face and she saw she'd said something wrong. "A person? Do you know his name?"

"No—but I do have a name that might help. I think the bag contains human ashes." She felt a sudden resurgence of her desire to cry, and quelled it.

The policeman's older companion moved closer, as if he had nothing more urgent to do than listen to a language he couldn't understand.

"Ashuss?" said the young one. "What is that?"

"Ashes," she said, a wave of despair beginning again in her tired feet. "From a person, after he is dead—cremation. I mean, dust." She tried to remember the word the taxi driver had taught her. Since they stood frowning, she got out her paperback dictionary and laboriously looked it up. "*Prah*." She showed them the page.

The young policeman said something rapid to the older, who shook his head. Did that mean yes or no, in this case? Alexandra wondered. Next the young policeman rubbed the top of his very short hair, as if embarrassed for her, or for the person whose ashes she'd stolen. "Show me."

She lifted the black bag and set it on the counter. "It's in this, but I would rather not open it here." Then she realized they might think she was carrying something dangerous—a gun, a bomb. The two policemen stepped out of the cubicle, and a couple of women walking into the building turned their heads to gape at her.

"You must to open the bag before we can help," the young one said firmly.

Alexandra unzipped it for them, showing the velvet inside and then the lid of the fine wooden box. She hated this. A life, exposed to ruthless bureaucratic staring.

"See, there's a name on the box." She uncovered the etching and pointed it out to the young policeman, who pointed it out to the older, whose lips moved as he read. Then she carefully covered the box again and zipped the bag. The plane trip seemed so long ago that she felt she had arrived in a different year, rather than earlier in this one long wobbling day.

"Okay," said the younger. "You must come with me and we will see somebody for missing peoples. They have a computer system to find missing peoples. Come with me."

The older one had lost interest; he returned to his tea at the battered desk. Alexandra thought to herself that Stoyan Lazarov was not so much missing as dead, but she followed the young policeman's muscular, neatly pressed back toward an elevator. She couldn't help feeling uneasy, after her taxi driver's remark about police who still beat people up in a democracy; this particular policeman could have broken her neck with a casual gesture. What if they concluded she'd stolen the ashes—or just stolen someone's bag—and decided to put her in a cell? She probably didn't have enough money for bail, or whatever it was she might have to pay to get out—a fine, a bribe. Would the English Institute even let her teach, after that? Perhaps, she thought, she should have gone to the American embassy instead, but it was too late now.

The policeman held back the elevator door for her and then stood beside her rubbing his neck and watching an antiquated needle search for the right floor.

Nine

After Jack's disappearance, I plowed through high school, graduating early, and went on to college, where I studied English literature. I dropped my first name, which my family had always used for me, and took my middle name, Alexandra. It was less painful; Jack had never uttered it. In college, I began to write poems and stories outside of my classes, although I never wrote about dead boys, and to prepare myself in the blind way young writers do for the work they will later undertake. I washed dishes in the college dining halls and worked at the college library, where Jack seemed sometimes to be working beside me. And I tried, haltingly, to teach myself my new craft.

Along the way, I fell more deeply in love with books, although I had trouble falling for people, even when I wanted to. My few relationships with men—or, rather, undergraduate boys—involved attraction, conversation, and sometimes birth control, but no lasting affection. I realize now that what I most enjoyed was breaking up with them, the look on their faces when I asked them not to call me again, the light going out of their eyes. At home, my parents split up as well—felled by silence, I could tell, not by fighting. I knew about silence; I knew the symptoms. They informed me together, both red-eyed, during spring break of my freshman year, and then divided my time equitably between their two smaller new apartments. They knew it was unfair to me, they said, since none of this was my fault. Each was kinder to me than ever; when they talked on the phone to each other they were kind, too, and I wished I could ask Jack to set a fire in a living room or kick a hole in one of their tidy separate kitchens.

After college, I lived at my parents' apartments in Greenhill and worked at the library shelving books. That left me a few hours a week to volunteer at a local Montessori school, in case I wanted to teach children later on—a vague notion—and to write short stories, and to read. I knew my parents both worried about the fact that I was "not moving on," but I avoided their eyes at our breakfasts and dinners. On summer evenings, I sometimes went out with friends from high school who came home to Greenhill to visit. The friends never asked about Jack and I never talked about him, which is maybe why they never asked—a perfect arrangement.

I remember those nights as well as anything in my life. My friends and I would drive up the Parkway before sunset and sit at an overlook until it was too dark to see the trees along the tops of the far ridges. They drank beer and I elected myself to drive the car back to town, sober. As I watched their faces and listened to them laughing and talking about not very much, they always seemed to me less real than the boy on the trail, his big hairy sixteen-year-old arms, his handsome scowl. Sometimes I sat on the grass looking at the fading peaks and digging a sharp stick into the side of my leg, where no one could see it. One evening I realized we were all seated at the top of a very steep slope, a vertical slope, wooded but perfect for the plunge of a car to complete destruction. The sound of it, hitting, shattering against tree trunks, was more real to me than my friends' faces—yes, and for a minute more real to me than my image of Jack.

Later that night, in the second bedroom in my mother's apartment, I drew a kitchen knife slowly over the inside of my upper left arm, hard enough to give the skin a deep furrow of red. The pain I'd longed for brought me no relief, except that it jolted me to my senses: the ugliness, the cliché. It took time to clean up the blood, and the thought that I might have to call for help made me light-headed with shame. But I managed to stop the flow, binding my arm tightly for a night. I didn't do it again, and I always wore sleeves after that; even my parents never saw. Light as it was, the scar weighed and tingled on my arm. Strangely, it also made me stop writing, as if the stories and poems I'd tried my hand at for years had trickled out and been lost.

I stayed in Greenhill almost three years after the night I'd carved open my arm—working, reading, lingering there for my parents without understanding that my own sadness couldn't comfort them. I wasn't ready yet for graduate school, but one autumn morning as I walked to my job at the library—now tediously full time—I realized that I wouldn't be able to stand my memories much longer. Soon after, I began to apply for positions to teach English abroad: in Bulgaria, for example, which caught my eye online because it was our secret, the pale-green mystery that Jack had loved, that Jack would now never visit himself.

Ten

The upper corridors of the Sofia police station were lined with polished granite in gray and beige —walls, floors, stairwells, ugly square columns, and benches where a few people sat reading newspapers. Alexandra thought they looked as if they were waiting for a bus that might never arrive. Along the walls ran a row of black-and-white photographs of men's faces with names and years on plaques beneath them; these dates seemed to be their terms of service, perhaps as precinct chiefs: 1961–1969, for example. The years wandered backward as she followed the policeman down the hall—farther on, she saw 1934–1939, 1932–1934.

Alexandra thought of the history she'd read in her guidebook, on the plane: 1878, the liberation of much of Bulgaria from the Ottoman Empire and the beginning of the modern Bulgarian monarchy, which had persecuted communists and anarchists and sided with Germany in two world wars. Then 1944, the advent of the communist regime, which had persecuted non-communists and a lot of communists, as well. And, of course, 1989—the fall of the Berlin Wall and the beginning of the regime's collapse. Since then, a parliamentary democracy, frequent economic chaos, the early return of many former communist leaders or their children to new positions of power, the occasional election of a progressive government. The men in the photos looked important, as if they'd been directors of everything, not mere policemen. As the years fell backward, their faces sprouted dark mustaches and they wore slicked-down hair and old-fashioned high shirt collars. She wondered if the end of the hallway would take them all the way back to 1878.

But the young policeman knocked on a door that interrupted the photographs from the early

1920s. He paused a moment, then ushered her in ahead of him. Inside, she saw a drab room full of bookshelves and file cabinets, a dingy rug, long windows backlighting a woman at a computer who looked up at them and pressed her cigarette into an ashtray. *"Da?"*

The muscular policeman seemed to Alexandra a little cowed by this woman; he bowed his head and gestured at the illegal bag, explaining something about it in Bulgarian; she caught the word *amerikanka*. The woman pursed her lips and got up, frowning at Alexandra. She wore a black skirt to midthigh, black pumps, a ruffled pink blouse. Her dark-red hair curved in a plastic sweep to her chin, and inside its frame her face was elderly, with winged blue eye shadow. She seemed offended by Alexandra's youth and appearance—her jeans and sneakers, her unwashed hair. Alexandra wished she could explain that her last shower had been on what now seemed to her another planet.

The woman turned and knocked on a door studded with brass rivets, and this let them into the presence of a man who sat behind a long desk, at the end of an even longer table. Alexandra thought, inevitably, of the Great and Powerful Wizard of Oz. The man was mostly bald, with bristling gray eyebrows. He stood up, quietly, and she saw that he had an empty holster at his belt, although he wore a white shirt and a tie rather than a uniform. The gun must be in a drawer nearby. The skin in his temples throbbed with veins; the lid of one of his otherwise benign brown eyes twitched and fluttered as she shook hands with him.

"*Dobur den,*" she said.

He asked her in Bulgarian if she spoke Bulgarian.

"*Ne,*" she said, too loud.

"Please, sit down," he told her in perfectly plain English. There was a small chair facing the desk. He dismissed the young policeman and the dragon lady, each with a nod. Alexandra wished that at least the policeman had been allowed to stay, since he seemed already something of an ally.

The Wizard went to sit behind his desk again and viewed her across its expanse. "Now—you have this luggage that is not yours."

"That's right," she said, putting her hands over the top of the bag. "But I certainly didn't mean to take it."

"You are American?"

She couldn't read his tone. "Yes."

"Your passport, please, Miss."

She handed it over and he examined it with quick precision; she noticed again that twitching eye, presumably fixed on her brand-new visa stamp. He wrote something on a notepad.

"How did this happen, the problem of a bag?"

Alexandra told him her story, briefly, describing the trio at the bottom of the hotel steps, the frail old woman with her purse dangling beside her, the younger man in his black and white clothes—dressed for a funeral? When she'd finished, the Wizard pressed his palms together above the desktop, as if praying horizontally. The light from a row of windows shone off his scalp. "I see. So you wish to return this item. And there is a name on the box, you said?"

She showed him. "I have a picture of the people, too." She pulled out her camera and found it, enlarged the image to hold up to him. She hadn't really caught the tall man's beauty. The Wizard glanced at it, but without apparent interest.

"Now—Stoyan Lazarov," he said. "There could be many people in Bulgaria with this name. You say that they, the family, are not from Sofia. Perhaps this will help." He turned to a computer that stood at the side of his desk. Then he smiled—at the screen, rather than at her—and began to type something.

She waited, cradling the bag, but it took a few minutes. He read something, touched a key, read more. "No, that is someone who lives in Sofia. Someone else in Sofia. Someone not in Sofia but who is still alive, no, and this one, also alive."

Then he stopped and studied the screen more closely with his elbow on his desk, leaned in with a sudden slow attentiveness she never forgot afterward. He pressed another key. He looked up at her. "You do not know exactly when this person died?"

"No. Well, recently, I guess," she said, with her hand over the top of the bag. "I couldn't know that, because I didn't even know there were ashes in the bag when I kept it. Has anybody come here to ask for it, maybe, or called you about it?"

The Wizard seemed to examine her words in the air, then shook his head. "May I see the photograph again, if you please?" She handed the camera to him, feeling uneasy. He studied the three figures; his eye no longer seemed to be twitching. Alexandra reached again for her camera as soon as she politely could.

"Is there something unusual about these people?" she asked. "They seemed rather— ordinary, to me."

He touched his chin. "I will make a telephone call. Excuse me. I will see if I can help."

He drew a cell phone from his jacket pocket, dialed, turned away toward the window as if to concentrate. She heard his rapid speech with a feeling of impotence. It was odd to think that six months from now, if she studied hard and made friends and listened carefully, she might well understand such a conversation. He was nodding, silent, then speaking in that quiet measured tone. She watched the skin on the smooth hinge of his jaw move back and forth with the sounds. He hung up, sat down, did something at his keyboard for a few minutes. Then he faced her. She had the sense that he didn't at all mind keeping her waiting.

"I am sorry to tell you that we cannot directly find the people you need," he said. "But if you would like, we can give you an address where you can look for them. It's not far away from Sofia. Maybe it is better, in such a personal matter, for you to go and explain what happened, if you have the time."

He bowed a little, as if aware she must be busy, in her draggled clothes. "They are probably very worried." His hands prayed to the surface of the desk again. There was a broad silver band on his right ring finger—European marriage. "Or"—he paused—"if you would like, we can keep the bag for you safe here and you can return with the owner and he can receive it from us. We would take care of it until you come back. That might even be the best thing."

Alexandra hesitated. The weight of the urn on her lap felt strange, but she couldn't imagine abandoning it to a storeroom. What if it got lost in some labyrinth of bureaucracy? She might find the old couple or the man with the beautiful eyes and then bring them here to discover their treasure gone, or irretrievable. What would her apology mean then? She put both hands around the bag. The long scar she'd carved on her arm began to prickle, and she willed herself not to scratch it.

"If you don't mind," she said. "I would like the address—I want to take the ashes to them myself. I'd feel better about that."

He looked at her gravely, his eye jumping now as if it belonged to some other nervous system. Then he spread his hands on the table and shrugged.

"If you like," he said. He opened her passport again and recorded some information from it. He took out a clean sheet of paper and sat making a drawing, which he handed her: a neat little map, with words underneath. "Here is the route. It is a town near Sofia. Do you have an automobile?"

This seemed to Alexandra unnecessarily sarcastic. She thought that in a minute he might offer her a ride in a police car.

"Oh, no," she said hastily. "But I have a friend who can take me."

He nodded. Perhaps he just wanted to be rid of her, after all. "Why don't you call me, in fact, when you have returned the bag? You can let us know it is finished. Here is my business card. Do you have an address or phone number in Bulgaria?"

"No—I'm sorry," she said. "Not yet, I mean. I'm hoping to get a phone soon." She didn't add that it would depend on how much that might cost. "But I'll be teaching at the Central English Institute." He wrote this down. His card was in Cyrillic, and she put it into her billfold with the new Bulgarian tens and twenties.

"Thank you," she said, reaching out a hand. He shook it pleasantly, but without speaking further, and saw her to the door. Again, Alexandra wondered if she'd imagined his sudden interest—maybe he actually hadn't wanted to be bothered with such a small matter. The dragon lady did not get up to see her out.

In the hall, Alexandra looked at what he'd written down for her: an address, neatly lettered in Cyrillic and then in English, but with no phone number. The map showed a road from Sofia to a black dot in the east; *120 km,* he had added in tidy script—not far, although much farther than Alexandra had bargained for. It was peculiar that he hadn't given her the name of a person to search for, but she wasn't going to knock on any of those doors again to ask him. She'd hoped for the name of a tall man dressed for a funeral.

Outside, the street was sunny and warm; she had a skin-creeping sense that she'd emerged from a crypt, alive again. Trees and buildings swam under her fatigue. Then her taxi driver looked up from his newspaper and waved through the windshield, and for a moment she felt almost at home.

Eleven

When she slid into the taxi, the driver said, "I see that you still have it." His face in the rearview mirror was placid, but his eyes watched her.

"Yes," Alexandra said. "A police officer found the address of the family. I didn't want to leave the urn with them." She handed him the policeman's card.

"Hmm," he said, and gave it back. Then she showed him the hand-drawn map. "Bovech," he said.

"What?" said Alexandra.

"That's the name of the town. It is a small place. In fact, I have never been there."

Alexandra shook her head. "I don't know what to do—I don't know if those people will stay in Sofia looking for me now, or leave without the urn. They might not be home yet. Maybe they won't go there until tomorrow, at least." She took the paper from him and folded it again. "Now I think that I should have left it with the police, after all, so if the people go to the station to check, it'll be there, waiting for them."

The driver shook his head. "It is not a good idea to leave things with the police," he said, as if irritated that she'd even considered that. "Do you want me to take you to your hotel to rest?

You could wait a day and then travel to Bovech. Too bad the police did not give you a phone number for these people. I do not think you can find them in Sofia easily, even if they are staying here. The city is too big."

Alexandra leaned forward again to touch the back of his seat. "The tall man spoke to me before I helped them with their bags," she said. "He asked me if I was in Bulgaria for vacation. He told me they were going to Velin Monastery— I knew the name from my guidebook. He said it was beautiful and famous and I should go see it someday."

The driver's face cleared. "They were traveling to Velinski *manastir*? That is near Sofia. They probably wanted to have a service there, for this man, in the monastery church. Maybe they will still go there, because they know that *you* know that they had this plan." He checked his cell phone. "We have lost only about fifty minutes— unless they traveled there with a bus, and then we will be faster than they will, anyway. Do you want me to drive you there?"

"Yes, please," she said. "But maybe it's too long a trip for you, to go out of the city."

He gazed over the seat, considering her with his bright eyes under the fringe of hair.

"I will charge you only the cost of the petrol, so far," he said. "This happened to you by an accident. And you can pay me just for the travel outside Sofia, to go to the monastery and come back. The total will be about forty-five *leva*, maybe fifty."

This was still a lot for her, but she didn't want to stop now to change more money or argue about the cost. More daunting was the fact that she didn't know this young man, or his culture, and now she and all her luggage would be leaving the city alone with him. Probably the jet lag was affecting her judgment. He was being generous, but he seemed a little cranky, too, at moments— did that mean he was an angry person at heart, perhaps even violent?

On the other hand, he was a professional, and how else was she going to return this bag? Alexandra, fidgeting under the taxi driver's gaze, also began to wonder if the old people would forgive her, when she found them. For a moment, she imagined that they would be grateful to her for tracking them down, rather than upset by her mistake. Maybe they would invite her to stay for the funeral, once she had given back the urn. She would refuse, with humble thanks, in order to allow them their privacy. The tall man would smile down at her—without reservation, this time, his face lit in wonder at her conscientiousness. He would squeeze her hand before he turned away. The old lady would have tears in her eyes. Alexandra would say goodbye to them quietly and respectfully and ask the driver to bring her straight back into the city to her hostel. She would take a shower, with lots of soap, and sleep for twelve hours, no matter how early it still was. After that, her real stay in Bulgaria could begin. First, though, she had to finish this troubling errand. *"Because I could not stop for Death—"* she murmured, *"he kindly stopped for me—"*

"Pardon?" The driver's eyes were fixed on her, puzzled.

"Nothing," she said hastily. "Thank you. I really appreciate this."

"I can drive very fast," he added.

"Oh, please don't," said Alexandra. She wondered again what Jack would have advised her to do if she could have told him about this situation. But he was not there. She felt a stab of resentment, almost defiance. "Let's go," she amended quickly.

The driver reached out a hand to shake hers. "I am Asparuh Iliev, by the way," he said. She could not make any sense of the sounds, and he tipped his head to one side, relenting. "Asparuh is a famous name here—the king who established the first Bulgarian state, in 681. Even I get sick of it. You can call me by my short name, Bobby." He pronounced it *Bo-bi,* clipping the syllables. Alexandra noticed again his odd accent—he sounded like a London cabbie in a movie, not a Bulgarian one. She nodded, too, and left her hand in his for a moment. His palm was warm and dry, his hand thin but pleasantly padded, like the paw of a monkey.

"I'm Alexandra Boyd," she said. "I should have introduced myself before."

"Alexandra of Macedon," he said, smiling. "Do you know what your name means?"

"No." She felt that she should have, since she'd lived with it so long now.

He nodded. "It means 'defender of men.' Are you going to protect me?"

This time Alexandra smiled. "Certainly," she said.

Twelve

The drive out of Sofia was unlike anything she had ever seen. There were signs everywhere, and in the crawling traffic she could make them out plainly: Cyrillic, sometimes English, occasionally French, German, or Greek. There were street signs directing the traffic and the pedestrians, signs pointing toward small hotels, signs for key copying shops, bicycle repair, and fresh meat; signs for flowers, with flowers in buckets all around them. She noticed brass placards on monuments to soldiers and statues of gesturing men in long frock coats, some of the pedestals sporting bright-colored graffiti.

When Bobby stopped at a traffic light, she

stared at the ads taped to lampposts and tried to figure out what they meant: tear off this number and call today to learn English, lose weight, acquire a wheelchair, travel to Greece or Turkey, report a found dog—this last was obvious, with a grainy photograph in black and white. In fact, there were dogs on many of the streets, something she hadn't noticed before; they appeared not lost or found but feral, dodging the traffic with little fear, urinating on the curbs, sniffing one another, sniffing the pedestrians—who held their packages or skirts or hands away from them. To Alexandra, they looked like wolves, trotting in packs along the edges of the parks, at large but absorbed in their own errands.

More than dogs, there were people, and she couldn't help staring at them through the taxi window: people thronging the sidewalks, people in the shops, people talking at café tables, people selling used books under canvas canopies, selling new shoes in the windows of shops, begging for coins, pulling their children away from people begging for coins. She saw people pouring out of the university buildings and the change bureaus and bakeries and churches, carrying books or purses or cigarettes or old plastic bags. She saw the people of Sofia checking cell phones or watches or their breast pockets or—in little mirrors—their lipstick, getting into other taxis or stepping up into the blue and yellow trolleybuses beneath webs of electrical lines. There were old men with carefully preserved frayed jackets and bottle-thick eyeglasses, greeting each other and stopping to shake hands. She saw young women in tight jeans and curled glossy hair and fantastically long eyelashes; grandmothers in orange-and-brown print dresses, with a child on each hand; young men smoking with the sole of one shoe up against the side of a bank building; middle-aged women hurrying somewhere in high heels.

As they left the center of the city, they passed more apartment buildings, some recently built but most looking at least a century old. They skirted a park; several monuments went by too quickly for her to see well, although she caught a glimpse of a huge pedestal bristling with figures and rifles.

"Excuse me," she said, but Bobby didn't seem to hear her. Then she realized it was one of the few images she already knew from her guidebook—a monument to the Red Army, which had occupied the country in September 1944. *"An invasion by the Soviet Union—or a communist revolution, depending on whom you talk to,"* the book noted. She wondered whom she might get to talk to, herself, and whether people were actually still talking about this, and where. In line at the grocery store? At parties? Back home, World War II was ancient history—except in Hollywood—and had been buried with honors. Her great-uncle, recently dead, had flown over these lands as a teenager, bombing Romania and Bulgaria; she wondered if his plane had ever dropped a bomb on the park where the monument now stood.

Bobby's taxi gathered speed on a wide boulevard and the center of the city fell away, followed by a zone of ramshackle stores—furniture, fabric, clothing, wares displayed beside the front doors or behind dusty plate glass windows. Suddenly she could see some of the massive housing complexes she had observed from the air a few hours earlier. Bobby pointed in that direction and spoke, and she leaned forward to hear over the warm rush of wind and traffic. The taxi did not seem to have air-conditioning, or perhaps he just didn't like to use it; he'd left the front windows open.

"I'm sorry?" she shouted.

"I was raised there," he shouted back. She turned to stare at clusters of giant buildings; from this closer vantage they appeared fragile, with weedy fields around them and construction barriers in some of the parking lots, or groves of scraggly young birch trees at their feet. She had no idea which of twenty or thirty structures he was pointing to. They weren't white, as they had seemed from the plane window high above. And although they were clearly modern, they looked already like a great ruin, some of their outer layers cracked and dropping off in sections.

"*Panelki*—that's what we call them," he shouted; it would be days before she actually learned the word and understood what he had said. "Because they were made of panels, pre-fabricated." She didn't see any panels—only rows of metal balconies, many with laundry on them, some full of flowers and even green trees in pots.

He waved to her again, over his shoulder. "The official name for them is *blokove*. I grew up right over there." They all seemed disastrously the same to Alexandra; she would have preferred a vista of little villages. Besides, she wished he would look only straight ahead.

The road left the city in two lanes with a chipped concrete barrier between them, nothing like a highway. She watched some houses go by, a suburban area—squat stucco in various colors and conditions, most with red tile roofs, many with chain-link fences outside, or concrete walls. In front of one house there was a wire gate with two big dogs barking wildly behind it. In another yard she saw a sweet-eyed donkey looking over a wall, and she wondered if they were now officially out of the city. Alexandra thought about trying to write down some of what she was seeing, but what was the point? She would never use those scrawls for anything, now that she had no stories to tell.

Instead, she leaned out the window with her camera and photographed the houses, the yards with newly leafed apple and peach orchards in them. Kitchen gardens flourished everywhere, vigorous potato plants, peas and beans climbing up strings, tomato stalks with small green tomatoes already swelling on them. She saw an elderly couple in their garden; the woman stood with her hands on her hips, the man leaning on his hoe. Alexandra realized that the taxi was the only car on this road now.

She bent forward to shout to Bobby again. "How far did you say it was to the monastery? I mean, how long?"

"The time?" Bobby suddenly slowed. Five or six chickens crossed, officious, leisurely. He honked at them.

"Yes." She had to lean even farther forward to hear.

"Do you want to sit in the front seat?" he called out. He stopped by a wall made of something speckled black and white, like the chickens. She didn't like to leave the bag with the urn alone, but finally she set it on the floor in the back, bracing it with her own luggage so that it wouldn't tip over.

When she stepped out of the taxi everything seemed suddenly different, inside of her and out. She did not feel sleepy anymore, or had moved beyond sleep to a brilliant new fatigue. She had the urge to touch the trees leaning over the wall beside her, a couple of weeping birches and a peach tree with hard-looking fruits the size of walnuts. The air was soft and fresh and clean-smelling, after Sofia. Alexandra filled her lungs and climbed in next to Bobby. It was odd being close to another person in this new place, his denim knee and his hand on the gearshift. She resolved that if he put that hand on her, anywhere, she would open the door and threaten to jump out. The front of the cab was more worn than the back, although it seemed clean; the seat showed a fringe of loose stuffing around her thighs. From the rearview mirror he had hung a string of beads that ended with something that looked like an ancient silver coin. She could see an owl on one side of the coin—and then, when it twirled around, the profile of a woman with her hair in a knot at the nape of her neck.

Bobby pulled out into the road again. "You don't have to use your seat belt," he admonished her sharply. She was hunting for the buckle. "I am a very good driver."

"I can see that," she told him. He was apparently an odd bird, annoyed and somehow annoying, and she thought without wanting to of Jack's frequent moods. She said, "I promised my mother that I would always wear a seat belt, even if I went to the moon."

He laughed, turning in her direction. His face seemed suddenly older, perhaps because wrinkles leapt into play around his eyes, so that the blue almost vanished. She was relieved when he looked ahead at the road again.

"I promised my mother, also," he said. "Not

about the moon—only to use the seat belt. Especially since I must drive every day."

"Do you do this full time?"

Bobby frowned, picking up speed again. At the edge of the suburbs, open fields spread out on both sides of the road. In the distance she saw mountains coming closer, steeper than the ones that loomed above Sofia. In the taxi's side mirror, she got a glimpse of her familiar self, the freckled pale oval of her face, the serious green gaze and thin mouth, her father's rusty eyelashes and eyebrows, her fierce obsidian earrings. It was like encountering an old friend in an unexpected setting. As always, she saw Jack in herself, too, although her hair was more brown than red and her skin fair instead of ruddy like his. But they'd had the same eyes.

Bobby stretched his arms, settling in behind the steering wheel. "Drive full time? No, not really. Maybe thirty-five hours a week."

This seemed to Alexandra rather close to full time—perhaps Bobby had to hold down two jobs, in this economy. She felt delicate about asking more, so she just nodded. "How long did you say it'll take us to reach the monastery?"

He smiled. "I did not say. It would be about another hour."

Alexandra felt her insides lurch. "An hour? But we've been on the road at least half an hour, haven't we?"

"Yes, well—naturally." She wondered if he was making fun of her. "Velinski *manastir* is not so far away. The problem is the road. Very twisted, with a lot of turns. It's up there, at the beginning of the Rila Mountains"—he pointed through the wind-shield, toward the high forest—"so we can almost see it now. But the route is complicated."

"Your English is really good," she said, partly to distract herself from the thought of that mountain road and partly to express appreciation for his driving her up it for relatively little money. "I'd like to learn some Bulgarian. I know only five or six words, so far."

"I'm certain you can learn a great deal," he said. "But it is a hard language. We have difficult verbs." He laughed, clearly proud—his verbs stumping foreigners.

"That's not good news," said Alexandra. They grinned at each other. Then she grabbed the sides of her seat. A car was coming straight toward them, in their lane. She tried not to scream; she willed herself not to seize Bobby's arm. Her mother and father flashed through her mind, and then the car swerved back into its own lane and she saw it had been passing a slower driver. Her heart raced in her throat, in her temples.

"Are you all right?" Bobby said.

"That car," Alexandra said weakly. "Almost hit us."

"No, no—he was just passing. It is a passing zone here. I would not let him hit us."

Alexandra did not know what to say. She felt that their headlights and the headlights of the oncoming car had practically kissed. She had seen very clearly the driver of the other car, head on, a man in a bright green T-shirt—his eyes, his expression of concentration. He must be a couple of kilometers behind them by now, at that speed. On the interstates back home, he would already have been pulled over and given a great big ticket.

"Oh," Alexandra said. "I'm used to American roads, I guess. There's some speeding there, too, of course." But she couldn't get her blood to stop fizzing. She focused on the view of fields.

Bobby was speaking to her again. "Where are you from, in the U.S.?"

"North Carolina," she said. "It's in the South."

"I've heard of it." She saw that for him it was an obscure name, as *Bulgaria* had been for her, and for Jack.

"What is an American doing here, in any case?" He shifted down; a hill rose ahead and she saw the road had turned now in the direction of those soft dark folds, the higher mountains that held their destination.

"I'm going to teach English." She tried to compose herself. "I have a job starting at the end of June, tutoring at a language program. I wanted to come here early—to travel around before I begin work."

"Well, you are traveling already," he said. "Is your job in Sofia?"

"Yes—it's at the Central English Institute," she said, examining his face for further sharpness, but he looked approving.

"Brilliant. They have an excellent reputation and many students. First rate." He took a curve into the shade of woodland. They were leaving behind the crops, the vast fields and distant villages receding to smudges of red and beige. The forest was deep, sprinkled with sun; the trees were mossy spruces and stands of oak and beech.

"So you think Sofia is a good place to work?" she ventured.

"It is the only place," he said solemnly. "You can do a lot there, see the theater and go to lectures and concerts. Of course, those things often cost money."

"Have you ever lived anywhere else, in Bulgaria —I mean, outside Sofia?"

He shook his head. "No."

"Or anywhere else? Another country?"

Then she felt she had been rude; probably he had never had the chance. He surprised her: "Yes, in England."

"Why England?"

"I worked some construction there."

"Really?" she said. So that was how he'd acquired the accent.

"You see, I am a Sofia intellectual." He smiled at her. "We sometimes go to do construction in England. I took one year of time off in the middle of my university. Liverpool. Some friends arranged it. I learned a lot of Polish there, too, actually."

She felt too jet-lagged to process this. He was a Sofia intellectual and he drove a cab? And what in particular made him call himself an intellectual? Was that a kind of title, here?

"It must have been very interesting," she said lamely. "Is that why you speak such good English?"

"It's not so good," Bobby said. His brusqueness seemed to have returned. "I also went to Sofia University in English philology. I can tell you all about George Bernard Shaw, if you want. But I am forgetting a lot of words."

She stared at him. Then he laughed. "Are you hungry?" He was looking her over—more as if he thought she might be showing the first signs of starvation, she thought, than as if he found her attractive.

"Yes, a little. Mostly very tired." That reminded her of something. She unbuckled, leaned over the back of her seat, and caught the handle of her purse. Inside was a packet of airplane pretzels. She offered him a few, which he accepted with alacrity.

"Thank you. We can stop for some lunch later, if you would like," he said. "I just don't want to lose the time."

"I don't want to, either." She wished she had a bottle of water and hoped his proposal of lunch wouldn't lead to dinner, or a room for the night. If she had to ditch him, she would keep the urn with her, protect it, find a ride on to the monastery.

But he was looking at her with amusement. "I thought that your mother said to you to wear your seat belt."

"Well, see—I'm buckling it again," she told him. She felt a pang of relief. Here she was, sitting right next to him, and he seemed respectful—no hand on her knee, just a friendly question or two.

After that they didn't speak for a while. She kept thinking about a normal meal, and a clean bed, and a hot shower, but she was thankful for her empty stomach as the mountain road became dizzying.

Thirteen

Near the end of their journey Bobby turned off into a narrow lane; Alexandra saw a brown sign that said ВЕЛИНСКИ МАНАСТИР/VELINSKI MANASTIR with a white symbol next to the words, a church or a castle. This new road was dirt, although hard-packed and clean; it wound among rocky cliffs half-hidden by trees. She had definitely been awake long enough now to stop minding being awake at all.

"Here we are," said Bobby, and they drove in past stone pillars and an iron gate that stood wide open. He steered along an alley of enormous peeling sycamores. The walls of the monastery rose up before them, forbidding but also mellowed by profound age, a sight that made Alexandra's heart leap—this was the kind of thing she had hoped to see. On one side, vines had grown densely over the stones. Small towers and slate roofs were visible above the walls.

Alexandra scanned the parking area, which contained four or five cars, but Bobby had already been looking. "There is no other taxi here," he said flatly.

"They could have told the driver to go back to Sofia," she proposed. "Or come on a bus, like you said."

"Yes, of course." He pulled the hand brake. "Probably yes. Especially if they were going to sleep in the monastery for a couple of days." Then he looked doubtful. "But they would not do that without the urn, I think. They would be looking for you, or going home to wait."

"So you can stay here? Even if you are not—a monk?" she asked, thinking again of a bed, a door with a lock.

"Yes," he said. "You can stay for a month if you

make a reservation. People do that for a rest, sometimes, or if they are very religious. If your people are coming by bus, we will need to wait for them here for a while, at least half an hour."

She took the bag and her purse with her and Bobby locked her computer in the trunk with her suitcase. The urn seemed heavier than before—she didn't remember its weighing so much on her arm in front of the hotel, before she had known what it was. She thought of a life, a face she had never seen and couldn't imagine, a real human body full of its own experiences, its memories. And now this. Perhaps he had been young, with a firm jaw and a startling smile. Perhaps the old man and woman had lost their other son, or a teenaged grandson. Now he was ashes, in the arms of a stranger. She thought of the tall man, standing with one hand on his son's shoulder. The son would be a little shorter, but even more beautiful; the man would grip him with that big hand. She could feel the warmth of it for a moment on her own shoulder. The son would be smiling, shy. How such a thing could happen at all: Alexandra carrying his urn across a parking lot, in a holy place, under these palatial trees. She felt tears of anger spring to her eyes.

Bobby had put on a denim jacket as worn as his jeans—it was cool here, after the Sofia streets. "This way," he said, and she saw that the doors to the monastery were open—smoke-darkened nicked wood beneath a stone arch. There was a painted sign above them, an elaborate Cyrillic she could not even sound out.

Bobby saw her looking. "It says something like, 'This monastery is to the glory of God and of the Holy Virgin Mary, 1349.' That is when the oldest part of it was built, I think. The rest is a little more new, from the early time of the eighteen hundreds." A group of tourists had surrounded them and were looking at the words, too. Alexandra could hear them speaking French, the women pushing sunglasses up onto their hair.

"Come," Bobby said.

Inside, the courtyard was drenched with sunshine, apart from the shadowed wooden galleries that ran around the second and third stories. A small stone church basked like a hen in the middle of the yard, digging itself in, pointed cypresses clustered around it. Underfoot the yard was cobblestone, and she noticed a dog lying in the sun, all its swollen nipples on display. Beside the gate was a glass kiosk—definitely not medieval—with a placard: POLITSIYA, she sounded out. In the kiosk sat a single figure in a uniform.

There were a few people walking here and there, or entering the church, but she saw no sign of an old man in a wheelchair, an old woman with weirdly auburn and gray hair, or a tall upright man in a black vest looking all around for the foreigner who'd taken their bag. It had seemed so real to her that they would be there that she felt shocked not to see them. They must be somewhere else, inside the buildings.

Bobby took her elbow, then seemed to think better of this and dropped his hand. Alexandra was not sorry. "They might be in the church," he said. "They might go inside to see if you are there, maybe. Or to pray."

For their treasure to be returned to them, she thought. She got a tighter grip on the bag and followed him. The church had a small wooden porch; haloed portraits flanked the door, a man with a long black beard and a man with a long white beard—twin bodyguards. She walked between them into darkness that suddenly became musty candlelight. In the dim entryway, a woman in a cage was selling books, postcards, and thin yellow candles. Alexandra felt terribly lonely. The air in the church was chill and damp, like the breath of a cave. Yes: she and Jack had gone to Dixie Caverns in Virginia once, on a rare road trip with their parents, and this had been the smell down there, the four of them huddling together along wooden walkways. Earth, the depths of it, cold rock and trickling water. If there were a hell, she thought, it must be cold, like Hades, a land of shadows with this frightening stillness emerging from nowhere. The Greeks had it right—no fire, just the chill breath of the Styx, a river that flowed underground, carrying away everyone you loved, the sound of oars dipping too quietly into dark currents.

Bobby stopped in front of the cage and bought several candles. "One is for you," he said in a gentle voice, as if he had guessed the nature of her thoughts.

She followed him into the nave, and the inside of that was a surprise, too—a high space, entirely painted with smudged figures. Light filtered into it from the dome above. It contained no pews, only a row of tall chairs like thrones along the walls. Across the far end, she saw a screen of gold branches and leaves, purple velvet curtains, crowned faces taut with resignation. Here and there stood candelabra with those yellow candles dissolving in them, the smell of incense and flame, beeswax. There were four other people in the chapel—a young man in a track suit, two women in black skirts and high heels crossing themselves in front of an icon, a little boy in shorts who stood twisting one foot around the other. And behind them Alexandra herself, with that weight in her arms, and Bobby—Asparuh— somehow dignified in his jacket and jeans. They turned and looked at each other. Alexandra felt the long scar on her arm begin to sting. She stretched her other hand toward it, across the urn, to calm herself.

"We can search in the monastery," Bobby told her. But first he went to the nearest candelabrum, lit one of the candles he had bought, and set it into a holder.

"Up here at the top is for the living," he told her in a low voice. "And down here, in the sand" —he indicated a tin box below filled with what looked horribly like ashes, for a moment—"is for the dead." He held a second candle out to her. "This one is for you," he said. "Do you want to put it somewhere?"

Alexandra shrank back.

"Where shall I light it?" he asked patiently.

"Down there, please," said Alexandra. "In the sand."

Outside they walked around the courtyard, to check in every direction. Alexandra saw a monk hurrying along one of the wooden galleries on the first floor—how old, how unbelievably ancient it all looked, even the monk, who appeared as time-worn as the frescoes inside the church. He wore a tall black hat like an inverted chimney that seemed to have sprouted out of his black hair and black beard, his dark robes. Bobby went to speak with him. Alexandra kept her distance; she recalled reading somewhere that monks did not like even to speak to women, lest they be tempted. Bobby made shapes and signs with his hands. The monk kept his own hands at his belt, holding them as still as if he had captured a pair of birds.

At last the monk spoke, and she saw Bobby shake his head. He came slowly back to her.

"They aren't here," said Alexandra.

"It's strange. They told you they were coming to Velin, and they did not return to the hotel. If they came directly here, they left at least thirty minutes before us. And this priest has just told me that there is no bus coming today—it is not one of the right days of the week for a bus. So they could only come by taxi, or borrow a car, something like that. They should be here already. He also said that no visitors who look like those people have registered today for sleeping here."

"I see," she said. She wished she could set down the bag, leave it quietly in a corner of the chapel, so that someone else—maybe that monk—would find it and take care of it. Perhaps he would simply bury it here, or wherever their cemetery was. That would be almost right, in the larger scheme of things.

"Maybe they went to the police station, instead, but after I left it." A familiar taste was welling in her mouth—the trail behind her empty, no one stepping energetically over the tree roots. She hadn't managed to do the right thing in this situation, either.

"I think we must walk into the remainder of the building, to be sure," Bobby was saying.

"Are we allowed to do that?"

He shrugged. "If someone doesn't like it, they will tell us."

They went all around the lowest gallery, looking

into each open room. The floors were flagstones, the lintels of the doors massive horizontal stones, the doors themselves worm-eaten dark wood. There was a library, lined with crumbling books, and a bare room with a long table and benches, perhaps the old refectory. There were empty rooms and rooms with locked doors.

When they came to a flight of wooden stairs, they took it to the second-floor gallery. Up there they found a big echoing dormitory bathroom, with elderly porcelain sinks and spiders in the corners. Alexandra stayed behind to use one of the toilets, which flushed by means of a long chain overhead.

All the other doors on the second floor were shut. "Probably the monks live up here," Bobby told her in a low voice.

They took another staircase back down to the first floor. There was one more open door to check there, which let them into a room full of brittle-looking documents and church paraphernalia in glass-topped cases, and a second room of the same beyond that—a museum devoted to the history of the monastery, apparently. The yellowing index cards next to the exhibits were typed in English and French as well as Bulgarian. There were no other tourists or monks here. Bobby shook his head and led the way back toward the gallery.

The door through which they'd entered was shut, although Alexandra was sure they had left it open behind them. Bobby pressed on the handle. He pushed. He turned to her.

"What?" she said.

"I think it is locked." He tried the handle again. It was old and heavy, iron bolted into wood, and it made an impotent clanking sound.

"But we just came in here," she said.

Bobby's face drew down into concentration; she felt almost afraid to look at him, exhausted and confused as she already was.

"Bloody hell," he said, and it sounded like something worse. "Somebody has locked it from the outside."

Fourteen

Alexandra was not only very tired, but also young, in both years and experience. The loss of her brother had prepared her to a significant degree for the imperfection of the world, but that event had been thrown into relief for her by the very fact that it followed a childhood of kindness and simplicity: Jules Verne and digging potatoes, and the protective love of her parents. Her most recent life—four years at a good college, and then a few years of shelving books—had given her a vague sense of freedom with no disorder attached, apart from her inner misery.

In other words, nothing in her previous experience had prepared her for the feeling of being suddenly locked in a monastic room with a stranger five thousand miles from the Blue Ridge Mountains, holding an urn containing the ashes of another stranger. In addition to being tired and afraid, she was suddenly a thief, a vagrant, and a prisoner. Is it any wonder that when Asparuh (whose patrician first name was just a mumble of sound to her) announced that they were trapped alone together, her first thought was terror? He was not a nice guy after all; he had locked the door on purpose himself. He had some kind of Balkan switchblade in his pocket, and a predilection for foreign flesh. The door was not actually locked, but he'd decided to tell her it was, and now he would—what? He had seemed so respectful, helpful, if a little sharp-edged. She took a step away from him as they stood there. Then, feeling she had to know at any price, she made herself go quickly to the door and try it. It really was locked—for a minute she felt relieved.

She turned to Bobby. "Do you think it just got stuck somehow?"

To her surprise, he put a finger to his lips, bent his ear close to the bolt, and listened. Then he shook his head.

"No," he whispered. "No. I heard feet outside, a minute ago, and now the feet are leaving the hall."

"Maybe they close the museum at this time of

day," she whispered back. "Shall we knock on the door until someone hears us?"

But he stopped her with a quick movement. "We were talking normally in here, and anyone could hear us," he murmured. "Let me think for a moment."

Which he did, visibly, standing in total silence with his thumbs hooked in the front pockets of his jeans—Alexandra stood there also, watching him and feeling a strange trust. But why on earth didn't he just bang on the door until someone realized they were shut in? Was he paranoid by nature, or had she missed something, very possibly, that he had understood?

"I think there was another door," he said at last. He turned and walked silently back through the two rooms, Alexandra following with the urn. One wall of the far room was hung with dark curtains, as if to shade the exhibits from sunlight. Almost out of sight, beyond the last cases of reliquaries and rotting manuscripts, there was indeed a door she hadn't noticed. The lock looked modern, with an ordinary keyhole and a steel handle. Bobby knelt to peer through the hole before slowly trying the handle. This door was clearly locked, too, and Alexandra felt a quiver of panic again. Perhaps he really was crazy, and she was still shut in here with him, even if he hadn't locked the doors himself. Then he groped in the lining of his denim jacket and brought out what looked like a tiny screwdriver, which he inserted into the lock, working the handle gently with his other hand. After a few moments something clicked.

But the door did not budge. "Hell," he whispered. "It has a big—bolt thing—on the outside."

He turned to Alexandra. "Come. We are going to look for another way, but very quiet, okay?"

She stared at him—*He knew how to pick locks?*—and then nodded, and he began to check the long windows and sills. Everything seemed to be bolted or nailed shut. Suddenly he stopped short, and she heard steps outside, coming toward the door on the gallery corridor. She could see the inside of that door through the opening between the rooms. The worst part was that there were no voices, no one speaking outside, just the sound of a key going gently into the lock. Someone had trouble with the bolt and tried again, and in that moment Bobby put a hand out and pulled Alexandra with him behind the curtains. *We won't fit back there,* she wanted to say.

To her surprise, and perhaps also to Bobby's, they stumbled around the curtains into a larger space, a room for presentations, apparently—plastic chairs in rows, a video screen on one wall, posters with photos of the monastery. At the other end were two more doors. Bobby opened the first with a quick movement and drew her in. They found themselves in a closet, which contained a few boxes and a broom. He closed the door with silent speed and they stood wedged together in the dark; Bobby's hand seemed to be doing something to the handle—locking it somehow, from the inside. She felt rather than heard him let out his breath.

Then there was the thud of heavy steps—at least two people, from the sound of it. Alexandra, with the urn squeezed between her stomach and Bobby's back, wondered why they were hiding. Her heart jumped around uncomfortably and she prayed she wouldn't feel his hands on her in the dark, fiddling with her as they had with the lock. But he stayed still, listening. She could smell him very close—a scent of light sweat and after-shave, as if he kept himself radiantly clean. She hoped he would explain everything when this was over. The darkness pressed against her face, her eyes, and she thought this might be part of an extended dream. Perhaps she was really in a hostel bed in Sofia, or in her mother's apartment in Greenhill; the rest of it, what was actually happening, was too bizarre to be real.

But Bobby's absolute quiet kept her motionless. There were no voices outside—just firm steps starting and stopping. The sound came closer. Someone was now in the presentation room; she heard whoever it was bump into something. For an awful second the sound halted and she thought that the people in the room must be listening hard, as she and Bobby were. Then footsteps again, and somebody tried the door of their closet, roughly. In the dark, she felt she might faint with apprehension; Bobby closed a hand on one of her wrists, as if to warn her not to move. There was a grunt outside, and the hands seemed to be trying the door next to the closet, which didn't open, either. Her knees had begun to quiver and she squeezed them together. Then both sets of footsteps moved away. Alexandra heard the outer door open and shut—the sound of keys again, the rattle of the handle, a bolt dropping into place.

They waited again in the dark so long that Alexandra thought she might doze off in the midst of her bewilderment. At last Bobby softly unlocked the closet door. He opened it and put his head out to look before beckoning to Alexandra. She drew a long breath, but silently. There was no one in the presentation room, although she could see that two of the chairs had been knocked out of line. Bobby tried the door next to the closet—it was locked, as the searchers had discovered, but he took the mysterious tool out of his jacket and worked at the keyhole until the handle moved. Again, he looked out first, then motioned Alexandra to stay close behind him.

The door led into a short dark passage. At the end was a larger door, a very old one, that ejected them directly into sunlight. Alexandra got a glimpse of scraggly trees and a stone well just outside. She followed Bobby down several steps onto bare ground, trying not to trip in the brightness. Mountains loomed just above them and she realized that they were emerging into an orchard —apple trees laden with green leaves.

Bobby began to make his way along the outside of the monastery, staying behind the screen of trees and touching the outer wall for balance once when he tripped. Alexandra thought they must look suspicious doing this, even if they had been locked in through no fault of their own, and she hoped nobody was watching from the slits of window far above. She kept close to the wall, imitating him, and tried not to stare up at the massive building. He took a long way around the parked cars and unlocked his taxi without haste. He started the engine gently, looking around him.

They were back on the main road before Alexandra felt she could ask anything. "What was—"

He broke in at once. "I'm sorry if I made you to be nervous," he said, and she saw the sober blue of his glance, checking her. She had automatically gotten into the back seat again, but he said nothing about that. He peered into his mirrors several times, as if he thought someone might follow them; she turned around, but the road behind them stretched empty through the woods.

Bobby straightened at the wheel. "I didn't have a good feeling about the first door. Somebody heard us there and locked us in, not by accident. There is no other explanation. We were talking quite normally in the museum and we were not far away from the door. And then someone else came in to look for us, or maybe the same people."

"I thought so—I heard that, too." Alexandra reached down and touched the urn where she'd settled it firmly between her feet. "But why would anyone lock us in?"

She watched Bobby's eyes flicker again to his rearview mirror; this time he spoke without looking at her. "I am not sure."

"Then why did we have to hide?"

Bobby raked his hair off his forehead with one hand. "When people want to lock me into a room, I do not want to meet them."

"But what do you think they would have done if they'd found us?" said Alexandra. "Whoever they were?"

Bobby answered her only with another question, and she saw she would get nothing more from him. "What would you like to do now?" he said. "Shall I drive you back to Sofia?"

Alexandra clenched her hands together in her lap. "I guess I ought to go to the Bovech address, the one the police gave me. I think it's on the other side of Sofia from here, a lot farther away." Part of her couldn't believe she was saying this, but where else could she take the urn? Bobby seemed to be driving even faster than he had on the way to the monastery; maybe he was just tired of the whole thing now and wanted to dump her off in Sofia so he could get on with other work. Now that it was over, their standing squashed together in a dark closet seemed as unreal to her as her arrival in Sofia had before.

"So you want to go to their home?" he asked.

"Well, I feel I have to try," she said.

"Of course," he agreed. "If this were the funeral of my own grandfather, I would like somebody to try. But I see you are very tired. Maybe you need to rest, first."

"How did you know what to do with that lock?"

This time his eyes were smiling at her in the mirror. "One door of my taxi is sometimes difficult to open. So is the door to my apartment. I always carry with me some tools for that. Are you hungry, by the way?"

"Am I hungry?" she said—she almost shouted —and he began to laugh. She realized he'd already turned off the main road, and then onto another road, well out of sight of the first, and slowed the car.

Fifteen

They had come to a wooden building under trees, with a dirt parking lot and some potted vines on trellises in front.

"*Dvorut*," she read out loud. "What does that mean?"

"It means 'The Courtyard.' The name of this restaurant. I hope they are open."

Bobby led the way into a single room lined with windows and filled with sunny tables; Alexandra could see a stream cascading off the steep slope just behind. A television sat on a shelf above the cash register and there was a tinny murmur of folk music from a loudspeaker in the corner. Two waiters leaned against the counter, watching the television, and a woman with bleached hair sat nearby typing on her cell phone. Some of the windows were open to let in the sound of rushing water and the crisp vegetal smell of mountain air. There were no other customers in the place, and apparently they were to seat themselves.

Bobby chose a table near the back and slumped opposite her, stretching his arms.

"You must be tired, too," she said.

"Certainly. I get up at four o'clock in the morning."

And you just got locked into a monastery, she added to herself. "To drive your taxi?"

"No," he said. "And I am not as tired as you are. How long does it take to travel from your part of America? Twenty-four hours?"

"Almost," she said. "I live in a small city, so I had to fly to a much bigger one, and then to Amsterdam, and then to Sofia. Maybe twenty hours. Counting the waits between flights." She wished he would explain why he got up so early, but he didn't seem to like answering questions about himself. She hoped that was not a bad sign.

"I've never been to America," Bobby told her. He was looking around the restaurant, as if he thought someone he didn't like might walk in. She had begun to realize that he was one of the most alert people she'd ever met—more like a bird, or a wild animal, than a human being. He pulled a cell phone out of his pocket and read some texts, but without replying to any of them. A waiter listlessly approached their table and handed them a couple of menus. When he was gone, Bobby began to explain the dishes to her.

"Do they have trout?" she said.

"Trout? Yes. In Bulgarian it's called *pusturva*. How did you know there is trout?"

"I come from mountains, too," she said, smiling. "This stream looks like some of the ones we have at home. Probably really cold water, and clean. But I don't actually want any trout."

In the end, he ordered for her—a soup of thin beef broth and vegetables ("Very good for you after traveling," he said, and she decided not to tell him that she normally didn't eat meat), a salad of cucumbers and tomatoes heaped with shavings of feta, and a plate of French fries. For himself, he ordered several large meatballs, a salad like hers, and three steaming cups of black coffee, one after another. He also insisted on getting Alexandra a Coca-Cola, although she protested that not all Americans drank it.

"It will make you feel stronger," he said, and in the end she swallowed the whole thing, with a pang of nostalgia for childhood—when it had been a rare treat, with equally rare pizza. She told Bobby about this and he laughed. "Here you can have both of those things any time you wish. Bulgaria is full of pizza. And Coke, everywhere. But it was not like that when I was a child. We had a Bulgarian kind of cola called Altay. Same problems for our teeth, however, with either one." He looked quickly around the room, as if he'd forgotten for a moment to stay on guard. "I was fifteen when the changes came, so I remember the old drinks quite well. And some other things, too."

"The changes?" Alexandra was still eating her salad, which was good.

"In 1989, when our communist dictator was deposed. And our change to democracy, the next year—or at least to a new kind of capitalism," he said. "First we had the Turks, then we had the Russians, and now we have Coca-Cola." She got the sense that none of these things had worked out very well, in his opinion. "We have not solved our other problems, either."

"Yes, I read about 1989," she said. "I didn't know what you called it, except the fall of the Berlin Wall."

"That fell far away from here," Bobby said. "Maybe too far away. I have always thought it was strange that Ronald Reagan congratulated himself about the end of the Wall, and then the governments on our side of the Wall congratulated themselves also. Actually, it was all to the credit of Pink Floyd. They built The Wall and they made it fall down one little piece at a time."

Alexandra had no idea what he meant, but she saw it was partly a joke—partly—and smiled. He had become so talkative that she thought she could ask him again the thing that weighed most on her, after the urn itself.

"Back there, in the monastery," she said, carefully. "Our getting locked in. You said it wasn't an accident, so who do you think *would* do that?"

Bobby sighed. "I told you—I don't know, but I didn't like it. You lock someone in if you don't want them to leave. That's why I wanted us to leave right away. Or maybe somebody just wished to scare us."

Alexandra was still puzzled. "But if somebody tried to keep us there, for some reason, wouldn't they follow us afterward?" She glanced around the restaurant, as Bobby had been doing since they sat down. Maybe, she thought, anyone who had grown up under communism had some natural paranoia. Apparently it was contagious, too.

"No one followed us—and they would not look for us here," he said. "It is well hidden from the road—and they would expect that we will drive fast back to Sofia, probably. And I don't think that they were watching for us to leave, because they must have believed that we were somewhere else in the monastery."

Alexandra wanted to ask him if he thought the police could be following him still because of the demonstrations he had been in, but now he was staring at the television set in the corner; she saw that a Bulgarian news program had come on.

"Shh," he said, not very gently.

It was hard for her to hear even the unintelligible language over the sound of the rushing stream outside. Men and women with news cameras and microphones were moving rapidly around a broad-shouldered man in a suit. The man had a wide, pale, elderly face dominated by a brown beard and mustache. His curly chestnut hair reached almost to his shoulders—a mane, but tight and neat, and somehow not natural. Alexandra thought it must be dyed, since it was chestnut, not gray. He looked harassed, turned away, then turned back to say something. He raised a hand to the cameras, got hastily into a limousine. A woman at a news desk was talking now, with a photo behind her of a ravaged mountainside and construction machinery—front loaders and bulldozers, trucks tipping dirt onto piles. She smiled dismissively and set aside a piece of paper. This was followed by an ad that even Alexandra could understand was for laundry detergent; it showed a mother transforming dirty little shirts into objects white as snow for her twin babies. A blissful vision of the Alps, and the mother gazing upward, completely happy for the first time in her life.

"What was it?" Alexandra asked.

Bobby picked up his coffee again. "A story about Kurilkov. He is our Minister of Roads, a very powerful man. With the Minister of the Interior, he is opening some old mines I told you about—the thing that we were demonstrating against, you know—and he had a press conference about them today."

Alexandra watched the disgust flicker across Bobby's face. "So these mines are an environmental problem?"

"There is that. A lot of water pollution and poisoning of land. Also, people are saying that Kurilkov received bribes from some companies to reopen the mines, and they will have a share of the profit, but he denies this in the press. The mines are in a rough area in our central mountains, not good roads—they must build new roads to support the project, and Kurilkov will give approval for this."

Alexandra thought of the demonstrations at home—mountaintop removal, minimum wage, the nuclear plant proposed for a river valley downstate. "Isn't there anyone who can stop him? Somebody else in government?"

"Nobody dares to tell him no in the government because he is very rich and popular. And also maybe because people are afraid of his connections and his reputation for—I don't know how to say. He is very correct and clean and very hard on anyone who opposes him. They always lose their positions, in the end. He calls himself the Bear." Bobby shook his head, thoughtful, displeased.

"Why don't other politicians get rid of him, then?"

Bobby shrugged. "Many people think he will be the prime minister of Bulgaria someday, so they want to stay on his good side. His whole career is built on the idea that he cannot be corrupted, like the others, although he was once in our communist-era parliament, long time ago. He even wears his hair that special way, to show he is somehow different. If people oppose him, he accuses them of being corrupt themselves."

Bobby tapped his spoon on the table. "He calls it the 'new purity,' in his campaigns. No one is certain about him, but no one can prove anything against him, either. And he is like magic, for some people, who love the idea of a Bear to protect them. This is our system, Alexandra."

Alexandra felt that she had waded into deep waters, and she was too tired to consider much more. One thing was clear to her: Bobby was like the people she'd grown up with—her parents, her aunts and uncles and professors, all of them talking about history and politics. It made her feel strangely at home with him.

The waiter, who hadn't smiled at them a single time, now came through the long empty room to bring their check. Alexandra grabbed it and told Bobby that it was hers.

His face fell. "You are a visitor here—a guest," he said. She remembered with a little shock that she wasn't a guest at all, but a passenger in his taxi. "I will pay it myself," he said. He pushed her bills gently away and counted out several from his own wallet, weighting them with coins in the middle of the table. She sat frozen, wondering if she should protest. What did it mean? Would she owe him something later?

But he smiled at her, a normal, pleasant smile. "You've had your first Bulgarian meal, and it was not such a bad one, was it?"

Sixteen

By the time they reached Sofia, the streets were thronged with evening traffic, people escaping in masses at the end of the workday. Her hostel turned out to be an old apartment building painted entirely light blue and sporting a little café in the garden.

Then Alexandra discovered that she was already asleep and Bobby was shaking her awake, with the door to the cab open and her arm wagging back and forth. She gasped out loud.

"Do you want me to carry you upstairs?" he said.

"No, no. Please." She began to collect her bags, realizing all over again that she would have to take the urn with her.

He lifted her suitcase out of the trunk. "I will bring this for you."

She followed him into the blue building and leaned against the counter while he coaxed her passport out of her and gave it to a girl with green hair and purple earrings. "This is a nice place," he said encouragingly. "You will like it here. They have lectures and readings some-times, too, in the courtyard."

Alexandra looked at the room key in her hand. She remembered vaguely that keys opened doors.

Bobby had somehow put her luggage upstairs in her room already and then come back down. She appreciated his not trying to enter a hostel room with her, even just to drop off her luggage; she found she could no longer recall whether he was an old friend, a criminal, or simply another total stranger.

"I need to pay you," she said, opening her wallet.

"You are incredibly tired." He gave her shoulder an unexpected squeeze, which she found she didn't mind. "And you said you need to go to another town tomorrow—Bovech, right? All right, thirty *leva* for part of today, to make you feel better." He took the bills from her limp hand and counted them carefully, showing her the amount. "It is not so far to Bovech. Eight o'clock tomorrow morning, okay?"

She was suddenly afraid to see him go. "Do you have a cell number? I don't have a phone yet, but—"

Bobby wrote it down for her, with his full name in Latin letters. "You should go to sleep as soon as you can. Here is a bottle of water for your room, in case you want the mineral kind." He had thought even of that, apparently. He looked at her for a minute, his head tilted to one side. "See you tomorrow. Eight o'clock. Don't forget."

She wasn't likely to forget, unless she never woke up, which she thought a possibility.

But lying alone in her first Bulgarian bed—a

narrow twin with rough, very clean white sheets and a plaid blanket—she could not sleep, at first. Her luggage was ranged at the edge of the locked room she had longed for, only her suitcase open where it had disgorged pajamas and toothpaste. She had pulled down the shades and closed the curtains because it was still light outside. There was a weird electricity in the room—a low hum of life that drifted toward her from the bag in the corner, the polished urn. She was frightened, but she liked this new country—at least, she was glad she had not stayed home. Once she became drowsy, she forced herself to stay awake as long as she could, wishing not to be alone with a man whose life had completely fled, or with memories she couldn't begin to imagine.

Then sleep reached her, a sucking undertow, and she went over backward.

In the morning, Bobby was already sitting in the garden café when she entered it with the bag in her arms. Alexandra viewed him with some self-consciousness, because she had been so dazed when he'd last seen her. She felt now all the comforts of her long sleep and a shower, clean clothes. She had also been able to send her parents an email: *Safely in Sofia. It's beautiful here, with a lot of interesting old buildings. Taking a day trip today with some colleagues.* She'd expanded Bobby into both a colleague and a group so that

115

they wouldn't worry further. She had sent the English Institute a message, too, to let them know she'd arrived and would be ready to teach in late June, as planned.

Bobby stood up politely when she approached. He wore a different denim jacket, this one black with ragged cuffs, and a pair of ironed khakis, and he looked shaved and combed. He was shorter than she remembered, thinner of limb, his hair longer, his elbows cocked out.

"How are you this morning?" he said. "We can have breakfast. I hope you are hungry—again."

She smiled and sat down opposite him. There was a tree just above their table and no one else in the garden. The girl with green hair came out to take their order, except that this morning her hair was purple and her earrings red. Bobby said something that resulted in their being brought two cups of tea. Each cup had a small saucer over the top to keep it warm, with a slice of lemon, a packet of sugar, and a plastic stirrer resting neatly on top of that, a degree of ceremony that held Alexandra's newly recovered attention for several minutes. Bobby brushed the table clean with a paper napkin from his pocket and arranged the plates of cheese-toast that followed their tea. He gave Alexandra his second piece of toast and an extra slice of cucumber. "How did you sleep?"

Alexandra considered. "I slept well—very well —except now I remember this howling noise that

I couldn't quite wake up for." She had heard it in her dreams, through the window, and wondered if it was the crying of a baby, or a woman screaming. Then she'd startled to it again and realized it must be cats on the streets below, shrieking at each other. "Alley cats," she said. *In heat, probably.*

Bobby speared a slice of tomato. "Are you ready for another trip?"

"Yes. I think I should get this over with. I mean, I want to return the urn as soon as possible—I won't be able to think about anything else until I do."

"I understand." He put an avalanche of sugar into his tea. "It is lucky that the police had an address to give to you. Probably the people went home to wait for some news, so they will be very happy to see you."

"I hope so." Alexandra felt a stab of real, wide-awake curiosity about what she and Bobby might find in that small town—what kind of house the old people lived in, and perhaps the middle-aged man with them. Or maybe he lived just up the street with his own family. Unless the ashes did mean that he had lost his only son. Maybe he was a widower, too, and was now terribly alone. Chewing her toast, she imagined again their gratitude, their surprise. The old woman might cry a little, and press Alexandra's hand between her swollen ones. The tall man, with an arm around each of his frail parents, would ask her what they could possibly do for her in return. He would drive her back to Velin Monastery with them, and they would all light a candle together in the church, for Stoyan Lazarov. Then the tall man would kiss her cheek, and ask quietly if he could come to Sofia to take her out to dinner, as a thank-you. But perhaps he couldn't afford that, or wouldn't think of it. Probably he wouldn't let her pay for a meal, either, like Bobby. She put her hand to her cheek, to protect the sensation there.

"Alexandra?" Bobby ran a hand through his hair, moving it fruitlessly out of his eyes, and she saw a shrewd, canine glance—he was like one of those surprising blue-eyed Siberian huskies in *National Geographic.* "Miss Boyd," he added, as if trying out the rest of her name. "You said *Boyd,* right? Alexandra—are you Russian?"

She laughed. "No. My parents just liked old-fashioned names. And Boyd is English, I mean English from England."

"Boyd," he said. "It sounds like *Bird,* and you are a little like a bird. Shall I call you that?"

"I guess so," she said, but she wasn't sure she liked it—was this too familiar of him? Bobby stood up. "Come on, Bird. You've finished your breakfast, I think?"

This time she climbed into the front seat of the taxi and put the bag between her feet, noticing again the medallion that hung from his rearview mirror. He pulled adroitly into the street, wending his way among parked cars; many were actually parked on the sidewalk, their rear ends sticking out into traffic. She had registered for a week at the hostel, enough time for her to explore the city; then she could think about some other destinations, find a train to the Black Sea coast with her bathing suit and a good book, begin her month of wandering. It would have to be cheap, cheaper than hiring taxis to small towns every day, but at least the hostel itself was not expensive, and it seemed clean and secure.

"How long will it take us to get to Bovech?" she asked him.

"Not very long. Two hours, if the traffic is good."

They turned onto a boulevard lined with sooty façades, shops, a window full of high-heeled sandals. The traffic did not look good to Alexandra, but Bobby was whistling, adjusting his mirror as if pleased with the state of things. She studied the moles at the corner of his mouth. There was something attractive about him, she saw now—maybe his restlessness. "I feel guilty for taking so much of your time."

"Stop," he said cheerfully. "It is a pleasure for me. My life is mostly boring. I'd rather help you figure out how to return the bag. In my own life, I have less to figure out, right now."

"I doubt that," she said. "What do you do, besides drive this cab and go to environmental demonstrations?"

He regarded her for a moment. "Well, I go to a lot of demonstrations, not only environmental ones. It is time for us to have our country back. In my generation, we must take it back ourselves, for people to have better jobs, more normal cultural life, to act really part of Europe instead of feeling like—lost souls." He buckled his seat belt.

"But you still haven't told me what you do all day," Alexandra said. "Although I know you drive thirty-five hours a week."

He frowned. "No—now I am telling you what I *believe* all day, not what I do. Okay, when I'm not driving, I organize lectures and write petitions, and I help to edit a magazine about politics and literature. I meet with friends almost every day. I go running, for exercise, but I also like a challenge. I have a plan of running on every street in Sofia before I die."

"Really?" she said. "Even though you have to drive every street already?" She wondered if he also met with a girlfriend almost every day, but maybe he didn't have one.

"You are a smart girl." He was silent a moment, smiling again, shifting gears. Alexandra wondered if she should say, *Don't call me a girl.* Or, perhaps, *You have no idea what stupid things I've done. And one terrible thing.*

But he was shaking his head. "No, I don't feel tired of Sofia. I want to see every street on foot, not only in my car. Sofia is for me like my skin, my own shell. I have already run on about twenty-five percent of the streets in the whole city. Maybe you will think that is not much, but some of them are very long and the city is very big. I keep a map of where I have run. I started three years ago."

"I'm impressed," she said. "When do you run? At four in the morning?"

"Sometimes." He smiled. "But usually I have other things to do at four in the morning."

A girlfriend, after all. That might explain his gentlemanly reserve. He was obviously a private person, except about his political beliefs. She had begun to wonder, too, what kind of life he had that he could abandon so easily to drive a stranger around the countryside. Didn't anyone need to know where he was?

"When do you have time for your running, then?" she said.

"Late at night, after I'm finished with work, or before breakfast, or sometimes both."

Alexandra watched as he accelerated up the boulevard; she could believe he loved to run. His forearms were knotted with veins, and she understood now the thin, hardened look of his frame behind the steering wheel. She thought of her brother's much sturdier body, his compactness across from her at the dinner table. Alexandra pushed the habitual surge of loss down with a firm hand. Not in a new country; she was here to start fresh, at least in the first weeks. Grief would always be available, waiting to catch the corner of her eye.

"That man," she said, "the tall one I took the bag from—he told me that Bulgaria is a place where anything can happen."

Bobby kept his eyes ahead, on the complicated streets.

"Yes," he said, "and where a lot of things usually do not happen." But unlike the tall man, he was smiling.

Seventeen

As they left Sofia again, they seemed to be moving away from the mountains rather than into them, although there were always gray-blue peaks on the horizon. Bobby said they were going due east. At a stoplight just before the highway, Alexandra saw two young women in short black skirts talking with each other, idling on their high heels. One of them momentarily stuck out a thumb, then dropped her arm.

"Do they need a ride?" she asked.

Bobby shook his head. "No. They need a client."

Alexandra, shocked, tried not to stare at them. They were very young, maybe just teenagers, and one had black hair to her waist. The other girl was checking her phone, her high-heeled foot propped on a couple of bricks for balance. They stood out against the dusty exit, with its shrubs coming into leaf, as if transported there from a bar in a city.

"In the middle of nowhere?" she asked. "Don't the police see them?"

"Yes," said Bobby shortly. "Probably the police are their clients, too." As if to cleanse himself of these thoughts, he turned on the stereo. A familiar American growl filled the taxi.

"Is that the radio?" Alexandra asked, surprised.

"No." He shook his head, as if she'd said something preposterous. "A CD. The other Bobby. Do you like Bob Dylan?"

"Sure," said Alexandra, who'd been raised on Mozart and Vivaldi.

"I'll say this, I don't give a damn about your dreams," Dylan growled. Alexandra, looking out the window at the industrial suburbs of Sofia, thought—not for the first time—that when you got right down to it the man couldn't really sing. But she understood suddenly that that wasn't the point.

Farther away from the city, they passed a cart loaded with branches and pulled by a drooping horse. Cars sped up to swerve around it. The cart was driven by a man and woman in faded blue coats that looked like some kind of ex-uniform. The woman wore a flowered scarf on her head, the man black trousers tucked into boots. His trousers were splitting open down the thighs, his knees exposed. They turned deep-tanned faces to the taxi as it went by; Alexandra saw a flash of silver in the woman's teeth.

"Gypsies," Bobby said. "They collect wood the old way, in carts, instead of trucks. No bad emissions. It's strange—they are actually ahead of us on the environment. Although we can go so much faster in our ridiculous cars and we like that."

A few minutes later, Alexandra saw more of these carts gathered at the edge of a field, the horses tied loosely and grazing under trees while people in old clothes, the women in headscarves, moved around at the edge of a wood. They were collecting branches from the ground, piling them in the carts. More gypsies—Roma, her guidebook called them.

"Where do they live?" she asked Bobby.

"In towns. In their own neighborhoods, like ghettos. These probably come from the ones on the edge of Sofia. The children don't always go to school."

Bobby was driving along a valley now, with newly green trees in the distance where a river must be flowing out of sight. Along the roadsides she saw broad fields, some of them plowed and planted, some apparently lying fallow, then long ruined buildings—brick and wood, their roofs caved in, timbers collapsed, weeds engulfing their foundations.

"What is that?" she asked.

Bobby turned to look across her. "Those are farm buildings from communist times, the collectivized farms. Some of the fields are rented for crops now, but no one will ever go back to the buildings. Look at all this old stuff." He waved—beside the ruins lay rusting machinery, the broken teeth of a harrow pointing toward the sky, weeds and vines claiming a tractor. *Brontosaurus,* thought Alexandra.

"People come and take them for the metal if they are not too rusted," Bobby said. "But most of this will go back into the earth. Maybe in a thousand years, or five thousand."

They passed through a village, then another. She saw a new house—concrete, metal beams, whole tree trunks—going up in an empty lot. "Bovech is farther than I thought it would be," she said.

Bobby seemed to be musing at the wheel; he looked at her with absent eyes. "Oh, it is close," he said, and she didn't ask more.

She saw the sign at the edge of Bovech before Bobby did because it was spelled in Latin letters as well as in Cyrillic. Next to that sign there was another, a blue marker with a ring of yellow stars on it, which Bobby said was the symbol for the European Union and had been put up only a year or so before; it was already rusting at the edges. Bovech looked larger than the villages they had passed through, a sprawling settlement on its own flat plain, its outermost buildings abandoned. Alexandra saw a huge black-and-white bird opening angular wings above a nest. The nest sat on a wooden pole.

Bobby was looking at it, too. "That is a— *shturkel*, what is the word? *Stork*—a stork. They make nests on the chimneys, which can be a problem, so people build this kind of post for them."

"Do they bring babies?" Alexandra asked.

"Well, here they bring good luck. And they bring us the springtime—when they come back, beginning in late March, we know the spring is really here. When they go away in the autumn, I always feel a little sad."

She watched the bird stretch up onto one long leg; it flapped its wings and then folded inward, settling over the enormous nest again as they passed. "Where do they go?"

"For the wintertime? To northern Africa. Even South Africa."

Alexandra caught her breath, feeling the stretch of this new world. Across Greece, across the whole Mediterranean, to another continent.

In the center of town, Bobby stopped the taxi, took the address from Alexandra, and jumped out to ask a man sitting at what looked like a bus stop. The man raised a hand, seemed about to point up the street, looked at the address again, shrugged. Then Alexandra saw Bobby approach a woman who carried heavy shopping bags in each hand, like a well-balanced ox. She bent her head attentively and said something staccato, jerking her chin in the right direction.

Bobby returned looking satisfied. "The street is at the other side of the town. But it is not difficult to find."

In the end, however, it was quite difficult to find, and they drove around on that side of town looking for the sparse street signs and seeing few people to ask for further directions. Bovech seemed to be a sleepy place, even on a weekday morning. There were tattered posters with photographs of giant faces on them, exclamation points and a few words Alexandra could recognize in Cyrillic, including *Bulgaria!*—perhaps for an election long past. She pulled out her camera, resisting the urge to glance again at her photo of the tall man. The houses on this side of town looked neat and prosperous. In one yard, an old woman in black sat in the shade, knitting something pale. She looked up and smiled at Alexandra's face in the taxi window. Alexandra felt tears start to her eyes, for no particular reason, and tried to smile back. At another house, behind a low-gated fence, a mother sat on her doorstep with two small children in red shoes playing around her. The public sidewalk was rutted and weedy, the street riddled with holes, which looked strange against the freshly painted walls and fences, the tidy yards and crisply dressed children.

"That is it. Probably," said Bobby, and he pulled to a stop. They climbed out and compared the address with their note; the house just next door to the young mother's had a pebbly wall in front of it and the right number on its gate. Alexandra felt her stomach surge with anticipation. They looked around for a bell at the gate, and finding none, opened it and went up the walk to a green door. The house was not the oldest they'd seen in this town, nor the newest; it sat somewhere in between, mellowed and probably often repaired, the stucco painted recently enough for uniformity. There was no one working in the yard, to Alexandra's temporary relief, or twitching the sheer curtains aside at the windows. She stood with the urn in her arms; she didn't dare let the bag dangle from her elbow, much less set it down on that speckled cement step next to the pots of flowers.

Bobby straightened his jacket and his posture. Then, putting up one hand, he rang the bell.

Eighteen

They waited side by side. They could hear but not see the children playing next door. Alexandra couldn't pick Bulgarian out of their talk, any more than she could have Japanese, and for a moment she entertained herself by converting their sounds into English words: "stove," "Buddhist," "derby hat," "Why not?" Beneath this distraction, her heart was pounding hard.

But nobody inside seemed to have heard the doorbell, so Bobby finally rang again, holding down the button a little longer. Alexandra wondered whether both the old people were deaf. The urn grew heavy in her arms.

"They aren't at home," Bobby said decidedly. "I suppose they have not yet returned from Sofia."

She shifted her weight, feeling a twinge of exasperation. "How can you be sure? Couldn't they be upstairs?"

"Nobody has been outside this morning," he said. "In a house like this, in nice weather, there would be shoes in the front, here, and perhaps some dirt on that thing—" He indicated a boot-scraper fixed to the edge of the walk. "The door is locked in two places, not only in the handle. Also, the flowers in these bowls have not been watered. I don't think they are at home, these people. They haven't yet come back from Sofia. And something is not right here." He shook his head and Alexandra stared at him, wondering again why he got up at four in the morning and didn't like to talk about his life.

"Maybe they're just out shopping and will be back soon," she ventured.

But Bobby turned away. She followed him out of the yard and watched as he shut the front gate carefully behind them. He went along the sidewalk and knocked at the neighbor's gate. The young mother was setting rolls and juice on a wooden table and propping her children up in two little chairs beside it. She had tied a bib on the smaller child, who seemed to be a boy, although both had buoyant dark curls. She came to the gate and opened it. Her face was as pretty as her children's—inquiring, soft-eyed; she looked like a little girl herself. Bobby held council with her for a few minutes, during which the woman glanced repeatedly at his foreign companion, as if expecting her to join the conversation.

At last he interpreted for Alexandra. "I asked if the family called Lazarovi live next door. I didn't tell her about the ashes. She says they lived there until about three months ago, and she has lived here herself only half a year. She didn't know them well, but they left an address in Plovdiv and a mobile number. She says there was an old man and an old woman, and a younger man who was getting old, too, because he had never found a wife. The mobile number is his. He only visited them here from time to time—he works somewhere else, maybe on the coast. She is not certain."

Bobby paused to listen to the woman again. She gathered her curly hair back from her temples with both hands as she talked; her nails were painted pink and she wore a small gold ring. Bobby turned to Alexandra. "Now she watches their house and keeps it clean for a little pay-ment until they can sell it. Or maybe they sold it already—she is not certain. She is waiting to hear from them. She asks if we are here to buy the house. She can show it to us, if we like."

"Oh," said Alexandra. She seemed to have slammed up against a wall, but the wall was inside her chest. She wished she had left the urn at the police station after all. What had possessed her to press forward like this, with so little information? But the Wizard at the station had seemed sure this was the right address—and it was, except that the family was not here anymore. And the tall man had never gotten married, so it was probably not his son whose ashes she carried. Perhaps, like her, he had lost a brother.

The pretty mother was bending over her chil-dren now, putting a red shoe back on a miniature foot, taking them out of the chairs and setting them upright again, restraining the boy from eating something in the flowerbed.

"I told her we might be interested in buying the house and we would like to see it." Bobby adjusted his jacket, confident, smiling.

"What? Why did you say that?"

"Because of course we *want* to see it. Be quiet, Bird, or we will lose this chance, you know? Don't tell her what you are carrying." He smiled hard at her.

"Okay," she said.

The woman took the children inside and they heard her speaking to someone. She returned alone, holding a key, and led Alexandra and Bobby back to the locked house. Alexandra reflected that she—a foreigner here—was now not only a thief but also possibly a trespasser. Bobby wiped his shoes on the mat before they entered.

Inside the house, everything had a damp smoky smell, the musk of absence. Alexandra noticed at once that, although they were furnished, the rooms looked bare, as if all the ordinary life had been sucked out of them. Her heart sank further— this long trip, and for nothing. There were crocheted doilies on a table in the entryway, but no keys or vases or magazines, no jackets on the hooks by the door. The curtains at the windows had been drawn; their panels let in a silent greenish light. In the small parlor, Alexandra saw an afghan folded over the back of a chair, and a television in one corner, but no plants or photographs. The sofa and chair were upholstered in scratchy orange fabric that had received years of people's skirts, trousers, seated weight. The carpet, very clean, was a scuffed brown. An empty cut-glass dish sat on a coffee table, as if someone had tried to make the room look less bare.

Behind the elderly television were several shelves of books, which Alexandra lingered over while the young woman showed Bobby the light fixtures and the view of a back garden. She could sound out some of the authors, if not the titles. *Hemingwei*, she read with surprise. *Charlz Dikenz*. They were matching sets—maybe forty or fifty years old, some a little mildewed on the spine. There were many Bulgarian books—histories or novels, apparently, and biographies of composers: Bach, Mozart, Stravinsky. There were several books in French and quite a few in German, and a couple of newer, Western-style photographic volumes with colorful spines: London, France, Italy. Then more about Italy, including two on Venice.

Bobby had come to stand beside her and he was gazing at the books, too. The lowest shelf, just behind the television, was packed with yellowing music scores, although there was no piano or other instrument in sight. She set the bag with the urn in it on the coffee table, thinking this would be more respectful than carrying it from room to room.

Across the hall from the parlor was an equally tiny dining room—again, all the aging cheap furniture still in place, and a cut-glass vase on a sideboard. A cabinet next to the window contained stacks of teacups in flowered porcelain, but every other shelf was bare and free even of dust. Perhaps this house had been too full of memories of the man whose ashes now sat watching the blank television; maybe his relatives had left as soon as they could find another place. They had gone somewhere else, possibly to die themselves. But why hadn't the pretty neighbor mentioned another man, the one whose ashes these were? Had he actually died elsewhere? An awful thought seized Alexandra: the old people had gone to a nursing home, if there were such things here, and now she would never be able to find them. She tried to calm herself by gazing at Bobby's competent black denim back, moving through the rooms ahead of her.

The kitchen, at the rear of the house, opened onto a small garden; the neighbor said she tended it herself and pointed proudly to young pepper plants and clumps of parsley. A fence overgrown with flowering vines looked into other back yards and then away to fields outside the town; beyond that, very far, Alexandra saw a mountain range disappearing into haze. An old woodstove stood in one corner of the kitchen, which explained the smoky smell—lifting the plate carefully off the top, she caught a glimpse of wood ashes. Yes: it was exactly the smell of her family's mountain house during the long summers. Plates and cups were arranged on shelves above a rust-stained, well-scrubbed sink; a colorless rag had fossilized over the tap. There was no food in evidence except a faded scent of frying. Alexandra felt the old urge—to kick in a wall, the way Jack had so long ago. The linoleum was clean but had cracked open across the middle of the floor, as if an earthquake had taken place here. Behind the kitchen table stood an iron bedstead, to Alexandra's surprise, with pillows and a blanket folded on the bare mattress.

Upstairs, they found two bedrooms; someone had painted the walls a soft peach color. Again, everything neat, clean, silent, sad. In the larger of the two rooms stood matching narrow beds, stripped. In the smaller bedroom, Alexandra stopped, astonished. The double bed was made up with white sheets and heavy blankets, pillowcases waiting immaculate for heads that no longer rested on them. A comb, brush, and razor lay on a nightstand. Across from the bed hung a tourist calendar from 2006, open to a photograph of maidens in some kind of traditional dress dancing around a wooden-roofed well: ЮНИ/JUNE. Alexandra stood in front of it and thought of a poem. *"Stop all the clocks, cut off the telephone,"* she muttered.

"What?" said Bobby.

She turned. "And look at this."

Someone had left behind at least a dozen photographs, which stood framed on the bureau or hung on the walls. The photographs were mainly black-and-white, some brown or yellowish sepia. Several of the images looked very old; these were wedding groups in stiff clothing with something Eastern about it, young people staring transfixed into futures now long past—the men in leggings and caps and woolen vests, the women in heavy dresses and short veils or wreaths of flowers. Here and there, a square of brighter paint revealed where a photograph had been removed; perhaps the Lazarovi had taken with them the most valued images of all. There was one photograph Alexandra found particularly striking: a young woman in a V-necked blouse and Hollywood pose, marcelled hair setting off her longish nose, skin luminous as a dewdrop, her eyes raised trustingly to the viewer. She wore a short string of pearls and pearl bobs on her earlobes. Alexandra could not look away from her gaze.

The neighbor had come in behind them and Alexandra guessed that she and Bobby shouldn't be lingering so long. But Bobby was pointing at a black-and-white snapshot, a couple with a little boy, the man in a jacket and tie, the woman in a dark dress and bouffant dark hair; they sat close together on a divan. The little boy looked six or seven, long-legged and solemn, standing between his parents. Maybe, thought Alexandra—yes, maybe he had grown up to be a tall man.

"Ask her if she knows who the people in the photos are," she instructed Bobby. But when he put the question, the neighbor gave a quick nod, which Alexandra realized after a moment was the venerable "no" she had been watching for.

They bent to see the last few. There was a

snapshot of the same little boy, at a party, seated between his mother and father. This time the boy looked younger, perhaps four years old, his face soft and round. He had glanced away from the camera at the last second, toward his father. There was another group seated out of doors, a birthday or holiday, people raising glasses of wine around a feast. Alexandra found the gangly teenager in the background, and his still-lovely mother sitting next to him. The father didn't seem to be with them; perhaps he'd taken the picture, gesturing for everyone to lift their drinks. The boy was sullen or shy, his face closed but inevitably handsome, that heavy lock of hair on his forehead.

Above the head of the bed, apart from the other photographs, hung the image of a young man in a thick dark suit and quaintly high white collar. It was a larger print than the rest, and the frame had a look of expense and Art Deco. The young man stood alone next to a pedestal with a potted plant on it. He held a violin before him in one hand, and in the other a bow, pointing toward the ground. The quality of the photograph was exquisite, Alexandra thought, and at the lower right she read in gilt letters: K. BRENNER, FOTOGRAFIE, WIENSTRASSE 27, 1936. The man had a fine, rather thin face, dark-eyed and clear-browed, as if he could see farther than most and was gazing beyond his photographer to distant mountains. He wore the unsmiling expression of a studio pose, but Alexandra had the sense that there was something eager and energetic just under it. His next movements would be vigorous, even arrogant —he would tuck the instrument under his chin in a single swift gesture. She smiled at him for no reason, except that he was youthful and beautiful and, sadly, could no longer smile back.

"I wonder why they left so many pictures here," Alexandra said.

Bobby shrugged. "Maybe to make the house look nice—to help sell it."

"But these are precious, and personal." *Or maybe they couldn't bear to look at them anymore, after the death of Stoyan Lazarov.*

The neighbor made a move to go; of course— she had left her children with someone at home and probably had work to do. She spoke to Bobby and he nodded. "She says we can look around a few more minutes, and that we should pull the door behind us—she will come back to lock it."

He seemed to listen hard until they heard the front door close behind her and then he dug inside his jacket, took out a pair of latex gloves, and put them on with a faint snap. Alexandra stood frozen. He carried gloves? But Bobby went matter-of-factly to the bureau, opening each drawer and searching it, although most were empty and the one that wasn't held a couple of ancient under-shirts, neatly folded.

"Wait," Alexandra said, aghast. "Should you do

that? What are you looking for?" She was a little afraid again, as well as shocked. Did he rob houses, on the side, with his gloves and his lock-picking tool? Could he be the nicest criminal one would care to meet?

"There might be an address book," he said softly. "Old identity cards. Or more photographs. Something that could help us find them more quickly, if the address in Plovdiv doesn't work either. We should look while we're here. They probably took it all, but I want to see."

He searched the other bedroom in the same way, disturbing nothing, but it was equally empty. She trailed him downstairs, nervous and confused, and watched as he peered into kitchen cabinets and drawers—a few forks, a pile of pink paper napkins, a mousetrap—and in the drawer of the television table in the tiny sitting room. That one held what looked like an outdated phone directory. He went to the bookshelves and pulled out a volume or two, ran his hand down behind all the books, one shelf at a time, standing on a chair to reach the top. From the second shelf, he retrieved a few coins, which he replaced. He moved the television table and reached behind the densely packed row of music scores, feeling around.

"Bobby!" Alexandra said. "Who do you think you are—Sherlock Holmes? We could get into terrible trouble here."

He grinned. "I love Sherlock Holmes," he said.

Then, as if sensing her worry, "Don't be afraid. I'm not trying to steal. I'm just checking all the places people might put things."

He moved his arm deeper, out of sight. After a moment, he drew something up from behind the music. It was a box—a tightly lidded box made of tin that might long ago have contained candy. It had apparently had a picture on the lid, worn now to shapes in red and gray, illegible.

Bobby set the box on the coffee table, next to the urn, and they looked at it. *Probably nothing important,* Alexandra started to say, and then stopped herself. She didn't want to open the tin box, but she suddenly felt that she wanted Bobby to. After examining the lid, he did, and they both bent over it.

She thought for a first queasy instant that there was a dead animal inside, or maybe just the decayed, shed skin of a snake. Bobby's gloved fingers touched the contents, and touched them again. He lifted an object out—two objects, long and sinewy and brownish—and draped them over the table. They looked as if they had once been fabric but were now stiff with age.

Alexandra felt a creeping of skin along her arms and neck. "What are they?" The words tasted garbled on her tongue, as if she'd fallen between languages.

Bobby had gotten down on his knees. He held one of the shriveled ribbons carefully to his nose and sniffed it. When he glanced up at Alexandra, there was perplexity in his eyes, and a faint disgust.

"They stink," he said, and his words were caught somewhere far off, like hers. "But in a very small way, like from a long time ago. Dirty."

"Are they bandages? Old bandages?" That brown stain, dried over time—her stomach shifted.

Bobby was still staring. "I don't think so. They do not look exactly like bandages. But something rotten. Something very bad."

After a moment, he took his phone out and photographed the two objects, without explaining. He coiled them back into their box and replaced it carefully behind the scores. Alexandra noticed that he glanced around the room before they left, as if to be sure he'd put everything back in its exact place. She picked up the bag with the urn, wondering for a moment if they should simply leave it there. Bobby kept his gloves on until after he'd pulled the front door shut behind him.

Then they went next door again; at Bobby's request, the neighbor fetched a scrap of paper and copied out on it the address in Plovdiv to which the Lazarovi had gone, and a mobile number for the middle-aged man. Bobby thanked her and bowed a little instead of shaking hands, and Alexandra said, "*Mersi mnogo*," which made the woman beam at them and ask Bobby a question.

"*Ungarka*," he said, and she raised her eyebrows but seemed pleased.

"What?" said Alexandra.

"I told her you're Hungarian. Be quiet, Bird." He smiled pleasantly at the woman and shook hands this time. "She doesn't need to know every damn thing, right?"

In the cab they sat for a long minute, not speaking, with the windows rolled down.

"Why did you want to go into the house?" Alexandra asked, at last.

"I thought that we might learn something there."

"So, did you learn something?"

"Yes," he said. "But I am not sure yet what it was. And you?"

"I learned that they're the same people—I mean, the people we're looking for. I'm certain of it. I should have shown you before, but I didn't think of it." She rummaged in her purse and took out her camera. "Here they are."

It startled her to see them after having been inside their house, the handsome tall man leaning close to his mother in the back of their taxi, and the blur of the old figure behind them. The tall man's face was familiar to her now, with that sadness around his eyes, and the old woman looked almost pretty.

Bobby peered at the screen. "Yes, they could be the same. I see it. They would be the right ages now, from some of those photographs."

Alexandra brooded over her one image of them, her head close to Bobby's. She carefully enlarged the younger man's face. It was even more striking up close, the eyes narrow and bright. "I think he was that little boy in the pictures. Of course, people change so much as they get older." Her words brought the usual stab under a rib: Jack, a one and only brother, would not be doing that. Changing as he got older was out of the question. She never heard such phrases—*get older, grow up, come of age, in the prime of life*—without pain, even when they came out of her own mouth.

"One thing is more important," Bobby said at her shoulder. "We do not know who Stoyan Lazarov was. Maybe he was the man in those photos, or maybe he was somebody else. But we don't even know for certain that he lived here."

"No. We don't." Alexandra was still thinking about Jack, how few photographs she had of him, even at home. She had copied her three favorites and brought them on this trip, including the small one that seldom left her wallet. It was safer than traveling with their originals—those could never be replaced, like Jack himself.

She said, "Maybe Stoyan was a younger man, their other son." *Cut down in his prime.*

"Yes, but if Stoyan was the old people's other son, there would probably be two boys in the pictures," Bobby pointed out, "and some sign of the one who died."

"Well, there were beds for four people, in the

bedrooms," Alexandra said. "If you count the double bed."

Bobby looked at her with what she thought might be admiration. "True. And the police sent you to this house. So even if he is not in the photos, Stoyan Lazarov probably did live here. Or is that what they said—that he was sure Lazarov actually lived at this address?"

"That's how I understood it. But maybe they meant that this was simply the address of his nearest relatives."

"That is possible," Bobby said, "but I wish you had asked."

"*You* wish I'd asked?" She smiled at him, although his criticism nettled her a little, and put away the camera.

He was looking serious again. "So you showed the police this photo?"

"Yes—I thought it would help somehow."

"I see." Again, she felt he wasn't pleased. Then he nodded at her, blue light in his eyes. "Well, now we have a phone number, so we can see if they answer."

He got out his cell phone and the paper from the neighbor. Alexandra hung her arm out the taxi window and watched him, thinking of the tall man with the amber eyes. She could hear ringing at the other end, but at last it simply stopped.

"No one answers," Bobby said. "And no way to leave a message."

Alexandra chewed the inside of her lip.

"Want to go to the address in Plovdiv?" he said. "I have more than half a tank."

"That's an even longer trip for you," said Alexandra nervously. Why would he be willing to keep driving her around like this? Either he was going to charge her far too much, or he was going to proposition her, sooner or later.

"Please," said Bobby. "We already decided that this is not about money. I want to know who this Lazarov was, just like you do."

Nineteen

First they went to look for some lunch, and it was Bobby who suggested this. Alexandra was beginning to like many things about him, despite her unease; one of them was this propensity to pause often for meals—as a still young, still thin person, she was never without an appetite herself. She'd noted long before that many people ate infrequently, or only at mealtimes, whereas she began to feel woozy and stupid after two or three hours without food. Bobby, with his wiry, compact runner's body, was not so different from her: always famished.

They left the cab where it was parked and walked toward the center of Bovech; Bobby had seen a café open two streets back. The sidewalk was rough here, too, full of holes. Alexandra picked her way carefully along behind him. There were more houses similar to the Lazarovs', with more walled-in yards. One was fenced from the street by a row of young fruit trees painted white up to the middle of their trunks. The sun drummed on the back of her head and she felt summer coming quickly to this place, probably a hot summer. They passed what looked like a mechanic's garage, with cars parked in rows outside but no one in sight to fix them, a padlock holding the doors shut, something painted in dripping white Cyrillic letters across the front wall. She would never know what it said—it was another of those many mysteries of travel. And of loss; she'd also never know what Jack would have thought of this place.

She tapped Bobby's shoulder. "What do those words mean?"

He turned, frowning. "It says, *Ne parkirai pred garazha.* Do not park in front of the garage."

"I see." She had to laugh. Some mysteries were not really mysteries.

The next lot was protected by chain-link fencing, with a hole bent into the front of it. Inside, Alexandra saw a strange exhibition: dozens of pieces of playground equipment and yard sculpture, massed together. Much of it appeared used, even battered; concrete birdbaths leaned exhausted against each other and a large plastic slide in the shape of a clown's head lay on its side, the orange smile broken off in one corner. Most of the pieces were sculpted animals—wolves with their noses thrown back in a frozen howl, lions pacing nowhere, a towering bear painted pale green, a cartoon skunk raising its tail.

One of the animals suddenly moved, the only real one, and then Alexandra saw it hurrying among its paralyzed brethren. It was a medium-sized brown-and-black dog, brindled of coat but with a long black face and a white chest, as if it had recently pushed through a snowdrift—a least-common-denominator dog, five or six different breeds mixed together so that they all canceled each other out. The only thing left was its dogness, its alert chestnut eyes and a friendly pink tongue hanging out of one side of its mouth. This dog was headed for the gap in the fence, and Alexandra went forward to greet it.

Bobby suddenly stepped in front of her. "Go back," he said. "We don't know if it is mad."

"What?"

"Lots of dogs in Bulgaria are mad. They bite people."

The dog stopped a few feet away, sat down, and looked calmly at Alexandra—she was certain he was looking at her. It was definitely a he. He was too thin, but sitting there he seemed even more collected and peaceful than the concrete yard animals behind him.

"He likes me," she said.

"Do not be sure," Bobby admonished. He was standing still now and scrutinizing the dog. "This is a wild dog. But he does seem intelligent. And clean."

"Yes, he looks as if he could speak."

"In English?" Bobby said. "Come on, let's go for lunch."

Alexandra turned away, reluctantly; she had the thwarted feeling of a child who is told not to pat the dog, the cat, the sweet mouse. As soon as they moved on, the dog followed them; she watched him over her shoulder.

"*Kush,*" said Bobby, waving a hand, but carefully, as if not to anger him. The dog sat down again. When they started up, he started up, too, trotting after them without hurry.

"He actually likes *you,*" Alexandra said slyly. "I'm sure you're the one he likes."

Bobby shook his head—enough. They had reached the café and he held a gate open for Alexandra. The dog sat down on the sidewalk, shut out.

There were tables in front of the café and Bobby chose one in the shade. A kind of music Alexandra had never heard before poured out of the building—singing, somehow Middle Eastern, complicated. "There will not be real lunch, but you can order a coffee and some toast with cheese," he explained. A teenaged waitress came

148

sauntering over and smiled back at Alexandra; she wore silver-sequined shoes and a black T-shirt that said, in English script, *Get Me Going!*

While they ate their toast and drank black coffee, the dog sat quietly outside the gate, where Alexandra could see him. He watched them in silence. A shining thread of drool fell from his jaw. "He's hungry," she said.

Bobby shook his head. "Don't give him any attention."

She wondered at this acceptance of bad things: hunger, loneliness, mad dogs on the loose, dangerous driving, broken sidewalks. Why did people have to be so damned accepting? Including her, of course. "I'm going to save him part of my toast," she insisted.

Bobby shrugged. The sun was high now and it filtered through the leaves to dapple their empty plates. "Third meal in Bulgaria," he said. He regarded her with his head on one side.

"Yes," she said. "I'm already losing count."

On the sidewalk, she lagged behind him and let the portion of her toast slip from her fingers. The dog pounced. Alexandra stopped to watch him, and Bobby turned and sighed. She said, "He's really hungry."

Bobby folded his arms. "*Yes, of course* he is hungry. He's a street dog."

The dog backed away, wolfing his treat, and sat down at the foot of a tree, next to the sidewalk.

He gulped and tossed his head, then set his front feet together and stared at Alexandra, giver of bread. There was a laminated piece of paper stapled to the tree just at eye level. The dog sat erect beneath it, gazing at them. They looked, and Alexandra saw that the Cyrillic letters printed on the paper were familiar to her, as was the black-and-white photocopied face. Bobby leaned close, despite the dog, who didn't move.

"Yes," he said.

It was the full name, STOYAN DIMITROV LAZAROV, 1915–2006, and some other printed words, which Bobby read for her: ONE YEAR, IN SORROWFUL MEMORY, PASSED AWAY JUNE 12, 2006, AGED 91. The man in the photocopied image had deep-sunk eyes, a long narrow nose, black hair, black sideburns, a look of the 1970s. Certainly it was not the image of a very old man. It was also not one of the photographs from the house they'd just toured, but Alexandra already knew that face—serious, intense.

"Oh," said Alexandra. "So he did live in Bovech. He must have been the man with the violin, but much older here, you see? And he was born—" She paused. "During the First World War. But why is his picture on a tree?" She remembered now having seen other such black-and-white sheets on walls and gates in some of the towns they had passed through; she'd assumed, vaguely, that they were advertisements for something.

"This is a *nekrolog*," Bobby told her. "You put it up when someone dies, and then you put up other *nekrolozi* on their death anniversaries."

"We don't have these at home," Alexandra said.

He touched the paper. It had faded and wrinkled, even under the lamination. "There are two things here not right."

She found herself staring at Bobby's profile. He was different from anyone she'd ever met, and not because he was Bulgarian. "What?"

"First thing—that is what was wrong at the door to their house. This should have been on the door, or on the gate in front, not only here in the town. When we were there, I couldn't think exactly what was missing. A house with a recent dead family person would always have a *nekrolog* on the door."

"Maybe the family removed it so the house would look better to sell."

"Maybe. But lots of houses are sold with *nekrolozi* on the door, because they have become empty."

Alexandra glanced down at the dog. He was still sitting politely near their feet, and Bobby seemed to have forgotten him.

"What is the second thing wrong?" she asked.

"Can you tell me?"

She pondered. "How would I know?"

"Think about it. See the dates."

"Well, it says he died in 2006." She looked at Bobby. "That's two years ago. This paper has been here for almost a year, if it's for a one-year anniversary."

"Yes."

"Oh," Alexandra said. "You mean, why was he not buried sooner—or his ashes, rather?"

"Why?" said Bobby. "Yes—why."

"Sometimes in the U.S. you hear about people keeping ashes in their houses until they decide where to bury them. Or they even keep them forever." *In fact, I might have voted for that, given the choice,* she thought, although she couldn't imagine her parents approving, and there hadn't been any choices.

"We have cremation here, too. But often we bury people. My grandparents were all buried, no ashes, in the communist times." Bobby combed his lank hair back with his fingers. "I think that is because we are an Orthodox culture, in our heart. The Orthodox Church believes that people need their bodies later on, when Jesus comes back to find everyone who was good. Then you will need your whole body to get up and come back to life so you can live in it again, in the new heaven on the earth."

"I see," Alexandra said. She couldn't tell whether he believed this himself or was just explaining. If this were all true, by some chance, a person who'd somehow killed her own brother would probably not be getting back up to live in a new heaven. She suddenly felt tears prickling behind her eyes and hoped Bobby wouldn't notice. But he was pondering their original question.

"Why *was* Stoyan Lazarov not buried?" he said. "Well—his ashes not buried?"

"Maybe they were saving up for the funeral." Alexandra cleared her throat. "When I met them they didn't look very—prosperous, and we saw how simple their house is."

He shook his head. "A funeral is a funeral. You must find a way to do it even without enough money. And the house is very decent, not poor. There is even a third problem. Who is the other old man?"

"The other?" Alexandra said.

"Yes, you know—you met an old man who had these ashes with him, but Stoyan Lazarov was old when he died, too, in 2006. He was ninety-one, as it says here. He could not have been the other old man's son."

"I see what you mean," said Alexandra.

"Maybe he was the brother of that old man. Yes—that would be possible, with their ages."

Bobby fished out his cell phone and took a couple of pictures of the *nekrolog*. The dog turned around suddenly—which caused them both to jump back—and put his front paws on the tree.

He raised his nose to the blurred poster, as if acknowledging their interest. Then he sat again.

"It seems this is a good-luck dog," Bobby said. He squatted down and looked the animal over carefully. "Smart. And he appears to be healthy, like you said, but if he had a home he might wear a thing on his neck. What do you call that? I forget the word—like on a shirt."

"A collar," said Alexandra.

"A collar," he agreed. He put one hand out, palm up. The dog sniffed it briefly, then settled back, courteous, collected. The eyes in the dog's dark face were oddly human—a cliché, Alexandra thought, but in this case true.

"I think you are right—he is friendly and calm," Bobby said. "And he found for us this *nekrolog*." To Alexandra's surprise, he reached out slowly and stroked the dog's head.

She took this as her own permission. Leaning over, she scratched the dog behind his ears, rubbed his neck, worked the skin on his back with fingers long-practiced from her childhood pets. The dog leaned against her and his ropy strong tail thumped her sneakers. His coat was clean and smooth, only his paws dusty. She hadn't been able to make anybody this happy in a long time.

Bobby laughed. "You are a funny one," he said. "And he likes you best."

They walked on to the taxi and Alexandra looked back a couple of times—to her sorrow, and secret pleasure, the dog was following them again. But when she turned to say goodbye, Bobby opened the back door and the dog jumped in as if he'd been living there all his life.

"What if he belongs to someone?" she said, although she could hardly believe her luck.

"I don't think that he does. Not anymore." The dog settled himself and Bobby closed the door, mindful of a tail. Alexandra got into the front without speaking and glanced into the back seat just once, in love. Bobby started the engine.

They were well up the street before she realized she had forgotten to look back a last time at Stoyan Lazarov's house: 1915–2006.

Twenty

The highway toward Plovdiv rolled out between fields. On every horizon Alexandra saw mountains, some of which were blue and very distant, beyond a great plain. Others were closer and rubbed with darkness like long smudges of soot. The sun was dropping: midafternoon already. Bobby tapped the steering wheel with his thumbs; he seemed to be pondering something, and after a silence he spoke to her. "It will be evening by the time we return to Sofia, even if we find the Lazarovi quickly. Would you like to stay in Plovdiv? It is a beautiful city."

Alexandra's heart jumped into the back of her

throat. Here it was, the inevitable proposition, the conversation a young man always had to have with a new young woman. What if he did have an unmentioned girlfriend back in Sofia? Almost as bad a prospect, what if he didn't? She searched for words that would sound clear, firmly rejecting, but not ungrateful. After all, he'd been driving her around for two days now without laying a hand on her.

"I'm not sure." She straightened her seat belt. "Couldn't we just go back to Sofia?"

"Certainly," he said, as if they were discussing nothing important. "But then we will arrive there rather late. I thought you might be tired."

"I'm already paying for that room in Sofia," she said. "If I get—I mean if we get, if we each get hotel rooms in Plovdiv—"

This sounded terrible, and she stopped. It was all too complicated; in fact, it was becoming ridiculous. Why didn't she know when to give up? The scar on her arm began to twitch and she scratched it viciously through her sleeve.

But Bobby was looking surprised. "I didn't mean hotel rooms," he said. "That would be very expensive. My aunt lives in Gorchovo, which is about half an hour east of Plovdiv, and we could stay with her."

It was Alexandra's turn to be startled, and also a little ashamed. "But she doesn't know me."

Bobby smiled. "That does not matter," he said.

"I am her favorite nephew and she will be very glad to see me and to meet you. I will explain to her—except the part about the police, I think. And maybe not the part about the ashes."

"Shouldn't you call her first?"

He scratched the back of his head. "Her phone often does not work. I always try to make her fix it. In any case, she will enjoy this more— if we surprise her."

Alexandra's doubts returned in a dark flock. What if there was no aunt, in reality? How could she know where he was taking her? To an empty house or apartment somewhere?

But Bobby didn't seem triumphant, only pleased to have settled a practical matter. "She is very nice and she cooks very well. My cousins left home a long time ago, and her husband is dead, so she likes me to visit whenever I can. When I was little, she spoiled us all, especially me. She still spoils me. In fact, she gave me this coin—" He pointed at the charm dangling from his rear-view mirror, the woman with her knot of hair. "Athena. She says it is to help me remember always to be wise when I drive."

"Did you live near her, growing up?"

"No, I lived in Sofia, but I went to her for the summers, when my parents were too busy for me." A cloud had crossed his face; he drew down the visor to shade his eyes, as if blinded by sun instead.

157

"I have an aunt like that, too," Alexandra said, to distract him, and to distract herself from the questions on the tip of her tongue. (*Why were your parents too busy for you?*) "My aunt lives on a big lake in the state of Georgia, and my brother and I would go visit her for a few weeks every summer. We loved it there, because she let us do all kinds of things our parents wouldn't, like go fishing alone out in the middle of the lake."

"Your brother decided not to come to Bulgaria?" He smiled over at her and she saw that the road was curving along a river now. A lane of packed dirt ran beside it. An old man in a cap was bicycling there with heavily filled plastic bags tied to his handlebars. Lines of low, pollarded trees clung to the road ahead of him; afternoon sun caught the leaves in their shorn crowns.

"My brother is dead," she said. She had tried many versions of her announcement, over the years, and had finally settled on the simplest one. "He died twelve years ago."

"I'm very sorry." Bobby shook his head. She had the impression that he wanted to raise a hand to touch her shoulder but had stopped himself, although she hadn't seen any movement.

"Yes," she made herself say. "He was—he always wanted to travel. He would have liked seeing Bulgaria." She didn't add that he had wanted to come here, or why; that was too private.

"Was he older or younger?"

"Older. Two years older. He was a wonderful boy," she added, without having meant to. Was he still a boy, on the other side of death, or now a man? She pictured Jack sitting in the back seat of the taxi, leaning forward to laugh with this total stranger, comparing their tastes in music, maybe murmuring something just to her: *Didn't I tell you this would be fantastic?*

"I'm sorry." Bobby seemed slumped into himself, and then he shifted his wiry frame behind the wheel, straightened his neck and shoulders. He pointed with one ear to the back seat. "So—what shall we name him?"

Alexandra had forgotten the dog for a few minutes, and she turned to check on him, relieved to talk about something else. He was asleep with his spine wedged against the seat back, his head and legs limp, one eye half-closed in his velvet face. He looked inexpressibly vulnerable to her, riding along with them to a destination he could not even inquire about.

"What about your aunt?" she said. "Will she mind having a dog there?"

"He can sleep in the back yard. I don't think she will be unhappy about him. But he must have a name."

"Maybe he once did," Alexandra mused. She braided her hair over one shoulder, a habit with her when she was thinking. "But we'll never know it, I guess."

"Then he needs a new one."

"What do you call dogs in Bulgaria?"

Bobby considered. "Well, people used to call them *Sharo*," he said. "That is 'Spot.' "

"Oh, he needs a more interesting name than that," she said. "He's an interesting boy." She reached toward the dog's dusty paws, then decided not to startle him in his sleep.

"How about *Prah*?" Bobby suggested.

"You told me that means 'ashes,' " Alexandra said indignantly. "That's a little sick, isn't it?"

"You're a good student." He glanced at her. "Good memory."

"No, give him a nice name." She left off her braiding and looked around the long sunlit plain, the distant willows. "How do you say 'hope'?"

"*Nadezhda*," Bobby told her. "But that's feminine, and it actually is a girl's name. Also the name of a big complex in Sofia where some of my friends live."

"How about *Stoyan*?" she said.

He laughed. "That is even more sick," he said. "But—all right. It's a good name for a dog because it means 'enduring,' if that is the right word in English, and this dog is very enduring."

"No, he's *endearing*," said Alexandra, and this time she rubbed the dog's bony foreleg. He woke and raised his head, rolling one eye dreamily. Then he lay back, stretched longer across the seat, and fell asleep again.

"We could call him Stoycho," Bobby suggested. "That would be kind of like Stoyan, but different, so it might sound more respectful. You can also say *stoy* to a dog—then it means *stay*." He glanced over his shoulder. "*Stoy*, Stoycho! See? He listens."

"All right." Alexandra raised a hand. "I christen thee Stoycho."

Plovdiv appeared under what was already late afternoon light, reddish, tawny, rising from the plain in shapes that looked half ancient and half science fiction, thought Alexandra, ravished. It was much larger than the other cities they'd passed; it unfolded on a series of escarpments and tumbled into urban valleys—a riot of distant houses, old churches, walls, trees, and on the out-skirts more groups of high-rise apartment buildings.

"Do you like it?" Bobby grinned and drummed his steering wheel. "Plovdiv is very interesting, very old. It was a Greek city, called Philippopolis, for Philip the Second of Macedon, the father of Alexander the Great." He glanced over at her. "Some people used to think that Alexander belongs to us, you know, because he came from here. But now we let the Macedonians and the Greeks fight about him. Everybody loves Alexander. Your namesake."

"Thank you," said Alexandra.

Bobby adjusted his visor against the sky. "There

161

is even a Roman theater on one of the hills—Plovdiv is built on seven hills, like ancient Rome. I think now we will go directly to my aunt's town, because it will soon be sunset. It is very nearby. Tomorrow morning we can go in to Plovdiv to see the Lazarovi and you can also view a little of the old city, okay?"

Alexandra did not think she could disagree—it was his aunt and his car. He took an exit swiftly, and a shiny black SUV cut him off, its tires screaming, and sped ahead. "Cover your ears, Bird," he told her. "I need to do some swearing."

"If it's in Bulgarian, it doesn't matter," she said. He swore a blue streak and she listened with interest. "What did you say?" she asked when he'd finished.

"I said to that driver that a cat should eat the organs of his mother."

"Really?"

He laughed. "No—of course not. I said the usual stupid things, just like in English."

The exit took them away from the vision of the city on its ancient hills, and they rolled south toward a small town. At the edge of the town, they passed a wall that stood right on the road; the wall was covered with graffiti, and along the top of it sat a row of Roma children, waving and shoving each other. They were deeply tanned, dressed in a hodgepodge of clothing; the smallest of them appeared to be only four or five. The wall was at least ten feet high and Alexandra felt a school-teacher's surge of anxiety that one of them would fall off into the traffic. Bobby shook his head, but he raised a hand and waved, too.

Alexandra was pleased to see that the center of his aunt's town was old, and filled with freshly green trees. The effect was only partly ruined by a huge concrete building on the main square, with Cyrillic letters falling off the front. Bolted above the letters was a rusty metal sculpture of a girl at least twenty feet tall, in a long dress and long braids, her feet missing. As in Bovech, people here seemed to be moving slowly, now on their way back from work or errands, carrying plastic shopping bags. A truckload of men passed them, one of them taking off his cap to scratch the top of his head, and a ring of elderly people in dark jackets and sweaters stood outside the concrete building with its gap-toothed metal slogans. Alexandra saw an old man touch an old woman's shoulder as if to remind her that they should be leaving; the old woman turned to kiss another old woman on each cheek.

Bobby stopped in front of an apartment building with cornices of gray stone and decaying stucco walls. Alexandra's heart sank. "We don't have a leash for Stoycho," she said. "I mean, a rope, some-thing to hold him with."

"He will stay near us," Bobby assured her. "He will want his dinner." He let the dog out of the back of the car. Stoycho staggered for a moment and then stretched his legs deeply.

"You," Bobby said in a stern voice. "Come with me." He pointed at his shoes and the dog followed them around the back of the apartment building, where there was a courtyard.

"Stay here," said Bobby. "We will bring you some food and water."

The dog urinated heavily on a bush, sniffed the wet patch, and then sat watching them; Alexandra saw his tail whip the dusty ground. The courtyard was shocking to her, a sea of dried mud with atolls of struggling grass here and there, a pit in one corner into which some-one had thrown the skeleton of an old-fashioned baby carriage. The wall that surrounded the yard was crumbling, and the top of it was studded with shards of glass stuck into cement, many of which had broken off again and fallen to the ground—she hoped Stoycho wouldn't step on any of them. Alexandra stroked his head and made herself turn away.

The front walk of the building, when they went around to it, was cracked and muddy. She wondered how Stoycho would endure this night; she wondered about herself. She wished she were at home, in Greenhill, with its smooth sidewalks. She almost wished she had never come to Jack's favorite pale-green country on the map.

Twenty-one

Bobby rang one of eight ancient doorbells and backed away, looking up. After a moment, someone called down to them. Alexandra saw that a red-haired woman in a housedress was leaning over a balcony two floors above, smiling and waving hard.

"Oh!" she cried. "Oh, Asparuh! *Kakvo pravish tuk?*"

Bobby stood there smiling, too, his hands in his jacket pockets, and then shouted something back. He explained to Alexandra: "She wants to know what we're doing here, and I told her I could not live one day more without her cooking."

The woman raised a hand to Alexandra and gestured rapidly for them to wait there. Alexandra waved back, feeling with sudden new conviction how insane this all was. Then she heard someone on the stairs, and Bobby's aunt opened the front door of the building. She was much shorter than Alexandra and squarely built, without fat. She had pinned up the back of her red-brown hair, the color of which certainly came out of a bottle. She wore a flowered smock with big pockets, and fluffy slippers on her feet; her bare legs were a fresco of veins. She kissed Bobby on the cheeks four or five times, audibly. Bobby introduced

Alexandra and his aunt shook her hand first in one of her own and then in both.

"Pavlina," she told Alexandra several times.

"That's her name," Bobby said. "She says you can call her by her first name. She says we should come upstairs with her immediately. But first I will explain to her about Stoycho."

This information seemed to sober Aunt Pavlina for a moment, and the way she looked at Bobby made Alexandra think that this was probably not the only time he had turned up with something as odd as American women or stray dogs. She had hoped his aunt would invite Stoycho in with them, but that didn't seem to be forthcoming. They followed her to the third floor; Alexandra tried not to mind the filthy staircase. Pavlina unlocked her door and then shut it behind them.

They were in a front hall with closed doors leading off it on each side. Evening light came through an opening to the kitchen and touched a parquet hall floor so clean it looked like polished amber. The walls were painted some pale hue that seemed to be part of the light; Alexandra saw on one of them a watercolor of boats pulled up onto a beach, dark waves lapping their sterns. Bobby hung his coat from a rack with an old mirror. Alexandra caught half her own face there, where it looked unfamiliar and faded, like something preserved in a daguerreotype. Copying Bobby, she took off her sneakers and put on a pair of wool slippers that reduced her steps to a shuffle.

Then Aunt Pavlina hurried them into the kitchen, where the air was full of aromas of boiling potatoes and frying meat. Bobby sighed with satisfaction and threw himself down on an old daybed in the corner. A cutting board and knife sat on the red Formica table; potato peels lay in the otherwise spotless, worn sink. The floor looked scrubbed to its bones and late sun came in through windows whose glass was almost too clean to be visible. Aunt Pavlina gestured Alexandra to a seat and turned down the noise of a small TV set, where a man in a tuxedo was giving away a sports car to anyone who could answer the next question. It was an American show; the words on the screen read "What is the largest body of water in South Dakota?" The dressed-up man provided a set of choices— Alexandra knew only that it was not Lake Victoria. Maybe South Dakota didn't have any water?

Before she could find out, the program switched to a news bulletin. Bobby sat up and put his arms around his knees. A reporter was standing in front of a podium where a young man seemed to be introducing an older one; the older man stepped to the microphone, glancing out at his audience with a smile. He looked vigorous, despite his age, and his hair made a neat, dense mane almost to his shoulders. This time Alexandra could see not only his thick brown beard and mustache but also a band of heavy scarring across his upper cheeks —she thought of the ritual mutilation on faces in the *National Geographic* issues of her childhood.

The man read a brief statement and there was applause from people standing nearby. "Isn't that the guy with the mines?" she asked Bobby. "What's he saying?"

Bobby didn't answer until an advertisement came on—cheese, made by happy sheep. Then he slumped back onto the daybed.

"Wonderful," he said grimly. "Yes, that was Kurilkov, the minister I told you about. He just more or less announced his intention to run with a party of his own in two years, as everyone predicted. If his party wins enough seats in the parliament, he will become prime minister, the most powerful position in Bulgaria." Bobby scowled. "He cannot yet start a formal campaign, but he tells us his slogan already: *Bez koruptsiya* —without corruption. He gives everyone warning of his serious intention, and they clap for him."

"Why do you think that's so bad?" Alexandra studied his face.

Bobby picked at the tassel on one of Aunt Pavlina's cushions. "Politicians who talk about purity usually end up deciding who is pure and who is not. Kurilkov already told one newspaper that any Bulgarian who does not contribute in a positive way to society should be found and put to work—hard work, through our prison system—to rebuild the economy. This is very unusual, very strange, but many people love him for it. I think he means anyone who opposes his party's campaign, when he begins it formally."

He looked up at her, stern, but Aunt Pavlina interrupted him, pointing toward the stove. "She wants to know if you like meat," said Bobby. "She has heard that many Americans are vegetarians."

"Please tell her I love meat," said Alexandra, although she had been completely vegetarian until two days before. "I wish I could speak with her, too. She doesn't know English, right?"

"Unfortunately, no—only Russian and French. She studied some French at her school in Plovdiv, and everybody her age speaks Russian, whatever school they went to."

"*Madame, je m'excuse que je ne parle pas votre langue,*" Alexandra said clumsily, and they both stared at her.

Aunt Pavlina came over to the table and seized Alexandra by the shoulders, bent to kiss her hair, pressed Alexandra's cheek against the solid shelf of her brassiere. "*Oh, ma petite! Et tu parles français comme une française!*"

"Not really," Alexandra said, turning hot and trying not to struggle.

As they ate their meal—infinitely better than

what Alexandra had tasted in any restaurant since her arrival—Aunt Pavlina asked her in French and Bulgarian about her family, her home town, and her plans for work in Sofia, but didn't question her about their journey. Alexandra felt with some mortification that she assumed they were a couple. She asked Pavlina in turn about her profession; apparently, Bobby's aunt had worked for thirty years in an elementary school. She said, in French, that her husband had died a decade before, after being hit by a truck: "I didn't sleep for two years, *chérie*."

I didn't either, Alexandra wanted to say, but instead she hunted for French terms of condolence until Aunt Pavlina laughed, surprisingly, and stopped her. "Grief comes to everyone," she said. She taught Alexandra Bulgarian words for sorrow, for potato and table and spoon, and made her copy them down in her notebook.

After dinner, Pavlina washed the dishes and cleaned the kitchen to laboratory standards, refusing Alexandra's help. Bobby did not offer; he stepped out onto the kitchen balcony and leaned against the railing, looking at the sky. Then Alexandra remembered Stoycho and they all went down to give him scraps from dinner, Pavlina in her housedress and a different pair of slippers, keeping her distance. Stoycho's backside wagged hard and he circled them until Bobby made him sit. He inhaled the food, stretched. They tied him up with a rope Aunt Pavlina had found and he lay down quietly on an old piece of blanket from the taxi. Alexandra didn't like to leave him outside overnight, but Bobby said he was certain the dog could handle—destroy—anything that might trouble him in the darkness.

When Aunt Pavlina went back into the building ahead of them, Alexandra seized Bobby's sleeve and made herself speak.

"How will we sleep?" she said. "I mean, are there enough—bedrooms?"

Bobby's eyes searched hers for a moment and she thought he might be angry. Then she thought he might be laughing at her.

"Don't you want to sleep me with, darling?" he said.

Alexandra gulped. "Well, it's not that—I mean, I like you and—"

"Bird," he said. "I wish you would stop worrying. I love *you* already, but I'm gay."

"What?" said Alexandra.

"I'm gay. That is what you always say in America, right?" She saw his defiant smile, but also the briefest flicker of uncertainty—how would she take this?

"But that's—" She was still surprised. "That's fine. I just didn't know. That's wonderful. I mean, I don't mind." Worse and worse. "In fact, I—"

"Also," Bobby said, "my parents know about this, but my aunt doesn't. Or maybe she does not want to. I don't want to force her. And my parents had a very difficult reaction. My mother still speaks with me. My father, less."

"I'm sorry." She made herself look at him—that deep shadow over his face. *Grief.* "I won't say anything to her. Of course."

"This is another reason I don't like the police, Alexandra. They like to make lists of people."

They stood looking at each other. She wondered if she should ask whether he had ever been arrested for this. She wondered if she should ask whether he had a boyfriend.

She tried again. "I didn't mean, before, that I didn't like you. In fact, I was even thinking just now that if you weren't gay—" But this was so awkward that she began to giggle, in spite of herself, and clapped a hand over her mouth. She couldn't remember the last time she'd felt that kind of laughter well up in her chest.

"Exactly," said Bobby, grinning, and he put a couple of fingers gently on her forehead, as if anointing her with his friendship.

Aunt Pavlina provided Alexandra with a pink nylon nightgown five sizes too wide and reaching just to her knee, a towel the consistency of starched cardboard, a clean toothbrush, and finally a shower cap, as if this were an American motel. Alexandra locked the bathroom door and took off her clothes, checking her alert face and shallow breasts in the mirror; at least her body was unchanged. The bathroom defied all her previous experience. The toilet flushed with a cord from a tank near the ceiling. A boiler was attached to one wall, and she thought to herself that she must be quick, if that contained all of Pavlina's hot water. Most strangely, the shower ran into a drain in the middle of the bathroom floor, with no walls or even curtain around it. Every surface looked strenuously clean and smelled of nose-burning chemicals.

Alexandra washed her hair with something she found in a plastic bottle, dried her skin with the immaculate, starchy towel, and discovered that she had not known to put the toilet paper out of range of the spray, so that it was soaked. Even the toilet paper was unfamiliar to her; it was dark pink and pliant, as if woven from some kind of rubber. Now it seemed ruined. She had left her socks near the toilet and they were also soaked; she congratulated herself for having hung up the rest of her clothes, at least, on a hook on the back of the door. Again, for a moment, Alexandra simply wanted to go home. She put on Aunt Pavlina's broad nightgown and wrestled her hair with the comb she found on a shelf.

Aunt Pavlina had made her up a bed in one of the rooms behind the closed doors—it contained bookshelves with a row of paperbacks and framed photographs of various children.

Alexandra was sure that the boy of about eight with the straight pale hair and the long-sleeved blue shirt was Bobby; his eyes were just the same as now. In another photo, Pavlina sat cheek to cheek with a man in nacreous thick glasses. The bag with the urn rested on a chair. Alexandra wished she could see Stoycho from her window, but this room looked out at the building next door, a buffer of anorexic trees in between.

Pavlina came to the doorway with her hair wrapped in a cotton scarf, to ask her if she needed anything more. Alexandra went forward instinctively and put her arms around Bobby's aunt. The older woman was like an animal, firm and large-muscled. Aunt Pavlina held her tight for a long minute, although Alexandra towered above her, and murmured in Bulgarian. Then she turned out the light, closed the door, and waved through a pane of frosted glass. Alexandra watched Pavlina's shape—and once Bobby's—moving quietly back and forth, a kingdom of shadows. It was the first time in years she had felt safe just before sleep.

But much later she woke from a dream that something was uncoiling under her and coming horribly to life. Then, just as suddenly, it lay still. The room was dark. Without intending to, Alexandra screamed and leapt out of bed. She could hear a wail from the street: car alarms, going off all around them. In the next fraction of a second, Bobby had burst in and seized her by the hand and they were running down the hall to the door of the apartment. He seemed to be wearing only white shorts, his underwear. She could see Aunt Pavlina ahead of them, moving quickly in her nightgown, her hair in the same cotton wrap. The floor trembled again and Alexandra cried aloud without meaning to; she had seen all this only in movies. In the dirty stairwell, lights flickered off and on and they stumbled forward, down, through the front door. There were neighbors tumbling out with them, dim human shapes, voices calling what sounded like questions or commands. A streetlight illuminated the sidewalk; some of the parked cars were still howling. Alexandra saw people grouped in front of the buildings on the other side of the street as well. A dog barked wildly in the dark, another farther away.

"That was strong," Bobby said. "And long." He brushed the sweaty hair from his forehead.

"An earthquake?" Alexandra said, to be certain.

"Yes."

"I've never been in one before," she said. It came to her for some reason that Jack had never been in one either, and never would. Now that it was over, she could feel her knees trembling. She was barefoot; she remembered to look around for broken glass, and then thought of the dog.

"Oh, no!" she cried. "That's Stoycho barking! And the urn is still in my room."

She turned, unsure which to rescue first, but Bobby clamped a hand on her elbow. "We can't go in again, for now. There might be another shock. The urn will be all right, but I will look for Stoycho. I must look at my taxi, too. Stay here—help Lelya Pavlina," he added, although his aunt was chatting with two younger neighbors, as if earthquakes were a welcome social event.

He disappeared around the building, his bare back pale in the streetlight. When he returned he had Stoycho with him. It was the first time Alexandra had seen the dog cowed. Stoycho's coat had risen in ragged hackles and his head was nearer the ground than his shoulders. He shivered, slinking toward Alexandra until he could lean against her knee.

"It's all right," she murmured, crouching. "My sweetheart." She stroked his head and ears and scrubbed his chest with her fingers.

"I will go check my taxi," Bobby told her. A couple of people nearby were unlocking cars, turning off alarms.

The next shock came just then, thinner but still sudden and violent, and it returned to every cell of her body the feeling of the first one, the wriggling horrible mass under her, the terror in her bones. There was a faint shriek from everyone in the street. Bobby put his arms around her, his fingers digging into her skin. A few pebbles tumbled from the roofs onto the sidewalk, like petrified rain. She had just enough presence of mind to keep Stoycho's rope fast in her hand. The earth stilled again at once.

"It's all right," Bobby crooned to her, as she had to the dog. He kept his hand on her arm, propping her up, and Stoycho crouched miserably over their feet. "It is much weaker now. If there are any more, they will not be bad. Maybe there will be none at all. I think there could be damage in other places, where it was probably stronger. We will know soon. Come with me—let's look at my car."

Alexandra was glad not to be left among the crowd. They were talking again, excitedly, Pavlina in their midst. Alexandra and Stoycho followed Bobby to the cross street, where he turned the corner and stopped short. There were people outside on this block, too, standing in small groups in front of the buildings, an old man in a bathrobe that dragged the ground. An alarm was still sounding, but farther away. Bobby's taxi sat parked under a streetlight, which glowed unaffected by the quake. Across the windshield was something that Alexandra thought at first might be a police marker; it proved when they got closer to be a couple of words scrawled in yellow paint. Bobby swore and hurried over to touch it. Then he stood staring. Alexandra thought the look on his face was very strange.

"And it is still a little wet," he said.

"What does it say?" asked Alexandra. But Bobby was turning around, alert. Suddenly he ran up the block, disappearing for a moment around the next corner, darting between two apartment buildings.

He returned with clenched fists. "Sometimes people break into cars when there is an earthquake, because the alarms are already so loud. But they don't usually make graffiti."

"What does it say?" she asked again.

He shook his head. "It says, *Bez koruptsiya*. Without corruption."

"Like your favorite politician's campaign," she said, trying to make him smile.

His face was dark. "Yes, like that." He touched the paint again and rubbed his finger on the seat of his shorts. "Maybe Kurilkov has some graffiti artists in Plovdiv. In fact, he has many followers in these smaller towns. But they did not hurt any of the other cars." He leaned close to the windshield. "I wish that I had my phone, to make a photo."

Then he looked at Alexandra and lowered his voice. "Don't be frightened," he said. "It is just some mischief. I'll clean it in the morning."

In Pavlina's spare bed Alexandra lay curled, quivering, and it took her an hour to fall asleep again—or rather, she dozed and woke, fearful, waiting for the mattress to come back to life. She wished she could have brought Stoycho into the room with her, or even Bobby. When she finally slept, she dreamed not of earthquakes but of a handsome tall man dressed in black and white. He smiled at her, but there was blood on his forearm, as if he had peeled it open with a knife. He leaned into a car to give her something with his other hand, the clean one, but she couldn't tell what it was.

"You see," he said, but she didn't see. She wanted to seize his hand and kiss it, whatever it held, except that he was no longer there.

Twenty-two

"This family name is not Lazarovi," Bobby said. "The neighbor lady in Bovech gave us a different one."

They were sitting in the taxi in bright morning sunshine, he was unfolding a scrap of paper, and Aunt Pavlina was waving from her balcony. There was no sign of disturbance from the earthquake. "Amazing—not even roof tiles," Bobby had said at breakfast, although the morning television news had reported cracked walls and two deaths in a town farther south. "Even the old city in Plovdiv is not damaged, except for one car that rolled down a street and hit a wall. Very lucky."

Stoycho was turning around and around on the back seat, trying to fit his long legs somewhere. "This does not say Lazarov," repeated Bobby. "I should have noticed it yesterday."

"Maybe they're staying with relatives from another side of the family, so the name is different. Or with friends?" Alexandra suggested.

"Yes, maybe. I tried to call the mobile number of the younger man again, but there is still no answer and no message. Possibly that is not a bad thing—it would be difficult to explain on the phone, and if we say that we have something that belongs to them, they might be suspicious of us, or afraid. We're so close that now I think we will simply go there and show them."

Alexandra wondered what they would do with Stoycho when they returned to Sofia, their mission completed. She hoped Bobby would have enough room to keep him and that she could see them both sometimes. They were driving slowly out of town now. In the center, near the concrete building with the giant folk-girl bolted to it, a group of old people sat around a dry fountain, perhaps the same people she'd seen there the night before. Probably they were talking about the earthquake. What had they witnessed, in their eighty or ninety years? Maybe some of them had lived in villages before communism and had been moved in a wave of modernization to cities, been lifted out of poverty or plunged into it, or arrested for trumped-up crimes against the state. They seemed to her completely separated from history now, waiting there for the approach of a pigeon or the handshake of an old friend.

When they entered Plovdiv, she saw that the lower part of the city was dense, a jumble of small stores and houses, apartment buildings, a church. Alexandra caught a glimpse of a shop full of marble gravestones and beside it a diner with fogged plate glass windows and a sign in English: *HOT FOOD.* She rolled down the car window and smelled baking bread, diesel fuel, excavated soil, fried meat, and a delicate morning freshness underneath everything else. There were people on the sidewalks and people crossing the streets. She saw a walking street lined with freshly painted buildings, their red-tiled roofs like hat brims; hotels with giant words sprouting from their tops, the names of banks and car companies; vast-trunked sycamores; three boys with skateboards. She saw a mosque with its lovely minaret pointing upward. The sidewalks were clean.

"Do you like it?" Bobby glanced at her and slid his hands around the steering wheel.

"Not bad," said Alexandra, smiling.

The taxi crawled along another street, narrow buildings in gray, ochre, cream, blue, lapped by café umbrellas—an Eastern Paris. Then they were climbing. The heights of the old city caught sun from across the plain; she could feel the reach of that light from mountain to field to hilltop, over centuries.

At the next intersection he consulted their scrap of paper and the map Aunt Pavlina had given them. Alexandra watched three young girls come out of a shop and put their arms around one another's waists. A man with a monkey stood next to a bakery window, but then she saw that the monkey was not real. It was a marionette, and he manipulated it for anyone who would throw coins into a basket. A woman coming out of the bakery set a bundle in a napkin on top of the coins: breakfast for the man in his ragged jacket. The monkey lunged hungrily at the bundle. Then the light changed, Bobby drove on, and she couldn't see what happened next.

"We're close," he said. "They live exactly in the oldest part. This will be spectacular for you."

He steered up one of the hills, until the streets became steep stone cobbles and walls grew up around them, with red tile along the top edges, arched entryways. Looking ahead, she saw houses with overhanging second stories supported by wooden beams, some decorated with painted swags and flowers and medallions. Then a balcony hung with brightly geometric rugs; in a few minutes they had reversed several hundred years. Easy enough to imagine, up here, that the twentieth century simply hadn't occurred.

She wished for Jack, although she suspected he would have preferred the raw strangeness of the Sofia housing complexes.

"We must park here," Bobby said. "This is as far as we are allowed to go with a car. We will have a short walk now."

"What about Stoycho?" Alexandra glanced into the back seat. The dog was sleeping as if he had years of wakefulness to make up for.

"We will have to take a risk, just for a short time. I will leave the windows partly open."

"Would anyone try to steal him?" She couldn't help asking it.

"He would not permit that," Bobby said firmly. "But you must bring the bag with you now."

"So we can return it," said Alexandra with a rush of pleasure. As they walked up the hill, she felt the urn light in her arms. The sidewalk was so steep that it bent her feet toward her shins; she held the bag tightly, since this was the last distance she would ever carry it. They turned their steps into a second narrow street. The address in Bobby's hand seemed to be leading them to a mansion decorated with curling acanthus against blue stucco. A sign on the wall outside said МУЗей/MUSEUM, and the house number was almost the right one, although not quite.

But when they went through the gate, they found a tiny two-story dwelling whose number matched their address, sitting inside the walled

183

courtyard of the grander building. Alexandra began to smile at the sight of it. The little house was stucco, like its neighbor, but painted a fading, rosy red. To its left, sheltering the tiled roof, stood a tree she didn't recognize, something like a beech but with weeping arms like a willow; every branch was covered with miniature yellow-green leaves. Above the front door rose a carved wooden sun. Alexandra and Bobby, holding hands, could easily have stretched their arms across the whole façade. The windows on each side of the door were covered with wrought-iron grilles, through which a profusion of flowers grew. The number they had been looking for was displayed in white lettering on a blue sign fixed to the stucco.

"It's so pretty," she said.

"Yes," said Bobby. "It's not the real Bulgaria, but it's pretty."

"There's no one around," whispered Alexandra, already fearing another empty house.

"And there is no bell," Bobby observed, but he raised a hand and knocked.

Almost at once the door opened and they saw an old woman standing very upright in front of them. Her hair hung white and loose to her shoulders, and she wore a long purple sweater buttoned over a black dress. The dress was pinned at the collar with an enormous brooch, which Alexandra noticed at once because of its size and because it caught the sunlight through the doorway—enamel in the shapes of lilies and irises, green leaves. The woman's face was like a beak, and her eyes were as dark as her hair was pale, which gave her the look of an image somehow reversed. Alexandra thought at first that she might be a ghost, and then that she must be a museum guide. She gazed at them without smiling, without fear, and possibly without curiosity.

Bobby spoke to her in his polite way and held out his hand, a gesture she hardly seemed to register. Alexandra caught the word "Lazarovi," and *"amerikanka."* The woman turned to stare. Then she raised a crooked hand, which she moved as if stirring a soup pot upside down in the spring air; it could have meant surprise but seemed also to say, *I should have known there would be trouble.* But she beckoned them in and even held the door for them, stepping back unsteadily.

The hall inside was tiny and paneled with dark wood, and Alexandra saw another sunburst on the ceiling, this one carved with storks flying out of it in four directions. A wooden chest sat against one wall and a striped woolen rug lay on the floor. A very small staircase disappeared up into the second story. Even with these simple furnishings, the hall seemed crowded. The walls were covered with oil paintings—trees and windows, houses, but especially faces, in dense confusion from floor to ceiling—narrow-limbed, weary men; sad-eyed women; drooping girls with long hair or hats. *A gallery of sorrow,* she thought, looking from one to another. The old lady waved a hand toward the walls, as if acknowledging Alexandra's interest, but said nothing.

They followed her into a tiny parlor that looked as much like a museum as the hall, but had the advantage of a wash of greened sunshine. Here tree branches swept the windows and the light fell on wooden benches and across a round brass table. The floor was highly polished and the flat rugs colorful, and again all the walls were covered with small paintings.

The old woman sat down and gestured them to a bench, and then a younger woman came in, also without speaking. She was dark-haired, delicately built, perhaps thirty-five, dressed in blue jeans and carrying a tray of coffee cups and a fragrant carafe. Alexandra was astonished; after all, they'd been in the house for about four minutes and had arrived unannounced. The woman set their coffee on the table, smiled, and left the room just as quickly.

When she was gone, the old lady addressed them again, hoarsely, opening crooked hands toward the tray. "*Zapovyadayte, molya,*" she said. *Please,* an invitation—Alexandra knew the second word, at least.

Bobby thanked the old woman and stirred sugar

into his mug. Alexandra put the precious bag beside her and followed his example. Bobby had stopped speaking, too, and was apparently waiting for their hostess to begin the conversation. The old woman sat across from them in a straight-backed chair, her hands on her knees; she ignored the coffee, although there was a steaming third cup. Alexandra saw that the brooch pinned to her collar was almost as big as the woman's forehead, full of birds as well as flowers. Sunlight made harsh work of the ancient face above it. Just as Alexandra was beginning to doubt that anyone would ever say anything, the old lady raised a hand. Her fingers were long and pale, almost blue, and they bent sideways from the big thumb joint.

"You may speak English," she said. Her voice was cracked, or perhaps it was her English that was brittle. Her accent was British, somehow old-fashioned.

Alexandra started. "Oh, thank you! I was wishing I could talk with you."

The old woman did smile, then. She was missing a tooth at one side of her mouth and she wore pale pink lipstick, unevenly applied. "You said that you have something to return to the Lazarov family," she said.

"Yes." Alexandra shifted in her seat. "We heard that they live here and we're hoping to talk with them right away."

"I am sorry, my dear," the old lady told her. "They come to visit me sometimes, but they are living in the mountains now, for Vera's health. She is my sister—you understand?" She turned to Bobby suddenly.

"Yes," Bobby said. "I speak English, too."

"She is my sister, Vera Lazarova. I expected them here this week, because they were going to Sofia. But she called me yesterday to say that there is some complication with their travel and they will not come here at once. She said that she will call me again soon."

Alexandra's spirits fell heavily. She had felt the presence of her people right here, in this room, in this house like a museum of miniatures, had known beyond fact that they must live here— had been sure the tall man was out walking the beautiful streets and would return any minute. She had been wrong again, as in a bad dream.

"Do you know how we can get in touch with them?" she asked.

"Well—" The old woman seemed to consider this, fiddling with her brooch. When she took her fingers away, Alexandra saw that there was a beast among the birds and flowers, a white wolf or perhaps an Arctic fox, a masterpiece of lifelike enamel. "I do not know. I thought they might come here to visit me on their way home. I hope to hear from them again in the next days."

"Do they have a mobile phone?" Bobby asked.

"My nephew does." The woman smoothed her hair. Alexandra had not understood until that moment how remarkably interesting this old lady was. The edges of her large eyes no longer fit—they were like Stoycho's eyes, darkly human, looking through the mask of something alien. A mask of age, in her case, rather than an animal face.

The woman cleared her throat. "Vera would never carry a mobile. And my nephew uses his only for his work. He shuts it off when he is not working, because he says he wants to live in peace. He does not even keep a real telephone at home anymore. I have often told him it would be a convenience to me if I could telephone them more easily."

So the tall man must be the old couple's son, as they'd speculated. Alexandra pondered this, and also his unusual bid for peace. "Their neighbor in Bovech gave us your address and a mobile number," she observed, "in case someone wanted to buy their house there. That's how we found you." She hoped she wasn't saying more than Bobby wanted her to.

"Yes, my dear." The old lady seemed to be looking at her more closely now. "Yes, they hope to sell their house. As I said, they live in the Rhodope Mountains now. Vera is too fragile to worry about business, and Radev is even more so. The mobile number is probably for my nephew."

Alexandra sat puzzling all this out, remembering how Vera had carried a wheelchair by herself down the hotel steps. But perhaps she was fragile mentally, not physically. "Your nephew is the tall man with dark hair who travels with them?"

"Yes," said the old lady. "But now, before I tell you more, you must tell me some things, too. What is your connection with my sister?"

"I really don't know her," confessed Alexandra. "I met them outside a hotel in Sofia, and then I accidentally kept something, a bag, that belongs to them."

The old lady frowned. "I don't understand."

"She helped them with their things while they got into a taxicab," Bobby prompted. "She kept one of the bags with her, but only by accident."

"And are you her husband?" The old lady turned to him. Alexandra realized that they didn't yet know her name.

"Oh, no," Bobby said—more firmly than necessary, Alexandra thought. "I've only brought her here to see you. I'm a taxi driver."

Alexandra nodded. "Your nephew told me that they were traveling to Velin Monastery, so we went right away to try to find them, but they weren't there."

"Yes, that is where they were going," said the old woman. "And you wish to return this bag to my sister? This is quite honorable, that you have looked so carefully for her." She sat musing, her crooked fingers at her lips for a moment. "Well, we must find her, then. Or, if you like, you can leave the bag with me and I will tell her about it when she calls me."

Alexandra glanced at Bobby, who asked quickly, "So the older man she travels with is her husband?"

"Milen Radev? Oh, no. He is their good friend. My sister's husband is dead. He was a musician. A very fine musician. In fact, they were on a sad trip, to bury him, at the cemetery near the monastery. He had a connection there, later in his life—he loved the monastery. I am sure this trip has been quite hard for my sister, and I am eager for them to come here to rest for some days. I said I would go with them to Velin, but they did not want me to try. I do not travel much, now."

Alexandra drew a long breath.

"And the younger man, your nephew—he was the musician's son?" Bobby asked. He was sitting forward with his hands dangling between his knees, coffee forgotten.

"Yes, Neven. He went with them to bury his father, of course."

"Neven," Alexandra repeated. She had wanted his name but not wanted to ask for it. On the old lady's lips, it rhymed with *seven*.

Bobby sat silent and Alexandra decided that she would leave it to him to figure out what to do.

"Bird, do you have the camera?" he said, at last.

She took it out and brought up the picture. Looking at the younger man's face, the peculiar sorrow in his smile, she told herself that at least she finally knew his name.

Bobby handed the camera to the old lady. "Can you see this photo?"

She held it close, studied it. "Yes, of course. That is my sister, and Neven. And, I suppose, Radev, inside the car. I am Irina Georgieva, by the way." The glance she gave Bobby was sharp and quick; he need not have worried about her eyesight. "You took the picture?"

"I did," Alexandra said. "They were the first people I met in Bulgaria and they were kind to me, so I asked them if I could photograph them."

"I see." Irina Georgieva returned the camera and studied Alexandra's face with the same thoroughness. "Do you have the bag? Perhaps I can give it to them." She pointed. "Is it that one, there?"

"Yes." Alexandra got up. She stood next to Irina Georgieva's chair for a moment and then set the bag on the old lady's lap. She unzipped the canvas for her, thinking that perhaps this would be hard for gnarled hands.

Irina Georgieva kept an arm around the bag and drew back the velvet inside. Her fingers touched the lid, and then Alexandra helped her tip the urn toward the light. In the sun from the windows, the name etched into the side had a benign look, softened.

Irina held the bag firmly in her arms, but Alexandra saw her tremble.

"Oh, my dear," the old woman said. "What a terrible mistake."

Tears sprang to Alexandra's eyes, but she felt somehow better than if the woman had told her it was nothing, really nothing, being handed the remains of her brother-in-law by an idiotic stranger. She felt that this old woman had spoken justly and would punish her now, and with the greatest fairness.

"Help me to put it down," Irina Georgieva said, with a quivering mouth.

Twenty-three

Alexandra took the urn from Irina Georgieva's hands and gave it to Bobby. She waited, still standing; she wondered if she should excuse herself, if they should quit the house and drive away. But the old woman appeared to be thinking, and after a moment Alexandra sat down again. Irina's fingers tapped her brooch, which had gone green in the sunlight.

"You know, I am an artist," she said. "These paintings are all my own work, every painting in this house. I have been selfish. I never allowed any others in, because it is my—temple, you might say. The only other artist I ever truly loved to have here was this musician, Stoyan Lazarov, the husband of my sister. He brought his violin many times, and he filled this house with his art."

She paused, breathing audibly. "All my paintings have listened to him, his Mozart and his Paganini, and his Bach. He taught me about music. My own brother died very young, and Stoyan was a brother for me, in his place."

Alexandra sat with her head bowed, hoping no sob would escape her.

But Irina Georgieva's voice went on, implacable. "I am sure you understand how serious this is. You did the right thing to come and find me, but my sister must be terribly upset."

She was silent again. Bobby touched Alexandra's arm. Then Irina Georgieva stood, with difficulty, holding the back of her chair. Alexandra and Bobby rose to their feet, too, ready for dismissal, but the old lady came toward her and took her hand. She could feel long fingers like branches, closing gently around her bones.

"My dear child," she said. "Now I must thank you for your kindness. This strange thing has happened, but it was not your fault. And often we don't know the reason for things when they happen. You did not have to bring me the urn, but you did, with a long trip to come here. Tell me your name again."

Alexandra told her, and Irina kept her hand

captive. "What a nice one it is—an old Russian name, you know. I am pleased to meet you, my dear, even in this difficult situation. As I have said, we do not know why fate has brought us together, but you can be sure there is a reason. Do stop crying, now."

Alexandra had no tissue, but Irina Georgieva apparently kept a supply in her sweater pockets. She dealt them out slowly, like cards, then gave her hand with equal formality to Bobby. "Let us put this very special object in a good place. Then we will have some lunch and I will call my sister."

She directed Bobby to take the urn from the bag and set it on a shelf nearby. The helper in blue jeans appeared immediately with a tray of lunch dishes, which smelled to Alexandra like the return of something normal. Irina Georgieva moved a candle from another part of the room and put it in front of the urn. She stood contemplating the polished wood for a moment, then touched the carved border around its top edge.

"This is quite interesting," she said. "Beautiful work, and by hand."

"Yes," said Alexandra. "You see, there are a couple of animal faces in the leaves, kind of like in your—" She pointed at Irina Georgieva's brooch, but saw that she had been wrong; there were only flowers and vines on it.

Irina touched the urn again. "My sister must

have paid someone to make this. What are these animals, do you think?"

Alexandra had not looked carefully, before; she had always kept the urn in its velvet casing. "One is a bear," she said. "And this other one might be a cat's face, but I don't know." Bobby leaned close and scrutinized the carvings over her shoulder. She felt uncomfortable, as if they were staring together at the dead.

Then the three of them sat down at the table. The food was exquisitely good, and Alexandra felt that it fed more than her empty stomach. Irina watched them eat. "After lunch, I will try myself to call my nephew on his mobile. He is probably with them still, wherever they are. I will also call our house in the mountains, where there is a telephone, in case they have returned there already."

The helper came in to clear their dishes. Alexandra had begun to feel nervous about Stoycho; Bobby must have been thinking the same thing, because he murmured to her that he hoped his taxi was all right inside. She practiced saying their hostess's last name to herself before she got up the courage to use it. "Madame Georgieva, I'm sorry to tell you that we must go back to our car for a little while. Our dog is shut in there and we're worried about him. Would you mind if we took him for a walk and then came back here to say goodbye?"

The old lady regarded her. She sat easily as tall as Alexandra. "What kind of a dog?"

"Just a—general dog," said Alexandra. "Really sweet and nicely behaved, though."

"Well, if he is a good one, you could bring him here. Perhaps he needs water, on this warm day? I will call my sister and nephew while you are out."

Alexandra thought she would have liked to be there while Irina made those calls, but they assented and Bobby shut the front door quietly behind them. The sunlight was brighter now, even filtered through the trees of the old town, and the air was warm and heavy. They found Stoycho sitting up in the cab, looking out the partly open window. He rushed at them, nose against the window and whip-tail thwacking the seat, then restrained himself and sat down again.

"See what a fine dog, just like we were saying," murmured Alexandra. Bobby took the rope and helped him down, and Stoycho went for the nearest bushes and along the old walls. At last he paused under a sycamore and looked up at it, t en at Alexandra. His tongue hung out one side of his mouth and his teeth showed white. He sat upright and vigorous, brindled back muscular in the sun, but Alexandra thought his eyes were sad. She bent down and put an arm around his neck. He licked her ear, politely.

"Let's take him back to Irina's," she told Bobby. When they knocked at the door of the little house, it did not fly open as before. They heard soft steps and Irina's helper let them in; she showed them out into an arbor, with the museum and its courtyard visible beyond. She put glasses of juice for them on a table, under the leaves and tendrils and first tight pendants of green grapes. She brought a bowl full of water for Stoycho, carrying it in both hands. Stoycho waited to be invited, then drank the whole thing. Next she brought him a dish of food scraps; he ate these more quietly and lay down with his back against a potted lemon tree and his head where Alexandra could reach it with her fingers. Alexandra imagined Vera and old Milen Radev seated at this table, and Neven with his long legs stretched out and the shadow of a tree across his lap. And earlier, a thin-faced man holding a violin in front of him. Soon, she thought, they would leave his ashes here, to be delivered safely to his son. She knew she should feel relieved of a burden, but there was an empty place in her chest that the sunlight couldn't reach.

In the warm silence, Bobby offered her a cigarette, which she refused, and smoked one himself. It was the first time she'd seen him smoke, and when she commented on this he explained that he seldom did it, since he was a runner. This reminded her that he was missing not only several days of work in Sofia but also his running routine. Well, he could go back to it soon, and she would check in with the English Institute in person. She hoped again that she and Bobby would keep in touch, that she would see him often.

When Irina Georgieva came out onto the terrace, holding the back of a chair for a moment to steady herself, they stood up at once, ready to say their goodbyes. Bobby quickly stubbed out his cigarette and kissed Irina's hand, which didn't seem to surprise her. Irina had changed her clothes; now she wore a white linen dress, more rough than stylish, and a thin black cardigan, as if no summer weather could ever warm her. Her hair was pinned up, away from her chalky face, and the brooch held her collar shut. It shone under the arbor, and Alexandra noticed that some of the flowers worked into the enamel were actually grape leaves and ripe grapes. Stoycho had gotten to his feet, too. Irina Georgieva seemed to see him for the first time.

"This is your dog?" she said. She put out her hand. Stoycho touched it with his nose; she stroked his black velour head, and his tail made a powerful circle. "He is a very, very nice dog," she said. "I would like to paint this dog." She gestured for them to sit down with her.

"We want to thank you for all your hospitality," said Alexandra.

"Of course, my dear." Irina Georgieva opened her hands on the table. She wore no rings and

Alexandra thought that none would have fitted over those uneven fingers anyway.

"Did you reach your sister?" Bobby asked. Alexandra held her breath.

But Irina shook her head. "I have called each of the numbers and there is no answer. I suppose they are traveling by now, maybe coming here with Neven on the train. They may even have gone home to the mountains, although there is no answer there, either. They would not have a place to stay in Sofia, and it is already two nights since they lost the urn. I will call them again this evening."

Stoycho had crept to Irina's knee and was leaning against it, his eyes open but dreamy. Alexandra thought again about the old woman who was Irina's sister, and the man in the wheelchair. She tried not to think about Neven. She had hoped to see them again, but at least they would know she had returned their treasure.

"Madame Georgieva," she said. "Before we go, I wanted to ask if—whether you could please just tell us a little more about Mr. Lazarov."

"*Gospodin* Lazarov," corrected Bobby. "Alexandra is learning Bulgarian."

"*Gospodin*," Alexandra said carefully. "It's none of my business, but we know only that he was a musician—and your brother-in-law."

Irina kept her hand on Stoycho's head. "Yes, of course I can tell you a little. I knew him quite well. He was a great violinist, and a complicated man." She sighed—Alexandra had never heard such a sound before. "He was a child prodigy, which always makes life hard for people, you know—he played a solo with the orchestra in Sofia when he was only twelve. And then he studied in Vienna before the war. He went there while he was still a teenager."

Irina looked up into the leaves of the arbor. "I have always felt certain that he would have been an internationally famous musician—not only a great one, you know—if he had lived in a different time and place. But the regime never allowed him to perform solo, or to make any recordings. Just after the war, he still played in one of the orchestras in Sofia. Also, he played chamber music, mainly with his friends. Later he was in the orchestra in Burgas, but only now and then."

She cleared her throat. "He sometimes played here in Plovdiv. They would not let him teach at the music institute, but once in a while he worked in the orchestra when other violinists were sick or on a holiday. Whenever he came here, he would always visit me and we would sit up until very late. Sometimes he would bring Neven, whom he adored, or Vera, if she could leave her job. After dinner, Stoyan would play for us, for hours. It was always worth it, to lose sleep with such a musician in the house."

Irina hesitated, stroking the dog's ears. "For a

few years he lived far out in the countryside and he did not play there, I'm sure. He worked in some factories, too, as many people did in those days. But he was always an even better musician when he returned and got back in practice. He loved all the baroque composers, especially the Italians. I had not heard about Geminiani or Corelli until he played them in this house."

Bobby leaned toward her. "Why was he not allowed by the regime to perform solo?"

Irina stroked her brooch and it caught the finely scattered light. Stoycho twitched and shuddered against Alexandra's feet. Then Irina raised her hand, as if pointing to the sky. "He was very quiet about himself, sometimes in sad moods, or difficult. He told me once that although he had never talked about himself enough, the story of his life could be found in his music. I understood what he meant—I often think the same about my paintings. When Stoyan Lazarov played his violin, it sounded exactly as I think his own voice would have, if he had talked more. He said the violin should be able to tell the truth and it should be able to cry."

It seemed to Alexandra that the old lady had not answered Bobby's question about the regime, but when he spoke up he simply asked a different one. "We were confused to see that *gospodin* Lazarov died two years ago, but his family did not have a funeral. Why is that? We found his *nekrolog* in Bovech. Also, I am surprised that after his death he was—Alexandra?"

"Cremated," said Alexandra.

"Yes," Bobby said. "Is that not unusual, in his generation?" He didn't say, *in your generation.*

Irina nodded. "It is somewhat unusual, and Vera did not tell me why this was done. Perhaps it was her wish. I have never asked."

Bobby took the rebuke calmly. "But then she didn't bury the urn somewhere, in two years?"

"I suppose she had too much grief to decide where that should be. Or perhaps she had some difficulty saying the last goodbye to him. I was pleased when she told me they would bring him to Velinski *manastir*, a place he liked and sometimes visited. Perhaps it required a long time. It is not easy to get permission for burial at such a place. Also, my sister can be not so— definite about things, and she has had many troubles. She loved him very much, you know. They met when she was still in high school. They both liked to tell the story of how they first saw each other, although Stoyan told it best. It was one thing he did like to talk about."

Alexandra sat on her hands, thinking of the luminous face and marcelled hair in the photo-graph at Bovech. Had that been Vera Lazarova? "Do you remember it?"

Irina smiled. "Of course. I have not yet forgotten the important things."

BOOK
2

Twenty-four

The man stepping off a train in Sofia's central station had a newspaper under one arm, a newspaper already two days old: The Vienna Gazette, *May 20, 1940.* He had rolled it into a tube like a telescope through which to view the mountains of his home country as they filled the window of the sleeping compartment. Now he held the paper under one arm and gripped the handle of his instrument case a little too tightly.

The headlines in the *Gazette* contained all the reasons he was returning. All the reasons except two: his mother and father, waiting at home for him while Europe began to burn. He had sent a telegram to tell them that yes, he was coming back for a while, and the time of the train. He wondered if it had reached them in Sofia—there had been no reply. Perhaps the telegraph lines had already been interrupted by all this absurdity. He'd stayed in Vienna as long as he could, not wanting to leave his hard-won seat in the Philharmonic, or his new string quartet. But the last weeks had made him wonder whether he would actually be able to get out of Austria if he waited any longer. It was two years now since the Jewish members of the Vienna Philharmonic had been expelled—Bruno Walter himself, after that, for all intents and purposes. It made Stoyan ill to remember, and maybe the Slavs in the orchestra would be next.

In his free hand, Stoyan Lazarov carried a leather valise; his father had given it to him seven years before. His other luggage had been shipped and he would never see it again, something he'd guessed while accepting the ticket stub. He had placed in the valise the thing he most cared about, after his violin, folding a clean shirt around it. The valise also contained a shaving kit, two silver-backed brushes, and his address book. At the last minute, he had added a small knife. The knife could have been for cutting up cheese and salami if he hadn't possessed money for the train's dining car, which he did.

Stoyan's hair was well cut; his lightweight suit—hanging on a tall, thin frame—was a little worn from his years abroad, especially in the right elbow, but it had begun and would end a very good one. Over it he wore a light summer coat and hat. His face was already not quite young. Instead, it was firmly intelligent, carefully clean-shaven, with bright dark eyes and surprising, curly lashes like a little boy's, his skin pale but not fair—it looked merely in need of more sun. Under the left side of his chin was a red-brown mark like polish on a stone. His mouth was gentle and could have formed a generous smile. Just now his lips were pressed together as he stepped down among the other passengers and glanced around.

He set his valise on the platform in Sofia—but not his violin, never that—and stood there a moment. People were finding and greeting family members; a nicely coiffed young woman he thought for a moment he recognized—but he was wrong—lost her hat to the embraces of two old people who must be her parents. The father picked her hat up for her, and as he bent over, Stoyan saw the fabric of a homemade shirt rough under a rusty black jacket: villagers. He would never know their story, nor why he could remember them decades later.

When it was clear no one had come to meet him, Stoyan took off his coat, folded it over one arm, and picked up his valise. He tested its weight in his hand. As of this morning, he had the wrong money in his pocket: the new *Reichsmark*, a German gift to Austria. Clearly, his telegram, like his luggage, had never reached Sofia. He would walk home. But as soon as he left the station, with the pigeons circling under its handsome roof, he felt better, felt that he belonged with the people around him. He was dark-haired like most of them. He heard a man calling out to another man and immediately understood the scrap of their exchange, even if it made no sense: "—just chew it a little more slowly, brother!" Literal advice, or a metaphor? And the second man, closer to Stoyan in the crowd, laughing and waving as he turned away.

The streets themselves were as he'd always known them—apartments and shops, and in the center the grand Parisian-style buildings stained with coal smoke, cobbles slippery underfoot, the occasional horse-drawn cart clattering past with a load: food, coal, wooden crates, piles of scrap metal. A man sitting on an upturned pail called out, endlessly, the offer to shine gentlemen's shoes. Stoyan reminded himself that it hadn't been so long since he'd left these streets; in fact, since his last visit three years earlier, the only changes were a few new omnibuses and the shorter skirts of the women, who dressed less fashionably than women in Vienna but were more beautiful. A street sweeper stopped work to wipe his face; he greeted Stoyan in a raspy too-familiar voice. "Fiddle player? That your *tsigulka*? Play some-thing, *maestro*!" Stoyan smiled and would have touched the brim of his hat if his hands hadn't been full.

He kept moving; now he felt Bulgarian again, included. The linden trees had blossomed out, his favorite time in the city. A brindled dog passed him on the sidewalk—handsome, polite, trotting fast as if on an urgent errand. Stoyan remembered walking in Vienna only two days before, saying goodbye to the trees there, where it was always colder. Strolling in those parks he had often pictured himself in childhood, in Sofia, looking at the lindens in bloom—full circle now. Even coming back was not so bad. He would be reunited with his parents and sleep in his old bedroom in their apartment. Bulgaria was neutral and likely to remain so—safer than Austria, certainly. If he had to stay home any length of time, perhaps a few months, he would get a room of his own and some practice space at the music academy.

Turning a corner, Stoyan felt the swing of his coat over his arm, the familiar weight of the violin in its case. He thought of histories he had read and discussed with other students in Vienna—Europe's wars in the *cinquecento*, in the *settecento*, the sordid comings and goings of armies and tyrants while Handel, Mozart, and Beethoven went on with their work. He thought of Beethoven and his Sinfonia Eroica, dedicated first to Napoleon. When Napoleon had declared himself emperor—the legend went—Beethoven had scratched out the dedication in a rage.

He turned another corner. He hoped that sooner or later Hitler would be scratched out, too, on someone's dedication page. Then he, Stoyan, could go back and resume his swift climb upward. Sooner than later, the Queen Elisabeth competition would be renewed and he would compete for it again. He'd qualified the first time, by dint of enormous work, although he knew it would take him some years to actually win. He would not simply be famous in his country. He had known since childhood that he would make his country famous in the world.

He heard music starting up, but someone else's music. On the sidewalk ahead of him stood a dusty-haired man with a violin under his chin, striking up a tune for the bear beside him. The animal stood upright, leashed with worn red leather, galumphing on its back legs, its small eyes looking straight ahead, its coat coming off in patches, even shabbier than the man's clothes. It held out its paws as if they belonged to a different animal. The man danced, too, while he played, with the same awkward shuffle; perhaps he had learned from the bear instead of the other way around. The bear's gaze darted here and there, fixing on Stoyan's violin case, and then the man dipped and bowed to him, acknowledging a fellow performer. Stoyan nodded, wished he had a little money to give him. The fellow wasn't half bad, as a musician—rather good, in fact, in a traditional way.

He hadn't reached his own neighborhood yet, but it wasn't far now. He passed a bakery in the warm sun, doubled back without thinking, and went in. The scent of bread made him suddenly ravenous, a surge of hunger for home. The baker, a huge-fisted man, fished out a roll for him before Stoyan remembered again that he had no *stotinki*. Warm on his palm, the day's second baking. It was strange to be so poor for a few minutes that you could buy nothing at all, not a tune or a piece of bread. He stood there, childishly hungry.

"What's wrong?" The baker patted his missing waist, stretched. "You won't find fresher any- where in the city."

"I'm sure of that," Stoyan said, feeling Bulgarian easy on his tongue. For a few months, he would no longer have to gird himself for the struggle with German, the constant regret that he had studied French in school instead. "It's just that I'd forgotten—I'm fresh off a train, with none of our money in my pockets. I'm sorry to have given you the trouble." He set the roll down on a clean towel spread out beside the man's abacus.

The baker leaned forward against his counter, one floury hand pressed on the edge. His ovens would be in the back, or even underground. Bulgarian bread, baked on stones, sliding in and out on long wooden paddles, a tablecloth trick. Stoyan thought for a moment of Vienna's pastry shops, the delicate displays in the windows, the wrought-iron chairs and Art Nouveau maidens frescoing the walls, the baroque cherubs on the ceilings, the thin china cups. At Demel's, he had seen a cake that reproduced Napoleon's second attack on the city, complete with sugar horses pulling fire engines, the Hofburg palace deliciously ablaze.

"Where've you been?" the baker said.

"Austria."

The baker's eyes glistened darkly in his face, and Stoyan realized that it was hard to tell whether the man's hair was going white in the midst of the flour. "A powerful place these days, isn't that?" he observed. "Little brother to the Germans. They're saying *gospodin* Hitler will return Macedonia to us, once Europe is properly redivided."

"I don't know about that." Stoyan thought of moving on, toward home and food he didn't have to pay for, but the pleasure of speaking Bulgarian with this man kept him a moment longer, even if the man's views were likely to irritate him. He'd known a few other Bulgarian students in Vienna—when they used their own language together it had felt like something illicit, useless. This man had probably never even considered learning another language; his Bulgarian was forever enough for him, as natural as his own skin and the wooden counter he leaned on.

"There's no other reason for Bulgaria to get mixed up in their doings." The baker brushed his hands together as if wiping away the crumbs of further possibilities. "We don't need them and the good Lord knows they don't need us. But if they restored our territory, wouldn't that be worth a little scuffle? I'd roll up my sleeves and do it myself, if they wanted me. But I'm too old, and I've got a bad hip. Very bad."

"I'm not sure it'll be a little scuffle," Stoyan

said. "You wouldn't believe the size of the armies parading in Vienna these days."

For some reason, he wished he could make the baker see the parades, this man who would never leave Bulgaria, who probably took a train out of Sofia once a year to go back to his father's village—a man who'd perhaps never traveled to the Black Sea at the other end of his own country. Odd, how some people were destined to see the world and some not. He thought of what he himself had already witnessed—horses with tightly braided bundled tails like women's hair, in a park in London. An aging harpsichordist in a Paris drawing room placing his hands on the keyboard, while a girl with blue satin shoes sat beside him to turn pages. The towering spikes of the cathedral in Prague. The even wider arc he would see in the future suddenly lifted Stoyan, and he felt almost faint with gratitude for the adventure of his life. He took off his hat and wiped his forehead, as he'd seen the street sweeper do earlier. The door swung open behind him, letting in traffic noise, and another customer entered.

The baker looked up and pushed the roll back to Stoyan. "Here, eat this. But don't go away," he said. Clearly, he hadn't finished reclaiming Macedonia. He turned to his new client.

"Oh, it's Vera," he said. "What can I get you, *moyto momiche*?"

She was just a girl, Stoyan saw, a schoolgirl in skirt and jacket, her dark braids roped together with a white bow.

"Two loaves, please." She put some coins on the counter and the baker turned to fetch her order.

The girl glanced at Stoyan, then averted her eyes and didn't look at him again. Well-bred, and grown up almost into a woman, probably a student at the *gimnasium* nearby. Her skin was pale, her nose a little long and delicately shaped. Her eyes, in that glance, were radiant, the pupils a sur-prising golden color, the lower lids rounded as if permanently swollen with tears, although it was clear that she hadn't been crying. She fidgeted with the cuff of her jacket in order not to look at him or anything else.

Stoyan kept his hat under one arm and watched her without meaning to, both of them waiting for the baker to bring the loaves. While she examined the edge of the counter, he observed that her mouth was wide and held in check at the corners, which seemed to produce a dimple. Her ear was small and tendrils of hair escaped around it, like a baby's. He watched the horizontal sweep of her eyelashes—dark, like her hair—and then the horizontal sweep of her cheekbones, the knitted brow that didn't want anyone looking. She might be as old as twenty or as young as fifteen, with her jacket fitted neatly over her breasts, her legs slim in their white cotton stockings, her shoes buckled and polished. She must be at least five years younger than he was, already a lifetime behind him.

The baker returned with the loaves in brown paper. "Give these to Mama," he said briskly, taking her coins. "How is your father, by the way?"

The girl named Vera glanced up. "He's better, thank you. We're going to the sea next month, for a cure."

"Well, may he be completely healed, God bless him." The baker shook his head. "Here, wait."

He pulled a tray of cheese pastries off a shelf and began to wrap one in more paper, which it spotted with grease. "These are the best of the day. They'll bring him some nourishment." He glared at Stoyan under white eyebrows. "A fine man, her father, and he was hit by one of those new buses right in front of his own house. What can happen at any moment! There, my dear— give him those, no charge."

The girl still did not look at Stoyan. He wanted to murmur an apology for life's hardships, in particular hers.

The baker was leaning over the counter now; he had spotted Stoyan's violin case for the first time. "What? A musician? Why didn't you say so? You can play for your snack! Are you any good?"

Stoyan laughed aloud, and felt it was the first time he'd done that in a week. "They say in

Vienna that I'm not bad." He was rewarded by the feeling of the girl Vera's eyes finally resting on his face, and he was careful, in turn, not to look at her.

"Is that so?" The baker's mouth had broken into a capacious smile and now he leaned back with his arms folded. "Prove yourself, then, son. Light up the old man's shop a bit."

Stoyan had frequently refused to play even for friends, if his fingers were stiff or his mind out of sorts. Now he found himself opening his violin case on the well-swept wood of the bakery floor, where flour had cemented the cracks like ice on a terrace. He removed the violin from its velvet nest and lifted it to his shoulder. Without looking, he could tell that Vera was facing him. He placed his bow on the A string and pulled a rich sound from the instrument, tuning it—it seemed very loud in this space—and heard the door open again behind them. More customers.

Without turning around, he began to play: the Chaconne from Bach's second Partita in D minor. He knew the piece as thoroughly as anything in his repertoire; he had begun to learn it at the age of fourteen and had worked at it ever since. But now it seemed to him a new set of notes, fresh and passionate, an almost unrecognizable melody that his fingers happened to find on the strings. It fell all around him into the high-ceilinged old room, into the smell of bread, the greasy front windows, onto the sleeves of his carefully brushed jacket. It shimmered on the face of the girl staring at him— he glanced frankly at her for a moment over the music and saw that she was more than a girl, her eyebrows raised in critical pleasure, her lips pressed together to keep a smile inside. The baker gestured over Stoyan's head to other people in the doorway; a small crowd seemed to be gathering behind him, then the sound of the door held or propped open, its bell clashing briefly with a phrase of the Chaconne, voices from the street pressing in. Around his own body he felt silence, as he always did while he played, the music coming to life inside him but also reaching his ears from a long way off, across fields, mountains, now whole countries. When he drew his bow through the last note, the silence broke behind his eyes and dizzied him for a moment.

Then the baker began to pound his hands together, and the people who had pressed into the shop began to clap and cheer. He turned to acknowledge them, to bow a little, holding the instrument near his heart.

"Just back from Vienna!" shouted the baker, as if he had arranged the concert and invited them all in ahead of time. "One of ours! From Sofia?" he asked Stoyan.

Stoyan nodded and bowed once more, beginning to feel foolish, but his eyes had found Vera again. She was the only one not clapping;

she didn't have to. Her schoolgirl expression had fallen away completely and he saw only the Bach on her face, the mobile twitch of her mouth, surprised and alert, the kindled look of her eyes, close to raw pleasure. She had forgotten him and heard only his music, or the composer's, or both. He bowed to her alone, and then packed away his instrument. The baker was wrapping up three loaves for him, swiftly, waving off Stoyan's protests. People were making way for Stoyan as he passed out of the store.

"That one will climb far!" a man called out.

"Go with God! Come back and play any time!" shouted the baker. The people in the doorway drew apart. Vera walked out with him, as if that was natural, and he fell back to usher her ahead, looking down at her neat, proud shoulder and the long braids tied together with white organdy. At the curb, she glanced at him again, more tentatively, then hurried away; she had seemed afraid that he might say something, or that she might, herself. He watched her, followed her at a short distance with his valise in one hand and his instrument case in the other. She crossed among the carts and cars—graceful, diffident, proper— and went up a side street without looking back.

When he reached the corner, he saw that she was letting herself into a gate in front of a four-story apartment building. He watched from nearly a block away as she shut it behind her. The building was a handsome one: a front garden with an old tree, wrought-iron balconies, long windows that had a look of lace curtains behind them. He noted the name of the cross street. A church bell had begun to ring somewhere down the boulevard. His parents would be overjoyed to see him, lunch soon spread on the table, his mother fussing over his one bag, his father's kisses on his cheeks. Hot water for his face and hands, a clean shirt.

Stoyan turned away. But he knew where she lived, and she had looked at him with her eyes full of music.

Twenty-five

Irina Georgieva walked them to the door and kissed Alexandra's cheeks, then Bobby's.

"Thank you, my dears," she said. "Travel safely. I will call you when I hear from Vera, so that you will know the end of the story."

She was still standing there, with her hand on the doorframe, when Alexandra turned back on the sidewalk to see her again. Alexandra wished she had taken a picture of the old lady, and of the small painted house, but it was too late now. She had also forgotten to say goodbye to the urn, although of course that would have made no sense.

They walked down the cobbled streets until

they found the right corner. It was quiet there, the heat filtering through the old trees, no one in sight. Then Bobby stopped sharply with Stoycho's leash in his hand, and Alexandra stopped just beside him.

The taxi sat where they had left it an hour earlier, but across the top of the windshield was a smear of yellow, although it didn't look like a word. Then she saw that two bullet-sized holes had been punched into the windshield, one where the driver's face would be and one for the passenger's. Long cracks radiated from each hole.

"Bobby?" she said. He stood there silent, his eyes narrowed, not looking at her even when she pulled on his arm. There was a piece of paper folded under one of the windshield wipers. He glanced quickly around, drew the paper carefully out and opened it.

"What does it say?" Alexandra begged. A quaking had started in her knees, which made her suspect that she didn't really want to know.

It took him another moment. "It says, *Varnete ya*," he told her flatly. Alexandra could see for herself that there was no exclamation point. "That means, *Give it back*." He paused. "Or it could mean, *Give* her *back*."

"Give what back?" She kept her hand closed on his arm. "And why would anyone put holes in your windshield?"

But Bobby was searching the street. He hurried

to the other end of the block, darting around parked cars, scanning walls and gardens. Stoycho ran beside him. Bobby returned to the taxi, bent close to the paint, stepped away to see the whole effect. He scratched some up under his fingernail and sniffed it. "Still a little wet, of course."

"Why would someone do this?" Alexandra asked again.

"I don't know," said Bobby harshly. "I see a lot of graffiti these days, a lot of vandalism of cars. But this is the second time. And *Give it back*—"

He fished out his phone and took a picture of the windshield, then of each of the holes in it. "We can't drive it like this. Watch for traffic. I don't want to attract any more attention than we have to."

He opened the trunk and got out an old blanket, which he spread over the windshield and began to fasten down with duct tape. Alexandra wondered how they would get back to Sofia now. The street lay quiet, but no longer peaceful, she thought. Stoycho sat gazing at them.

"Why would someone do this?" she asked again.

"That is not the right question," Bobby said, tearing off pieces of tape. "The first question is, *Who?* Let's say this is not something silly, someone making a joke. It could be, but the message doesn't sound like that. Especially after what happened at Lelya Pavlina's—twice in two days. If we knew who, we might know why. And, second, what are they saying we should give back? What do we have? I don't think they mean a person, unless I am supposed to give you back to someone."

He turned toward her, but still as if distracted, almost exasperated.

"We have Stoycho," she said and immediately felt foolish. The dog moved on restless feet, looking up at her. "We have the urn, or we did until a few hours ago. But who would want it back? I mean, except the Lazarovi?"

Bobby taped across the top of the windshield; she held the blanket smooth for him. "Well, let's say it is most probable that someone who wrote this means the urn. That is the only unusual thing we have—except that we don't even have it, now, as you said. And *who* knows that we had it?"

"The Lazarovi," Alexandra said again. "But we're trying to find them to give it back. And also Irina knows, and probably her helper." She thought for a moment, wiping paint from her fingers. "And the police, those two guards I spoke to at the station in Sofia, and maybe the receptionist there, and the officer I talked to about it."

"Yes," Bobby said. He was still glancing around the street every few seconds.

"But I had the urn right with me, at the police station. If they'd wanted it, they could have taken it then, and they didn't insist. I mean, I actually brought it to them. Anyway, why would they want it?"

"Yes, why?" Bobby said.

"There is one weird thing," Alexandra said, hesitantly. "I might be remembering it the wrong way now, or making too much of it. You know, at the station, I talked with that police officer for a few minutes—he gave me the address in Bovech. We were alone together, in his office. He didn't seem very interested in me except at one point, when he looked up Stoyan Lazarov's name in a database or something. Then he kind of flinched, and he made a call on his cell phone, which of course I couldn't understand. But he seemed a little more attentive after that, or just— interested in a different way."

She looked at Bobby. "That was when he asked if I wanted him to keep the bag, but after I said I felt I should do it myself, he immediately told me that was better and that he could give me an address. I guess the police could find anybody quickly on their own, much more quickly than we could. So I don't know why they haven't done that—I mean, if they're even the ones who want it back. And they wouldn't write threatening graffiti, right?" She wasn't sure that was right, however, in this country where it turned out she knew less and less about everything.

"What did he look like, this officer?" Bobby asked.

She described him: the nearly bald head, the winking eye, the long intimidating office with the big desk.

"The one who gave you his business card. Yes, that was the chief," Bobby said, straightening up. "I'm sure of it. I was surprised that they took you to him, but maybe it was because you were a foreigner and you were carrying human— remains. That doesn't happen there every morning."

"Why would the police want us to give back the urn now?"

Bobby shook his head again. "I don't think this was done by the police. You are right—that is not the way they do things. They would come find us by looking for my license number and maybe even go bang on Irina Georgieva's door, if they knew we were there."

"But no one else knows," Alexandra said.

"We can't be sure that is true," Bobby said quietly. He stretched the bottom edge of the blanket tight over the windshield. "The police could have told someone else, from what you are describing. Irina could have told someone this morning while we were out, or her helper could have told her own friends. And the Lazarovi would not be able to find us or the taxi—if they could, they would be here already, to ask for the urn."

"Unless they went to the police themselves, but

after I did," Alexandra said. "And the police had already traced us and decided to give them the license plate number of the taxi. I mean, in theory."

Bobby looked hard at her, then leaned over and pointed at the side of her head. "You are a very smart girl," he said.

"Not a *girl,*" she said, automatically.

"Right," Bobby said. "But I don't think the Lazarovi would come to us like this, with a paint can, or break windows. They are normal people, old people, and probably very sad and upset. They would ask the police to help them find us, and then they would ask us in a normal way for the urn."

"I don't like this," Alexandra said. "I feel as if we should tell someone about it."

"What—do you want to go back to the police?"

"Not really," she admitted. "At least, not right away. Maybe Irina will reach the—Lazarovi—today, and if she does she will let us know everything's all right." But her heart was sinking.

"I don't like this, either," Bobby said. He tore off a last piece of tape almost viciously and stretched it down the side of the windshield. "Also, if someone who is angry wants the urn for some reason, how can we leave it with this old lady? What if they discover that she has it now?"

"I was thinking of that, too," Alexandra said. "And we might still be able to help her find her sister." A little warmth, a little relief, broke through her uneasiness.

When they returned, Irina Georgieva was sitting under the grape arbor drinking water and slowly taking some pills. She looked up at them, apparently unsurprised.

"Without these medicines, I die tomorrow and the museum will get my house," she said. "They have a legal right to it, and they are waiting eagerly." She waved at the mansion across the courtyard. "Not my paintings, however. I am leaving my paintings to the art school. Did you have trouble with your car?"

"Yes," Bobby said. It was the perfect solution—car trouble. "Would you mind if we stay a little longer, while we decide what to do?"

"Unfortunate for your car," Irina said. "But fortunate for me." She smiled, her watery eyes bright.

"Do you mean that your sister called?" Alexandra asked eagerly.

"No, my dear. I wish so, but she has not. And I have been calling Neven and also the phone at the mountain house, again, and still there is no answer. I never liked that they went to live in the mountains, especially in winter. It is too small a place, too far away from everything. But I think we cannot sit here forever—they have certainly gone back there, or they will go very soon." She sighed. "If you get your car fixed quickly, we can reach the village in less than one day and take the urn to them ourselves. We could go tomorrow morning. Lenka will come, too, to help me." The younger woman's name, at last.

Alexandra glanced at Bobby. "Would you have time to do that?"

Bobby had folded his thin arms across his chest. The hair fell into his eyes and his skin looked pale and verdant under the leaves of the trellis. Alexandra wondered if he was handsomer than she'd first recognized, or if it was simply that phenomenon that makes people look better and better as you get used to them, familiarity softening their oddness.

He nodded. "Of course, Bird. We can do that. I will make a phone call or two, myself."

They all smiled at one another. In spite of everything, Alexandra felt a sudden sharp pleasure, this time from the faces before her, the long-short distance to home, the early summer light and warm sun.

"One thing we must agree," Irina said to Bobby. "Asparuh, I will hire you to drive us. You have been away from your work for several days, I think? I shall insist."

"Thank you, Madame Georgieva." Bobby inclined his head, respectfully. "If you feel safe, I will be honored to take you. My taxi is not very nice, however."

And maybe not that safe, actually, Alexandra thought. "And we have Stoycho," she said aloud. "But he could sit on my lap."

Irina patted Bobby's hand. "Then that is settled," she said. "One bed, tonight, or two?"

She put this briskly, and Alexandra was a little taken aback. On the other hand, perhaps an artist, however old, couldn't be easily shocked.

"Oh, two, please," Alexandra said, without looking at Bobby.

"Very well. And do you have some luggage? Other luggage, that is?"

Bobby told her they didn't. Then Irina said that she would show them Stoycho's lodgings. She led them unsteadily beyond the arbor, where they saw a doghouse, painted blue to match the houses of the old town; Alexandra felt certain it had not been there earlier. Food and water sat in front of it and a cotton mat was spread inside.

"My place is small, but your place is smaller," Irina Georgieva told Stoycho. "And it is in shadows enough to be cool for you." He went into his house, turned around once, and lay down with his head outside the doorway and his eyes already closing.

Lenka took Alexandra upstairs to a room whose ceiling was so low she could stroke it with her hand flat. It was lined in time-darkened wood, the trim carved into acorns and oak leaves, a smooth-faced girl looking down from the top of the doorway. Irina had hung her animal paintings in here—goats, sheep, chickens, doves, fish, and a surprisingly vivid hippopotamus. Alexandra thought at first that there was no bed. Was she supposed to sleep on the wool rug? But Irina's helper opened a cupboard across one wall to show her the bed inside: white pillows, a cotton coverlet, and for some reason a twig of dried herbs lying in the middle. Alexandra picked it up and smelled it and said, "Oregano?" Pronouncing it in as Slavic a way as she could think of.

Lenka laughed and said, "*Chubritza*," and they stood grinning at each other, unable to communicate further.

Soon after, Irina disappeared for her afternoon rest. Bobby proposed that they leave the house for a little while; he wanted to look around the neighborhood some more. Alexandra knew he was thinking about the holes in his windshield. They took Stoycho on his rope and walked through the old town toward the ruins of the Roman theater. It stood high above the city, on what must have been a commanding site in its own time as well. There was a fence across the top; they paid an entrance fee and went in. A columned back wall had been restored enough to shelter plays and concerts. Level with the last row of the theater stood a fine old building: the music institute where Stoyan Lazarov had not been allowed to teach. Alexandra wandered around looking at gigantic rough-quarried stones and then they climbed back up to sit on the top row. Stoycho lay near them in the aisle, his rope slack. From here it was possible to imagine every kind of classical spectacle—an already antique Greek tragedy played out against the marble, for example.

Bobby waved a hand. "It was built in the time of the emperor Trajan, in the second century."

"You know a lot about your country," Alexandra told him.

"I've always been interested in history," he said. "But a country has many myths about itself—mythology, mixed up with the history. Don't you know a lot about your country, too? Or at least some myths?"

"Maybe a few," she said, wondering when the Golden Gate Bridge had been erected, or Philadelphia founded.

"Well, your country is very big." He slung an arm around her shoulders, surprising her. "Probably you can't know all of it."

"I know my own region pretty well," she said. She imagined him with his arm around a boyfriend, but maybe he couldn't do that in public, here—or didn't have a boyfriend, anyway. His arm was comfortable, warm. The thought came to her of Jack, sitting on her bed to help with her homework; for once she felt no uprush of pain at the memory.

Voices clattered behind them and they watched

as a tour guide entered with her string of tourists in tow. The guide wore a navy pantsuit, like a flight attendant, and a bright red hat that said SUNNYTRIPS, and she waved a sheaf of papers at her ducklings to keep their attention. The tourists were dark-haired or swarthy-looking, mostly middle-aged, the men bearded and the women in skirts and sandals that looked bad for walking. There were a few teenagers, hanging back alone or in pairs, a lanky boy turning away from his parents to check his phone. Alexandra imagined the text he'd just sent to his girlfriend, somewhere back home: *Hi, another fucking ruin.*

"Greeks," Bobby said with interest. "But not ancient ones." He took his arm off her shoulders and pulled Stoycho closer. Stoycho looked sadly at him—did Bobby really think he was going to dash over and chew up a bunch of tourists? Light fell over the great stones in waves and Alexandra felt that she'd never really seen the sun before; it was different in this part of the world, as if a huge veil had been removed and the sky was shining with strength from an earlier time. Her skin felt washed by it, and by the warm wind coming up the hillsides. The stones they sat on looked almost silver. She saw weeds growing unheeded out of the cracks, a cluster of poppies in bright red bloom near the stage. This, she thought, was peace, which came over you when you least expected it. But it stayed in her veins only a moment, and then the image of a broken windshield hung before her.

Irina Georgieva's phone didn't ring that evening; instead Alexandra and Bobby sat near her for a while in the perfection of a May evening in the Balkans. Lenka had brought them cups of a tea that Irina said was from the mountains. The air stirred, but only a little, and the growing moonlight spattered everything in forms like the interstices of grape leaves and tendrils. Alexandra brushed her hand across the table and found that she could move her fingers but not those shapes of light and shadow, and that her hands added complicated new shadows. She described to Irina the old house in the North Carolina mountains, although she didn't mention Jack. Bobby explained his project to run all the streets of Sofia; Irina laughed approvingly and told them that she had once had a project to paint all the animals in the world—"Although how would you do that, from Bulgaria?"

"You mean because there are only a few species here?" asked Alexandra, who had already observed that Irina liked her forthrightness more than her politeness and had begun to avail herself of that discovery. "Because you'd have to travel so much?"

Bobby said softly, as if correcting an innocent mistake, "Remember, no one could go anywhere, under communism. I mean, most people could not. But you must have seen many animals in pictures and films, Madame Georgieva?"

Some of her white hair had come unpinned, and she tucked it back behind her ear, one of many youthful gestures Alexandra had noticed in her.

"Of course," she said. "Also, there was the zoo in Sofia. And before the war I did go to other places, mainly England. Our father worked in London from the time I was a little child until I was twelve, when we had to return. That's where I learned my English, you know, and we went to the London Zoo very often. As a child, I wanted to become a painter because of the animals there—for example, the way the elephant has these kind of—whiskers—along his back and around his ears."

She gestured with long bent hands, drawing the hairs. "But you are quite right. Most of us could not travel. I knew people who dreamed all the time about going somewhere else, and they let that ruin their lives. When you are not allowed to do something, it often becomes very important."

Irina stopped suddenly. She frowned at the table. She stirred her tea, releasing a swirl of moon and steam, and Alexandra watched this magic, fearful.

"Those are much sadder stories than mine, and to not go somewhere else was the least of it, my dears," Irina Georgieva said, after a moment. "You have a better life to look forward to, I hope."

She gazed at them out of her moon-speckled face.

Bobby leaned back. He looked older, too, in this tessellated light. Alexandra noticed that he listened keenly to any sound from the street, and looked around the courtyard from time to time, which made her shiver. The moon was high overhead now; she caught a glimpse of it through the top of the grape trellis and saw that it had become distant and cold.

Suddenly Bobby said, "You don't have a *nekrolog* on your door." Alexandra wondered if this would offend Irina Georgieva. She remembered Bovech, the green door with nothing pasted on it, the flowers drying in their pots on the front steps.

But Irina did not seem inclined to reproach him. "My sister asked me not to put one here, and I was not sorry. I don't like them. They are almost always ugly-looking, so they are not a proper honor to people. I would rather have all my memories of a brother than some paper to tell to strangers that he isn't here anymore, with a bad photograph."

Alexandra thought how completely she could agree with that.

Irina straightened herself in her chair. She glanced at Alexandra. "Would you like to know how Stoyan married my sister?"

"Yes," said Alexandra. "Yes, please."

Twenty-six

I remarked to you that Stoyan and I were like brother and sister, Irina said. This is true. There were no brothers in our family, except one who had died as a baby, before Vera was born—and you always need a brother, don't you? Because of this, Stoyan talked with me like to a sister, sometimes, when we got older—although as I told you he was also a very reserved man, so there must have been many parts of his soul I never knew. I was only fifteen when Vera met him at the bakery, but I remember well the first time he came to call at our house. Vera was almost eighteen. My father, who had become an invalid by then, told Vera that she could not see Stoyan alone because she was too young, and that she must wait until she was at least twenty-two to marry—I don't know exactly how he and our mother chose that age. But he allowed her to invite Stoyan to dine with our family every few weeks, especially since Stoyan had now been formally introduced to us by a friend of one of our uncles.

Stoyan came to dinner for years, all through the war, even when there was not much dinner and sometimes when other friends and relatives were present. I don't think he cared for the friends and relatives, but he liked my mother, who was sweet and kind and adored music, and he treated me to little jokes and anecdotes. Most of the time, he sat and watched Vera with glowing eyes as she moved around bringing cushions to my father or helping my mother pour coffee. After dinner Stoyan played his violin, which he always carried with him.

In those days, he was more talkative, and I loved his stories. He told us once that until his return to Sofia, the happiest two days of his life had been the day his father had given him his first violin and shown him the sounds it made, and the day he had stepped off the train in Vienna to study at the music academy there. Vera blushed. Stoyan told us about the musicians he'd heard in great cities, about the cafés of Vienna, about Notre Dame towering over its river. He told us about Rome, where his father had met him on a holiday a few years before, and had bought him his violin —this one, the best he'd owned—a gleaming piece of wood shaped by Giuseppe Alessandri. Alessandri, he said, was born in 1824 and was a student of a student of the great Lorenzo Storioni of Cremona. Stoyan's violin had been made in the 1860s, during the turmoil that formed Italy.

When he played that violin for us, I thought about his stories and the history he talked of, about paintings I had seen and books I had read. His violin made a smoky, mysterious sound. I heard in it the explosions of chestnuts cooking on a brazier at the edge of a river, and horses clopping across cobblestones in Siena and Florence, and also the rustle of leaves that fell on Garibaldi's troops as they marched. The violin sang *"Roma o morte,"* and it wailed for the mountains of dead in an American Civil War across the sea, and for Paris glittering with the Second Empire. It rose and fell with voices reading Victor Hugo aloud by whale oil, and it sang about dynamite, about Ottomans and Englishmen falling under their horses in the Crimea, and the feet of crowds shuffling through international expositions. Above all, Stoyan's violin sang about places—places its maker had been, places the teacher of its maker had been, places its current owner would someday see, and the many, many places where he would someday perform on it.

When Stoyan first came to us, dinner was as it had always been, except for a lot of talk about the war. In the beginning, the King kept our country neutral—although eventually he let Hitler have a few Bulgarian divisions—so the bombings and rationing didn't start for a long time. We lived in a big apartment, nicely furnished, with long curtains in the windows and French doors onto the balcony. Most of our relatives lived in the same building, which my paternal grandfather had put up years before. My mother had brought our furniture with her on her marriage, from her father's orders to Paris in the previous century.

Our parents were very proud of the lives they had made for us in that apartment. My mother kept everything beautifully clean and orderly, with our help, and she made the lace mats for the tables and the antimacassars that protected the chairs from my father's hair pomade. My father's hand beat time on the armrest of one of those chairs while Stoyan obliged his requests by playing a melody from Brahms or a romance by Beethoven—and if he played a tune from an opera, my father would silently shape the words in Italian. During dinner, my mother sometimes pressed a button with her foot under the dining table to call in our one servant—my grandfather had installed this technology for my grandmother when electricity first became available in central Sofia, and everyone was proud whenever my mother did that and the village girl appeared magically from the kitchen. No one else we knew had this system.

That was at first, during the time Stoyan was becoming a member of our family gradually, without our noticing it. We still ate meat from the butcher's, and pickles from my great-grandmother's in the village, because hers were the best. Vera and I changed into clean dresses for dinner. If Stoyan was coming, Vera spent an hour doing her hair and powdering her neck and face to make her complexion even fairer. She was beginning to wear more grown-up clothes and during those years she finished school.

Then the King joined forces with Hitler, who gave him control of Macedonia, and the first soldiers were sent there, and to Greece. The King was still very popular, because he was getting us back our territories. But Hitler also attacked Russia, our old ally. Sometime in 1941, I don't remember when, organizers in Sofia held a protest in the streets because they believed our men were dying for foreign causes and not for the glory of greater Bulgaria. They were right about this part, as it turned out later, but the King decided to crush their demonstrations.

After that, the communists and the anarchists grew even stronger, mostly in secret. Papa told us that someone had approached one of his younger friends about giving money to the partisan resistance, but this friend was still partly loyal to the King's government and said he could not. The King, our father told us, was a great man and would bring us through the war somehow. "Beware of secrets, children," Papa said, in the same way he did when we were little and stole sugar from the kitchen. "They will come back to hurt you."

The Allies bombed us in the spring of 1941, to punish us for joining Hitler, and people died, and we went to the cellar—but then these attacks ended as suddenly as they had begun. Later, we saw people going hungry. In the streets there were sometimes soldiers with only one eye or one hand, begging for bread. Vera and I would take a few coins and go to the bakery to buy some to give them. The soldiers ate it quickly, standing right in the street. People began to say that the King could send these soldiers to be broken in Greece or Macedonia but could not feed them when they came back. I understood from conversations at our table that Stoyan disliked both the German alliance and the Allies who were fighting us—he thought the war ridiculous, a waste, but not in the way the partisans did.

One evening he was very quiet at dinner, and he politely declined to play his violin afterward. When Vera asked him what was wrong, with her beautiful hand on his arm, he only shook his head. But after a while he said that he had realized the night before that even if the war ended well for us, he might not be able to return to Vienna right away. "My parents couldn't manage without me just now," he said, and stopped. We all knew that he didn't want to admit that his family had no money left, either—he wanted to marry Vera and didn't want my parents to think he was too poor.

"But that's good!" I burst out. "Then you won't take Vera to Vienna and you can live here with us!"

Even my mother and father laughed at this,

although they had not yet given their consent to the young couple. But we all really were thinking, *How can they marry in the old way, when they have no money, no possibility for Stoyan to continue his studies, no work for great musicians, not even any chicken for dinner this week?* At last Stoyan said that it didn't matter—he would work at anything he could find until he had enough to go to Vienna when the war ended, and to support a family; he gazed right at Vera and her cheeks became red.

I think my mother and father approved of Stoyan, partly because of his patience and courtesy, his good upbringing and astonishing talent, and partly because he never asked to see Vera alone. He kissed her goodbye on the cheek only after the first year of eating dinner with us. Now that I'm an old woman and I know something about love from my own life, I think he must have burned for her. But he waited those first few years and I know that he practiced steadily at home. No one could pay him for lessons, so he did some other work here and there, I don't know exactly what—probably anything he could find. Once he came to dinner with his right hand in a bandage and said he had hurt it at a job, and he looked so embarrassed about doing labor that we did not ask him more about it. "Fortunately, it won't keep me long from playing," he said.

In the autumn of 1943 we celebrated Vera's

twenty-first birthday. My mother managed to buy extra beans and a little pork and concocted a big dish. I used the sewing machine to make Vera a skirt out of a pair of dark curtains put away in a wardrobe. The skirt looked very nice, fitted on her small waist. A friend cut Vera's braids off and waved her hair with hot irons, which made my mother cry. My father had a cousin who was a photographer; he took a photograph of Vera in my mother's pearls. Later, when Bulgaria changed sides and fought against Hitler, he was killed in Hungary, behind his camera.

On that evening of Vera's birthday, nobody said it, but we all thought that this was the beginning of the last year she would be at home with us. If Stoyan proposed to her, in another year, she would certainly accept him. A few other young men had spoken to my parents, but none of them pleased her, and my parents respected her wishes. During the birthday dinner, my father looked serious—thinking, no doubt, about her future with a musician who now had only his talent. My mother still looked tearful because of Vera's hair. Some of my aunts and uncles were there, and they nodded gravely, like my father. Vera seemed very cheerful, as if she was pleased to be counting off the last year.

When we'd finished dinner, Stoyan said he had a gift for her and we all sat down in the parlor. I suddenly noticed that the room was beginning to look shabby because we could not replace the rug or repair the furniture anymore. Stoyan stood in front of us with his violin in his hands and bowed to Vera.

"Dear Vera," he said, "*Chestit rozhden den.* May you have many more birthdays, all of them happy." He could be very formal, like that, even as a young man. I think Vera liked it, the dignity he showed, especially in front of our parents. He made a noise to clear his throat. "I do not have a gift for you better than the one I will give you now, although it is not bought with money and it is not something to wear or keep in your pocket. I hope you will keep it in your heart. This is something I have not played for anyone except myself, since I returned from Vienna. In fact, I am certain that no one in Bulgaria has ever heard it before."

Vera sat in front of him with her hands folded on her knee. Her neck looked very white, with her hair short. I hoped that at twenty-one I would be as beautiful and grown-up as she was, more or less engaged to be married, but with the war behind us.

Then Stoyan began to play, and I think from that moment on we all forgot everything else. The music was first very rapid, like cold water running over stones, but more orderly than water on stones. It sang with the voice of a woman, or a spirit of the wind. I thought of the *samodivi*, the wild maidens of folk tales, running through forests without touching the ground—and yet it was endlessly, neatly logical. The sound made me feel dizzy one moment and fulfilled in the very next phrase. In fact, I couldn't predict the next phrase—at least not the way I could when listening to Bach—but when it arrived I felt there was no other way it could have sounded.

After a long time the cold water flowed all the way down to the foot of a mountain and slowed, and the voice of the violin turned deeper and throbbed with a quiet emotion. My father's eyes grew wet and he wiped them quickly with the back of his hand. I remembered the way he had been when he could still walk. My mother's face was pale and I saw her as she must have looked when she was young, with the beautiful features Vera had inherited. Vera herself sat leaning forward, forgetting to be lovely or graceful, listening like a man with her feet set firmly apart. The room was completely still.

Finally there was a flourish, red and gold in the air, and Stoyan held his bow aloft for a second, until the resonance died away. We applauded, but our hands sounded hollow and inadequate.

"That is not Handel?" my father asked tentatively.

"No, sir." Stoyan let his shoulders drop, stretched his long arms a little. His eyes were very bright. As always, he had played with a somber face, but now his whole frame seemed suffused with happiness. "It was written by Antonio Vivaldi."

"Ah," my father said. "The Italian priest."

"Yes," said Stoyan. "He was the same generation as Handel, I believe. He lived in Venice, you know, and wrote many works there. This is a special piece of his. Special to me." He glanced toward Vera, where she sat looking up at him.

A few days later, the bombs began to fall on Sofia—Allied bombers, coming in from Italy and other countries, striking the city so that it shook. As I said, they had bombed us those brief times in 1941, to punish the King for joining the German cause. But this new attack seemed never to end. Buildings went up in flames and whole blocks fell down. We didn't know when our house might be hit. Vera was frantic whenever she and Stoyan were apart, thinking he must be dead. When he could, he still came for dinner with us, but the meal was often interrupted by air raid alarms. Once, I swear, he kissed Vera quickly while all of us were sitting in the blackout.

Then food became very scarce and we helped my mother make bread from odd things, lentils and acorns. We were always at least a little hungry. At all hours we had to go to the basement and sit there with our knees against the knees of our relatives, shuddering. I hated feeling other people's bodies shaking—it made me tremble, myself, when I wanted to be brave. My father said that everyone knew now that the King, who was dead by then, had made a terrible mistake. We had thrown our lot in with a barbaric version of Germany—not the Germans he had known in his youth, he said, before the First World War.

The new year came, 1944, and by spring we were bombed so constantly, so hard, that it was like a nightmare no one could wake from. There was little food, and what we could buy cost the rest of our savings. My father said that Stoyan could marry Vera earlier than planned. In case we were all killed, I suppose—he didn't want to deny them that much, although he did not say so. Sometimes Stoyan played his violin for us by feel, in the dark, although never in the crowded basement. He said the planes flew too high to hear him. I'm sure that if those Allied pilots had been able to listen, they would have stopped their bombing and left us in peace forever.

So he proposed to my sister, but in private, at some moment when they felt they could safely—or not so safely—meet outside together. She told me later that first he made her promise that she understood one thing: when the war ended they would have to live all over the world for the sake of his music. They got married very quietly one afternoon, in a chapel not far from our neighborhood, with all of us standing behind them. Just as the ceremony was ending, the air raid alarm began. Fortunately, the priest had already knotted them together. My father and mother had given them some rooms in our building that had stood empty since the death of a great-aunt; but they spent their first wedded night in the basement with us, Vera holding my hand as well as Stoyan's.

Oh, dear, Irina said, wiping her eyes with her sleeve. *Well, it was a long time ago.*

Twenty-seven

In Irina's low-ceilinged upstairs hall, Alexandra stopped Bobby. "Can I talk with you before you go to sleep?"

"Sure," said Bobby. She realized that he'd probably picked up that little word from her.

They crept down the hall together, past the heavily textured paintings in their frames. When they went by the room closest to Bobby's, Alexandra saw that it was lit from inside with a glow, which seemed at first to be without any source and then became candlelight. The door stood ajar and through it she caught a glimpse of an ornate bed with two figures lying in it. One was the helper, Lenka, still wearing shirt and jeans, her eyes shut, and in her arms Irina Georgieva. The old lady's eyes were closed, too, her face bereft of color, her hair loose and draped around her like Spanish moss. Never had Alexandra seen one body hold another so tenderly, the younger woman's lips against the older one's sere scalp, her arms cradling the wrinkled shoulders and neck above a pink nightgown.

Alexandra and Bobby sidled past and went into Bobby's room, where he shut the door with care behind them. There were papers everywhere, some covered with a tiny handwriting, some half-written-over, some a scatter of empty leaves. They lay on the table, next to a candle in a tarnished holder, or fluttered off the chair onto the floor; they drifted along the wool rug and sat in piles under the window. They must have come out of his satchel, Alexandra thought. She couldn't see the writing very well, and besides it would be in Bulgarian.

"I'm sorry for the mess," he said, and began moving around to collect it all.

"What are you writing?" she asked.

"Nothing important. Just notes."

Again, a blank wall, which made it seem impossible to ask a second time. For a disagreeable moment, Alexandra entertained the idea that he was making notes about her, and then had the wisdom to see how narcissistic this was.

She turned away. "I should go to bed. We're getting up early."

"Do you want me to wake you?" he said, as if in compensation.

"Okay," she told him, and lingered for a moment.

"What did you want to talk to me about?"

"Oh." She had nearly forgotten. "I just thought I should ask if I can finally pay you. I know Irina is going to cover the trip to the mountains, but you've already driven me a long way. Please."

He looked at the floor. "I don't really want you to pay me, at this point," he said, his voice dropping. "It would not feel right to me. In fact, if you mention it again, I might have to get angry."

He smiled, but she felt he meant it. She vowed to herself that she would repay him, and more, in the end.

"Besides, I may be causing you more trouble than you know." He stood by the dark window, combing his hair out of his eyes with one hand, a quick, apologetic gesture.

"What do you mean?" she asked, but he had looked away.

She tried again. "What are we going to do about the windshield?"

"Yes—well, I will show you tomorrow."

In her wall bed, the sheets smelled like that strange herb. She left the doors to the cupboard open, in case the house was haunted rather than just magical. With its own thrill of dismay, her body remembered the shivering mattress at Aunt Pavlina's, the serpent uncoiling beneath her.

The next morning Irina Georgieva was ready before everyone else. Coming down to the front hall, Alexandra saw a tightly packed plastic bag and a basket with a cloth over it. When she and Bobby went out to the terrace, the light still looked pale; the old lady was already eating bread, cheese, and salami, and Lenka was serving three more plates. For the first time, Irina's helper sat down to eat with them. She had braided her dark hair thickly back from her temples and Alexandra could see now that it was threaded with gray.

"It is always important to have a good breakfast before a trip," Irina told them, as if she traveled every week. Her chalky face was flushed, her eyes bright. Today she wore her complicated brooch pinned to a pink blouse. She had balanced a walking stick against her chair, a long wooden staff with a knobby head, as if they were going to be hiking instead of getting into Bobby's cab. Stoycho sat beside her, waiting for pieces of salami to fall from her awkward hands.

"Bird," Bobby said, putting jam on his bread and feta, "do you know what you're going to see today? The Rhodope Mountains—*Rodopa*—the most beautiful mountains in the world."

"I'm sorry, but *my* mountains are the most beautiful in the world," Alexandra said, smiling at him.

"Yes, I only wanted for you to have a chance to say that. This way you will pay better attention to *Rodopite*."

"Children," Irina said, "Lenka and I are almost ready. Asparuh, I will show you my map. We are going first to Shiroka Luka and then south, very high into the mountains."

Lenka poured more tea for them and began to clear the dishes. She spoke to Stoycho in a whisper, then went to his bowl and scraped bits of bread and cheese into it. Stoycho followed gratefully, but looked back several times; Alexandra thought he seemed anxious.

Bobby was wiping his hands, glancing at his cell phone. "I will bring the car up in a few minutes, to get you, but first Alexandra and I have an errand."

They did? Probably he'd left the taxi at a repair shop, with that broken windshield. She followed him obediently through the museum gate to the street. Several blocks away from Irina's, he turned down a block she was sure they hadn't been on before. This one, too, was quiet, lined with old walls and newly green trees. At the far end, a young man was leaning against a shabby dark-green car with his arms folded. When Alexandra and Bobby drew near, he turned and faced them.

Alexandra took a step backward, remembering the damage to the taxi. But the man was smiling. He was black-haired and fit, taller than Bobby. He had large dark eyes—long-lashed, radiant. He wore a black polo shirt over trim muscles, black jeans, polished black shoes. Alexandra liked his alert look and the gentleness of his tanned face. He shook Bobby's hand, half-embracing him, slapping him on the back.

"My friend Kiril," Bobby explained. "He lives in Sofia, and we went to university together."

Kiril shook Alexandra's hand with sedulous politeness and stooped to admire Stoycho, who sat on the sidewalk, listening.

"We must go right now," Bobby said. Kiril slapped and hugged him once more; as she watched, each slipped the other a set of keys. Kiril shook hands with Alexandra again and sauntered away down the exquisite street. She realized only then that she had not heard him say a single word.

Bobby opened the car and gave Alexandra a nod she understood meant she should be quick, and she got into the front seat. Stoycho jumped in after her. Bobby started the engine up at once with Kiril's keys. The inside smelled of cigarettes but was very clean, and there was a figurine attached to the dashboard, a Mickey Mouse whose head wobbled like a gyroscope when Bobby pulled into the street. Stoycho sat up to look at it.

"Where's your taxi?" Alexandra tried to get comfortable in her new seat.

"Kiril will have it repaired and drive it back to Sofia—he can park it inside a garage near my mother's apartment," said Bobby. "I checked it this morning. There was no new damage." He glanced around as he drove.

"That's very nice of him."

"Well, he's a friend," Bobby said.

Alexandra wondered how many of her own friends at home she could have asked to bring her their car in another city, at a moment's notice, just in case someone was shadowing her. "But do you really believe we're being followed?"

"I think it is probable," he admitted. He turned his blue stare on her. "I just don't know why. Or by whom. Not yet. Let's tell Irina that the taxi was still having some problems."

"Well, it was," Alexandra pointed out. "What are we going to do?"

"Keep our eyes open," said Bobby. "Look in the—that—the glove box. Is there a map of Bulgaria?"

She clicked it open and saw the gun. "Bobby?" she said.

He glanced over. "Good. Cover it with the map."

She had never been this close to one before, and the sight of it terrified her. "Is this your friend's?"

"Now it's mine," he said. "Put the map over it, and that plastic bag. Make it look a little messy."

She did, trying not to touch the thing with even her fingertips. She was with a man she hardly knew, now he had a gun, and he wanted her to know it was there. She looked over at him;

he was shifting gears up the hill, and his face was calm.

As the car drove away from Irina's house, loaded with all of them, Alexandra turned one more time to see the high courtyard wall, the massive trees. She was sitting in front with Stoycho heavily across her lap and the bag containing the urn at her feet; the two older women sat in the back, their basket and Irina's cane between them. Alexandra looked at Bobby in his familiar place—he was carefully keeping to a low gear over the cobble-stones. The car lurched slowly down the hill past Plovdiv's mansions; morning sun had begun already to scatter patches of light on the blue and ochre walls, the wooden gates. Five days ago, she reminded herself, she had never seen any of this before, or these people. Or this dog. She embraced his dusty neck and he touched her cheek with his nose.

Half an hour of weirdly uncultivated farmland, deserted farm sheds, and open skies brought them south. As they traveled past a meadow, Bobby suddenly pulled off the road. "Look at that," he said. "I must take a picture." He unbuckled his seat belt. "Excuse me," he added to the two women in the back seat.

Alexandra peered through the window and then stepped out of the car, following him. In the field beside them stood a doorway, all by itself—no house, no door—just the frame and a few concrete blocks, as if someone had contemplated living there and wanted first to practice stepping into the unbuilt dwelling. Insects ruminated in the grasses around them; a couple of birds—swallows?—darted through the field and rose high above the empty doorframe.

Bobby was photographing it with his phone. "I've never seen something like this," he told her.

"Why is it standing alone here?" She had never seen such a thing, either.

"I don't know," he said. "But I was just thinking that literature is like that, like a door in a field." His face was absorbed; he typed a note into his phone. She watched him with amazement. From the first, he had reminded her of someone, and now she realized that that someone might be herself.

Soon the edge of the mountains loomed in a green-black mass just ahead of them. The road seemed to go straight into this wall, hemmed in on each side with cliffs and precariously rooted trees—an opening blasted through by modernity, thought Alexandra, although perhaps much earlier trails had once wound upward into the mountains. The road cowered below the high forests and crossed noisy mountain streams. She had just glanced back to see if Irina Georgieva was enjoying the scenery when Bobby braked hard in the middle of a bridge. Stoycho sat up, digging his nails into her knee.

"Oh, *my God,*" said Alexandra. On their right side, nearly a third of the bridge's width had crumbled into the river, railing and all, so that the pavement hung by threads of metal. She could see the rocks and white water forty feet below. Whole dead trees were suspended on the steep banks, caught in the forest as if in a tangle of hair.

"Damn," Bobby said. "This is probably from the earthquake. Or maybe floods—or both." He set the parking brake. She watched with trepidation as he got out and walked ahead a few feet, craning into the abyss.

Irina tapped Alexandra's shoulder. "What is the problem?"

"Just a bridge," Alexandra said, touching her hand. Perhaps it was a good thing that the old woman apparently couldn't see the damage from where she sat. "I think it's nothing to worry about. Bobby is checking the route."

Irina Georgieva folded her hands in her lap and nodded to her helper. "I'm sure Asparuh knows what to do," she said. Lenka stroked the old lady's cheek and reached into the basket, from which she took a small bottle of pills; she handed one to Irina, then gave her a sip of water.

Bobby returned to the car shaking his head. "I think we should go forward," he told Alexandra in a low voice. "Otherwise, we must drive about two hours back to a different road. This probably happened a few days ago—maybe even a few weeks—that might be the reason they have not fixed it yet. Of course, if it was the earthquake, it is very recent. But they could have put a sign here, to tell people." He looked ready for one of his outbursts of swearing, then paused, as if considering the presence of the ladies in the back seat.

"All right," Alexandra said, although she was terrified. "But should we get out and walk, maybe?"

"That would be more dangerous, especially—" He meant Irina, of course, with her cane and unbalanced gait. "In any case, the pavement is not hurt on the left side."

He started the engine and began to inch forward. Alexandra squeezed Stoycho's neck. If she fell off this Bulgarian bridge in a little green car, her parents would have nobody; all her memories of Jack would disappear with her, too.

Bobby brought them slowly to the middle of the bridge, steering into the left lane, and Alexandra was careful not to look out her window into the wild current just below. Because she was staring straight ahead, she saw the oncoming car even before Bobby did, and her cry stopped him short. The opposite approach was a blind curve. A moment hung between the two vehicles before the other car stopped hard, too, swerving away from the broken edge, so that they sat facing each other precariously near the gap.

"Agh, no." Bobby was gripping the wheel. Stoycho sat up straighter in Alexandra's lap, and she held him tightly to calm him. Bobby shook his head. *"Politsai."*

The policeman had stepped out of his car already. He was a tall man with a pleasant and even wistful face, very different from the policemen Alexandra had met at the Sofia station. He made his way to their car and peered in, examining them. *Dog,* thought Alexandra. *American tourist, old lady, pretty helper, basket. A full house.*

The policeman and Bobby blandly exchanged words, as if they were meeting over a grocery counter instead of at the ragged edge of a precipice. Bobby gestured toward the cataract below and the policeman shook his head. Then the policeman pointed at the glove box. Alexandra froze, but when Bobby leaned over to open it and take out some papers, there was no sign of the gun. Had he somehow put it under a seat? Or in the trunk? When had he managed to do that? The policeman carried Bobby's ID and papers back to his own car and sat inside with them for what seemed an interminable time, while Stoycho drove nervous toenails into Alexandra's lap, trying to see. What if the policeman identified them as the people who'd had the taxi? Surely, she thought, this system could not be that well organized, even with computer records. And whoever had painted the taxi, especially if it had been the police them-selves, wouldn't have recorded that act. Besides, it probably hadn't been the police. Bobby's way of thinking—his paranoid way—must be rubbing off on her.

"He could at least back up his car, off the bridge," Bobby murmured, and she understood that if any other vehicle came around the curve behind the police car, they were all in trouble.

Which, strangely, was what happened next. The new car was upon them, going too fast, before anyone could draw breath—a big pristine black BMW with tinted windows. The driver braked so hard that his tires squealed and Alexandra heard Irina give a choking gasp behind her. Bobby's hands flew to his wheel, although there was nothing he could do. The BMW hit the back of the police car with a scraping thud, making it jump like an animal, so that Alexandra got a glimpse of the pleasant policeman hopping forward inside it, his face astonished, his mouth open. The bridge shuddered. Stoycho yelped.

But the police car had been well parked, and its quivering leap didn't reach Bobby's front bumper. Bobby exhaled heavily and whacked the steering wheel. The policeman leapt out, then seemed to remember the yawning gap in the other lane and steadied himself. The driver of the

BMW had climbed out as well and was already raising both hands in protest. He wore a dark jacket and cap and looked huge enough to repair the bridge with his two hands, like Paul Bunyan. He bent to examine the damage to his front bumper and to the back of the police car, and Alexandra thought that he probably did want a cat to eat the organs of the policeman's mother.

"Aw, no." Bobby drummed his dashboard with impatient fingers. "And it's a car of the government. Now we will never get anywhere." The huge man was still talking with the policeman. "I hope I get my papers back someday," Bobby said gloomily.

"Should we go out and help?" Irina's voice came from the back seat.

"Oh, no, Madame Georgieva." Bobby turned to her, and Lenka patted her knee. "They will decide things between them, and then perhaps we can travel onward."

As they watched, the huge man in the cap looked around and gestured at the rushing water and at the policeman's car.

"What is he doing?" Alexandra asked.

"I think that he is wishing he could give the policeman a little—bribe, you might call it," Bobby explained. "But he can't, because we are sitting right here to watch."

"Oh," said Alexandra. She had never seen

anyone being offered a bribe and she thought it would be interesting.

"So instead they will argue," Bobby said. "Which takes a longer time."

The two men did argue, the big driver pushing his cap back and then pulling it forward, the policeman carefully pointing out the damage that had been inflicted on his own vehicle. Bobby put his elbows on the steering wheel. Irina patted his shoulder. "Don't worry, my boy. They will finish soon. And I have some biscuits here if anyone is hungry."

Suddenly, the back door of the BMW opened and another man stepped out. They all watched in surprise; Stoycho gave a startled growl. This man was not as tall as his driver, and he looked much older, but for some reason far more imposing. He was dressed in a dark-blue suit—expensively cut, was Alexandra's first thought—that made an odd contrast with the mountain scene around them. She wondered what he would think if yet another car came around the curve behind him and hit the BMW in turn. He didn't look as if he would take it well, and yet there was something infinitely calm, and also infinitely familiar, in his appear-ance. His posture was upright, although he moved rather stiffly inside the suit. He had a reddish-brown beard and a heavy mane of hair, receding from his forehead but thick and curling at the ends, as if you could lose a pencil in it. In the light filtering over the cliffs, that hair looked both dark and bright, metallic, not quite real. The man's face was much older than his hair, broad and lined and somehow desiccated, heavily scarred over the cheeks. Alexandra would have thought him striking if his expression had been lively or his body more animated. But he was too collected, too quiet.

Beside her, Bobby leaned forward, peering through the windshield. "What?" he said. "I'm sure that is Kurilkov."

"Who?" said Alexandra. She was calming Stoycho, who had begun to growl softly again.

"Mikhail Kurilkov. The Minister of Roads, the one they call the Bear, who wants to be prime minister—I told you about him, from the television. I saw him in person once before, giving a speech where we had a demonstration."

"Oh—from the TV at Aunt Pavlina's," said Alexandra. "And the trout restaurant. I thought he looked familiar. But what is he doing here, in the middle of nowhere?" Then she remembered the slogan on Bobby's taxi windshield: *Without corruption.*

"Maybe he really *likes* roads," muttered Bobby, but he didn't take his eyes off the man. "I hope he does not come over here. I have never wanted to meet him."

Irina was leaning forward again. "Who is it?" she asked.

"We think it is Kurilkov, the Minister of Roads."

"Out here?" Irina said. "Ah." She fell silent, but Alexandra thought she looked strange— thoughtful, almost wary. Perhaps, like Bobby, Irina disliked the man, or politicians in general.

Now the three men were in conference together, and Alexandra saw the Minister of Roads reach out to shake the policeman's hand. The policeman seemed as startled as Bobby had been; he shook Kurilkov's hand, and bowed slightly. The huge driver had backed away, and Kurilkov and the policeman talked alone. Then the Minister signaled to his driver, who made his way toward Bobby's car. Alexandra saw the driver stepping gingerly along the damaged bridge, as if he feared his own bulk might be the straw that broke its back.

"Go away," Bobby muttered, but he rolled down his window again. The hackles on Stoycho's neck rose under her hand. Stoycho was showing yellow teeth now, snaggled over his lower lip; she wondered what would happen to her dog if he bit a minister's bodyguard.

But when the driver got close, he only said something to Bobby in a courteous tone, glancing around as if puzzled by the abundance of passengers. Bobby nodded, waved to him, and reversed carefully off the bridge and onto the narrow shoulder against the cliff. Irina and Lenka were placid, in the back seat, as if it was a matter of course to them, by this time, to get stuck above white water in the mountains.

A few minutes later the policeman came over to return Bobby's papers, without comment, then started the police car and drove past them. He gave a sedate wave; he seemed to be counseling Bobby to forget all about it. The man called the Bear waited for his driver to hold open the door of the BMW. Alexandra saw his strange hair disappear first, his stiff polished boot last. As the luxurious car passed them, driver and passenger were completely hidden by tinted windows. She wondered if he'd turned to look, if she had met his narrow ursine eyes without knowing it, through Bobby's windshield. Stoycho's head turned, too, and his gaze seemed to follow the BMW until it was out of sight. Alexandra suddenly felt that she should not have stared so directly into that dark glass.

Twenty-eight

The first Rhodope villages Alexandra ever saw clung to the sides of ravines above a mountain river, and the first thing that struck her about them was the roofs. They were not fluted red ceramic, like the roofs in the towns they'd already driven through; instead they were made of gray slate, laid in complicated scalloped layers. She remarked to Bobby that the rough stone houses looked as if they'd sprung up there naturally, or been piled up by giants. Bobby said that in a sense they *had* grown out of the mountains, since they had been created by people with only the natural world from which to build them. "The original environmentalists," he said.

The road was very steep now and it took them up hillsides of pastureland and then to a plateau, a large village with a flat streambed down the middle and a statue of a man holding a tattered bronze flag. There was a yellow building on the other side of the stream, old trees leaning over it, a tumble of stone houses on the higher slopes. When she rolled down her window, Alexandra could hear running water and smell the sharp, clean cold of mountain air just under the sunlight. She saw several signs for hotels, with three stars and arrows pointing uphill. Then she noticed a couple of men attaching a poster to the side of a store. One man was on a ladder, holding the top of the poster against the wall.

"Look," she said to Bobby. He slowed and peered across her: it was a huge photograph of a man with hair to his shoulders, smiling out at them.

"Kurilkov," Bobby muttered. "Again. *Bez koruptsiya*! It doesn't say anything specific about his purity campaign, but that will come next." He shifted gears. "They are choosing the poorer areas to put these in."

They climbed higher, past more of the ancient houses and into forested mountainsides. Alexandra saw a sign that promised Gorno in four kilometers.

"But there was an earlier sign that said three," she told Bobby. "How can it be getting farther away?"

Bobby shrugged. "Ask the Minister of Roads." He had the map on his knee as he drove; Irina's hand sometimes reached for his shoulder, or pointed the way. The roads were even narrower now, pressed between towering slopes; the villages they passed were very small, the feet of the houses almost on the pavement. Some looked empty, a cross of iron over the windows, glass panes broken in. They passed an old man sitting outside a house with curtains at the open windows, chickens in a small yard, and a tiny church with a surreally bent-over, folded-up woman locking the door. Everyone they saw was old. Alexandra had only imagined such places, but here were people living in them, finishing out their days.

"Do they have television?" she asked Bobby.

"Television?" He seemed to be driving somewhere else, in his head, a million miles away.

"Here, in these villages," she said.

"Oh, certainly," he said. "At least most people. A few might be too poor, but almost everyone has television."

She wished again that they could stop at each village, knock on doors and go in to see. Another woman, her head covered with a flowered scarf, was scraping something out of a pan into her garden. She looked up, so close to the road that Alexandra could see her gold earrings, the stains on her apron; she could have been fifty years old or eighty. Her face was full of a guarded curiosity, no smile. Alexandra hoped the woman had a dog like Stoycho, to protect her in her yard and give her someone to take care of. But no dog was visible and a moment later the woman was behind them and the road was winding through heavy woodland, higher and higher, with steep views opening out to their left.

"I think this is it," Bobby said suddenly, and Irina waved him into a turn. There was no village in sight, only a worn wooden sign, which Bobby read aloud: GORNO, 2KM.

"Is that what your village is called?" Alexandra asked Irina, turning around.

The old lady was peering forward, as if for landmarks. "It has several names—one from the deep past, perhaps Turkish. Now it is just called Gorno, which means 'high.' Or maybe, in English, 'upper.'"

"Upper *what?*" Bobby asked. The road was dirt now, but steeper than ever, and he had to steer around large holes and ruts, going slowly. Stoycho sat up on Alexandra's lap and gazed out the window, then at Alexandra.

"Only Gorno," Irina said. "You can invent the other part if you would like."

Bobby smiled at Alexandra and she thought about squeezing his hand.

A few minutes later they drove in among the first houses, which were all stone, growing out of the earth. The road had become so slippery and crusted with big rocks that Bobby slowed the car to walking pace. They passed a tiny chapel with a spray of briars over one side, an empty store with peeling yellow letters on the window. A middle-aged woman dressed in black was walking past it; she turned to stare at them, apparently astonished to see anyone new. The road leveled out into what could have been a main square except that it was made of packed mud and was only a little wider than the road itself. The next stretch, between the houses, looked very steep; Bobby shook his head.

"I must stop here," he said. "I don't think that I can drive farther."

"Yes, this is a good place," Irina said. She gripped the back of his seat and Alexandra saw that her face was white with fatigue. "Here we are. Our house is in the second street, a very easy walk."

But when they got her out, she had to lean against the side of the car to steady her legs.

"Shall I carry you there?" Bobby asked her. She

said something to him in Bulgarian and smiled for a moment. He chuckled, but she only took his arm.

Alexandra stood gripping Stoycho's rope and smelling the wind with him—wood smoke nearby, and a sharp freshness beyond. It had been a long time since she'd felt this slight breathlessness, the pressure in her ears. The air was extraordinary, like sips of a thin white wine. Alexandra drew it in: hikes with her parents and Jack, in the old days, before the bad one. From here, in the middle of the road, in the middle of the village, the world spread beneath them. Some of the roofs on the lower streets, a few yards away, were level with her feet. A rusted turquoise truck sat wedged among the trees in one yard, its tires collapsing into the earth and smaller trees growing up out of the dirt in its bed. She wondered why anyone would build on this steepness, in the path of winter weather, even with sheltering higher peaks around it. At home, in the Blue Ridge, the old farms huddled in their coves and hollows; these Rhodope houses strode defiantly up to an alpine meadow. Far below, she saw the villages through which they'd come, and still farther away a long plain and even a city the size of her thumbnail, tiny white and red tombstones. Beyond that, mountains again.

She thought, *A whole country—I am seeing a country whole.* Now the meadows and roads smelled like grass, a clean warm scent blown toward her on rising wind; just around her there was the smell of mud baking in afternoon sun, and of animal dung. Looking up, she saw that the sky was enormous, laced at the edges with light clouds. A single green cone symmetrical as an extinct volcano sat in front of the darker ridges. Looking down, Alexandra found she was standing next to a trough full of muddy water, a long stone hollowed out and ancient as the village itself.

"Come," said Irina, leaning on Bobby's arm, and they all turned and picked their way into a street where the houses sat well back in gardens. One house had a pen of hay in the front yard, another some cages of giant fierce-looking rabbits. At the third, which was joined to a small stone barn, Irina made Bobby stop. She tried the door, found it locked, and then rapped with her carved stick instead of her hand. They waited. While they were waiting, Alexandra tied Stoycho carefully to a tree in the front yard, in case he wasn't supposed to come into the house with them. Any minute, she thought, they might see Vera or Neven.

When there was still no answer, Bobby knocked gently at one window, where the curtains were drawn. "Perhaps they are asleep?" he said.

They waited again. Alexandra could hear the wind coming softly up the valley, riffling through the hay next door, turning the leaves of old poplars in the yards. Everything looked so somnolent, so green, that she felt she might fall asleep herself, despite her anxiety. Lenka had gone to the other window and was peering in, standing on her toes. A curtain was drawn there, too.

"I don't think that they are here," Irina said flatly.

"Maybe they went out," Bobby proposed.

"No—my sister would be resting, at this time of day. She would leave the door open and sit in the kitchen, or lie down in her bedroom."

Bobby turned to look up the street. "Shall I ask your neighbor?"

"Yes, dear. On that side. He keeps the keys for us." Irina let him go and Lenka came at once to prop her up. Alexandra noted again how tall Irina was and how straight she stood even when she was clearly exhausted. Her hair had come unbound around her face in a white cloud, and her brooch glowed in the shade of the house. Alexandra thought they should get her inside to rest as soon as possible.

Next door, Bobby was conversing on the front step with a man in a plaid shirt and worn pants. When the man saw Irina he hurried over and shook hands with them all, speaking rapidly. Irina's rectangular face grew even longer: apparently, the house had been locked for almost a week. Yes, Vera and Milen Radev had been living here for many months, with occasional visits from Neven—but then they had left with him, maybe six days before, to do something in Sofia. No, they hadn't given him any details of their plans. He and his wife had been away themselves the past few days, and had just returned.

At last the man went to fetch a large iron key, then left them to return to his work while they opened Vera's house. Bobby squeezed the latch and the door swung inward, revealing a step down onto a flagstone floor; the house breathed out at them, cold and dank.

"Come, children," Irina said wearily, and they went ahead, to help her.

Twenty-nine

In that first moment, Alexandra could see nothing of the inside of the house, partly because she was still turned toward Irina and the sunlit doorway, and partly because Irina suddenly lost her footing. Alexandra's heart constricted; for a weird second she was back in Sofia, watching Vera Lazarova stumble forward next to the taxi. She caught the old lady's upper arm and felt a bone so thin she was afraid it might snap. But the strength of her hand kept Irina upright. The old woman gripped Alexandra's shoulder and then stood there a moment, panting. Lenka had darted forward and was holding Irina's other arm.

"Oh, my dear." Irina looked around at Alexandra in wonder; her watery eyes reflected the bright day in the doorway. "Thank you."

"You're welcome," Alexandra said humbly. "I just didn't want you to—" She thought of the graceful old woman writhing on the floor with a shattered hip, and found she couldn't finish her sentence.

They led Irina to a chair beside the door and helped her sit down. The room was dark and surprisingly cold, as if it bore no relation to the spring afternoon outside. In the yard behind them, Stoycho had begun to whine, and then to bark.

"Where can my sister be? I cannot understand this." Irina sounded as if she might cry with frustration, or worry, or sheer fatigue. "She should have returned days before now, or called me."

"Let's bring some light in," Bobby said stoutly. He drew aside the curtains at one window and Alexandra went to open the others. Now she could see enough to make out a lamp in the corner; she turned it on. They stood staring, and Irina sat without moving, Lenka's hand on her shoulder.

The room was wrecked. The other chairs, upholstered in faded blue fabric, had been turned upside down, splintered. On the far side of the floor lay books, rocks, and broken shells, as if someone had swept a shelf clean with a powerful arm. One of the little tables had been smashed against the flagstones. It was amazing, thought

275

Alexandra numbly, that the lamp on the other had survived. A small oil painting—Irina's work?—lay in the middle of the mess, its landscape rent across, perhaps by a knife, its frame asunder. There was a fireplace of smooth river stones; broken glass sparkled on the hearth. Alexandra was thankful that Stoycho was still outside, where she had tied him up. Through an open door on the other side of the room, she could see what looked like a kitchen. The wall beside the doorway was white, and it bore sprawling hieroglyphs of reddish-brown—a word. They all stared at it.

"Bobby!" Alexandra said. His hand closed over hers for a moment.

"What is that?" Irina asked, her voice a quaver. Even with her sharp eye for details, she apparently couldn't see the word well enough in this half light to read it.

Bobby's voice was controlled. "It says *Znaem.* 'We know.' "

"Know what?" Alexandra said.

"Who would do this?" There was rage in Irina's tone, and a sob.

Bobby suddenly left the room and hurried into the kitchen, where they saw him turn on an electric light. They heard him running up wooden stairs and then above them on the upper floor. He was back just as quickly, going out to the yard again.

When he returned, he stood breathing hard,

looking at the word on the wall. "There is no one in the house or outside," he said.

"Our *house,*" Irina said softly. "Is it—all like this?"

"No," Bobby said. "They smashed up only this room."

Irina gasped, a long intake, rattling. "And my sister! Could they have hurt Vera?"

Bobby turned to reassure her. "No, I don't think so. There is no sign of a struggle with people, and everything else looks as if your sister left it normally, for her trip. I think that this happened after they departed. Please, everybody—" He held up one hand. "Please, don't touch anything. I've got only my torch, but—"

He took a small flashlight from inside his denim jacket, and Alexandra was reminded of the tool he had produced to let them out of Velin Monastery. *Oh, God,* she thought. They had been locked in there, from the outside. Then the writing on the taxi and the holes in the windshield.

Bobby was examining the paint, the upended furniture, the broken glass underfoot. Alexandra saw him shove something farther into a corner with his foot, behind the divan. He took out his phone and photographed the smeared word and the damaged room. Irina gave a sudden groan. Lenka stretched an arm around her shoulders.

"Bobby," Alexandra said.

"Not now," he told her in a low voice, and she

knew he meant they should not talk about whatever was in the corner, or the words on the taxi, or anything else, until they had taken care of Irina. But Irina herself spoke up, as if she had regained her voice.

"Here, my dear—" She beckoned Alexandra close. "Could you and Lenka help me to lie down in the little bedroom? Behind the stairs. Bobby, it is so cold in here. Would you build a fire in the stove? There is no other kind of heat here, you know. The wood is inside the barn. As you say, we can clean up later."

"Do you want me to call the police?" Bobby asked her.

"No," said Irina. "No, I do not think so. The police are a long way from here, down in the big town, and they will only question all the neighbors and then everyone will talk. I have known our neighbors for—generations, and I am certain that none of them would do this to us."

Alexandra wanted to point out that if outsiders had done this damage, perhaps the police would be the ones to find them. Then she thought of the word on the wall—maybe neither Irina nor Bobby wanted the police looking at that word?

Alexandra and Lenka got the old lady into a chamber under the stairwell and took a dusty sheet off the bed. They helped Irina lie down and covered her with blankets from the wardrobe; the blankets were made of tufted wool, warm and dry to touch even in the chilled air. Lenka sat down beside the bed to take the old woman's hand. Irina thanked them and closed her eyes as if content, but Alexandra thought she looked half dead.

Then Alexandra went back to Bobby. He was standing in the rubble of the sitting room.

"Bobby," she ventured. "What is it?" She pointed to the corner behind the divan.

"I don't know if you want to see," Bobby said irritably. "But go ahead."

She hesitated. "The word on the wall—that's blood?"

"Yes." He stood with his hands in his pockets and his head bowed.

She stared at him. "Not—"

He shook his head. "Not human. But it is awful."

She went slowly to the corner and looked behind the divan.

"Oh, God," she said. There was a gory, disheveled object on the floor and the first thing she recognized about it was teeth, three sharp yellowish ones snaggled over a lower lip. A head. Then a wild yellow eye, half-closed in the middle of ragged fur. Beside it lay a paintbrush, also smeared with blood. She thought for a split second that she might vomit.

"It's—isn't it a wolf?" she said.

"I think so." Bobby scanned the word on the

wall, his hands still in his pockets. "Another strange thing is that there are very few wolves in the mountains anymore."

Alexandra tried not to look at the head again. "Isn't that, I mean, it must be illegal, to kill a wolf?"

"Illegal?" Bobby snorted.

Alexandra wished she hadn't seen it. There was so much brown blood on it, and in the corner; she could smell it now. And there was that other horror, the animal's final struggle.

Bobby knelt carefully beside the divan and checked the floor with a finger; Alexandra could tell he had already done this several times. "Dry," he said. "But blood dries quickly."

She didn't want to know how he knew this. "We can't let Irina see. And I don't think Lenka noticed."

"No." Bobby pulled a paper napkin from his pocket and wiped his hand. "I will take a picture, and then I will bury it in the yard. But first we must find a box or a bag to put it in, so that we can dig it up if we need it for some reason."

"You mean you will call the police?"

He looked at her—but thoughtfully, without annoyance, and shook his head.

The kitchen turned out to be a cave of stone, dim and cold until they lit the stove. It was very neat, even clean—a few pots hung on nails along a whitewashed board; braided onions and garlic dangled from the rafters above them. At one end was a fireplace with a wide bench of hearth. Alexandra had always been sensitive to the smell of a new place, and here she had to restrain herself from sniffing audibly. The kitchen had a complicated aroma—cold, earthy, as if the house had been built into the mountain. She imagined the winter wind, deep snows, driving rain. The house had survived it all, year after year, like a well-sheltered grave. The bright day outside seemed to have vanished until Bobby pried open the single kitchen window and let it in. Lenka filled a kettle with water from the tap and added a handful of herbs from her bag. There was a telephone in one corner, although not the old-fashioned kind Alexandra had imagined for Irina's house in Plovdiv. Ants ran up and down the sugar pot and stitched a border along the oilcloth on a shelf. When the tea was ready, Lenka took a cup out to Irina.

Bobby and Alexandra sat at the battered table, drinking hot water with the herbs strained out of it.

"What should we do now?" she asked him. "What if whoever is writing these messages comes back here? Maybe we should leave right away?"

He had rolled up his sleeves and washed his face in the cold tap, smoothed his hair so it lay damp.

"I don't think that Irina can travel again yet,"

he said. "But I also don't think we should sleep here tonight, even with the doors and windows locked. We will have to find another place. And maybe the Lazarovi will arrive tomorrow, if they have been traveling in this direction. Irina can help me to keep calling Neven's mobile."

"If they don't arrive, what should we do?"

"We must see how Irina is."

"Do you think she's sick?"

Bobby shook his head. "No—only very old and very tired. I should not have permitted her to come."

"I think she is the one who permitted us," Alexandra said. "But she doesn't look well now."

"Tomorrow or the next day we can take her home. Then we can go back to Sofia and try again to find them," said Bobby. "Or to Bovech first. Although I am worried about leaving her alone, even at her house. Especially at her house, if someone knows we were there and that we had the urn. I am glad now that we didn't leave her alone with it."

"I am, too. But why would we go back to Bovech?"

"Only an idea," he said. "Let's see what happens."

Lenka returned with the empty cup and began to wash the dishes, refusing their offers of help. While she was at the sink, Alexandra touched Bobby's arm. "Why does the word say that?

We know? If the other graffiti was about the urn, this one must be, too," she said.

"Probably." He picked at a rough spot on the table.

"Well, so someone knows that we have it—that's what they *know*."

Bobby leaned back, stretched his shoulders; she felt his eyes sharp and blue on her. "But that is exactly what the other one seemed to mean, on the taxi—that someone knew that we had it and they wanted it back. If we are correct about this."

Alexandra thought for a moment. "Maybe this one is saying they know something about the urn, not just that we have it."

"You mean, whose ashes are in it?"

This time she nodded. "Yes, or maybe they are saying they know something about the man, as well. About Stoyan Lazarov," she added in a low voice. It seemed embarrassing to her now, disrespectful, to speak of him as ashes.

Bobby sat fiddling with a saltshaker. "I'm not sure. This musician who died very old, in a small town—not so interesting, in a way. He was not rich, or a criminal, or with a public life. He never became famous. What is there to know? Maybe it is about his son, Neven—maybe he is a criminal."

"Then wouldn't the police just find him and arrest him?" Alexandra said.

For a moment, they sat staring at each other, listening to Lenka slosh the cups under the faucet.

With Lenka, they put the front room to rights, scrubbing off the blood, and Bobby buried the wolf's head in the back garden. Lenka asked no questions, but there was fear on her quiet face. Afterward, they went into the room under the stairs to speak with Irina Georgieva. Irina lay with her eyes closed; her pink-veined eyelids looked huge. Alexandra saw that the old lady had removed the brooch and set it on a bureau—she had a nervous feeling that Irina might fade away without it. She sat down on a chair beside the bed. She remembered sitting this way beside her mother, in the weeks after Jack's disappearance; sometimes her mother's reddened face had relaxed into a dull normality, and occasionally she would reach out to touch the hand Alexandra offered.

"How are you feeling, Madame Georgieva?" Bobby asked.

Irina opened her eyes. "I confess that I am tired. The trip, I suppose. And the shock of the house."

"We've cleaned up the front room," Alexandra told her.

"Thank you, dear." Irina raised a hand to smooth her hair. "I am sorry to delay you—I do not believe that I will be able to travel back until tomorrow, at the earliest."

Bobby bent over the bed. "That is what we thought, also. But I don't advise we should stay in this house tonight."

Irina stirred against her pillow. "You are right. I do not want to, in fact. Perhaps we could stay with Baba Yana, up the street. She is our oldest friend here—extremely old, and she knew all our family, my father and mother, Vera, Stoyan. I am sure she will welcome us." She made a motion as if to sit up, but feebly. "Baba Yana is blind."

Bobby was studying her. "I'm sorry."

"Well, she is not sorry. She was not born that way, you know—I heard that it happened on the day she became one hundred years old. And some people say that she sees things. Go up and ask her for me if we can sleep there tonight. She lives on the main street, three houses after the church. And ask if she knows anything about where my sister and Neven are. Maybe she sees them with her special vision." Irina closed her eyes again. "I don't believe anyone will disturb us now—especially not in the daylight."

Alexandra bent to kiss the old woman's forehead, which smelled like mint. Lenka was waiting for them in the passage outside and she went in to Irina at once.

Bobby and Alexandra locked the cottage door behind them and walked toward the main street of the village, Stoycho following them briskly without his rope. The sun had dropped already toward a horizon of mountains; Alexandra regretted not having worn her sweater. The trees along the village streets were beginning to leaf out with a thin, bright foliage that looked almost transparent. She and Bobby paused for a minute at the wide place on the road to watch a man herding a dozen goats toward the ancient-looking trough. There was a dog with him, a tall alert animal with ears that stood up in aggravated triangles as it drove the stragglers toward the herd. Stoycho ran over to meet this rival, hair rising on his brindled back, but the strange dog looked around, without rancor, then hurried on: *Sorry, I'm working just now—can we talk later?*

The shepherd turned on a tap at one end of the trough to run water into the hollow stone while his goats shoved forward. They wore small brass bells that rang with every movement; when they pushed each other they sounded like a complicated instrument playing itself. Alexandra went close enough to look into the horizontal slits of their eyes, which made her want to turn the pupils upright. She put her hand on one ridged and bony back, felt the surprisingly soft coat, the flesh warm underneath. The goat shied a little but pressed forward for water without looking at her.

Then Bobby started up the main road again, and Alexandra hurried after him. They passed an old woman peeling potatoes in her dooryard, a cascade of roses over a wire fence, stone houses and barns shored up against the slopes. Alexandra noticed suddenly that Stoycho had slipped away. Her first thought was to call for

him, but Bobby pointed to a church spire at the|
top of the road, which they'd nearly reached.
From here most of the houses lay below them,
scalloped stone roofs fanning out, stained with
lichens. She could see a cloud of dust on the road
below the village where a truck lumbered
upward. Around the village spread endless
meadows, mostly wild and golden-green with
what Alexandra guessed was future hay.

The church stood alone, flanked by spruces. It
had a stone lintel over the door, and the outside
was whitewashed, although here and there
pieces of stucco had fallen off, showing the
skeleton of rocks and clay underneath. Stoycho
had flopped down on the front step, waiting for
them. Around the church was a little yard whose
gravestones were tall and slender or short and
broad, with a bed of earth outlined in stone for
the body that must lie beneath. On the graves sat
candles, lanterns made of red glass, vases of
wilted flowers, on one a pile of rounded pebbles.
The newer headstones were glossy black or gray
granite, polished to a sheen that reflected the
surrounding colors of meadow and shrub;
Alexandra saw her own form in one, when she
bent close to it.

"Ivanka Belechkova," she read. There was a
photo of a face etched with eerie precision onto
the granite, an unsmiling curly-haired woman
trapped in the stone. Alexandra thought she

looked ready to move or speak—dark magic. But it was a pleasant place, quiet apart from the wind. It offered the best view yet of the village, and the best view of the valley. It looked out toward mountains in three directions, the forested shoulders of the highest peaks. *Jack would have liked to rest in a place like this,* she thought, where he could see mountains and be up high, but still among people.

Alexandra reached for Bobby's sleeve. "Why didn't they bury him here?"

"Stoyan Lazarov?" He was reading names on the oldest-looking stones.

"Yes. He must have liked it up here, visiting with his wife's family. It's so peaceful."

"I suppose," Bobby said. "But we don't know if that was his wish."

"I guess he wanted the monastery, and it's not for us to decide, anyway," she said.

Bobby shook his head. "Maybe not even for Irina Georgieva to decide."

Alexandra looked out toward the peaks, where the light still hung in hazy layers. "Do you ever think—sometimes I have this feeling that we're walking along the edge of a precipice. I mean everyone, all the time."

"A precipice? Like a cliff?" Bobby thought about this. "Yes, of course we are."

"You feel that, too?" She watched the light in his fair hair, the narrowing blue of his eyes.

"Yes," he said, and then was silent for a moment. "I also believe that my country is doing that. If we fall, we will fall a long way." He looked straight| at her, but she couldn't see what he was seeing.

"What do you mean?" She touched his arm.

He turned to the panorama spread below them—the village roofs, the fields. "If you grow up here, you know this is the most beautiful country in the world, even when you sometimes hate things about it. But we have these memories of how we were shut away from the world and forced against each other. It happened quickly, once it started, and not very long ago—my grandparents were already alive then. If we accept the wrong government, it could happen again."

"That's true in any country, the part about the wrong government," Alexandra objected, although she knew she was out of her depth.

Bobby suddenly grasped her shoulder; she thought for a moment he was going to shake her. Then he reached up and tucked her hair behind her ear, his fingers gentle. "I know," he said. "But when you accept an intruder for too long, you sometimes invite him back later as a guest."

He turned and looked again across the village, down to the fields. Alexandra tried to follow his gaze. "My country has come a long way in a short time, in spite of everything. I think we have something special to give the world—culture, and lessons from history. And beauty. It would be tragic for us to go backward. We have already suffered too much."

Sunset had begun to pierce the village as they passed out of the churchyard and down the road on the other side; it carved out alleys between the houses and made fissures in the trees. Alexandra knew this rapid disappearance of the sun, the way it plunged out of sight behind peaks instead of setting gradually. She could smell wood smoke again, and some kind of meat cooking. She thought of the urn, and then of her own luggage, abandoned in the hostel room in Sofia, and the fact that she didn't have clean clothes to change into; it hardly seemed to matter anymore. The scar on the underside of her arm was itching. Stoycho stayed close to their heels, without his rope. The evening sank and cooled, moment to moment.

"This is like the mountains at home," she told Bobby. "The sun sets so quickly. You want to grab it before it disappears."

"Are you homesick, Bird?"

Not for a place, she thought. "No. But this does remind me of being in the Blue Ridge."

They were climbing the narrowed part of the street now—barren yards, one house partly collapsed, its slate roof fallen in and the chimney topped with birds' nests. Then a yard with a little boy and a girl shaking rugs under a tree, laughing, snapping the fringe in each other's faces. The first children they had seen here.

"A blue ridge?" Bobby asked.

"Yes, the Blue Ridge Mountains," Alexandra said. "I told you—I live in the part of them that is in North Carolina. They're like this, but more—*blue,* softer. Not so rocky."

Bobby suddenly stopped walking, and she realized they'd reached the third house above the church—a stone cottage with a few pots of flowers in front. A woman was sitting in a chair just outside the door.

Alexandra had imagined a big round old woman with blank eyes, but this person was tiny, like a scrap of dark fabric. She was dressed entirely in mourning except for an apron that might once have had a pattern in red and green but was now threadbare. Under the apron she wore—to Alexandra's surprise—the black clothes of a man. A very small man he would have been, and dressed for winter: pilled wool trousers with black patches sewn onto the knees, tiny black rubber shoes mended with some kind of tape, a shabby black wool jacket. She had planted a stick in the ground before her, her colorless hands gripping the handle on top. Her head was covered with a black scarf, folded in some complicated flattened way around the cheekbones and drawn tightly under a miniature chin. Her face was less a face than a crumpled piece of origami. She was possibly the oldest person Alexandra had ever seen. If the woman had eyes, seeing or not, they seemed to have disappeared into the folds of her skin, along with her eyebrows and the color of her lips. Alexandra thought she could trace some delicate lines there, in the thin, transparent nose and arched forehead. Eighty years ago, Baba Yana might have had a birdlike beauty—might have been the tiniest belle in the village. Perhaps she had never grown up, only grown old.

Bobby called a greeting, but in the moment they'd stood staring, the old woman had already swung around as if she heard or smelled them. Her small face lifted; she cocked her head sideways, and then for the first time she had eyes, unhooded —not the blank white weirdness Alexandra had dreaded, but a pair of dark buttons. Stoycho darted toward her and for a moment Alexandra and Bobby both froze. Then the dog's tail whirled with joy and he nosed Baba Yana's rigid hands gently until they opened. Her face unfolded with an equal pleasure; she stared up into the sky, caressing his head, her mouth stretching to show a last tracery of teeth. Her hand was a claw against his coat, patting him, greeting him.

"*Babo Yano*," Bobby began politely, but the old woman interrupted him with a string of words. Her voice was much larger than she was.

"She says," he murmured to Alexandra, "that she knew we were coming." He bent to take Baba Yana's hand and spoke to her, using Irina's name, and Vera's, and she looked blankly up into his face for a moment. He watched her and listened. "She says she has not seen the Lazarovi in several weeks. Or years—she isn't sure." The old woman reached around, patting Alexandra as she had the dog; she seemed to be ascertaining that there were two of them.

An hour later Irina was settled in bed again, this time in a small room Baba Yana had chosen for her. Irina put her head on the pillow with evident relief. She spoke again, faintly, as Alexandra left the room. "Ask her about this house," she said. "And our family."

Alexandra found Bobby sitting outside the front door, talking with the blind woman; he patted the empty chair beside him. Before Alexandra could make any request, Baba Yana looked up at the twilight, the first stars, as if she could see them. Her voice was loud and gravelly.

"Stoyan Lazarov," she said.

Thirty

I tell you even if you don't believe me that I saw the Turks driven out of these mountains. My father said to me, You will remember this moment all your life, even if you live to be a hundred and twenty. You see, the rest of Bulgaria had been free for a long time. Then, when I was already a young mother, some Turkish officials who lived in the big village down the mountain heard that the Bulgarian army was in the Rhodopes for the second time—this was in 1912 or 1913, the First Balkan War. The army had come at the time of the first liberation of Bulgaria and then they had lost these lands again. But this time the army was taking us back for good. So all the Turks from the villages around here left one night with their wives and their livestock and never returned. There were only a few in Gorno, but they went, too. They left with their horses and mules, very noisy, in a long line.

A week later a government man rode into Gorno and put his banner in the square. He said it came from an Assembly, with many important men. He brought newspapers to prove this. He said it was the end of an empire and Bulgaria had helped to bring the whole thing down like a building falling in an earthquake. I remember how his hands moved up and down to show the stones crashing to the ground.

I didn't know what an Assembly was—I thought it might be a kind of festival, the sort we have on *Ilinden*, bringing in the hay and the beginning of the harvest. I thought they would elect who would sing and who would dance. I thought my father might be invited to this festival, because he was one of the most important men in the village, and he danced very well, especially when he was drunk.

Instead, my father stayed here and helped to

collect the money for the new church. Actually, it was still the old one, but they put new stucco over the outside and whitewashed it inside and put up those fine windows and made the steeple tall. Before that, it was a short church—by decree of the Sultan, everyone always said, who wanted every church shorter than any minaret, though there had never been a minaret in our village. The day the priest consecrated the new church with the taller cupola on the tower, my father and the other men hung a Bulgarian flag on the front. The Gorno children went to school down below and learned new Bulgarian songs, but things up here were much the way they had been before, except that we were proud of the news in the newspapers that arrived from Plovdiv every month— sometimes even in the deepest snows of winter.

I had not been in school much myself. My mother needed me at home with the younger children, and then I was married at sixteen years old. Now the young women go to university, and what do they learn? Anything more than we did? I could read and I could write, thanks to my father's teaching us all to do that, and I could add and subtract the *stotinki* in our metal box at home. I knew where England was on the map, and Africa. My first husband was a fine young man. He drank a little, like my father and uncles, but he never hit me and he often helped me with the more difficult chores once his own work was done. I remember him carrying two big sacks of potatoes like they were nothing, and smiling at me. We worked in the fields together, except hen he hired himself out to orchards down in the plains. He was eighteen when we married. Sometimes, when I'm feeling wide awake in the early morning, I remember his name.

In any case, that husband was killed in the Second Balkan War while our youngest children were still very little. He was a hothead like all his family. My brothers brought me beans and salt during the next winter, and my oldest son tried to help me—he was a good boy, and so was my littler boy, and later my daughters all helped me until they married, except for Maria. Maria didn't ever marry. She really was very pretty, and very sweet-tempered—just rather serious. I don't know what happened, but she lived with me until I outlived her. Their father was dead, you see, and I let them choose their own husbands, mostly good ones. I never forced them. They're all long gone now. My younger son was killed in a threshing accident down on the plain when he first started working, one of those new machines with the engines. I haven't touched a machine since. I don't need them, any more than I need you to tell me I can't be this old. Believe me, when you are this old, you know it.

After my first son settled with his bride in the lower part of the village and took over our fields,

I had my sons' children to look after, and then my daughters had a few children, too. When the grandchildren were just starting to arrive, Anton the Tailor asked me to marry him. You see, I remember his name with no problem. We had Anton the Goatherd and Anton the Tailor, and I certainly wouldn't have married the goatherd, who was not all in his head after the First World War. He saw things other than goats, in the mountains. Anton the Tailor had been to the First War, too, but only at the beginning. He got a bullet in the leg and was sent home for the rest of it. He limped forever, but that didn't mean he wasn't handsome—oh, dear Lord, he was. All the girls wanted him. When you're young enough, that kind of thing still makes an impression on you, handsomeness. Watch out for that, girlie.

But Anton really was kind and smart, he was something, and it had been so long for me. We couldn't keep our hands off each other. We had a son, my last child, because with Anton it didn't matter that I was getting on in years for a baby, and it didn't matter to him that I was older than he, by a little. He thought I was beautiful, and you wouldn't want to argue with that, especially when you already have little grandchildren running around. He lived to be much older than my first husband had, until the earthquake—I mean the real one, not the end of the empire I told you about before. He had a temper, Anton, but we all have our faults. When I see him in dreams now, it's always pleasant. In fact, he sends me my dreams, and he sends dreams to several of my neighbors. If you have an important dream while you're here, you can be sure Anton the Tailor sent it to you.

This was what I started out to tell you, about the earthquake and Stoyan Lazarov, but I hope you will excuse an old woman if she needs to tell some other things first. In fact, I should tell you the in-between part, so Anton's death will make sense. Some sense, anyway. The village got bigger and a little richer after I married him, because we do have good land here and we started to grow more tobacco. My father had died by then, and my mother before him, of fever, both of them. They left me this house because my two older brothers were also killed near the end of the First War, and then my younger brother stayed in Germany after it ended, heaven knows why. I have German great-great-nieces and -nephews somewhere out there. They're probably in Australia, by now.

The important thing to say is that this house was one of the best in the village—it still is—and do you know why? It may look small on the outside, but it was dug deep, very deep into the earth. We have a root cellar for vegetables and cold foods and wine and pickles. Below that there is another cellar for storage of everything else, especially things like flat stones to repair the roof, and below that is a third cellar where there is an underground stream with the best water in the mountains.

It is very unusual for a house to have its own spring. Some people say the village started right here, around my spring, in the old times of the Bulgarian kingdoms. I have wooden stairs going all the way down to the deepest cellar. Everywhere else, the village sits on rock and you could not dig into it like this, but someone knew long time ago that here you could reach down into the mountain, all the way to water. Or perhaps it was once a cave—even my great-grandfather could not tell us why this house was built so. The water flows in a trench out of our cellar to the side of the mountain. Professors came from Sofia years ago to look at the spring and take pictures. There is probably not another one like it in all the Balkans, all the way down to the holy mountain Athos. I told you—we were taught some geography, too. Do you get that at your universities? When the Turks first came burning things and conquering, people hid in our deepest cellar, but it was no use. And one terribly hot summer during the wars with Greece and Serbia, I slept down there with my children, and my neighbors slept in the first two cellars, and we were all comfortable. Later,if any child was too naughty to be tolerated, I sent him or her to the cellars for a spell, to cool off.

In any case, the village grew a little richer in the years after the First World War and our wedding.

Anton sewed clothes for people from all the villages, although he could never sit cross-legged like a real tailor. Not so much the everyday clothes as the special ones, for weddings and christenings and for a few rich people who could afford to wear suits to visit their relatives in the city. I made the grandchildren's dresses and their little shirts and he made everyone else's finer clothes and was paid in silver and big new bills with the King on them, or just in food. The grandchildren were strong and well and if any of them got a fever, they got over it, and if they got lice we put a good mix of kerosene, vinegar, and lard on their heads. But then other problems came. Anton liked to read newspapers and talk with visitors, and he went to the larger towns sometimes to fit his suits on people. More and more often he came home saying we would have another war. Hell, no, I said—enough, already. My grandchildren were growing up tall, black-haired like the rest of us and beautiful, and the oldest had already married his true love from another village and they had a little baby. He met her at a church holiday one year.

Then, yes, war came again. Once during the war we walked or rode down to town to watch a real tank drive through. It was the biggest parade I ever saw, except on television later on. Anton could not volunteer even at the end, when Bulgaria entered the fighting, because of his leg and because he was getting old—he could not have kept up with any marching. Instead he made officers' shirts, and for a few months he worked in a factory in town, where they sewed the uniforms. Very ugly those were, too.

One day near the end of the war, everyone suddenly started running out of their houses, and those who didn't know what was happening followed. When we got to the top of the first field below the older Goranov farm, we understood what the other people had gone down to see. There was a crowd of men standing in the field, not our men from the village but strangers, Greeks whose clothes hung from their bones. Some were splashed with brown blood and some were bandaged around the head with pieces of old shirts. Some had only one shoe or no shoes. One man was curled up on the ground. One had ripped his pants down the front, or something had, so his privates were out in the sunlight but he hadn't even noticed. They stood still and didn't speak. They just looked at us and we looked at them, and everyone was thinking that maybe they had come to attack us and take our food.

Then the whole village ran forward, all the women, and the men who were not away at the war or out in the fields, and the young girls like my granddaughter Vanya, who later became a nurse. We all ran forward and helped the soldiers slowly climb the hill to our houses.

Through the next days we were bathing and feeding these men, putting whatever medicines we could find on their wounds. A couple of them died in the night and we buried them in the churchyard—go up there, you can see their graves to this day. We learned they were partisans in Greece, where soldiers had chased them and shot at them until they ran up into the mountains. They had crossed the mountains to us without knowing where they were, not even that they were in Bulgaria. One of them who spoke some Bulgarian told me that he'd left his wedding ring on the end of a tree branch, hanging on a twig, so that it would not rot in the ground with him if he fell down and died. I guess he got confused about what it was for. But he lived and we took care of him and we tried to tell him that his wife was certain to understand. He was from somewhere near the White Sea, very young.

In a week some men in trucks came and got the Greeks and took them to hospitals in Plovdiv, but I do not know if they ever reached home. Maybe they became prisoners. One of the soldiers stayed in the village, I don't know why, and he got better and then stayed for the rest of his life. Lili, with the house near our closed post office, is his grand-daughter. You can ask her.

After that, we saw planes overhead sometimes, and a few young men went with the divisions to Macedonia. I remember the sky as gray in those years, everyone sad and tired, although the sun must have continued to shine since the vegetables and the apples and the hay all kept growing. There wasn't much food from outside, so we had to work even harder to feed ourselves.

Eventually the radio in the *mehana* told us that the King had died. We heard much later that he had gone to see Hitler and then came home sick and just died. Some people said Hitler poisoned him as he did the rest of Europe. Later the radio told us that there were demonstrations in Sofia— people were throwing stones through windows, people hungry and angry. No one wanted the war anymore or believed we were fighting for anything that could help Bulgaria. And in 1944 there was a glorious revolution—it turned out we had all been waiting for one without knowing it. The radio broadcast speeches by our new leaders, men with lots of energy who cheered for the tanks in the streets. The tanks turned out to be Russian tanks, which showed up for the celebration. Bulgaria changed sides and fought against the Germans, instead, and that was when many of our men went to the front. Later there were votes for a new government. Those who voted in the village at all voted for the agrarians— they were farmers like us—not for the communists, but don't ask me about politics. Old women who live long enough mainly count the bodies, whether we want to or not.

Thirty-one

Well, I am telling you more than you want to know, but we went on growing food and eating and sleeping and I cooked for a big crowd here every day, all my family. What else could we do? You just go on, if you have to. The war had ended. We got some special laws in the village, because we had achieved socialism, and a new cultural center in place of the *chitalishte*, the library from old times. I was sorry to see that one torn down, but they said the walls were cracked inside and it was a hazard. They threw out some of the books there, too. The church closed for repairs, which seemed to take forever, maybe about forty years.

We also got some new officials, and a few men from our village were on committees down in the town, and there was a red star on the front of our school. My first great-grandchild started kindergarten under the red star, tiny Marina with the curliest hair in the family. I remember her because she was so much like me, although I've lost the names now of the rest of them. One day when she was in about third grade some men came to the school from the big town called Smolyan, and asked Marina if her father had said at home that he wanted to leave Bulgaria because he didn't like the Revolution. She said no until they finally believed her and left her father alone. Then they asked if maybe our neighbor Lyubo, who was the goatherd's great-grandson, was the one who didn't like our new system, and she said she didn't know. So they took Lyubo instead. He was crying in handcuffs, and we never saw him again. The goatherds were all even crazier after that. They say in the newspapers that we can talk now about anything we want to, but do you believe them? My grandmother used to tell me—she lived her whole life under the Turks—that you *can* talk about anything you want to, if and only if you're an old woman. That's the one constant rule. So now it's my turn, and I keep forgetting what I was going to say.

Maybe you want to know where Stoyan Lazarov was in all this. I forgot to mention him again, too. First, I must tell you about the earthquake—that's what reminded me. Vera and Irina's family inherited their house from their great-uncle in Plovdiv, who had married a Gorno woman in the old days. They stayed here a couple of times when they were little, long before the war. They were city girls—I remember them in white city dresses that would get dirty in no time, and white bows in their hair, visiting. Their father was a nice man. He had a sad kind of accident and started coming here more often for his health, the fresh air, which didn't help him walk again. He knew how to smile, though.

I was already married to Anton when Vera and Irina first stayed in their house, and their father hired him to make some special trousers that were easy to put on—Anton's finest invention, he called them. He liked to tease Anton about being an inventor, not a tailor. Anton knew what it was like, not to be able to walk as well as other people. After the next World War began, we heard that Vera had gotten married, but not Irina. I imagine Irina was like a horse you can't break, and no one wants to try. She's an artist, you know, and they do whatever they want. You can imagine what a life of adventure she probably had. I hear she's still alive, an old lady like me.

During the war Vera and Irina's family didn't come to the village for a long time. Then, near the end of the war, the bombs were falling on Sofia like rain and we heard Vera's parents might bring them here for several months, to get away. But they didn't—they were sent somewhere just outside Sofia in the worst part. It was very lucky they were not all killed there. Later, we heard that Vera's new husband had gone to Hungary, to fight the Germans when Bulgaria changed sides. We heard he was wounded in the thigh after just a few weeks, and then got very sick, and then was allowed to go home. Because of this, we didn't meet him until after the glorious revolution had become a little less glorious and everyone was used to it. One day my granddaughter—don't ask me which one—told me she'd been employed through a letter in the post to clean out their old stone house for them. She opened all the windows, beat the rugs, washed the steps, all the proper things. It was like a grave in there, I'll tell you—I helped her, to make it go faster.

The next day was a beautiful one, with bright sunshine. A hired car came up to the watering place on the square and Vera got out. I wouldn't have known her, she was so grown-up and grand, with fluffy dark hair around her face like a photograph, and a pretty dress she had made herself, and little shoes from before the war. Her husband Stoyan was like a beautiful photograph, too. He wore a black felt hat that he lifted firmly off and then put on again with one hand when anyone greeted him. He had dark city clothes and he carried a *tsigulka* in a black case. He played it in a big orchestra in Sofia, for the Revolution. Vera told us it had taken him some time to be able to play his *tsigulka* again after he'd gotten a fever from a wound in the leg, in Hungary. My granddaughter was kept on to help them in the kitchen and to wring the chickens' necks. They came to visit all of us and Vera got tears in her lovely big eyes when I talked about my memories of her father, from when he was a young man. He was still alive in Sofia, but he had never really walked again, after his accident.

Anyway, they stayed for a week and visited with

many people in the village, making friends and seeing the children. Stoyan had a kind look to his face, but also sometimes sad, I thought—I supposed that was because they had no children. He never talked much. During the day you could hear him playing his instrument for hours, and it was fine city music like from the radio, not our mountain dances. I kind of prefer the dances, myself, but he made a wonderful sound, especially when he played in the evening and the tune wandered out of the chimney and went up to the stars. I liked to sit on the square and hear it. Then they went back to Sofia, since their vacation time had ended.

But they started coming more often after that— with Irina at New Year's one time when it snowed less than usual, and sometimes in summer for the *Ilinden* festival on the mountainside. Stoyan lay in the grass next to their picnic basket and listened to the men playing our kind of music—I think he enjoyed that. We got used to seeing them and it was like a little holiday, or at least a change, whenever they arrived. Stoyan still never said much to anyone, but Vera brought gifts for the children and one of the last things Anton ever made was a coat to thank her. He made it out of sheep wool, dyed dark bluish gray from berries in the forest and combed very soft. He cut it in a city style and sewed a collar on it made of rabbit fur. I liked it immensely and was even a little jealous, but it takes a young woman to look good in something like that. I was already getting old, although I could still bale hay with the best of them. Anton was amazingly strong for his age, too, in spite of his leg—some people said it was from living with me, and some said it was the water from the spring in our basement. That water is so good you can give a bottle of it as a present to someone and he will be happy for days, or recover from illness. Of course, Anton drank more of it than anyone else, living with me.

When he gave the coat to Vera she kissed us both and said that she would wear it forever and that old friends were always the best ones, and blessed us in the old-fashioned way. I really was attached to her, even if I didn't yet know Stoyan as well. Then they left for the city, and that was the last time Anton saw them, because for some reason they didn't return the next year, or the next, and maybe for some years after, and we just took care of their house and waited for some news. Vera sent a short letter once at New Year's to say that they missed us and that Stoyan had been away from home, working, so they couldn't come. She said nothing about children, and I thought they must still be waiting for some.

You don't get any warning about an earthquake. The first thing I knew of it, it was already over. This was early summer, almost nine years after the Revolution, and I was putting berries into jars in the kitchen, with a big fire in the stove and boiling pots everywhere. I needed more water, and Anton, who was in from the fields for lunch, had gone down to the spring, our deepest cellar, to fetch it up for me. He was like that, doing things in spite of his bad leg. None of the great-grandchildren were there, so I think they were at the fields, too. Suddenly everything shook around us, hard. We had not had any earthquakes in years, at least not a strong one. And it is such a strange feeling that I thought at first it was my brain that had shaken, or that I was getting sick. I ran outside without thinking what to do, and immediately the house caved in.

It happened so quickly that I didn't understand what I was looking at. It was my house, the house my great-something had built, and in two seconds it had fallen in. The earthquake had stopped as quickly as it started. Nothing moved except steam flowing upward out of the pots on the buried stove, still managing to find its way around the stones and the collapsed roof. The houses on either side looked the same as always— it was only our house that fell in, all alone. But the neighbors had felt the ground tremble and they had run out into the street, too.

Then I remembered that Anton was down in the deepest cellar and I began to scream and pull at the rocks. My neighbors understood at once and they rushed at the ruins of my house to help me.

And then the stove set fire to everything that was caught under the rocks—the clothes and the furniture and I don't know what else. I screamed for Anton, who had started downstairs only a minute before with the pail, wearing his old blue trousers with the strong patches, going down very slowly because he limped but insisted on doing this for me. In fact, he might have lived if he had not yet been coming back upstairs. If he'd still been in the deepest cellar he might have lived. And even coming back up the stairs he might have lived if it had not been for the fire. I don't know whether he heard me screaming, because he never screamed back.

Thirty-two

We buried him in the churchyard the next day. I don't want to think about what we buried. I couldn't say anything about him to anyone; I had lost my voice. When it started to return, I didn't feel like speaking anyway, so I stayed silent for a year. I had to live in Iliya Kaloyanov's empty house, two doors away—they had gone to Plovdiv to find work by then. I didn't cook much, or do much in that house except sit and survive. I was only a visitor there. I got up, I sat for a long time, and then the sun went down and I went to bed. I didn't let anyone touch my ruined house—if the grandsons came to try to work on it, I drove them off without speaking. I'm sure I worried everyone badly, but sometimes you just have to do what you need to.

The day I posted the one-year *nekrolog* on the door at Iliya Kaloyanov's, I said aloud to my granddaughter Milena, who was keeping house with me, "Let's clean Iliya's kitchen." The next morning we took everything out of the kitchen, which was pretty dirty by then, and we scrubbed even the bottoms of my iron pots. Someone had pulled them from the ruins for me, along with what remained of my furniture, which was almost nothing. We sprinkled the floor with water and swept it until it cried. Then we cleaned the rest of Kaloyanov's house with the windows open and repaired the front steps.

A week later, I was even gladder I'd cleaned up so well, because Vera and Stoyan suddenly came back. I had not seen them in years. They brought Irina with them—Irina went out right away with her painting equipment to the fields in her funny clothes and I don't know what else, but Vera and Stoyan came to visit me even before they had unpacked their luggage. Vera hurried straight in the door without knocking and she hugged and kissed me like a daughter, and Stoyan hung back behind her. She said she had not known about it until they saw the first *nekrolog* at the foot of the village, on a wall, and they had hurried up the street to find me.

"Oh, *babo Yano*," Vera whispered. "We saw your house, and then Ivanka's son told us what happened and where you were staying."

Stoyan had lifted his hat off to enter, but not with the same smartness. When I looked at his face in the light, I felt shocked. He was like an old man, twenty or thirty years older. His skin was gray and full of little broken red and black patches, and his fingers shook where they held his hat. His hands had always appeared so clever and fine, for playing that *tsigulka*, you know, but now they were like an old farmer's, brown and scarred, some of the fingernails gone. I knew he must have gone to work doing something other than playing music, to have lost his fingernails. I'd never thought to see him so ugly, when he used to look like a prince.

"Have you been sick?" I said.

He smiled, as if this cheered him up in some strange way, and said yes, but he was getting better, and that he would soon have a job again, back at home. We sat down together and I gave them *bilkov chai*, tea from the mountain herbs, which I remembered was Vera's favorite. I thought it would help whatever was wrong with Stoyan and I whispered to Vera to soak his hands in more of it in the evening. I also gave her a big jar of our spring water, from where it still came out farther down the mountain. I explained to them I'd been speaking out loud for only a few days and my voice was out of practice—I was glad they hadn't come before that.

Stoyan hardly touched his tea, and he kept stroking his hat on his lap as if he had a small child sitting there. Finally he asked me why my house had not been repaired. I said I didn't want anyone to touch it, after Anton. He nodded and was quiet for a while, listening to me and Vera talk about the news of the village, and she told me they had a little boy. He was at home with Stoyan's mother and father but they would bring him to the village soon. I was happy to hear they had finally managed this, especially with Stoyan looking like the shadow of death, although I didn't say that part.

Then they got up to leave, but Stoyan stopped at the door and said, "I will repair it for you."

"What, my *house?*" I said. "But I haven't let anyone touch it. Why would I let you do that?"

"Because you would be helping me, if you would allow me to," Stoyan said, and he put the hat back on his head almost like a fine gentleman again. I tried to protest, for all kinds of reasons, but he gave that little city bow and took Vera's arm to go. I was so glad to see them and to hear that they finally had their child, and to talk about Anton with someone new, that I didn't stop them. I understood that they were trying to make me feel better with their words, and I was grateful, even if Stoyan hadn't meant what he'd said.

You can imagine my surprise when I came out the next morning an hour after sunrise, to get some things from the store, and glanced from habit at the ruin of my house just up the street. The ruin was still there, with its broken spine against the front wall of the chicken barn. But Stoyan was there, too, in an old shirt and pants, his sleeves rolled up above the elbow. Two of our neighbors, men, were talking with him, but if either tried to lift something for him, move a stone, he drove them off just as I had all the year before. I couldn't believe my eyes. He had already made neat piles of about a third of the stones from the front wall and had brought a wheelbarrow to fill with the rotten stucco and old hay from inside the walls, and other debris. Now and then he stopped to mop his forehead.

I thought to myself that a *tsigulka* player ought not be working like that with his fine hands. Then I remembered how bad they already looked. He lifted the stones skillfully, in spite of his sickness. I could see that he was piling them in the yard, out of the way of his work but as close as conveniently possible to where the wall of the front room would need to be rebuilt. That was just as I would have done it. In fact, I had imagined many times doing it that way.

"Good morning, *babo Yano*," he called, when he saw me.

"Good morning, *Stoyane*," I said. He was getting closer, in his clearing-out work, to the spot where we had found Anton, so I turned away and went down to the store. When I came back, he had already stacked most of the stones—for the first time the place looked like something other than a wreck.

"You are wearing yourself out, *sine*," I said to him.

"Exactly," he replied, without stopping. "But maybe you shouldn't watch this part." He had begun scraping out what was left of my belongings—scraps of burned cloth, shards of dishes, some objects even I couldn't recognize. My grandmother's fine tablecloths and blankets had been in there, and eighty years of things after that.

"All right, I won't," I said.

I went back to Kaloyanov's house and made a big lunch for Stoyan and anybody else who might drop by, and believe me he was hungry when one o'clock came. Vera walked up, too, and my granddaughter Milena, and we all ate together and pretended not to look at the scratches and welts on Stoyan's arms.

"Just let him do what he wants, *babo*, if you don't mind too much," Vera whispered to me before she left.

So I did—let him do what he wanted, partly because I was curious about how he would do it, a city man who'd never worked on a farm in his life and who'd been ill on top of that. He didn't look as if he had the strength to lift a single stone and yet he hauled them all day long. The rest of the village was curious, too, and he let them come by to watch his work and even talk with him. But still no one could touch even a pebble there. He would stop anyone who tried to do that, in a way that left no doubt he was serious. People gave up trying, even my grandsons, who were angry because I hadn't allowed them to rebuild the house for me themselves and came to talk with me about it. But I silenced everyone. I didn't know what on earth he was doing, besides repairing my house, but I recognized that same need I'd had when I left it in ruins and didn't speak for a year. Maybe he was one of those people who just can't bear a mess, or a job not finished. Besides, there are things you have to do for yourself, even if everyone else thinks you're crazy.

In any case, Vera settled down here in Gorno for a while to let him do this work. She had some leave because she'd lost a baby after their first one, and been sick from that, I found out. And for some reason Stoyan was actually required by a special card to stay in the village for several months. Even when he was working on my house, he took a bus down to an office in town once a week to register himself there, walking all the way back—one of the Goranov boys drove the bus in those days, and he told us about it.

Vera must have sent for their little boy, because one day he arrived with his paternal grandparents, all the way from Sofia, and that was the first time I saw Neven. The grandparents were just what you'd imagine, city people with neatly mended clothes, clean and fine but not too proud. The father had Stoyan's strong jaw. But Neven looked like Vera, which meant he was the most beautiful child I'd seen in a long time, even with all my own great-grandchildren around. He was about three years old and very serious. He held Vera's hand, but he also stood apart from her, like a little pasha in the old stories. His hair was soft and dark, with a bit of red in the sunlight. It was a cool morning, and he wore a red sweater someone had knitted for him in beautiful patterns. His eyes were golden when the sunshine touched them, and his skin was soft and golden, too. His nose was straight and fine, like Vera's. But those were just the things in his face. Even though he was not much more than a toddler, he held himself upright the way Stoyan had always done before he got sick. I thought what a lucky child he was, touched with Vera's beauty and Stoyan's elegant ways.

The strangest thing about Neven was that as soon as you saw him, you wanted him to like you, although he was only a little boy. I went out to meet them and stooped down in front of him so I could look into his face. Most children would have shrunk back from such an old woman dressed in black, but he raised his sweet round chin up and looked at me with curiosity. I picked a flower from the pots in the yard and handed it to him. He took it and looked at it in the same way, softly, then looked back at me.

"Say thank you," Vera told him.

"Thank you, *babo*," he said in a clear voice, like a much older child. Then he smiled for the first time. That smile—so handsome it made the sun come out. I didn't even know what to say in return.

Vera brought Neven every day to see the progress on my house. Soon the rubble was all cleared, even what had fallen into the cellars. Stoyan had stacked the loose stones around the edges of the yard, with the few beams that were still sound placed neatly beside them. He asked me a lot of questions about the walls, both the ones that were standing and the ones that were gone. He bought bags of a cement powder down in the town—they were probably stolen by somebody from the factory there, but that's the way it was then. He mixed big pails of mortar like gray bread dough. This wasn't going to be like the old days, with just straw and mud. It took him a whole day to get the trick of putting the stones together, but he didn't let anyone help him, not even me. Soon enough, he could turn his wrist with those clever, scarred hands and mortar two stones together as smooth as my daughters filling *banitsa* for lunch.

The ground floor was built up in two weeks, and then he rested for the first time. The next week he found some logs in the old barn below the store, to make beams for the ceiling. He must have bought them from Petar Ivanov, whose father had hidden them there for years. After that, he had a serious problem: hauling them out of the barn and up our hill. Finally, he borrowed a wagon from Petar. No one really knew what he went through with those logs, because no one was allowed to help—some people believed it took him hours to move them even a few meters. He had to rest every two minutes, they said, because he was still weak from his illness, and it would have been a hard job even for a healthy man. But maybe he actually had someone help him at the barn, at least. I hope so. Vera and I both begged him to stop and let somebody else take the rest of the work—he had done more than one man could usually manage, anyway.

But he was determined and he no longer even argued with us. If we tried to reason with him about it, he just looked over our shoulders at something else until we stopped talking. He trimmed one side of each log with an adze. Then he borrowed pulleys and ropes that took nearly as long to put into place as the walls of the first floor of the house had taken to rebuild, and he used that contraption to raise the beams.

One day, he left his work and came to sit next to me in the shade, and I gave him water to drink. I had gotten in the habit of knitting or crocheting under the tree at the edge of the yard, now that the rubble was gone. He had something on his mind, I could see, but it took him a little time to come out with it.

"*Babo Yano*," he said finally. "What do you think of this. Could you imagine living in a house with one story, rather than two as it was before?"

I saw his point at once. If he put on the roof now, he could finish by himself. But even with his pulleys and ramps and his wife wringing her hands at the danger, he wouldn't be able to lift beams above a second story without help. And I thought about it before I answered. My great-something had built the house taller as well as deeper than most in the village, a big solid house that rose high above its cellars. There had been a second floor for living and then bedrooms in the attic, all fine big rooms.

"*Stoyane*," I said, after thinking it over. "What would be so bad about getting my grandsons to help, just with this part? They are very strong. If it would make you feel better, I would allow you to pay them something. Why not?"

He sat scratching the back of his head. There

was mortar dust in his hair. His shirt had long wet areas under the arms and down the front. His hands looked worse than ever, and sometimes he cradled them against his chest as if he regretted hurting them further. But I thought the work had done his health some good, actually—he looked stronger, his skin was brown, his movements more normal, and his appetite huge. He seemed to be trying to figure out how to explain something to me. Finally he looked right into my face.

"*Babo*," he said. "What if you did something terrible, and you wished you could undo it. But someone thought of what you'd done in a different way, and punished you for the wrong thing, against your will. And then one day you found a way to punish yourself for what you had really done."

"Go on," I said, although I couldn't think of anything terrible this man could have done. I looked at his wide, steady eyes, with the broken veins in them. He was good-looking, of course, or he had been—maybe he had cheated on his wife. Hard to imagine anyone cheating on Vera, though.

"Well—" He looked down and tried to brush some of the mortar from his hands. "Then let's say that someone tried to take from you the way you had found to punish yourself for the awful thing you had done. And you knew that if you let anyone take that away, you would have to go back to living with your terrible deed."

"All right," I said. "Go on."

"Wouldn't you refuse to let anyone take that away from you?"

"I suppose so," I said, trying to think of any terrible deed I'd done myself. I did sell a batch of lumber to the older Kaloyan once, for a little more than I should have. And I didn't tell Anton that I used the extra money from that for our third granddaughter's wedding, because he would have opposed me. And once I shouted some swear words at my oldest friend right in the middle of a work bee, and she shouted at me, and then we were friends again. And I used to scold Anton about small things, more than I should have. Apart from this, I've tried to lead a holy life.

Stoyan was staring hard at me. "There you are. Let me finish the house by myself."

"But what does all this have to do with me or my house, *sine?*" I asked him, seriously puzzled.

"Nothing at all," Stoyan assured me, "except that you have a good heart."

"Oh, nonsense," I told him, but it pleased me. "All right, then. I don't understand, but I'm an old woman and only Milena lives with me now. One story is enough for us. Just be sure you put in an extra bedroom, and build me three big beds for the great-great-grandchildren, for when they come to visit. They can share. And you can use the leftover stones to make a new wall next to the barn, for a courtyard."

He jumped up and clapped his hands as if I'd played him some fine music.

Now he whistled while he worked. When he didn't know how to do something, he asked the old men in the village to tell him. The main part of the house was done within another few weeks. It was almost as good as the old one, if smaller— four rooms, clean plastered walls inside, a kitchen with a stone hearth wide enough for my biggest pots. It was all very simple, even a little rough. Stoyan had built every bit of it himself, including the wooden pegs for aprons and jackets. And the stone windowsill to hold my cans of flowers. Under the summer sun, he hauled slates for the roof and fitted them above one another, the lowest row first, like trim around the hem of a dress— Anton couldn't have done it better himself. Stoyan built up the top of the chimney and set a big slate across it, with openings for the smoke to pour out. On the slab he set little pieces of rock shaped like teardrops, pointing up to heaven.

He finished putting those rocks in place two days before *Ilinden*, with half the village standing out in the street to watch. When he was done, he climbed down dripping with sweat and I reached up and gave him a big kiss right on his sunburned mouth. Everybody laughed and cheered, even my grandsons. Stoyan had built this beautiful house in an incredibly short time, and he had built it alone. It was not big, but it was just right for me and my granddaughter to live in again. Everyone was smiling and slapping him on the back, and Stoyan smiled, too, which was not usual for him. Vera clapped her hands and wiped her eyes, but she was looking at him, not at the new house.

Only one person didn't smile or cheer: little Neven. He stood next to his mother and looked at Stoyan with a soft and serious face. If he hadn't been just a baby, I would have sworn his eyes were full of pity.

Thirty-three

"You know that Stoyan Lazarov died," Baba ana concluded peacefully, as if she had no idea that she had left out the rest of the story. "I don't know where he's buried. Not here, although he might have liked that. Probably in some fancy place in Sofia, where his people lie."

It was dark now, and one electric light shone out of the kitchen window behind the old woman; Lenka moved across it. Alexandra sat looking at the house Stoyan Lazarov had built from a ruin. She knew that Bobby was tired from interpreting Baba Yana's story, but she had another question. "Ask her if she saw Stoyan again, if he kept coming to the village."

Bobby nodded. When he put the question to Baba Yana, she seemed confused, shifting her little black eyes in the light from the window. She uncurled one hand from her stick and rubbed it over the top of Stoycho's head, where he leaned against her. His tail hit the dust. "Well, I'm not sure. I think they visited here a few times after that, for a week now and then, and Stoyan began to play his *tsigulka* again, down at their place. He comes up here still when he needs to see the house he built for me. He was here yesterday, I think. Or the day before. Time is a funny thing, so I can't quite remember. I made lunch for him."

"But, *babo Yano*, you told us he was dead," Bobby reminded her softly.

"Of course he's dead," she said. "Everyone dies. Except me." She laughed without a sound, exposing that glint of long-ago teeth. Alexandra thought she must be able to eat only soup or yogurt; maybe that was why she was so small, in her men's clothing. She looked like someone's tiny widower, as if she had changed places with her deceased husband.

"Ask her again if she knows where Vera and Milen Radev are now—and Neven," Alexandra said to Bobby.

But Baba Yana seemed to have lost the thread of her earlier subject. "Do you want a cup of tea?" she said. "I don't have coffee. It hurts my insides, gives me the runs. Coffee is for young people like you."

326

They refused, with thanks. Baba Yana tapped her stick on the ground, yawned—that tiny, gaping mouth. "Tell Irina I said hello, when you see her." She had obviously forgotten that Irina was resting inside. "A strange bird. I've heard she had a daughter when she was almost too old, with a writer from Plovdiv. It was a secret and he's long dead, they say. But at least she has someone to take care of her now. I wish Vera were still alive, the sweet girl."

"That's Lenka," Alexandra whispered in amazement, when Bobby translated for her. "And tell her that Vera is alive."

Bobby shook his head.

"It is no good," he told her. "My great-grandmother became like this, too. She could not answer many of our questions properly."

"Your great-grandmother?" Alexandra was startled; her own great-grandparents had been born in the nineteenth century and died decades before she was born. But that story would have to wait. They stood up and Bobby shook hands with Baba Yana's curled mitts, thanking her again. The old lady embraced the top of Stoycho's head, her stick gathered up against his ear, and then pointed at Alexandra.

"What did she say?" Alexandra asked Bobby.

"She says, 'Tell the young maiden not to sit out in the cold on stones, the way she usually does, or she will catch a chill.' "

"I don't sit on stones," protested Alexandra, trying to remember if this was true.

"It's a wish for your good health. Or maybe a worry about the future."

"You translated very well."

"Thank you. I tried," he said. He put an arm around Alexandra for a moment, surprising her again, as if his effort had made him feel close to her. The road—steep and rutted, houses growing like mushrooms out of the ground, lights coming on here and there, fields sloping below—took on a suddenly heightened reality for her, a last glow before it became part of the dark mountains. She knew that moment, too, from home.

When they went into the house, they found Irina sitting up, drinking something hot. Alexandra felt a huge relief, not only because she liked the old lady so much but also because the idea of another dead person in their midst made her knees weak. Irina looked strangely young and fresh after their hour with Baba Yana.

"My dears," Irina said. "I began to worry, and Lenka has made us a little supper. How did you find my hostess Yana?"

"She's a force of nature," Alexandra told her, sitting down in the chair beside the bed. The room was small, with low beams across the ceiling. It smelled of cool water. "She described to us how *gospodin* Lazarov rebuilt this house."

Irina smiled. She had so many teeth. "Well, yes

—he did, although we all thought he was mad to tire himself that way. But in the end, it seemed to help him get well." She stopped, and Alexandra wondered if the illness had been something of a private nature, about which Irina was too polite to speak. "And did she tell you that he once played a concert at her house, small as it was—or, rather, in the yard?"

"No," said Alexandra. "When did he do that?"

"Well, I am not sure. I think it was to celebrate the new house after he built it." She sipped from a glazed brown cup, looking down into it.

"I don't suppose you have any news of your sister?" Bobby stood near the foot of the bed with his hands in his pockets.

Irina nodded slightly but definitely: no. "I wish I could tell you so. Lenka has asked everywhere now and everyone says the same thing—my sister and Milen were living here for many months and then they left about a week ago and did not come back. I am quite worried about them now, I will tell you. If you saw them in Sofia, and they didn't come to me, and they didn't come here, and Neven doesn't answer his phone, then where are they? Probably they are still in Sofia, trying to discover where *you* are, my dear. I'm afraid I've made a terrible mistake, bringing you all the way up here."

"Oh, not a mistake!" cried Alexandra. "We had to try."

"Do you want to go to Sofia to look for them?" Bobby asked soberly. "Or do you think that they could have left Sofia now, and might be waiting for you in Plovdiv?"

The old lady sighed. "I can't tell. I thought of this, too, and they do have a key to my house, I think. Lenka phoned there a few hours ago. But again there is no answer. Perhaps I should go to the police after all?"

She looked at Bobby as she asked this, and after a moment he shook his head. "Let's try a little longer to find them," he said.

Irina did not protest. "I think I will be much better tomorrow, and we can return to Plovdiv. Then I shall wait for my sister there."

Bobby seemed to ponder this. "I don't like to leave you alone at home," he said slowly, "after what happened to your house here."

"I will have Lenka with me," Irina said. "And there are always people in the museum, at least the people who work there. One of them sleeps there at night, in fact, to guard it."

Bobby nodded. "In that case, Alexandra and I could take you home and then return to Sofia to search there. I have several friends who work in hotels and I have called them to ask if they saw any people who look like the Lazarovi. They will ask all our other friends. Sofia is big, but I thought we should try this."

"And you could go back to work," Alexandra said.

Bobby looked sober. "Yes, I must do that soon."

Lenka had just come in, her sleeves rolled up. *Daughter,* thought Alexandra. Lenka certainly looked very different from Irina, or even from the way Irina might have looked decades earlier, and if she understood English, she seemed too shy to speak it. She had something to tell them—in rapid Bulgarian, which Bobby translated for Alexandra. "A man stopped her in the road while she was asking people about the Lazarovi. He told her that his employer had heard there is a guest from abroad and that he would like to offer the guest some hospitality—that would be you, Bird. He invited us to lunch at his employer's house tomorrow—a big house outside the village, around the side of the mountain. He did not give a name."

Alexandra marveled at how quickly the news of their arrival had traveled around the village. Was this typical Balkan hospitality, as her guidebook called it? But Irina was frowning. "The big house? Did he mean that monstrous thing on the hill road? I have always been thankful we cannot see it from here."

Bobby watched her closely. "Who is this employer?"

"The owner is officially a businessman from Plovdiv, who does not live here—he is terribly rich and with unpleasant connections. That house

331

was built only five or six years ago and it is one of the biggest in the mountains, like a ski resort—nobody likes it."

"Do you know who this businessman is?" asked Bobby.

"No," Irina said. She turned to Lenka and they spoke for a few seconds. One side of Bobby's mouth went down; Alexandra had seen that look before.

"What?" she said.

"Well," Bobby said, "they have heard before in the village that this house is actually owned by the Minister of Roads, who arrives at night when he visits. But he does not visit often."

Alexandra stared at him. "Kurilkov? Well, I guess that could be why we saw him coming out of the mountains, at the bridge—maybe he was up here. But why would he invite us to lunch, just because I'm a foreigner? Especially if he's already left the village?" Then a wave of heat went through her face: the slogan on the taxi, the smashed front room here at Irina's. "Do you think—"

He shook his head slightly and she stopped.

"Perhaps you should refuse the invitation," Irina said, but she was looking at Bobby again. "We must get back to Plovdiv, and it does seem very strange."

"I don't believe that Alexandra should refuse." Bobby shoved his hands more deeply into his pockets. "That might be worse than accepting."

Irina stirred against her pillows. "She cannot go alone to such a place."

"Of course not," said Bobby. "I wouldn't let her do that. But I do not especially want to go, either." He was staring at the floor now and Alexandra knew he must be weighing possible complica-tions. She was beginning to feel a cold pit at her very center.

"We saw him leave the mountains," she said again, mainly to reassure herself.

"Whatever this is, Bobby will take care of you, my dear." Irina smiled at Alexandra, but her face was as pale and anxious as before. "You can stay the shortest time possible, and after that we shall return to Plovdiv. I am determined to be ready."

Alexandra was almost too tired to be afraid, falling asleep in her musty clean bed in the back room. Bobby had set the urn in a kitchen cup-board, for safety; he was sleeping near it. For a moment, alone in the dark, Alexandra thought with a pang of the ashes and wondered if she was actually missing them. Stoyan Lazarov had played his violin in this very house, or in the yard. She pulled a pile of blankets over her. It was chilly for May, as if the stones here never warmed up, and she had gone to bed shivering in her sweater. The blankets made a suffocating load—layers scratchy or soft, with a faintly oily smell, like the animals they had come from. Death was in the room: Baba Yana's husband under a collapsed house, the Greek soldiers staggering toward the village, Irina's eyes shut in her white face; and of course, of course, Jack.

She drew the weight of the blankets farther up on her shoulder and made herself think about someone living—Stoyan's son, Neven, for example, who might be middle-aged but had looked youthful, vigorous and agitated, standing on the hotel steps in Sofia. She tried to remember his black vest, his formal shoes and the gesture of his beautiful large hand. That twinge of longing she had felt for him. Where was he now? Why did he not answer his phone, even when his aunt called him repeatedly? Before she could wander down the path of this new anxiety, she grew warmer and sleep took her away.

She woke while it was still dark, feeling sharply conscious and as if she must leave the house at once, for air. Suddenly she remembered her dream: Jack had told her where Neven Lazarov was—a hot, blurred place she had never expected to look. She had found Neven standing directly in front of her; she had set down the heavy urn and thrown herself at his feet, prostrated herself, because she could not find the right words for an apology. He'd lifted her up without effort, and to her sur-prise he had not been angry. He had kissed her, briefly. Then she had opened her eyes. Her lips still tingled.

She lay for a moment confused by the sweetness of being forgiven and the shock of being awake. Although she'd always been a coward about darkness, she found herself getting soundlessly out of bed. The doors to the other rooms were shut; she wouldn't wake anyone else. For a moment, she was afraid—someone had broken into Vera's house, just down the road, and painted a wall with blood. But she also felt that she would suffocate without fresh air. She stretched both hands in front of her in the dark corridor; she stumbled against something warm, which made her breathing stop. It was Stoycho—he stood up against her legs and went silently with her, so that she was no longer frightened. Groping around, she found her sneakers among the shoes lined up by the door. She lifted the latch.

Outside, there was a buttery twilight, which she discovered was the moon, still large and bright, hovering over the rooftops. The air was full of stirrings like dawn, although it might have been two in the morning or five—she had forgotten to check the time. Stoycho walked beside her. In the mottled light and dark, she could see a gleam that proved to be stone steps up the hill behind the house, then a path through prickling grass. The path climbed the hillside; soon she was looking down on Baba Yana's roof, scalloped with moonlight. She could see the shadow of the chimney long against the slates, the conical rocks on its stone cap showing sharp as beaks. The rest of the village lay around and below her, softly visible. She passed under dark trees and came to the edge of a high grassy plateau, which she remembered seeing from the road. There were no houses here, as if the area had been left sacred, or simply provided a playing field. She wondered at herself; at home she would have been afraid of strangers prowling in the night, or even of ghosts, and here she might be followed by someone who wished her harm. But Stoycho was with her, and every-thing was so unfamiliar that she felt protected, as if she weren't actually present. *I am the ghost, myself.*

The moon stood just above the peaks in front of her and the mountains lay around the horizon in a ring, black matter against a liquid sky. She found an outcropping of stones near the center of the hilltop and sat down on them as comfortably as she could manage. They were cold against her clothes. Stoycho sniffed the stones and sat down next to her, then stretched out in the grass as if she'd told him to. She could see the dark reflection of his eyes in the moonlight. The silence from the village behind her was eclipsed only by the enormous silence of the forests on the slopes; the moon had already fallen toward the highest peak and she saw where it would set—very soon. She waited without moving until the swollen lower rim of light touched the edge of the ridge and silhouetted something broken there, perhaps trees or jagged rock. The light moved faster, slipping away. She tried not to breathe. At the last second, the upper edge of the moon became very bright and disappeared in a rush, swallowed by the mountain.

Then Alexandra felt something behind her, the lightest touch on the back of her head, and realized with a start of horror that she and Stoycho were not alone. She whirled around on the rock. Directly behind her, opposite the moon and reaching over the massy shadow of mountains, she saw an infinitesimal bright gleam: the sun, rising in the instant the moon had set. The earliest ray of it had touched her across a great distance. This sliver quickened and pulsed and pulled up above the ridges, and then she remembered to stop looking directly into it. Stoycho moved beside her, raising his head to watch. Alexandra was trembling, because she had seen the end and the beginning. And the sun had reached out and found her, stroked her, chosen her.

Thirty-four

Just before noon, they left Baba Yana sitting by her door and walked to the big new house. The road branched off below the church and ran up over the shoulder of the fields. The big house sat on a rise by itself, mostly out of sight of the village but looking down on it nonetheless. Alexandra disliked the house as soon as it came into view—it was much too large for the landscape, where buildings were supposed to sprout up out of the stones as if they belonged there. This one loomed—huge but relentlessly traditional, giant Tudor beams crisscrossing it, balconies jutting off the façade, ten thousand folksy new slates slathered over the roof, an actual tower rising at one end. You could have put twenty of Baba Yana's little dwelling inside it. For a moment, Alexandra wondered what Stoyan would have felt toward this excrescence—had he known about it? After all, he had rebuilt her house with his own hands. This one was the work of bull-dozers and cranes.

The wall around the big house was punctuated in the middle with a pair of enormous wooden gates—like the ones she'd seen at Velin Monastery, but four or five centuries newer. An electric doorbell glowed at one side; Bobby rang this and they waited. Alexandra missed Stoycho, whom they'd left in Baba Yana's yard for extra protection. He'd pulled wildly on his rope, straining after them and barking, until they had to walk away. She wished he were here, against her knee, listening with his crooked ear to the foot-steps on the other side of the wall.

A moment later, a smaller door in the gate swung open and a burly young man in Rhodope costume stepped out. He looked like the dancers in Alexandra's guidebook, except that he was not happy. He wore wide shirtsleeves, a brown woolen vest, and pantaloons trimmed with black braid; at his belt hung a canteen of metal worked in patterns, along with what Alexandra felt sure was a real knife in a leather sheath. A cap of curly black sheepskin teetered on his head, and below his baggy pants she could see wool stockings wound with bands of leather. He was shod in elaborate leather shoes that turned up a little at the toes. The clothing itself could have been beautiful, but it was brand new, like the house, and this brand-new man wore it despondently, his arms huge in the linen sleeves. Alexandra noted his face with surprise; he looked much younger than she was, a rosy teenager. He nodded, shyly, although he could have killed either of them with a single blow, and turned to lead them up the stone walk to the front of the house. Alexandra gave Bobby a careful glance, but he was watching the door in the gate shut automatically behind them.

Inside, their escort took them through a gargantuan stone-flagged front hall and into a side chamber and gestured for them to wait on a bench, then bowed and left them. Bobby shot her a look that told her not to speak—how did she understand him so easily? They waited in a silence that seemed to fill the whole house, Bobby gazing around, memorizing something; Alexandra thought he must be looking for clues that Kurilkov owned it. This chamber, like the front hall, was surreally clean, as if the dirt roads of the village below did not exist. Alexandra took her cue from Bobby, sitting straight and still, but when their host entered the room, she stood up with an exclamation of surprise.

It was the Wizard of Oz, the chief from the Sofia police station with the large bald head— she knew him at once. He was dressed very differently now, in a pale green shirt untucked over silky trousers. He held a hand out to Alexandra.

"So nice to see you again," he said, smiling as if her shock pleased him. "Alexandra—Boyd, yes?" His hand was warm and friendly and his face relaxed: a professional on vacation.

"It's nice to see you, too," she said. "But—is this your house?" She felt a little surge of anger at the trick, and a larger wave of fear—why was he here? And why did he remember her so well?

"Oh, no." He laughed. "You are making me feel good. I am only a guest, like you."

She wanted to ask point-blank whether it was true that the house belonged to Kurilkov, but the Wizard had already turned to Bobby, as if noticing him for the first time.

"This is my friend Asparuh Iliev," Alexandra said, in what she hoped was a collected voice.

"Asparuh Iliev." He made a statement of it, shaking hands warmly again. "Very pleased."

Alexandra looked at Bobby, to see what he thought of this man. Bobby's face was a study in decorum and he bowed as he shook hands. But he had overdone it, that moment of irony; Alexandra was absolutely sure that he had met the Wizard before. That they knew each other at a glance, in fact. Then she realized Bobby must have recognized the Wizard from her description, and probably the name on his business card, before that. Did he know the chief personally? What if the Wizard himself had put Bobby in jail after the demonstration he'd told her about? Neither man said anything about a previous meeting, however. Alexandra trusted her intuition heavily, back home; here, it was like a compass whose needle swung around without bearing.

"Will you come into the dining room?" The Wizard gestured courteously to Alexandra. "I believe our lunch is ready."

They followed him, although at each of several

341

doors he stopped and ushered them carefully ahead of him. The dining room was a baronial horror, three stories high, with interior balconies and a fireplace big enough to roast a whole lion. The walls were hung with tattered flags and rugs, each giving Alexandra a sense of priceless history that didn't belong in such a place. It was like walking into a spanking new mansion in her home town and seeing it decorated with precious ragged flags—DON'T TREAD ON ME or JOIN, OR DIE. Here, she couldn't read the meaning of anything, apart from the fact that it had all cost a fearsome amount of money. One end of the acre-long table was set for three.

The Wizard saw them to their places and then sat down at the head, between them. He unfurled a huge red napkin and leaned back as if content. "So you have come to see our mountains," he observed mildly. "This is the best possible village to see them. I believe that we have the most beautiful views, in fact."

"It really is lovely," she said. A spirit of rebellion was creeping through her veins. "And you arrived on Tuesday?" That would have been two days ago.

She saw something like appreciation, but tightly controlled, flicker across Bobby's face.

"Tuesday?" The Wizard looked surprised. "Oh, no. I have just come yesterday, like you. Why do you ask?"

Alexandra smiled. "Well, because we met in Sofia on Monday, so I thought Tuesday would have been the earliest you could come here."

He smiled in return. She noticed that his eye wasn't twitching this time, possibly because he was away from his desk. He said, "I have only very short vacations, in my kind of work. This is the nicest place I know for a few days of rest."

A young man dressed in black came in, carrying a tray of dishes. He began to set plates of salad and bowls of soup in front of them, and little glasses of something clear. The Wizard raised his glass and toasted them—they raised their *rakiya* in return, although Alexandra noticed that Bobby set his down without taking even a sip, and she followed suit. She thought it would be better not to have any alcohol in her system for this conver-sation.

"*Bon appétit*," the Wizard said. "A special thing—this is tripe soup."

Alexandra tried to remember what tripe actually was—a kind of fish, or an organ meat? Or a collective noun, like *offal*? She concentrated on the fish idea. Bobby had not said a single word and she began to doubt that he would talk at all. The Wizard commenced to eat, delicately and with enjoyment, indicating that they should pick up their spoons. "Alexandra—so, your travels brought you to this beautiful place. And you were able to return something to somebody on the way—the remains of a person—to his family? As you told me. That was a welcome gift, yes?"

She considered for a hazardous second. "Yes, it was very satisfying," she said. "You can imagine. They were terribly relieved."

The Wizard put down his spoon, but Bobby kept eating, in silence. She didn't like the way Bobby's shoulders looked so straight—*Bird! What were you thinking?*

But the Wizard was gazing at her with interest. "How lucky that you found that family. Did the address I gave to you—you remember—did it help?"

"Very much," Alexandra said. "I was so grateful. Bovech really wasn't very far from Sofia, so it was easy."

"And how strange that you found them at home. You know, I thought later that I should have sent someone to help you, so I checked, also. Lyubenovi—no, Lazarovi, was it? And they had not lived there in at least three months. But maybe they returned after my officer visited? What day were you there?"

"Tuesday," she said, this time truthfully.

"Oh, before my man. He went there yesterday. He found things very quiet."

Alexandra imagined a police officer talking with the pretty neighbor next door, who must have told him about their visit. And searching the house—would he have discovered the lonely undershirts in the bedroom drawer, the tin box with the stained coils of fabric inside? There was a little silence, during which Alexandra sat very still. She didn't dare to pick up her spoon, in case it rattled in her hand. She remembered the pleasant-faced policeman taking Bobby's papers back to his car on that half-collapsed bridge. But how could those papers have connected them with a search for Vera Lazarova? Another memory came to her, as she looked down at the pinkish-gray soup, which had something floating in it. She had gone straight from the front door of the police station to Bobby's taxi, just up the block, and gotten into it, in plain view. In plain view, no doubt, of a security camera. She hadn't thought of that before.

The Wizard smiled at her, as if she'd simply made a mistake, which she knew she had. "So you couldn't find the Lazarovi, either, actually. Or maybe you found them somewhere else. Is that what you mean?"

"No—you're right," Alexandra said. "I guess I only wished very badly that I had found them. Wishful thinking." She wondered if the neighbor woman in Bovech had given the police officer Irina's address in Plovdiv. Had the Wizard looked for them there, too? Had he seen them going in and out of the museum courtyard? Or had he found Irina and Vera's connection to Gorno some other way? Why was he here at all? That was the important question.

The Wizard seemed to be reflecting. "Yes, of course you were sad. But I'm sure that you will find them, and I can help you if you wish."

Alexandra wished less than ever, so she said nothing.

For the first time, he turned to Bobby. "And you are showing her our country very well—maybe some things she would never see alone?"

Bobby inclined his head over his soup. The Wizard seemed unperturbed by Bobby's silence, and this made Alexandra's compass needle swing forcibly into place: they knew and hated each other.

The man in black came in, cleared their bowls quietly away, and dished out something with meat and vegetables. She wished more and more that she could jump up and run out of the house— at one moment, she felt she might actually do it.

The Wizard had set his fork down and leaned back, elbows propped on the arms of his shiny new medieval chair.

"You know, when we met, I immediately had the impression that you are a very intelligent young woman," he said to Alexandra. "Also, you have a big heart. And a very good ethical sense. I did not think that you had such interesting friends already, however." He gestured toward Bobby, who was eating with stolid concentration.

"One of our greatest young poets ever, a prize-winner."

Alexandra stared at Bobby. His mouth looked pinched, but he remained silent, chewing politely.

"Are you a poet?" she asked aloud, without even wanting to. His room at Irina Georgieva's, strewn with paper, and his tales of rising early, not only to run.

"Oh, a very good poet. And a famous one," the Wizard said. The way he uttered the word "poet" made Alexandra wonder what else he knew about Bobby.

The Wizard tapped the table with large fingers. "Didn't he tell you? Last year he received our big Bulgarian prize, which is normally for old men. I don't read poetry, but the newspapers say he is quite special. He publishes in the newspapers, too, you know—poetry and many of his opinions, also. I would say he has very good contacts with some of the papers. But the prize is real, the real thing." The Wizard paused, as if to resume eating. "He even gave up a good job for his poems. He drives a taxi, but of course he is better than the rest of the taxi drivers. As a poet, anyway. Do you read poetry, Alexandra?"

Alexandra had spent five days with Bobby, almost every waking hour. She had watched him with interest, and increasingly with affection, and she prayed now that he would not stand up and punch the Wizard in the nose. A *bad* movie, that would be, armed guards erupting from the passages, the Wizard bleeding down the front of his pale-green shirt, and certainly another arrest. But Bobby was quietly examining his knife, which was not sharp, and Alexandra felt suddenly that he would always prevail over anything and anyone less than he was. He wasn't better than the other taxi drivers; he was better than everyone.

"I do read poetry," she said quickly. "Very often. In English, of course. British and American poets, and sometimes translations." She put down her fork, not looking at Bobby. "Actually, I'm trying to read all the work of every great poet in the English language, and some from other languages, too. It's taking a long time."

She stopped, breathed—why was she saying this, here, except to distract them? "Last year, I read all of Walt Whitman, Gerard Manley Hopkins, W. B. Yeats, and Dylan Thomas. And Czesław Miłosz, and a lot of Auden, although I'm not finished." Alexandra slowed as she crossed the finish line, thinking of the public library and her ragged anthologies. "I brought Emily Dickinson to Bulgaria," she added. "She took up a lot of room in my bag."

The Wizard fixed her with startled eyes. Bobby raised his face, smiling. Alexandra met Bobby's gaze, which was blue and full of suppressed admiration, and felt something fill a long-empty cavity just under her ribs. She picked up her fork again and ate. Bobby was in trouble with her for this, though—hiding his vocation when they'd had such personal conversations already. Was he genuinely that modest, she wondered, or somehow ashamed of his calling? She doubted she would ever confess to him that she'd wanted to be a writer herself.

"Very interesting," said the Wizard, after a moment. She wondered if he recognized some of those names—maybe he had studied literature at university, too. But he merely cut a large bite of his meat. "The two of you must have a lot to talk about."

"We do," said Alexandra firmly, and Bobby returned to his meal, still smiling a little.

During dessert—which the Wizard explained was called *kompot*, a stew of fruits in syrup—the Wizard talked in a genial flow about the most beautiful places to see in Bulgaria, villages she must not miss because they had been preserved from the old days, and famous monasteries. When coffee came in on the tray of the black-clothed man, she felt a rush of boldness. "If you are a guest here, who owns the house?"

The Wizard put his hands together, praying horizontally, in that gesture she'd observed when he'd been behind his desk at the police station. "Well, this is not known to the public, because it is officially said that a certain businessman from Plovdiv owns it. But that is for privacy. In fact, it belongs to a friend of mine, a minister in the government. You have probably not heard of him, because you have been here only a few days, but I assure you he is very important. His name is Mikhail Kurilkov—our Minister of Roads, a man of great integrity. And power."

Alexandra felt a jolt of blood to her head. It was true, then. She stole a look at Bobby, whose shoulders were straighter than ever. He sipped his coffee and turned his eyes here and there, apparently more interested in the room than in the ridiculous talk; but she sensed that the same shock had traveled through him, too.

The Wizard tapped his fingers together. "Mr. Kurilkov is quite possibly the only politician in our country with a perfect reputation, no image at all of corruption. He is improving our roads at a great speed, when no one else could do it, even with money from the EU. He is very important, you see, for the morale of our country, after so many problems. And he has been in politics for many years, but rising straight from the people, with a clean record."

He frowned at them. "In fact, his friends know that his first promotion came because he saved the life of someone I will not mention, in a fire. This is why his face looks as it does, above his beard, if you have ever seen him on television. He could have lost his eyesight, or his life. So his bravery also makes him different from many others. You, young lady"—inclining the dome of his forehead respectfully toward Alexandra— "come from a country with far fewer problems and much less corruption."

"Oh, I don't know about that," Alexandra said drily, although her heart was pulsing in her throat.

"We are fortunate to have such a leader, because roads are enormously important. They bring trade in and out of Bulgaria, and they bring tourists, like you. They carry our people to their work and to the seaside for their vacations. They are the foundation of all our agriculture and industry, all our economy. So—you see."

He offered them each a second cup of coffee and poured one for himself. "And I am fortunate to have such a friend—my friend for years, in fact. This house has had many important guests, now including the poet Asparuh Iliev and of course yourself. You would like Mr. Kurilkov, I am sure. I was surprised and pleased—as he will be, too—to discover that you have a connection in the same beautiful village."

He cast a glance at Bobby, who was staring at a flag above the dining room door, as if trying to decipher its damaged gilt appliqué of Cyrillic letters, which ended with an exclamation point.

The Wizard cleared his throat. "He is of the people, but also a true gentleman. I believe he even reads poetry. In fact, he has a nickname from Bulgarian folklore—the Bear. Asparuh, perhaps you know from where his name comes?"

"No, I can't say." Bobby's voice was low and calm. Alexandra had almost forgotten that he could speak.

"Well, but you must know it—the he-bear, not the she-bear—in our story of *The Wolf and the Bear*. Or perhaps it is really called *The Wolf and the—Treasure Box*? Well, I am not sure how you would translate this in English."

"The treasure chest, maybe?" suggested Alexandra. She wondered what the Wizard would say if she told him that she had a name for him, too, and that she had no idea, still, what his real name was; she had never thought to memorize the Bulgarian on the business card he had handed her.

"Maybe." The Wizard seemed suddenly to have grown a little restless, as if an invisible list of transactions had been checked off and their lunch was de facto ended. "Would you like a tour of the house?"

Alexandra agreed with mingled relief and fear —what if he locked them into a room, or hurried them out the back door to an unmarked police car? Had he really brought them here only to tell them of his connection with Kurilkov? They trailed the Wizard from floor to floor while he pointed out views from corridor windows and opened doors into bedrooms furnished with traditional simplicity. Everything looked surprisingly unpretentious, in fact, compared to the dining hall —but there was so much of it. After the tenth guest bedroom, Alexandra stopped counting. The room she liked best was a long open hall on the second floor, with a kind of extra kitchen at one end and a two-sided fireplace in the very middle, brightly new antique chairs pulled up around it. *A place for a good book,* she thought, looking out to the mountains. She wondered if the Bear sat here to read poetry.

Their host returned them to the front door with great—if distant—politeness, bowing and shaking hands as if he had already half-forgotten who they were. The costumed young Titan, shyer than ever, escorted them to the gate and let it shut behind them.

Alexandra and Bobby walked up the road without speaking until they had passed over the first hill and were just above the village again. The early afternoon was soft and clear; Alexandra could see peaks far away, on an impossibly high horizon. The sun rested hot on their shoulders and birds rose out of the fields as they passed. She wondered what it would be like to spend the rest of her life here, perhaps with Bobby, the two of them in a small stone house like the one Stoyan had put back together for Baba Yana. Both of them reading; Stoycho sleeping in front of the fire. Then she felt an aching guilt. This was what she and Jack had always said, when they were children—that they would live in a cabin together once they were grown up, somewhere out in the mountains. She slipped her right hand up her left sleeve, to feel the puckered skin beneath.

Bobby spat on the road and ran his fingers through his hair, tugging it out of shape.

"Did you—" began Alexandra.

"Give me a few minutes," he said.

Thirty-five

When they'd walked a little farther in silence, Bobby slumped down on a stone bench at the edge of the road—at least, it was a stone, if not quite a bench.

"Do you think someone made this?" Alexandra couldn't help asking, although it was not the most pressing question. She was an ideal tourist, always curious about irrelevant details.

Bobby felt the edges of the stone. "Maybe," he said. "It seems very old—it might be from a building. Probably it is a stop for the village bus now. You see the footprints around it, here." Sure enough, the ground was trampled hard in front of the stone, a crowd of phantom shoes in the dust. Bobby kicked at them.

Alexandra sat down next to him and tucked a hand under his arm. "What the *hell* was going on, at lunch?"

He groaned and stroked his hair back as if

petting a dog, except that the dog was himself.

"You're a great poet," she added, wondering. "You should have told me."

"Not great," he muttered, but he smiled sideways at her. "But you are a great reader."

"Yes." Alexandra considered this. "I'm trying, anyway." She pressed his arm, edging toward some way to punish him a little, although she wasn't yet sure how to do it. No, she would not tell him that she had once planned to be a writer. It had been so long since she'd had the urge, anyway. Alexandra shook off the thought of the notebook in her purse. "How did that man know we were here? And didn't you already know him? He was the one I talked to in Sofia, like he said, but I couldn't even catch his name. The two of you looked as if you were going to have a duel."

"A duel?" Bobby thought about the word and then nodded. "His name is Nikolai Dimchov. He's the big boss, at the station. I'm still surprised that you were permitted to see him, there." He rubbed his face again. "I used to work for him."

Alexandra digested this rather slowly. "You worked for him—how?"

"Oh, not in a terrible way. Don't look at me like that, whatever you are thinking. That is why I quit."

Alexandra took her hand off his arm. "I don't understand."

"Until last year, I was a police detective."

Alexandra thought of Bobby's fingers neatly picking a lock at Velin Monastery, the gloves he kept in his jacket pocket. The *nekrolog* for Stoyan, posted two years late on a tree in Bovech, and his words to her: *Two things are not right, here.* Or, just now, *A bus stop—you see the footprints around it.*

"I know that," she said stiffly. "I guess I've known that for a while. Well, are you spying on me? Is that why you came on this trip—because I'm a foreigner? Or did I do something wrong?" She felt heat rising up her neck. "Is it because I took the urn? You know perfectly well that I didn't mean to. I didn't know anything about those people."

"No, no, no." He sat up straight and looked her in the eye. "No, I'm not spying on you. I like you, and I'm not a detective anymore. I didn't know anything about all this, either, except that you needed help and I wanted to help you, and —yes, your situation seemed interesting, but in a personal way. I mean, a human way. I'm sorry I didn't talk with you about these things. I don't usually talk about my poems and I thought it would be better for you if I did not discuss my old job, either."

He slumped back into himself, knotty runner's arms crossed on his knees. "When I won the prize I got quite a bit of money—and I had saved a little before that, living with friends who have a house. I didn't like some things the police were doing, arresting people from demonstrations and questioning them in illegal ways, and also putting them on lists." The bitter smile. "I suppose I became a detective years ago partly to prove something to myself. But that is over for me—you cannot be an activist and a policeman at the same time. So I quit. I gave a payment on my taxi so that I could just drive instead. And write my poems."

"And then you got arrested by your old colleagues, in a demonstration or two?"

He grimaced. "Yes, I did. I saw that to reopen the mines was a terrible idea, especially because Kurilkov seems to have a lot of repressive plans about it. And I spoke at some of the demonstrations, and I also published some letters in the newspapers. Mr. Dimchov was very angry, which is interesting, because they are not his mines and I already didn't work for him anymore. They belong to a company called Zemyabit. He called me into his office—from my jail cell—and told me that he was angry because I had been so recently a police officer and I had made a scandal for the station. He said they would let me out this time but that he did not want to see me make a second mistake—if I did, he would uncover some other way to arrest me."

Alexandra scanned Bobby's face. "And then

he found you with me—how? You didn't go into the police station with me, in Sofia. But I did get into your taxi, near the station."

"He has my identity card on file, of course, and my license," Bobby said.

"Also, a policeman inspected your papers when we stopped at that bridge."

He gave her another look, which could have been admiration, again. "Yes, that might be it. Maybe he invited us for lunch to make sure I understand that he is watching. He is serious, I'm certain, and he is a brutal person. Sometimes he uses his position to have people beaten while they are questioned, and he can make it all legal enough so that there is no publicity. I do not like at all that he is a friend of Kurilkov—the Bear. I am not surprised that they are friends, but I think it is strange that he told us that so directly, especially after we saw Kurilkov on the road yesterday."

"I know," Alexandra said.

Bobby damaged more of the footprints with his sneaker. "And I do not like the fact that Dimchov is concerned about me still. It is already more than six months since I was in that demonstration. But they never forget. I am afraid I am the one putting you in danger. Maybe putting the Lazarovi in danger also."

Alexandra looked around. The afternoon lay over fields of gently colored hay and the road stretched brown below them. The mountains seemed to be dozing, gray and green.

"Maybe he's not paying attention to you," she said haltingly, "but more to me. Even if he probably knew that you would come with me to lunch." He was listening with his elbows on his knees, his smooth face with the dark moles in one corner turned toward her, unselfconscious. She wondered if she would ever become as alert and confident a person as he was. Probably if you even wondered about how to be like that, it was a state you could never attain.

"Paying attention more to you?" he said, frowning.

"Not exactly to me. But something related to me. You know—" She groped for the farthest distance of those ridges, where one peak showed as broken rock emerging from the forest. "First, he's very interested in the urn. Like it said in the graffiti in Vera's house—someone knows something about it. And before that, we were told to give it back."

He let her speak, his eyes blue and intense.

"He must be paying attention to Stoyan Lazarov." She had dropped her voice. "We know he is interested in Stoyan's family, because the urn belongs to them. If Mr. Dimchov is watching us somehow, or following us, then he will know when we find them."

"If we find them," amended Bobby.

"Well, we have to." Alexandra was tempted to beat her fists on the stone. "And we don't know why he would even want somebody's ashes. Now I *really* don't want to give the urn to him. The strange thing is, if we take it to the Lazarovi, and he follows us to get it, he will get it back slowly when he could have had it more quickly at any time—I mean, by taking it away from us. He could have gotten it from us right here, in the village. So maybe he wants to find *them,* but without doing it himself, too obviously. Or maybe he simply has not been able to find them, either."

Bobby was shaking his head, but it seemed to be in agreement, this time. "And maybe he is warning us not to *fail*. But also to be careful. You should have my old job," he said. "I will tell Mr. Dimchov to hire you."

"What if Vera and Neven are already in some trouble with the police, maybe worse than you?" Alexandra clutched his arm again. "What if we are the only people who know they are being followed, because the police are following us following them?"

"Then we would have to warn them. But probably they know that themselves. After all, they do not answer their phone calls. Unless something has already happened to them."

Alexandra suddenly had a sense that it was all too dramatic. "I feel silly, making this up."

"I don't know," he said. "Something really is

strange. We keep receiving graffiti, even blood, and then Mr. Dimchov finds us up here and invites us, but does not try to get the urn from us. Possibly he wants to warn us about something, o keep us out of bigger trouble. Although he does not like me. And why is Kurilkov somehow in this?"

"I have been thinking—you remember when we were locked into that room at Velin Monastery?" She realized with surprise that this had happened only days before.

"Yes. Someone came in, and we never knew who." Bobby tapped her arm. "I have thought about that, too. But if it was someone from the police, they followed us to Velin immediately, very fast, after you were at the station in Sofia. Although I suppose the station could have called the police at the monastery. And they only scared us—they didn't follow us to the parking lot and try to take the urn."

"Who would care about an old dead man?" Alexandra said harshly, to hear it aloud. She could not imagine giving Stoyan up to anyone, except to Neven. She wanted Neven to appear on the road below them, to hurry toward them in his formal clothes. She clenched her fists on the rock so that she wouldn't imagine running to meet him. Then she remembered that she might already have endangered him in some way she couldn't understand.

"There are too many questions," Bobby said. "Too many we cannot answer yet, although we will when we can. The more important thing is to decide what to do."

"Should we tell Irina Georgieva?" Alexandra thought of Irina's fatigue after the trip through the mountains, her twisted hands on the blankets.

Bobby rubbed the side of his face. "I think we must. She might know something that could explain this better. Even if she does not, we should give her every possible piece of information. I still do not like to leave her at all, in Plovdiv, but how could we take her to Sofia with us? I don't know what we would do with her there."

"She will be so worried," Alexandra said sadly. "And their house here has already been vandalized, all because of me. It doesn't seem fair."

"It is not your fault." Bobby leaned over and kissed her suddenly on the ear. "What a kind person you are."

"I like her," Alexandra murmured, but she was pleased. They got up and started down the road, slowly, postponing for a moment the return to Irina and explanations. Bobby kept his hands jammed into his pockets. After a while Alexandra said, "The fairy tale about a bear—do you know it?"

"Everybody knows some version of it," Bobby said. "It was in my schoolbooks, when we were in the third or fourth class. I think it's a very old story, but I don't remember it well. You need someone who is a good storyteller for that."

"And you're just a poet?" Alexandra said, smiling at him.

"Yes," Bobby said.

"Would Baba Yana know it?"

"Probably," he said.

Alexandra threaded her arm through his. "It would give us an excuse to talk to her again before we leave."

Thirty-six

The Wolf and the Bear, *that's one I used to tell my children when they were little,* said Baba Yana. *It's not about Baba Metsa, the She-Bear— they liked that one even better.* But it's a good one. My grandfather told it to us, right here, while the Turks still owned our land, and he said even then that it was a very old story, so you can be sure it is. There was a Bear, you see, who was the strongest and fiercest of all the animals when Bulgaria was young. He was so big and so tall that you could see him walking over the mountains, and he roared like this—*aaaarrr.* That's the part where my children liked to scream, and my grandchildren, later. Everyone was afraid of this Bear because of his strength and his size. They said he could eat a sheep or a little girl in one swallow. The Bear wandered around the country-side and everybody stayed far away from him.

At the same time, there was a Wolf, who was big and strong but not as big as the Bear. But the Wolf was very smart, and one day he came into a village not so far from here, and he said to the villagers, "If you make me your Tsar, I will protect you from the Bear. Not only that, but I will get back all the sheep and goats that other wolves have stolen from you, shame on them, and give them out to everyone in the village."

The villagers were a little afraid of the Wolf, but they all wanted their livestock back, so they agreed. And the Wolf ruled over the village, and many other villages, and he brought back not only the sheep and goats that had been lost, but many others that he stole from rich farms and gave to the poor villagers. The villagers were happy and they did not ask any questions about where all the food came from. Sometimes people came from other farms and villages, angry, and tried to attack their village, but the Wolf drove them off and kept the village safe.

Now, the Wolf had a young maiden to sweep his house and cook his meals and she was beautiful enough to be a bride of Heaven. When the Wolf had ruled over the village for some years, he said to this maiden that he had to go on a journey and that she must keep everything in order and not look into the chamber under the hearthstone, where he kept his treasure box, and not let anyone into the house while he was gone. Then he went away, without saying when he would come back. She had not known there was any chamber under the hearthstone or that he had any treasure, but she agreed to his orders.

For three days, the girl cleaned the house and cooked up good food for the Wolf's return, and she did not open the house to anyone or touch the hearthstone. But he did not come back. Then she became so curious that she couldn't help herself, you know, and she locked the door to the house and carefully lifted the hearthstone, which was very light. *Give me my other sweater, there, sweet ones—the sun is starting to get lower and I take a chill at this hour.*

So she moved the hearthstone and she saw in the opening beneath it a flight of stairs. She went down these stairs and at the bottom was a chamber with a great big box in it. She was even more curious, but when she opened the box, she found it filled with the bones of the men from other villages whose sheep and goats the Wolf had stolen to give to his own villagers. The Wolf had apparently killed them to take what they had. It was a terrible sight, and the girl ran back up the stairs and quickly put the hearthstone back into place.

The next day, while she was sweeping the

floors, there came a knock at the door. Looking out, she saw the huge Bear, whom she had heard about but never laid eyes on, and she was very frightened.

"Girl, let me come in and warm myself by the fire," the Bear said through the window.

"I dare not," said the maiden. "Besides, the Wolf who lives here told me not to open the door to anyone."

"But I am not just anyone," the Bear said.

She would not open the door, and he went away quietly.

The next day he knocked again. "Girl, let me come in and warm myself by the fire," he said through the window.

"I dare not," said the maiden. "The Wolf has given me orders. Besides, if I let you in, you will eat me."

"I have not eaten anyone here, or you would have heard of it," the Bear said. But she would not let him in.

The third day the Wolf had still not returned, and now it had been six whole days—and the Bear knocked at the door again. "Let me in, girl," he said. "I only want to warm myself by the fire."

She could resist no longer and she let him come in and sit down by the fire. He was so quiet and like a gentleman that, little by little, she stopped being afraid and gave him some soup.

After he had eaten, he said, "This is a nice house, but it's very small for two people."

"Oh, it's not so small," said she, bridling a little. "There's even a big chamber under the hearthstone, where the Wolf keeps his treasure box." Then she wished she had said nothing.

"What treasure would a wolf have?" the Bear asked her.

"A treasure nobody would want," said the girl, shuddering.

The Bear looked at her with his little eyes and he said, "Then I would not want to see it either."

He went away and met the Wolf coming over the hills. They had never met before, but each had heard of the other.

The Bear said, "I have been to your house and I hear, Brother, that you have a treasure only a Wolf would want."

Then the Wolf was very angry, because he knew that the maiden had looked under the hearthstone and had let the Bear into the house. But the Bear said, "Don't worry, Brother—I did not look at your treasure, and I do not know anything else about it." The Wolf didn't dare to fight the Bear, who was bigger than he was, so he left him and went back to his house. The Bear followed him disguised as a great bird.

Soon enough, the Wolf went into his house and he said to the maiden, "While I was gone, you looked at my treasure and you opened the door to a stranger, so now I shall kill you." But he had left the door open behind him, and the Bear flew into the house and struck him dead.

Then the Bear in his own shape said to the girl, "Leave this place and do not tell anyone about the treasure. Now I am Tsar in place of the Wolf, but I will never look at the treasure box and I do not want to know what is in it. And you must never tell anyone about it."

The maiden left and wandered far and wide, while the Bear settled down and ruled the village as Tsar. He was kind and just. The villagers did not have as much to eat as before, because the Bear did not take food from other villages. But they lived in peace.

Meanwhile, the maiden went into faraway lands. A prince saw her and fell in love with her and they were married. She lived in a palace and slept on a featherbed. But she could not forget the Wolf or the Bear or the secret she had to keep, and she longed to tell someone. She did not dare to tell her husband. Finally she decided that it would hurt nothing if she whispered it into a hole in the ground. She went out into the forests of her new land and found a little hole in the earth. She lay down and whispered into it that under the Bear's hearthstone lay a treasure that even he had never seen. Then she was relieved of her secret and went back to her palace and her husband.

But under the earth was water, and the water carried the secret to the rivers and the wind found it on the surface of the rivers and blew it far away into the village of the Bear, and the villagers heard what it said. Then they thought that the Bear had been keeping a great treasure from them, while they did not have all that much for themselves. They went to the Bear and demanded to see it.

The Bear calmed them, saying, "If I have any treasure, may you take it all from me, as is only fair." So the villagers went into the house, and they pulled up the hearthstone and went down into the chamber. There they found a big box, but it was empty and clean. The Bear's goodness and strength had dissolved all the Wolf's wickedness without his even seeing what was in the box.

There is another version of this story in which a Dog comes to the village and digs up the bones and scatters them on the ground, but I don't know that one. And I have always wondered, myself, if the Bear simply took all the bones of the dead and hid them somewhere else. *Will you bring me some water, dear ones? Milena, my grand-daughter, will be here to make my dinner soon. She's pretty old, poor thing, so it takes her a while to get up here. You won't stay? My loves, goodbye and take care of yourselves—you, girl, don't sit on any more of those cold stones. I told you not to!*

Thirty-seven

Irina was better. Another neighbor had driven her and Lenka and the bag with the urn back down to their own house; Bobby and Alexandra found them in the kitchen, Irina drinking tea with her thumbs wrapped around the cup. When they came in, she looked up, her eyes full of questions. Stoycho lay on the floor beside the table, clearly in Lenka's good graces. He got to his feet and sniffed their shoes, licked Alexandra's hand, and lay down again. Bobby slumped onto the bench next to her and Lenka brought them cups of tea, which smelled of the hay and grasses outside. There were questions in her eyes, too.

"How was your lunch?" Irina said. Reluctantly, they told her everything, and the alarm in her face grew. She touched the brooch at her breastbone, as if for solace. Alexandra sat looking into the steaming cup—troubled, too, but by something else. What was it? It pulled at her. She had seen and not understood. Seen.

"If you are ready, I will bring the car," said Bobby. "We must get you home as soon as possible."

Irina sighed. "Thank you, dear. I hope that we can reach my sister, to tell her not to come back here soon. Unless she knows already not to. Yes, do bring your car. The urn is in the cupboard—will you get it, Alexandra?"

Alexandra opened a worn wooden door and lifted out the bag. It was heavy again in her hands and she felt a shift in her vision, a memory. "Wait, please," she said. "Bobby—Madame Georgieva, may I open this again? Just the bag, I mean."

They stared at her, but she set it on the table and worked at the zipper, peeled back the velvet inside. She touched the carving around the top of the polished box: a wreath, or a vine, with the face of an animal on each side, two faces, different from each other.

Bobby looked thoughtful. "These leaves," he said. "I think they are *zdravets*."

Irina leaned forward to see them better. "I believe you are right." She turned to Alexandra. "It is one of our national symbols. A very famous plant—the name comes from the word for health. I have always loved it because it is quite fragrant. You must have seen it in many places already. There are *zdravets* in my garden in Plovdiv, in fact."

"But the animals," Alexandra said. "Maybe this is just on my mind because of Baba Yana's story." A chill had come over her arms and neck. "That animal, the face in the leaves—I think that's a bear. Here—" She turned the urn slowly around. "This is not a cat, or a fox, on the other side.

371

That could be the Bear and this could be the Wolf."

Bobby was on his feet again, carefully turning the urn. He said nothing, but Alexandra saw the intensity of his gaze.

Irina looked puzzled. "From the fairy tale?" she said.

But Bobby did not seem to be listening. He had put both hands around the urn now—Alexandra flinched—and was lifting it carefully out of the velvet, looking at the carvings. "It is signed here," he said. "I didn't see that before."

"I didn't either," said Alexandra. "It looks like an *A*—two *A*'s, very small. Someone made this by hand."

"Show that to me," Irina said. They tipped the urn with care under her eyes—the two fine letters, almost hidden in the Wolf's carved ruff. "You may put it down," she said after a moment.

"Do you know this signature?" Bobby was still peering at it.

"I do," the old woman said. "I have a friend who signs this way, an artist. He was also a good friend of Stoyan's. His name is Atanas Angelov. Perhaps Vera asked him to make it—I have not heard anything about it, before this."

Bobby sat with his elbows on the table. "Do you think he would know who wants it, or why?"

Irina gestured helplessly with a big hand. "I have no idea. I wish that I could call him, but I do not have a phone number, not with me. In fact,

I haven't seen him in several years—he lives in the mountains almost two hours from here. We would have to drive there before we go back to Plovdiv."

"Which direction?" Bobby said.

"The wrong one," Irina told them. "We will have to go quickly."

The mountain roads took them down into the bigger town again, then up into a higher range, and finally along a narrow valley surrounded by green-black peaks. It was already late afternoon. Alexandra had begun to feel carsick, and also to come down with what she thought of as mountain sadness. The drive up to Gorno the day before had been so riddled with novelty that she had managed it better. But now the thought of Jack rose with her stomach until she could hardly swallow. He had disappeared among ridges not so different from these. He had ruined mountains everywhere for her. Her heart would always be ill from it, her gorge rising. Had he fallen down some steep slope like that one just above them? If so, he had fallen far from all roads, where his bones could become one more statistic: on average, two point five hikers per year in the National Forest, missing, inconclusive. Search suspended. At the word *bones* she began to jerk the leash of her mind: down, stop, not now. She gripped Stoycho's neck and tucked her feet around the urn in the bag, to keep it upright. She thought of the unknown man, his long life, his music. And he remained unburied.

"I believe our turn is here," Irina said, touching Bobby's shoulder. There was a little sign in Cyrillic and English, at the edge of the road.

"What does that mean—'Irkad'?" Bobby wanted to know. The sign said that Irkad was two kilometers away, a turn to the right.

"I think it is a very old name, probably Turkish," Irina told him. "We will ask Angelov."

Alexandra looked around for a village but saw only a cluster of houses with the same slate roofs, and a high stone wall. The place was so small it hardly seemed to justify its name.

"Please stop here, Asparuh," Irina said, rapping his shoulder.

They parked in front of a great pair of gates with iron handles, set into the wall. Bobby got out, stood staring, and then pulled the rope that hung down beside the gates. There was no address, no numbered sign. After a few seconds, somebody opened to them; Bobby drove the car up a ramp of worn stones and into a large courtyard. They all climbed out—Alexandra helping Stoycho, Lenka helping the old woman. The stone and stucco and wood building around them reminded Alexandra of Velinski *manastir*—partly because of its courtyard, but also because the second story had a long roofed gallery. In places the stucco had fallen off, revealing what looked like ancient hay under-neath. The courtyard itself was neatly swept, boxes of flowers sitting under the windows.

The man who had opened the gates was talking with Bobby, and after a moment he turned to Irina and kissed her on both cheeks. He might have been in his fifties, dressed in an old sweater, worn woolen pants, and rubber shoes. Bits of straw dusted all his clothes, as if he'd been mucking out a stable. His face was delicate and deeply browned, his short hair turning silver around the temples; Alexandra marveled again at a country apparently full of beautiful people. While she stood staring, the man shook hands with her and Lenka. He squatted in front of Stoycho and spoke to him. Stoycho sat beside Alexandra and listened to this man without growling, then allowed him to scratch his head. The man beckoned Stoycho to a water tap at the edge of the courtyard; the faucet was brass and set into a wall carved with letters that looked like Arabic. It had a marble basin beneath it that Alexandra thought must be very old. The man ran water into the basin and Stoycho drank greedily. The man looked up and said something to the rest of them, laughing, so that wrinkles came to life all around his eyes.

"He tells us that we didn't bring horses, like in the old days, but at least we did bring a dog,"

Bobby interpreted for Alexandra. "This is an interesting place, Bird. He says this was the *han*, the inn for travelers in this part of the mountains, almost four hundred years old. That is why there is a big gate, to drive in the horses and the wagons."

"Is this where the artist lives?" she asked.

"I believe so. I think this is his son. He says we can go in to see him. I will leave Stoycho out here. Just bring the urn."

The man in muddy boots took one of Irina's arms and Lenka took the other, and they went through more wooden doors. As they entered, Alexandra felt the urge to gasp; it was a large low space with wood-framed windows along one wall, and it seemed to hang over the valley below. She hadn't realized that this side of the village sat on a precipice. Out the windows was a long, long view: green mountains and miniature stone houses in the deeps, the march of enormous spruces along a range to the left, and on a far horizon the highest peaks she'd seen yet, bursting with sharp rocks—a land that looked nearly untouched by history, a Grimms' fairy tale setting in Alexandra's eyes. The room was lit by early evening sun. Along the windows sat benches and a table. On the floor lay a woolen rug of reds and greens in matted tufts, as if it had been pulled directly off some brightly colored animal. On the walls hung more wool, woven in geometric patterns, and faded pieces of embroidery.

Suddenly an old man rose from one of the benches. He had been in shadow; Alexandra hadn't seen him.

"*Irinche!*" he exclaimed, and there followed a great deal of kissing on both cheeks, including Alexandra's. The man from the courtyard had taken off his rubber shoes and was walking around in knitted red and gray socks, like a little boy. He settled Irina Georgieva near his father and she drew Alexandra toward her. With Bobby to interpret, Irina told the old man about her, although she didn't mention the urn.

"And this, darling, is Atanas Angelov," she added. It seemed to Alexandra that Irina uttered his name as one might say "Albert Einstein" or "Mohandas K. Gandhi." The old man shook his head in approval and gripped Alexandra's hand for a few long seconds. His own hands were large and looked strong, but Alexandra saw that his fingers were strangely worn down, almost as if they'd been sawn off at the tips. He was brown from weather, like his son, and his hair was sparse and completely white, with a pair of heavy plastic glasses perched on it. He was smiling at them, but whenever his face relaxed it fell into lines of a permanent sadness.

"Is he her cousin or something?" she whispered to Bobby, as soon as there was a chance.

"I don't think so," he said. "I think this man is a friend, an old friend, and he has bought some of her paintings, over the years." (*Old lover?* wondered Alexandra, and looked away.)

Bobby listened for a moment, the blue of his eyes fixed on the faces before them. "She calls him Nasko, his nickname—I think they are very fond of each other. He is a painter, too. Sometimes they traded their paintings or worked together. They have not seen each other for several years, as Irina said." He listened. "His wife is dead, five years ago, and he has written a book of poems about her that was published in Plovdiv last month. Irina congratulates him."

Bobby turned to Alexandra, and to her surprise she saw his eyes were glazed with tears. "He says that his wife was the whole universe for him."

She squeezed his shoulder. "Bobby, you have a heart," she said.

He looked stern. "Did you doubt that?"

"I didn't mean it that way," Alexandra said, shamefaced. "I only meant that I like your heart."

"You are the one who saves wild dogs," he told her a little sourly, and wiped his eyes.

Irina was leaning toward them. "My dears," she said. "This friend taught me much of what I know about painting. And he is still a great artist. Also, he is more intelligent than I am, so he chooses to paint only people. He always tells me that I have no real focus, but he likes my animals."

After a few minutes, a middle-aged woman in a tracksuit and a flowered apron brought them a tray that held glasses, a bottle of clear liquid, and a plate of sliced white cheese and salami.

Atanas Angelov poured for them all and raised his own glass to make a toast. "*Nazdrave!*" Angelov's glass made its way clinking around the circle, and when he reached Alexandra he bowed from the waist.

"To health," Bobby explained. The liquid went down with a severe burn; Alexandra coughed. "Don't!" Bobby said. "This is *rakiya*, grape brandy. Like at lunch today. You take just a little, then a little more."

After that she sipped, and the walls of the room relaxed around her. Irina's red-rimmed eyes were shining. Soon dinner dishes came in, carried by the woman in the tracksuit and the son in his socks. Alexandra felt that she had never before been part of such a charmed circle—these people, strangers, greeting her as a long-awaited guest, the old artist presiding as if nothing had pleased him this much in years. She wondered when they could ask him about the urn. The artist put Alexandra at his right hand, with Bobby beside her, and sat questioning Bobby about something. She caught the word *taksi*, and also *ecologiya*.

Irina, perhaps sensing Alexandra's alcoholic drift in a sea of Bulgarian, brought the conversation to a halt. "Now! *Gospodin* Angelov is not only a great painter, but also a great reader of people. Nasko—" she raised her forefinger in the old man's direction—"tell me what you see in this young woman. When you look at her."

Angelov set down his fork and turned to Alexandra. He sat forward and lowered his glasses on his nose. He gazed into her face for several long seconds, almost close enough to kiss her. Alexandra held her breath, in case.

"Beautiful, of course," he said.

She hadn't understood that he spoke any English. But he switched back to Bulgarian at once and Irina interpreted for him, magisterially. His eyes were brown and soft, with a sheen like fine wood.

"Sweet-natured," he said, "but impatient under that. Gentle, but capable of—causing great harm, if she is not careful. Unintentional harm. Sometimes very sad." Alexandra held his gaze as well as she could. "Young for a person of her years, although also wise from sorrow." Irina nodded.

Angelov put up a finger and touched Alexandra's forehead. "Always thinking. Thinking too much, and then sometimes not enough. You read a lot of books, yes? Soon you will learn from other sources, the real springs of life. And you will live to be very old."

Then the painter gave Alexandra a hearty kiss on the forehead, where his hand had been. She could feel the dryness of his lips. "A mountain of contradictions."

Alexandra tried not to give way to her discomfort, or at least not to show it. How had he known that she was secretly an agent of damage, that she had already caused great harm? She had hoped for something very different—the detection of genius, for example, or the prediction of a magnificent future. She felt Bobby smiling, his ironic twitch.

"*Gospodin*—" She hesitated. "*Gospodin* Atanas, could you look at my friend's face and tell us what you see there, too?"

Bobby grinned at her but sat still under the artist's gaze.

"Translate for me, Bobby," Alexandra said wickedly.

Atanas Angelov was leaning forward in his chair, staring hard, fists on knees. He could have been in his studio, Alexandra thought, before a model and a canvas. The rest of the room seemed to have faded from his view.

"*Da, interesno*," he said at last. Then he added a lot else, in Bulgarian.

"Bobby, tell me," prompted Alexandra.

Bobby reddened a little. "He says that my face is an unusual one. Slavic, not Bulgar, whatever that means. The face of—a revolutionary. Under that"—he shifted on the bench—"the face of a lover. A lover of life, not people. A philosopher.

Complicated." He quoted then: *" 'He will never belong to any woman.' "*

Bobby did not meet her eyes, but he fixed Angelov unflinchingly. *" 'His fate—well—' "* Bobby paused, and Alexandra saw that Angelov himself had looked away. "He says, *'Not everyone has good fortune. But he will leave a mark.' "*

Alexandra regretted her request. It was better, she thought, to be told one was to be a long-lived mountain of contradictions than to receive such an ambiguous sentence. She stroked Bobby's upper arm, uninvited, left her fingers there.

"Nasko," said Irina. "Do stop. You're scaring the children. Look at them."

Angelov clapped his hands. "Sorry! Sorry!" he said in English. "Old men—me—" He gestured helplessly, humorously. "Stupid. Now we will eat."

After the meal, Angelov brought them into his studio. It was on the second floor, so that the view was even more stupendous; Alexandra wondered how he could stand there painting people all day with his back turned to those vistas. She saw a canvas in progress, facing a low pedestal for a model. With a little shock, she realized that the woman half-painted before them was unmistakably the one who had served them their dinner and the *rakiya*, but without her red tracksuit or apron or any clothes at all. A

382

table held a rack of tools and several small wooden carvings of human figures. Along the walls she saw other canvases propped, some of Angelov's son—the younger man was dressed in most of them but casually naked in a few, hands on hips, looking at the floor as if absentminded about his own body.

"Will you be volunteering?" Bobby murmured.

"No," she said, but part of her wished, perversely, to stand in that crystalline mountain light and feel the artist study her, breast and flank, with his soft, objective eyes. A couple of Irina's paintings were here, including a bony rhinoceros. Angelov pointed it out with obvious admiration and Bobby explained: "He says she is the best of their generation, and she says he is the best of their generation. A perfect exchange of compli-ments."

Atanas Angelov cleared a table and set four chairs around it, then helped Irina into one of them and motioned for Bobby and Alexandra to sit down. After a moment's hesitation, she put the bag with the urn on the floor beside her, and thought she saw Angelov glance at it.

"My dear," Irina said, putting an old thin hand over Alexandra's young thin one. "You asked me about Stoyan, and Mr. Angelov is going to tell you some things. I have explained to him now what it is you carry and how we came to meet. Unfortunately, he has heard nothing from my sister or Neven—I have already asked him."

Alexandra felt her heart sink. Perhaps, she thought, she'd hoped for news more than she'd admitted even to herself.

Irina pointed. "Asparuh will translate for you," she said to Atanas Angelov.

Angelov rubbed a hand over his face. Alexandra saw again that the ends of the fingers were hideously worn down, stubby, the knuckles swollen.

"Stoyan Lazarov," he said. He nodded to Bobby, waiting for him to interpret. "Stoyan was one of the people I loved best."

He paused again. "You see, I met him many years ago, when we were both young and in very difficult circumstances. Then I didn't see him for a long time, and then later he found me through one of my paintings and came to visit me and meet my wife. Each of us had thought that the other was dead, so we were enormously happy to be reunited. He was ill and tired, and when he had a short time off work, he asked me if he could stay with us. It was a large request—I cannot explain to you why, just now—but I said yes, and now I am very glad that I did so. It must have been in the late 1960s. I used to know the year exactly. Write down a good record, you young people. It becomes easy to forget." He shook his head.

"In any case, Stoyan came to us for a couple of weeks. We were still young enough to stay up talking and drinking half the night, and then go to work—or practice music—first thing in the morning. I had already been living here for a few years, working at the parts factory in the valley. But at night I painted, even if I could not exhibit much."

Why couldn't you exhibit? Alexandra wanted to ask.

"Stoyan's hands were not well, after some farm work he had been doing out in the country that year. But he was healing them, and he began to play again while he was here. He told me that for the first week he would play only Bach—he said that was for him both the greatest exercise and the greatest medicine."

Atanas cradled his damaged fingers on the table. "But I understood that he was beginning to recover when he started playing Vivaldi again. People did not know Vivaldi's music so much, when we were young, but Stoyan loved it and talked about it often. He would stand in the middle of my studio and play his music while I worked. He could make his violin laugh, but mostly he made it weep. I believe he slept with his violin case under his hand—he always seemed worried that someone would take it away from him. I painted him with his instrument. His face was terrible sometimes, sad, much older than his age, which was forty-and-some."

"He was born in 1915," Alexandra said. "So he must have been in his early fifties then, right?"

"Yes—I suppose so." Angelov folded his worn fingers under his chin. "Yes. One night we sat up very late, and he told me for the first time many things about his music. He told me about the moment he decided to become a violinist—he was only six years old, already taking lessons in Sofia, and his father took him to a concert, some Beethoven. When he heard the violinists begin to play, Stoyan said, he saw stars in the air, above their heads, and he wanted a star for himself. He smiled when he said this, but bitterly. He told me about his studies in Vienna, where he played for fine teachers and great audiences. He said that he felt his life since then had been a series of traps, smaller and smaller, until he had only music left, and his love for his wife and son. I will leave the story of my life in my music, he said."

Alexandra nodded. It was a sentiment she had come to recognize, and it made her feel even sadder for Stoyan Lazarov.

"Then he told me about some things I had not known, a lot of things," Angelov said, "about the moment his life changed the most. He was too honest to be a really good storyteller, but he made me see everything through his eyes. In fact, I think sometimes that I remember these parts of his life better than I do some of my own."

He fell quiet for a little. "I am surprised that I find myself talking with you about this. Irina told me that you want to know more about him, and she is my very old friend. In those days, it was dangerous to tell people certain things, but he and I had every reason to trust each other."

Angelov sighed. "Stoyan had thick hair that grew too fast, and a beard that grew too fast—he was always shaving and trimming, trying to stay neat. I cut his hair for him that evening, outside, in a chair, and he started telling me. We watched the sun go down. Later, he kept talking, rubbing his new short haircut, like this, with both hands. And we ended up talking all night."

He turned to Irina, and Alexandra saw that tears were trickling down his brown face, like cracks in mud.

"Oh, I'm sorry," he said. "How did we get so old, my dear? With everybody gone?"

Thirty-eight

This happened in October 1949, five years after the Revolution and three months after the death of the first communist leader, Georgi Dimitrov. There was music in the streets of Sofia that morning.

Strangely for him, Stoyan couldn't remember later where the music had come from: a military band? Or merely a radio tuned to a military band, in some open-doored shop? His morning orchestra rehearsal was supposed to start at nine. There was a feeling of hurry in the streets, people quieter than usual and in a rush, as if the city itself was nervous. The trees curled over the promenades and dropped leaves with that mild-mannered brown of the Sofia autumn.

That morning the orchestra was to rehearse a Mozart symphony—No. 40, G Minor, a work he already knew almost by heart—this detail he did remember easily, years after. In the evening, his quartet would sit down to read a couple of works they hadn't attempted before. Stoyan carried his jacket, although the air was warm and the sun was full; it would be cold inside the hall and he liked to keep his arm muscles limber. He could see a young policeman standing at the corner, chatting with a boy in civilian clothes. This was Stoyan's favorite kind of morning; there was a smell almost like autumn in Vienna creeping into the streets from the parks, and a blend of sound he had known since childhood: the crash of something heavy being unloaded at the curb, a shout, the blast of an automobile horn, the creak of metal-rimmed wooden wheels, the hollow clop of hooves on cobbles, two old women on the corner talking loudly.

At the door of the theater, he left the sunlight and went into gloom and that smell of must and chalk that had mingled for him with rehearsals, these many years. It was the same scent as that of the hall in Vienna where the Academy orchestra had always rehearsed, and even of the Vienna Philharmonic. Perhaps every rehearsal in the world smelled like this. He found the orchestra half-gathered onstage, unpacking instruments, one of the clarinetists finishing a greasy stub of *banitsa* with cheese crumbling out of it, wiping his hands on a handkerchief before he touched his instrument case. Mitko Samokovski, the conductor, had already arrived and was directing the flutists to rearrange some chairs at the back. They shared the hall with other productions—the opera, sometimes a play—and everything was always in the wrong spot.

Stoyan sat down in the second-chair place with his violin case across his knees and looked up for a moment at the rows of curtains above, the familiar lack of light, lack of sky, the worn raspberry-colored velvet from the end of the previous century. He cracked his neck, then his shoulders—long habit, relief. He watched Samokovski searching in tight-stretched vest pockets for something or other, something he appeared never to find. In fact, everyone watched him before rehearsal, to see what sort of mood he was in. After several years of working under him, Stoyan hated the man. Samokovski was given to sudden rages at the first violin section; Stoyan particularly disliked his way of lowering the baton, rapping, evoking instant silence, then glaring without speaking as an extra measure of humiliation for whoever had missed a note. The conductor was a good example, Stoyan often thought, of someone who would never have gotten this job before the war; his tyranny of the orchestra was hardly justified by musical prowess. Stoyan remembered Bruno Walter in Vienna, the passionate face and quick ability to teach a musician anything on the spot; Walter had been driven out by the Nazis, along with the brilliant Jewish musicians in the Academy itself. But the Nazis had been destroyed, long since. If Bulgaria had opened her borders for citizens to travel after the war, he and Vera could have gone straight back to Austria. And in Vienna he would have played forever under such conductors, not for people like this scowling, second-rate egotist.

Lately, Samokovski had looked even more harassed than usual, his hair a sideways wreck. A rumor had circulated among the musicians that their conductor had recently been questioned by the police. "Or he reports to them, maybe?" Velizar Gishev had muttered. Gishev was the first chair of the orchestra, the concertmaster, second in importance only to Samokovski himself. No one hated the conductor more than Gishev, who had been Samokovski's particular target for the last two years, although—or perhaps because—he was one of the best musicians in the orchestra. Stoyan had to admit that Velizar Gishev was at least technically as good as he was himself, even if he was a peacock. He, Stoyan, should be the first chair. But Gishev was hellishly good, trained in Europe like himself, but in Paris. Stoyan could not have held together his quartet without Gishev's energetic playing and nearly perfect intonation.

The musicians were testing notes, plucking strings, screwing together pieces of instruments and then adjusting them with a delicate backward twist. One of the cellists left the stage to struggle with a window at the side of the hall, propping it up with a block of wood and startling a pigeon just outside. Samokovski rapped for order and they opened their bound scores of the Mozart.

They were starting not only on time, Stoyan noted, but a little early, and Gishev's seat next to him was still empty. Velizar always arrived at the last second, as if to spite the conductor. Stoyan had a brief fantasy of slipping over into the first chair, where he belonged anyway. If Velizar ever left the orchestra, Stoyan would certainly be promoted to his place, unless the conductor chose to bring in someone else. Which would be like him; Samokovski disliked Stoyan as well—in fact, he seemed to distrust all foreign-trained musicians.

Stoyan stayed where he was, but after the oboe had given the A, he led the violin section in their tuning. The other violinists glanced around, and then began to tune.

Suddenly Samokovski rapped on the edge of

his stand, and the tuning sprang to a discordant close. His face looked bleached and his free hand fiddled with a vest pocket. "Where is Comrade Gishev?"

No one spoke.

"Well, where is he?"

Samokovski looked straight at Stoyan. "Comrade Lazarov, is it true that you would prefer to be concertmaster yourself?"

What could he say?

"Well?" Samokovski searched his vest with a hand like a big grub.

Stoyan tried to sound easy, humorous, something he knew had never been his strong suit. "Comrade Conductor, doesn't every second chair in the world wish to be first?" There was an appreciative snicker somewhere behind him.

But it was as if he and the conductor were alone in the hall, and now Stoyan could see sweat dribbling from under the matted gray hair at Samokovski's temples.

The conductor raised a forefinger toward the proscenium. "I understand you said as much to your colleagues in a smoking break, just the other day?"

Stoyan felt the presence of something out of sight, as if he stood among dark trees—as if he had heard the crack of a twig. "The other day?"

"Well?"

It was true. He had said to two of the cellists, in

a misanthropic private moment, that not every-one with permission to sit in the concertmaster's chair would use the position so arrogantly. Earlier that same day, Gishev had leaned over in the middle of a movement—Beethoven—and pointed to their shared score, as if Stoyan had lost his place. Which he certainly hadn't. And later Stoyan had been smoking with the cellists and had said this thing, bitterly, implying Velizar's vanity and perhaps unworthiness. But who had repeated it to the conductor? And why would anyone bother? The whole orchestra knew already, with the accuracy of Byzantine courtiers, who resented whom.

Samokovski cleared his throat, harshly. "And is it also true that Comrade Gishev has spoken disrespectfully of his conductor, and of the People's Republic of Bulgaria?"

There was motionless silence among the ranks of musicians. Stoyan knew, and knew that everyone else knew, that the first part of the accusation, at least, was true.

"Well? Comrade? Did Gishev speak this way or did he not? Or should I perhaps ask what you have said about me yourself?"

Everyone sat frozen. Stoyan felt his mouth dry to starch inside. He held his violin upright on his lap, to keep his hands from trembling. He hadn't felt like this since childhood, answering his father's stern questions about a broken lamp. But that had not been deadly. He thought of era. Then he realized, as if he'd never seen it so clearly before, that if Gishev fell from favor, he, Stoyan, would ascend immediately to the position of concertmaster. Once he was there, he would certainly prove himself, even to the conductor. Would it hurt Gishev to take a little fall, for once? In their quartet rehearsals, too, Gishev could be unbearable.

"Yes," he said faintly.

"Yes, which?" The conductor seemed to be trembling himself, perhaps with rage.

"Yes, Comrade Gishev said—something about you." The statement tumbled into a leaden silence. Another of the violists shifted uneasily, next to him.

Stoyan was already beginning to regret his words. He cleared his throat. "But he meant no harm, I'm sure." He tried more strongly: "What harm could he possibly mean?"

As if in answer to Samokovski's question, Velizar Gishev himself appeared at the far end of the hall, hurrying and yet oddly bowed down in the gloaming of the theater. They all stared at this figure, which was full of a new meaning no one could quite read. At first Stoyan was relieved—perhaps now the questioning would end. But his heart pounded; had Gishev heard his betrayal, a moment before?

Gishev nodded curtly to them all and said something too muted for anyone to understand.

He settled himself in the empty first chair and opened his violin, brought his bow down on the A string with vicious force. The musicians began to tune again, everyone bleakly sober.

Stoyan, second chair, enemy of his neighbor, noted with shock the man's shaking hands and drooping shoulders, the way arrogance had been stripped from him like an overcoat too warm for the day. He observed for the first time how shabby Gishev's black leather shoes had become, although they were neatly tied and polished and his socks pulled gaiter-tight above them. He noticed the wrists of Gishev's suit-jacket sleeves, which someone had fitted with narrow black velvet bands, presumably in order to stop their fraying, the perfect work of a tailor or perhaps of loving hands at home. It had been a long time since Stoyan had examined his rival this closely. He averted his eyes as he fought to steady his own A, then glanced at him again. He studied Comrade Gishev's white shirt cuffs and the outline of a bony elbow. Anything to keep his eyes on the first violinist and at the same time to avoid seeing the violet welt blossoming along Gishev's cheekbone.

They played Mozart for an hour, stopping, starting, repeating passages, the wellspring of notes bubbling as good as new out of the worn pages. If only Gishev's eyes would stop looking so reddened, the edge of his face so haggard whenever he raised it to see the score. If only the silver upswell of the second movement could erase that bruise from everyone's averted gaze.

When the rehearsal ended—a last echo and rap, the conductor turning away—Gishev left the hall quickly, without a word. Stoyan packed up with clumsy fingers; he took off his jacket and folded it over his arm again, remembering the warmth outside. He walked back through the same streets: sycamore leaves curling brown and yellow, smooth cobbles under his feet, a dog sunning itself on a patch of grass, a pretty woman with a red band around her hat—politics or fashion?—crossing at the corner. He remembered the day he'd arrived in Sofia from Vienna, the friendliness of people on his walk from the station, the man in the bakery who'd persuaded him to play, his own urge to show off in front of the customers, especially Vera. What had become of that country? It seemed to him a place from his distant travels—a brief stop in some other world.

Thirty-nine

She was cooking his lunch when he arrived at the apartment; he smelled it at the door. As had become a habit with him these last months, he wondered at the moment he took off his shoes why they didn't have any children. Since his recovery from his weeks of service in the war, he'd had more of these patterns of thought than ever: this one with the shoes and the question about children; another rumination about his paternal grandmother and her last illness whenever he began to play any piece in A minor, as if that had been the key of her decline; yet another when he found himself at the edge of a curb, waiting to cross a street. That last habitual thought had to do with a small broken stove that they had inherited from one of Vera's cousins and that sat in pieces on their balcony; it was slightly larger than the one they were currently using. He knew he might never get to this repair, but for some reason he pictured it whenever he stood waiting at the curb for cars or militia trucks or horses pulling a cart to pass safely by.

Now, slipping off his shoes by the apartment door, he thought of the many times they had made love in their lumpy bed without producing the voices of children as he came in the front door: *"Tatko! Tatko's home! Did you bring me—?"*

He could hear her opening the oven door, in the kitchen, and when he went in he could see the ties of her apron first, her slim backside under the cotton of her dress, her legs with the heavy-seamed stockings below them. She was twenty-seven, and he knew she wondered if it would one day be too late for her. She dressed neatly even at home, often with a bow at the nape of her neck, always wearing stockings with her house-slippers, as if she had never completely escaped her school uniform. He had gotten glimpses of some of his friends' wives, slovenly at home and dressed up in the street. This proof of her natural elegance, her education, increased his pride in Vera.

When she heard him come in, she turned from the oven and set down her dish, then put her arms around his neck. He could feel their unnatural warmth against his skin. He kissed her lips and her nose. What a strange thing, to live with a woman. He had lived for years with his mother, of course, but she had never seemed like a woman to him; she had never been anything but his mother, with her heavy corseted figure, comforting but androgynous.

He washed his hands at the kitchen basin and dried them on the towel she offered, sat down at the table beside their one window, which was open today to the sounds of the courtyard below. She served him and then herself bowls of the steaming soup and a heel of bread. There was little meat these days, but he liked the smell of potatoes, greens, the broth made from whatever bones she could save for it. At some point they would go to his grandfather's village to see if his aunt and uncle there had received any meat for winter, trade something, soap or old sweaters. His aunt would give them pickled cabbage and onions from her garden. He wondered if there was an omnibus running out there this fall.

While they ate, he told Vera about the strange events that had taken place at the morning's rehearsal. He found himself lowering his voice as he spoke, leaving out the worst of his own cowardice and the bruise on Velizar's cheek. As soon as he'd begun the story, he wished he hadn't. Vera sat back from her soup and pulled her braid over one shoulder, fiddling with the ends of the hair. He watched her perfect forehead wrinkle and saw around her luminous eyes that puckering that seemed to affect everyone these days—worry, uncertainty. He could almost call it fear, when he saw it in her.

She shook her head. "You mustn't feel responsible, dear. He was bound to get in trouble with Samokovski sooner or later."

"I'd like to tell him I didn't mean anything by it." Stoyan made a grand show of eating his soup, to please her. "He knows I admire his playing, even if I sometimes find him—" He'd almost said *an ass*.

"You'll see him at the quartet tonight, right? You can always tell him then." She drew a soothing finger over his arm, where he had rolled his sleeves back to eat. He wanted to stand and lift her from the chair, put his face in the side of her hair, kiss her neck and chew her braid. He took another spoonful and patted his lips with his handkerchief.

"I suppose I could simply drop by and speak to him. He's home for lunch, I'm sure."

She was clearing up the meal already. "I'm going to my mother's this afternoon. If you're out, would you get some extra bread?" Neither of them said the obvious: *if there is any left.*

"Certainly, darling." He went to the daybed beside the stove, lay down, and covered his face with the newspaper he found there, all the warped headlines he'd read in the morning. She washed up their few dishes in silence and then he felt her move the paper a little and kiss him on the forehead. He kept his eyes closed, pretending to sleep. He knew her routine; she would change her dress in the bedroom they had arranged in a corner of the parlor, behind a sheet hung on nails, brush her hair, dust her neck with the last of her round box of perfumed powder, straighten the seams of her dark stockings.

He heard her pull the door quietly shut behind her, and then he lay there a while longer, trying to fall asleep. Her presence was even more palpable when she was out of the apartment; he felt her in the kitchen, her rounded long thighs under her dress, the firm snap of her movements as she wiped the table or chopped vegetables. He lived with her mystery right next to him, and something of the dislocation of that mystery eased for him when she wasn't actually there. He loved to look around the apartment and see her sweater and apron, hung on separate nails.

Sleep didn't come; finally he got up, put on his

400

shoes, and locked the door behind him. Then, not wanting to go empty-handed, he unlocked it again and went back into the front room. He took from among the music scores his most precious possession—something he had bought in Prague years before—and put it in his bag. He didn't intend to lend it to Velizar, but he would show it to him as a peace offering, tell him the story of buying it. Perhaps together they could copy it, arrange it for their quartet. It might be time, in fact, for it to be played again. Velizar would be fascinated; he would understand better than anyone, damn him, its significance; he would understand, too, that this confidence was an act of sympathy. Stoyan had already decided not to ask about the bruise on Velizar's face. He thought of confessing to what he'd said, and then thought better of that, as well. He would just show Velizar this wonderful piece and confer with him about it. That would straighten things out; it would be the work of a few minutes.

The streets were full of early afternoon somnolence, the air heavy, the sky clouding over now, children at home for their naps. The grandparents would be sleeping nearby on kitchen divans or horsehair sofas that had been pulled from the rubble after the bombings. He remembered suddenly the day five years ago when Soviet tanks had rolled into Sofia, the cheering, the guns, the flowers. Now it was all listlessness, the young policemen bored and leaning against walls with their guns at their belts—a quiet time between two and four, sacrosanct to the city. Bells rang somewhere in the center, perhaps from the Russian church. Stoyan didn't want to wait a minute longer than necessary to set things straight with Gishev. He crossed an old square, passing two fountains, now dry, and a bed of yellow and white flowers, then a dog leashed to a lamppost, relic of a more prosperous age, like any pet—careful, beast, someone might make you into soup. He nodded to the dog and it quivered but sat obediently on. He found the right street, a shady lane of houses from the end of the last century, their garlanded cornices beginning to crack and peel. The street seemed very long, quiet.

Like most of the other houses, Velizar's was four stories. Velizar and his family lived on the first floor, which they had to themselves because it was so narrow. It was a familiar enough place; he and Vera had been here twice for supper after orchestra concerts, and he had come here several winters ago on a regular basis to practice with their quartet. Stoyan knew that when he was invited in, he would recognize the parquet floor, the shabby antique armoire, perhaps even Velizar's black orchestra jacket hanging in the front hall. He had met Velizar's wife on several of these occasions, a little, dark woman with considerable beauty looking out of haggard eyes.

Velizar had two sons, one of whom was young enough to live at home still.

At the door Stoyan paused; to his surprise it stood slightly open and there was a sound of movement somewhere inside. He braced himself to encounter Velizar on the doorstep, with no warning to either of them, then turned the brass key that rang the old-fashioned doorbell. Because the door was ajar, he could hear the screech of the bell through the front rooms.

There was no answer, and after a moment he knocked on the door itself. He pushed the door farther ajar and called quietly in. He thought of going away again—or perhaps he could simply leave the score on the kitchen table. Velizar would understand at once whom it was from. But he knew he would never leave it anywhere, would never part with it for even an hour. He stepped inside and went through the tiny hall into the kitchen, from which he would be able to tell whether they might be in the garden.

There was a moment of complete unreality, and he actually turned his head away and looked back into the hall, because he could not register what he was seeing. Velizar Gishev was in the kitchen, but he lay on the floor on what looked like a red blanket; his wife lay next to him, and their son lay beside her with his legs thrown awkwardly apart. The blanket had soaked into their clothes. There was a gun beside Velizar's hand, just clear of the spreading red, an old gun of the sort people's great-grandfathers left behind, to be displayed in a parlor cabinet. Except that since the Revolution no one was allowed to have one, even without bullets, even to display. Stoyan saw again that velvet edge on the cuff of Velizar's jacket, except that now it rested next to a gun. Velizar's face was twisted in a snarl, much more expressive than the sardonic expression he often wore in rehearsals, and there seemed to be a dark hole at the top of his forehead. Stoyan found he could not look at that hole for more than an infinitesimal beat. He saw a spray of something red against Mrs. Gisheva's cheek and throat, and across the boy's oddly hollowed skull and calm white face. She had shut her eyes; her men—the one middle-aged and the other very young—had left theirs open, examining the ceiling.

Then Stoyan saw that the back door stood ajar, too, and there were two figures moving in the tiny walled garden. An acrid smell rose all around him. He felt he should go away, leave at once, but he hovered at the edge of the kitchen, where the seep of blood did not reach his feet; he found himself looking down at his shoes to see what that meant. The people in the garden wore uniforms, and they were leaving the garden through a gate. When Stoyan took a step back, one of them turned quickly and looked at him through the kitchen window. He knew the face, a neighborhood militia volunteer, but couldn't remember his name. Stoyan met his eyes through the window—the thinning hair, the narrow head; he saw the man recognize him at the same moment. Or had he imagined that? Maybe the man had not even seen him? Then they were gone, the gate shut behind them.

Stoyan backed farther away, next to the table. An arrest in broad daylight, Velizar with his old-fashioned liberator's gun, long hidden in a drawer. The neighbors home but unwilling to investigate—perhaps not the first time there had been shots in this neighborhood, with so many arrests taking place these days. No one in the streets. Three shots, maybe both uniformed figures aiming at once, drawing their guns quickly in self-defense or simply to murder. They had not quite remembered to shut the front door to the house. Somehow shooting without much noise. How? And many minutes before, since he hadn't heard the shots himself, when he'd turned into the street. The uniformed men must have been conferring in the garden when he came in, with their guns back in their holsters. People were arrested and tried and sometimes shot, or they disappeared; they were not shot in their houses, so Velizar had surely resisted and been killed on the spot for it. And left there—it would look like two murders and a suicide, a family crime.

Stoyan turned and hurried from the house, leaving the door still open, listening for steps

405

behind him. He ran for a moment, then forced himself to slow down, trying to calm his breathing. It had begun to rain, the misty fine rain of early autumn. He tucked the bag that contained his treasure inside his jacket and watched the pavement as he walked. He felt that getting the rhythm of his feet correct was very important; if anyone watched at all, they would see him putting one shoe forward in a normal way, and then the other. It was like being on stage: you brought your mind fully to bear on your bow and fingers, on anything but the silence of the audience, and you kept it there until the music itself took over.

Suddenly he thought of Vera—what was he going to tell her? Nothing, of course. That would be safest for her. But he had always told her everything.

He understood, then, that his punishment was already beginning, and that it would take many forms. It was already beginning, and it was only just beginning.

Forty

By the time Angelov stopped speaking, the last sun had moved off the windows of the studio, leaving his face in shadow. Alexandra's hands were numb where she had sat on them. She had been watching the artist's lower teeth; the tops were ground off so that an interior brown marrow showed in each, a horrifying but also fascinating sight. When he smiled, she forgot this spectacle completely and saw only his eyes, liquid in that broken-down room. And Stoyan had stood looking at three bodies on a kitchen floor.

Bobby rose slowly and found a light switch by the door, and the twilight sprang away again. Irina was shaking her head, her mouth turned down. "I knew that something happened with that orchestra. He didn't like to talk about them, ever. But I did not know it was this."

"My God," Bobby said. "It must have been very dangerous for him to see those things. What happened to him afterward? Did he tell you?"

Irina and Angelov were looking at each other, and Alexandra saw Angelov drop his gaze. Bobby translated for Alexandra. "He says there is more, but that he is not sure whether he should tell us." Then Angelov turned, pointed. Bobby looked at her. "He says to put the bag on the table and open it."

Alexandra obeyed. After a moment, the artist stood and drew the urn from its wrappings. "Yes, he carved this," Bobby said. "He says that Stoyan asked him to make it, and in a special way."

Angelov touched the border of leaves and flowers, raised the polished lid. Alexandra had not seen the urn open in several days, and she had never seen it completely bare of the velvet casing. She felt a surge of unease, as if there really might be a life inside. Angelov lifted out the plastic bag, its burden of gray and white ash shifting around inside, and placed it very gently on the table. Then he put his hand inside the empty urn and turned it. He lifted it again and pressed one side of the bottom, and she saw almost before it came apart that there must be another box fitted below, a sliding base nearly invisible except to the hands that had built it. Angelov set the top of the urn aside and showed them the separated box, with its own lid; his worn-down fingers shook. He stopped, spoke to them, and Bobby told Alexandra: "He says he is breaking a promise."

The lid of the box flew open. Inside sat a folded wad of paper, thick, yellowing. They all looked at it in silence.

Then Irina said, "My God." She leaned forward. "Does my sister know about this?"

"*Ne*," said Angelov. He picked it up, carefully. "Only me." Alexandra saw that his face had gone pale. He opened the folds of paper; they were thin—crinkled like old typing paper, and covered with a beautifully consistent handwriting in Cyrillic. He spread them flat on the table.

"There is a title," Bobby told Alexandra. "It says, '*A confession, by Stoyan Lazarov.*' Then there is a year—'1991.' He wrote this just after the changes." He was looking hard at the top of the page. "Above that, in a different ink, it says '*Only Milen Radev knows*'—but as if the sentence was not finished."

Irina seized Alexandra's hand and gripped it so that it hurt. "Milen Radev? What else does it say?" she asked.

Angelov spread the first couple of pages out for them. "It is a memoir, I think," Bobby said. "It seems to begin with—this is very strange. It begins with the story he has just told us, about the killing of the violinist in Stoyan Lazarov's orchestra in Sofia."

Angelov spoke and Bobby listened for a moment, nodded. "Stoyan asked him to make this box, to hide the story in it, and never to tell anyone unless a life depended on it. Now he wants me to read this to you. He says that his life does not depend on it, but ours might."

BOOK
3

Forty-one

1949

I had known something would happen, but I hadn't known what.

The knock at our door around midnight was almost a satisfaction, the closing chord to what had been hovering in my dreams all night. I moved as close to the back of Vera's neck as I could risk without disturbing her. She twisted drowsily, and I said, "No, no, just sleep—let me see what it is."

The knock came again, more sharply. I pulled on my old sweater, which I used for a bathrobe. I went around the sheet that served as our bedroom partition and through the front room to the apartment door. I opened it quickly, so that I wouldn't have extra time to think. There was no question of my not opening the door. That would only make things worse.

Three men stood in the hall, dressed in plain jackets and with ordinary black hats on their heads, no uniforms.

"Citizen Stoyan Lazarov?" one said. I realized instantly that it had been some time now since anyone had addressed me formally as anything but *comrade*. I had already been demoted from the Revolution.

"Yes," I said. "Can I help you?"

A second man laughed shortly and they all stepped forward, so that I had to step back to let them into the apartment. The last one shut the door behind him. The one who had spoken stood right in front of me, a little too close, willing me not to move, which I didn't. The other two went swiftly around our front room, pulling books off the few shelves, pushing the kitchen things here and there in the corner where we cooked, looking even under the stove lid. I couldn't tell whether they were searching for something in particular or just making a mess of my possessions.

As I'd feared, the noise had brought Vera from bed; she lifted the cloth that served as our bedroom door and stepped out among them, all too beautiful in her faded gown and ruffled long hair. I tried to move toward her, but the ape in front of me clamped a hand on my arm to keep me where I was. Vera looked at the disorder, at the two men searching through our things, then at me, and fear leapt into her face. She crossed her arms tightly and stepped back toward the bedroom. I swore to myself that if any of them touched her I would fight back until they killed me, but after a glance or two they returned to their work.

"Just books, comrade," said one of the searchers to the man who held me. "Some fascist books."

He held up a history of music I'd bought in Vienna, in German, and a French novel saved from my mother-in-law's library. "Fascist propaganda."

"The *roman* is in French, in fact," I said. "An entirely different language." Vera gave me an imploring look.

"Shame on you," said the man who held me. I saw that, weirdly, he was serious. "Hoarding dirty fascist propaganda."

"There's no propaganda here," I said as clearly as I could. "I returned to Bulgaria even before the war started. Besides, propaganda makes boring reading." I wondered why I was talking this way, but couldn't stop myself.

He shook me by the arm. His fingers were beginning to burn my skin. "In any case, you'll need to come to the station for an identification check. Don't bring anything except your card—it won't take long."

"I'm in my nightclothes," I said.

"Well, dress, damn you." He pushed me toward the bedroom. "And don't touch her. Sit over there, please, comrade," he said to Vera, pointing at a chair. She went to it, trembling. "And be fast, you."

I went into our bedroom, behind the sheet— although it was terrifying to be out of sight of Vera for even a second—and dressed as quickly as I could. Something made me reach for my violin, which I always kept near me at night, and push it under the bed. I hoped they would not search the bedroom—we didn't keep books there, so they might not be curious and perhaps the instrument would go unharmed. But I wanted it hidden.

I emerged in my street clothes and bent to kiss Vera as I passed her in her chair, although the head thug swatted at me. She was straining not to cry in front of them; her knees shook visibly. I got my shoes on somehow, next to the front door of the apartment, and kept my eyes fixed on her, my face turned toward her, until they made me stumble out the door. They shut it quietly enough behind me, perhaps not wanting to alert the neighbors on our hall. I didn't know why they should take this precaution, since they'd been throwing things around inside. But no doors opened; no one looked out to see who we were or where we were going. We clumped down the stairs without speaking. They had not handcuffed me or shown me a gun; I suppose they knew I would go without a struggle. Outside, the sky was dark, and a couple of streetlights glowed near the bridge. I wondered for a moment if they planned to tie me up and throw me into the river, or beat me up in an alley, but instead they marched me in silence toward the police station, which was only eight blocks away.

Fog had wormed into some of the chilly streets, and I could see my breath imitating it in miniature and hear our footsteps on the pavement as if we were far away from ourselves. One cart passed us, horse-drawn, a delivery wagon. The driver's head was down; he seemed asleep in his seat. There were no lights on in the house windows and I wondered if I would ever see lights again. I knew what they would tell me I'd done wrong. And I knew what I had really done wrong. I talked silently with myself about what I would say when they questioned me. There was the matter of the truth, and then there was the matter of Vera, and what might happen to her if I told the truth.

When we reached the police station, they walked me in a back door. I had been inside the building several times before, on the first floor—for my registration and Vera's and to get our identity cards, after the war; and then once to report the death of an elderly neighbor, whom I'd found lying peacefully across the threshold of his apartment one floor below us. I thought for a moment of his little smile, his look of having chosen to nap in an unusual place. I had heard the thud in the hall and come out with my violin and bow still in my hand. Vera and I had taken him back into his apartment and placed him on his bed, since the neighbors who shared his apartment were all at work and his wife was long gone. Vera had cried over him, although we had known him very little. And I had walked to the station to tell the young officers on duty: a death quietly accomplished and duly reported. I wondered who would report mine if I one day slumped over my threshold. I hoped I wouldn't have my violin in my hand, at least, so that it wouldn't be damaged, and that Vera wouldn't be the one to find me. I hoped she wouldn't worry herself sick while I was at the station. When they released me, I would walk straight home—walk, not run, but swiftly.

The station was dimly lit inside, rationed power for the small hours, and a guard sat half-dozing behind the desk. He didn't look like the young man who'd come with me to see my peacefully sleeping neighbor. He nodded to the officers and one of them adjusted his grip on my arm, but no one spoke. They led me to a stairway at the back of the entrance. My stomach began to quiver at the realization that we were going down rather than up. For some reason, I had expected to be taken to an upstairs office for questioning. I knew better, of course, but at these moments you try not to actually remember what you're remembering, to forget the whispers you've heard. The staircase was dank, the walls stained with moisture, as if we were entering a cave. Our footsteps were shuffling and soft. I wanted to turn and run, but I told myself I was not going to do anything in front of them that could either be interpreted as fearful or make them hold me any longer than necessary.

At the bottom of the stairs there was a small damp hallway, and one of the men produced keys and unlocked a door. He opened it and I stood there a moment, not wanting to enter unless I had to, and wondering if they would lock me in there if I did step inside, and for how long. The man seemed to be waiting for this, or for any sign of hesitation. It happened so quickly that for a moment I wasn't sure where the blow had come from. The side of his hand crossed my nose with numbing force, as if a train had whipped past my face. The pain seemed to arrive even before the blow. I saw comets and clouds around me and I felt myself sway. A sense of liquid coming from my nose and dripping, with its taste of rust, into my mouth, was more surprising to me than the pain. Most surprising of all was the clarity of my thoughts: I had not been hit since fifth grade, when Dimitar from the next street over had punched me in the mouth for liking his sister. I'd punched him back, if ineffectually. Before and after that, no one had ever hit me. This time my arms hung stunned at my sides. My parents didn't believe in striking children, and since childhood I had lived in a world of musicians, who did not hit each other even if they longed to, for fear of injuring their own hands.

One of the men shoved me forward and I walked so that I wouldn't fall instead. Inside, the room was larger than I'd expected, and filled with a cloudy darkness that I feared was only my vision. I clamped my sleeve over the gush from my nose.

The door shut behind me and the lock turned noisily. The darkness in one corner began to move—a boy stirred in his place on the floor and stood. Another man remained sitting, in dark coat and cap, his face shrouded, watching me. The boy spoke, but softly. "Are you by yourself?"

I wiped my nose and put a hand to the wall. It was hard for me to think, let alone to make sense of this question, with the ringing still around my head.

"By myself?" I said. "No. I'm with you."

"No, no." He raised a hand in explanation. "Did they bring anyone else in with you? They said they would deal with us when there were four of us."

"I see." He folded to the floor again and I slid down to sit next to him. Our voices had already dropped to a whisper. "What else did they say?"

"Nothing," the boy said. "They brought me in from the street at midnight. My mother doesn't know where I am." He put his face in his hands.

"You'll be back home soon enough," I said, as much to myself as to him, and we both wiped our noses. The other man had not spoken at all, even in a whisper; I couldn't see him clearly, but he seemed to be older than I, perhaps middle-aged, his face a half-disc under the shadow of his cap.

"They told us not to talk to each other," the boy whispered, and we both stayed silent until there was a commotion outside the door. It was unlocked again and the three men reappeared, dragging someone who seemed very drunk.

"You fucking criminal," said one of the policemen. The drunk man stumbled forward. He had blond hair and a flat face, and there was blood and dirt on his shirt, which had once been white. He also wore a white apron, like a waiter from better times—this, too, was stained. They pitched him forward into the room and the boy beside me ducked to keep clear. The policeman said, "What are you looking at? Haven't you ever seen a *nemets* before? A Hitler pig?"

"But I'm not German," the man mumbled, in Bulgarian. He was so drunk that I couldn't tell if he spoke with an accent.

"It doesn't matter," said another of the policemen. "German or Bulgarian, you're a thief and a gambler. Get down on the floor. And you others, don't think you're too good for this kind of company. Actually, you should be cleaning his boots. At least he's an honest criminal and not a spy. Unless he's a German spy."

The boy cowered against the wall. The man in the cap hadn't moved, although the light from the door showed me the shift of his dark eyes. My face seemed suddenly to wake to its ordeal; I felt my nose begin to pulse with pain. The officers looked at us all. Then the biggest one, who also seemed to be the oldest, spoke. "The chief needs to ask you some questions, before anything else."

Before what? I wondered. I had expected questioning, but what else would there be after?

He folded his arms, as if we were keeping him waiting. "Well? Who wants to go first?"

"Oh, just choose one," muttered the policeman who'd called the blond man a fascist. The larger officer, who seemed to be their superior, either by rank or by unspoken agreement, ignored him.

"Well? Who's first?"

Some part of me wanted to volunteer, since that might get me back to Vera more quickly and I was certain I could answer any question they put to me, except maybe the hardest one. *Did you see anything unusual recently?* Or, perhaps, *Where were you yesterday afternoon?* If I really had something to confess, it was not what they wanted to hear.

Suddenly the man in the hat got up, still without speaking. The three policemen looked at one another and the large one shrugged. Then they took the man away, locking the door behind them. It was almost dark again in the little room and at first I could hear the voices of the policemen in the corridor as they opened and shut another door, somewhere across the hall. Next there were some thumps and scrapes, like furniture being moved. Then a long quiet period during which I heard a murmur that gradually rose to yelling, against the closer sound of the drunken prisoner snoring in the corner. There was a smell like mildew all around us. The boy seemed to be trying to sleep, but he breathed unevenly and I doubted he'd been able to drop off, in his fear. The yelling was a sound of impatience, a scolding, not pain, and I began to wonder if the man in the hat had remained silent. Maybe he had something large to hide. So had I, I reminded myself; what would I say when my turn came? The something I had to hide was not a crime of my own. In fact, it was more serious; it was their crime. If the man in the hat had stolen something or really owned fascist propaganda, he might be keeping silent to protect other people.

Then came a sound worse than a scream: the wild groan of someone determined not to scream. I had heard that sound once before, as a child, when my aunt was giving birth with the doctor attending her in our family house. I was not supposed to be there, in the hall; I had come back in against orders, for a ball I wanted to take to the schoolyard. That loud animal moan through clenched teeth—I had sensed even as a child that the feeling behind it was not courage but a belief that screaming would make it hurt more, a conviction that once screaming began, it would never stop.

So this questioning was not merely questioning. Were they punishing the man because he'd remained silent? Or because of something he had already said? And what was the punishment? My hands and neck were bathed in sweat.

The boy next to me crawled closer, pushing against my elbow in the dark. I wished he would stay away so that I could focus on this new sound, but I let him rest there. God only knew what would happen to him when they took him in his turn; I resolved to go before him, at least.

The door across the hall was opened, roughly, and our door unlocked again. It was the largest of the policemen.

"Hopeless," he muttered, as if he'd been dealing with some inferior machine that simply couldn't do the job. "Come on, all of you. Maybe you'll inspire this no-brain."

The boy clung to my arm and we moved across the hall together, but two of the policemen had to drag the drunken man with them. I envied his oblivion, although what would he wake to? In the brighter light of the second room I saw the man with the hat lying on the floor on his back, his legs up over a chair. There was a policeman standing beside him, one we hadn't met before. The man's feet were bare; his shoes and roughly darned socks sat in a pile on the floor. I had an unexpected vision of Vera's hands, neatly lining up my two pairs of shoes and one pair of boots on the low shelf in our front room.

The man's cap had fallen from his head, or perhaps been knocked off; it, too, lay near him. His bared head was bald, with a fringe of gray around the ears, and a raw red welt bloomed on one side of his glossy skull. His face was ashen, purple over the cheeks. When we stumbled into the room, he turned slightly, panting, and then turned away, as if embarrassed to be seen in this position. From my new place in the corner, I could suddenly see that the soles of his bare feet were bleeding, crossed with long open cuts. Then I realized that the policeman held a cord in his hand, except that the cord was made of finely braided metal, and I saw that there was skin and blood on it. For a moment I wondered at the modesty of the punishment, just the soles of the feet, not the naked back or the medieval rack or boiling oil. But I saw again the man's gray-green face, and remembered the exquisite sensitivity of that area, the bottom of the foot—he looked near fainting and we had heard his groans.

The new policeman ordered us to stand in a row. "You see how uncooperative this man is? He's a traitor, but still things would go better for him if he would tell us the truth about it. Is this how you want things to go for you?"

The boy trembled beside me and I closed my hand firmly around his wrist, willing him to stay still. Surprisingly, it was the drunk who spoke for all of us. He lolled against the wall, grinning. "No," he said. "No, no, no. Not wanting any trouble."

The biggest policeman rolled his eyes. "No trouble? You're already in trouble, my friend."

"I suppose so," the drunk man said, but amiably.

"You two," said the policeman with the cord in his hand. "Shall we just question you all together? There's not much time for all this."

This made my heart jump with hope. Clearly, they intended to release us before the day was well under way—probably they had other work to attend to, or perhaps they didn't want the publicity of holding people through the workday.

"Yes, please do," I said, as clearly as I could manage.

"Well, you can be first, then." He pulled the chair out from under the silent man's legs, which fell to the ground so hard I feared they must be broken. The man twisted a little onto his side, holding his feet heavily away from him, and groaned again.

"Sit down there."

I sat down on the chair. It was still warm, under my backside, from the man's burning legs.

"My colleagues tell me you're here for the possession of fascist propaganda."

It wasn't a question, so I remained silent. That was one thing to try, anyway. But it seemed only to annoy him.

"Well? Have you been hoarding fascist propaganda?"

I looked carefully at him, although my heart was throbbing hard and sweat ran down the sides of my neck. Like the man with the slashed feet, this policeman no longer wore his hat, and I could see comb-lines in his pomaded dark hair—it lay in hoops over the top of a round head. His skin was the kind that breaks into whisker stubble within hours of shaving, something dark constantly pushing out through the pores. His eyes were large and intelligent and would have been pleasant in a gentler face. I wondered who he was—besides Bulgarian, like me, and only a few years older than I—and where he had come from, who his parents were. His shirt looked very clean. His speech was Shopski, from the Sofia region but not of the city itself—he sounded as if he'd come from the countryside.

"No, I haven't been hoarding anything," I said.

"We found some interesting materials in your apartment," he said, lowering his voice as if this was just between the two of us. "Books in German, for example, and other decadent works."

"I do have some books in German," I said. "Poetry and histories of music. No propaganda."

"So you have time to read German poetry?" he said. "You have time to read the words of our enemies while your colleagues are busy building a new nation with their sweat and blood?"

I thought of the blood on the very cord he held. As if he'd read my mind, he handed the whip to one of the other policemen and carefully rolled up his shirtsleeves, which were already partly rolled up. He came closer to me. "Why are you against the Party?"

I tried to clear my throat. "I didn't say that I am."

"Are you from Vienna?"

"I only studied in Vienna—for some years," I said. "I am from Sofia."

"And what brought you back to Sofia from your new homeland?"

The other policemen shifted from foot to foot or stretched their shoulders. It occurred to me that they didn't like the talking part of all this.

"Bulgaria is my homeland," I said firmly. "I came back here—" I had meant to say, *because my aging parents were worried about me,* but I suddenly didn't want to mention them. "I came back because of the war."

"You had the means to come and go to the other end of Europe, at will?"

"In Vienna, I was a poor student," I said. I kept my body as still as I could; I didn't want him to see me trembling.

"Poor you," he said. "Studying abroad while our peasants suffered at home under the capitalist yoke."

I almost laughed; for several years now, we'd seen this kind of line in the newspapers or heard it blaring from megaphones at political rallies; but I hadn't yet accepted the fact that there were ordinary individuals, even policemen, who spoke this way, and in all seriousness. I caught myself in time, horrified.

"I hoped as a musician to make my country

proud of me," I said. "That is why I went to study in Vienna. I was wounded in '45, fighting the Germans."

He stepped closer and looked into my face. I could see the purple beneath his eyes; he'd been working all night and was nearly as tired as I, although not as frightened. I wondered if he had a name. In face and stature, he looked very much like a boy I now remembered from my *gimnasium* class, an adult version, although he certainly wasn't that person. We were the same height; I could imagine the two of us playing ball in the walled schoolyard, shouting at each other.

"What instrument is yours?" he said.

"I'm a violinist," I said. Ridiculously, the love of it washed through my heart, even there, in a police cell. I loved those words and everything I had poured into them.

"Let me see your hands."

Then, for the first time, I was passionately afraid. I had not thought of myself as being vulnerable, like a drunk or a boy or a silent peasant. In my world, I had always been not merely worthy but exceptional.

"Your hands," he said slowly.

I kept them behind me for a moment, then held them out toward him. They had never looked so far away from my body, so naked, in all the uncounted, uncountable hours I'd spent gazing at them, on the bridge and bow. I could see them under that bare electric light; they were unnaturally long, slender but already a little gnarled around the joints, the haunch of each thumb muscular, the fingers squared off at the ends, the right hand a little larger than the left and with that precious callus on the middle left side of the index finger, another callus at the tip of the thumb, just to the right. People say sometimes, "I know such-and-such like the back of my hand," but I actually knew my own hands like the back of my hand, like precious objects. If I relaxed them both on a table, palms upward, the fingers of my left hand curled up more than those of the right. Like my leg, my left arm would always be a little stiff from shrapnel wounds. Holding my hands out before the Shopski policeman, I had a sudden strange feeling that he was going to read my fortune, or praise their extraordinary shape, as my first teacher in Vienna had. ("So these are the hands they grow in the Balkan mountains," he had said, patronizing and admiring at the same time.)

The policeman took one of my hands in his. He held it a moment so gently that I felt the calluses on his palm, and then with his other hand he swiftly broke the top joint of my little finger.

Pain didn't reach me as quickly as my grief and anger: sheer damage, which would take months to heal. And what if it never healed quite properly? Then a moment of relief. He had broken a bow finger, on my right hand, not my left. Then a searing heat shot up my arm. I tried to yank my hand away but the policeman held it with alarming strength. I thought of the silent man, now lying with his eyes closed at our feet, and I bit down on my lip. I wondered why I hadn't seen this coming, why I hadn't pulled away or ducked. If I'd lost my temper and attacked them, perhaps they would have whipped my feet or back and spared my hand. The finger was already beginning to redden and swell.

"Hurts, eh?" the policeman said sternly. "I guess it does. Your hands wouldn't be worth a thing all broken up, would they? I know that much about music, anyway. My grandfather was a musician. You don't want to risk another finger, do you? Or a whole hand? Wouldn't want to spread any more decadent lies around with your books, either, would you?"

He bent one of my other fingers back, warningly, and I thought again of the fact that he was threatening my right hand, not my left. One of the other policemen leaned toward him and whispered something in his ear; I couldn't make sense of it through the pulsing in my head.

The policeman who held my hand looked quickly at me. "You wouldn't want to report anything you might have seen in the last few days, would you?"

"I haven't done anything wrong." I tried to

speak slowly, to keep my voice from shaking.

"You mean, you haven't seen anything you'd like to report, have you?"

I heard in his voice that the correct answer was an emphatic no. He wanted me to remember that answer. I wondered why they hadn't chosen to speak to me alone, but I was glad the boy and the drunk were there with me, and even the poor man with his lacerated feet falling sideways out of his trouser legs. Perhaps they only wanted me to say no in front of witnesses.

"I haven't done anything wrong," I said. My hands were trembling now, too, with pain and their own terror. It occurred to me that if I kept saying this the policemen might not dare describe in front of the others what they knew I'd seen, if they even knew about it, and I would not have to lie—or admit to it.

"Oh, I suppose not," he said suddenly, dropping my hand. "Go sit down over there."

I sat against the wall, resting my hands on my knees, trying to reclaim them. It was the beginning of that long bifurcation that became my life: Obey and hate yourself, survive. Disobey, redeem yourself, perish. I thought later how simply and quickly they had introduced that concept to me, as easily as breaking a little finger. For some reason they had decided not to beat me.

The policeman tipped the chair on its side again, pushing the silent man out of the way with one strong foot. He said to the boy, *Take off your socks and shoes*. The boy cried a little, but bravely. When they started to whip his feet he began to scream at once, as if to get the screaming over with, or to establish the sound of it firmly in the room.

In my dreams, later, I rushed at them, grabbed the bloody braid from their hands, pulled it tight across their necks, tied them up with a rope from my pocket. The drunken man pulled himself together and lifted the hatless peasant over sturdy shoulders. I hoisted the boy into my arms and carried him safely home to Vera.

But only in my dreams.

Forty-two

Bobby paused and cleared his throat. Irina was very pale, leaning sideways against Lenka's shoulder. Angelov sat with his stubby hands folded on the table, his face drawn. For Alexandra this was the first time words had been not only a means of expression but something real. She had read poetry and novels, and they had given her pleasure; she had read some history, and it had given her pain. This was beyond both. In a minute Bobby would continue—in fact, he read out loud to the end of the crackling pages, translating slowly into English as he went; Alexandra would see their reality over and over in her mind's eye, during the remaining few days.

It was Irina Georgieva who thought of the next possibility. She was drying her face with the handkerchief from her sleeve. "Stoyan wrote on the first page that only Milen Radev knows about this."

"We do not know where he is, either," Bobby objected.

"No," Irina said, "but I am thinking of the niece of Milen Radev." She spoke briefly to Angelov, who shook his head in agreement. "My sister and Milen used to go often to see his niece Bogdana in Yambol, and she sometimes visited them, too. She is very fond of them, and of Neven. Earlier today, Lenka called her to ask if they all went to Yambol, by chance. If anybody else knows whether Milen Radev has more information about the urn, it might be Bogdana."

"And did they go there?" Alexandra started up from her seat.

Irina sighed. "I'm afraid not. Bogdana told me that they have not been to visit her in quite a long time. But Milen called her about ten days ago, to say that they were planning to bury Stoyan's ashes. She says that he promised they would visit her sometime soon after. He told her not to come to the burial, because they were going to do a very simple goodbye at Velin Monastery, she always has a lot of work, and it had already been two years since the death of Stoyan. She has not heard from them since, or been able to reach them. I had the feeling that she was worried about something, but did not want to tell me what it was. I explained to her that I have friends who have something to return to them, in case Milen calls her again."

Bobby looked thoughtful. "Do you suppose we could go to talk with her? Or that they might be traveling there already?"

Irina nodded. "Yes, I thought of that, too. And she knows her uncle well. I will give you her number and let her know you are coming. He might have spoken to her if he felt some worry, during the last two years. Perhaps she even knows what other information Stoyan gave him."

"Where is—Yambol?" Alexandra felt something like hope well up behind her eyes.

"In the east of Bulgaria."

She tried to picture her guidebook map, with the sea on the far right.

Irina propped her head in her hands. "But you must take me back to Plovdiv first. If we leave now, we can be home tonight, even if we arrive very late. I fear I am too tired for more travel, after this." Angelov reached out to touch her shoulder.

Bobby was frowning. "What if we do go to see Milen's niece, and that puts her in some kind of danger, too?"

"Well, you must tell her what you know, to

warn her. I think she would want to hear if her uncle and Vera are in any trouble." Irina smoothed her hair, but shakily. "I have decided I would like you to take the urn with you. I feel sure you will find them, or they will reach you, and then you can give it to them at once. But if this does not work, you must bring it directly back to me."

"I will ask *gospodin* Angelov to put the base on again," Bobby said. "It must not look damaged, to Vera and Neven." *Nor,* thought Alexandra, *to whoever else might try to seize it*. The old artist seemed to understand; he stood up and began to assemble it with delicate care, without replacing the manuscript.

Irina nodded. "Yes. I think that we should make at least two copies of these pages before you leave Plovdiv. I will keep one copy and you can carry a copy and the original separately, in your bags. When you find my sister you can put it back in the urn."

Alexandra went to sit next to the old lady; she put her head on Irina's shoulder, which felt like a rocky outcropping, and Irina reached an arm around her. "Oh, my darling," she said. "Let's go. Say your goodbyes to *gospodin* Angelov and we will hurry now." The old man had put the urn back into its bag. "You can spend one more night in Plovdiv with me and leave for Yambol early tomorrow. You will travel faster without an old lady on your backs."

●●●

The wall in front of the merchant's mansion in Plovdiv looked like home to Alexandra when they reached it in the small hours, and Irina's house like an oasis; inside, nothing had been disturbed. The next morning, under a very different light, they told Irina and Lenka goodbye. The air was already simmering, a hot day rising off the cobblestones.

"But goodbye only for now," Alexandra insisted, with one hand in Irina's and the other clutching Stoycho's rope. Bobby held the bag with the urn and a piece of paper with the number and address for Milen Radev's niece.

"Remember, if they are not in Yambol," Irina said, "you must bring the urn back here and I will keep it in my house for now. Please be careful. Please call us."

Alexandra looked around the courtyard—no tourists at the doors to the museum, the leaves on the grapevines a little greener and larger than when they'd first visited, the morning sky brassy above the trees.

"We'll come back," she said. "We'll find them. I promise."

Lenka kissed her on each cheek. Irina bent over and stroked Stoycho's head with her splayed fingers. He leaned against her knee, carefully, as if he knew he could knock her over with any sudden movement.

"If you hear from your sister or Neven, please call me immediately," Bobby said, and he added something in Bulgarian that made Irina shake her head.

In the car, Alexandra and Bobby were silent. The road toward Yambol unfolded in a long straight line, with plains to their left and a high range of mountains on the horizon beyond that. Stretching into the distance were rows of grassy mounds, each at least twenty feet high and strangely regular, around which crops were planted or fallow meadows waved. Bobby said these were tumuli, the grave mounds of the ancient Thracians, so many graves that only a small percentage had ever been excavated, although quite a few had been robbed, over the centuries. He drummed the steering wheel with his thumbs. "I have heard that there are people who go to worship at some of these graves—they believe in Orpheus, that his spirit lives there and also lives high in the Rhodopes—especially in the caves near Greece."

"What kind of people?" wondered Alexandra.

"Educated people, I guess, from the cities. They believe in the Thracian gods," Bobby said. "That began years ago, before communism, and sometimes continued during communism, too, always in secret. And even now. I have never seen this myself, but I heard that they dress in robes and dance for Orpheus and Bacchus. The real ancients were different. They had some terrible practices—human sacrifice, for example."

Alexandra imagined this—the frenzied dancers, and then a red-haired boy, tied hand and foot across the altar. Then an older man, tall and dark-haired, helpless under the knife, his violin smashed against the rocks. She shook herself and reached back to stroke Stoycho's warm neck.

Yambol, a couple of hours later, appeared as a jumble of houses and high-rise buildings like the complexes she'd seen in Sofia and Plovdiv—except that these were smaller and some of them sat at the very edge of the main road, their balconies festooned with laundry. Bobby stopped to call the number Irina had given them and left a brief message. "It's a workday," he said, "and this is her mobile, so perhaps she's busy. Let's go to her address and see."

The address Irina had given them was confusing. Eventually they found one of the tallest of the high-rise complexes, and then the right cement tower and the right parking lot. It was hot here; dust blew across the sidewalks and among the monolithic buildings, where there was more dried mud than landscaping. Two young children, watched by a grandmother, were playing in a patch of papery grass and stunted aspens. Alexandra wiped her forehead with her wrist and decided she couldn't safely leave Stoycho in the car; she let him wander around at the end of his leash, enduring the grandmother's stare, while Bobby disappeared into a doorway.

He was gone a long time, but eventually she found a bench to sit on, holding Stoycho near her. Some of the slats were missing from the seat. She wondered what her parents were doing at home—sitting up reading at their respective apartments, probably, now that the semester was over. They wouldn't expect a second message from her until the end of the week; that was their agreement, a minimum. She thought that she should ask Bobby to help her get a cell phone. Perhaps they could manage it the next day, if there was time and it didn't prove too expensive. She began to feel lonely—even when events don't become strange and dark, there are moments in a new place when you glance too far off into a distance or encounter the unwelcoming stare of a stranger and are suddenly displaced, a kind of travel within travel. This out-of-body sensation came over her as she looked at the cracked cement walks, the dusty trees, the shimmer of heat on the little boy's hair, Stoycho watching another dog nose around the garbage dumpsters at the end of the parking lot. The dog had apparently once been cream-colored, but its coat was falling out in big patches, so that it looked like a molting chicken. Stoycho stood up and growled and Alexandra jerked his leash harder than she'd meant to.

"No fighting," she said.

Then Bobby came back out of the building. "Miss Radeva does live here," he said. "But she is not at home. A lady told me where she works—as the secretary at an orphanage. We can look for her there. But I hope it will not be a shocking place for you—some of our orphanages have a very bad reputation. We should go now. I don't want to be seen here."

Alexandra remembered: sooner or later, whoever was following them might somehow find not only them but Miss Radeva, through them.

"All right," she said. She took Stoycho away from the old woman's gaze and they clambered into the car. Stoycho wanted to sit on her lap and she let him, even in the heat, gathering his long legs close.

Forty-three
1949

We slept in the cell the rest of that night—or, rather, lay on the ground dozing and waking. The boy and the man with the hat whimpered, awake or asleep. The drunken man snored; he had hardly been worth their trouble, and I wondered why the officers didn't put him back out on the street. I lay there and thought of Vera, and of getting a doctor to see about my broken finger as soon as possible. I would need to say I'd tripped and fallen, or something like that. It would take me months to be able to play again; if my conductor knew I'd been called in by the police, would he even keep me on? I wouldn't tell anyone, of course, but I'd have to show him my injured hand. We had very little money saved and I wondered if Vera's family might be able to help us until my finger healed.

For a long while, as I lay there, I harbored the hope, almost the assumption, that the large policeman would release me in the morning. One heard these things, whispered here and there—people held for questioning for a night, then sent home, where they became quieter than before. One heard other things, too, more publicly, and read them trumpeted in the papers, these last five years—the trials of enemies of the people. I pushed down the phrase as soon as it came into my head; I made myself sleep for an hour, my handkerchief stuffed into one ear to drown out the sounds of misery.

Sometime during the night, the door opened, light came in across the floor again, and the officers added three more men to our number. An hour later, they pushed another young boy in among us. The cell was nearly full and I wished I could stretch my legs better as I lay there, but I stayed as still as possible, trying to rest. The ache in my heart sharpened; why would they add men to the cell if they planned to release us in the morning? Perhaps they would take us all together before the courts to sentence us the next day, and send us to prison? There was the chance, if we went to court, that I could be found innocent, unless the judge had been told what I'd seen. Then I might hang. I told myself to stay alert, and a few minutes later two more men were put in. One of them stank horribly; it seemed fear had overcome even his bowels. He got more space to sleep than anyone else.

They came for us before dawn and took us from the back of the police station into the back of a truck; by then we were twelve men in all. The guards kept their guns lowered, hidden—so we would look like a group of workers being sent on detail somewhere, I suppose. My finger throbbed, my nose was stiff with dried blood, my clothes were rumpled and damp. They hadn't brought us water or food and I was beginning to feel those deficits as achingly as I did the pain in my hand. My nostrils were full of the odor of the man who had slept next to me, his rank coat and unwashed hair, and—worse—the man with the soiled trousers. It was funny to me, later, to think that at the time I'd considered this a bad smell. When they stopped the truck and urged us out, I caught the purity of morning, the streets very dark but with a breath like sunrise in the air.

The train said PLOVDIV; I didn't know whether that meant it had just come from Plovdiv or was bound there. We walked from an empty lot behind the Sofia depot toward our train car, without entering the station itself. A fellow next to me couldn't stand on the soles of his feet, where he'd been beaten, like the boy and the first man in our cell. Two of us automatically took his arms and supported him as we moved forward; I kept my damaged right hand carefully out of his way.

I saw that the lights of the train were off, and also the lights in the station. There was only a faint dark figure moving here and there, outside the coal car—no crowds of people, no friendly noise. It was like a station I had never seen before, or the ghost of a station I'd once known. For a second I had the feeling that I was actually on my way back to Vienna from Sofia, in clean clothes, with my instrument case cradled in my arms. And I thought again of my violin, sitting under our bed. Vera would discover it and put it somewhere safe. If I could just get back in a few days, that would at least shorten her suffering over my absence. I tried not to picture Vera's distress; that image was worse for me than what was happening in the present. Then my mind wandered and I found myself more in need—of something to eat and hot water to wash my sore limbs—than eager to see her, and I felt ashamed.

That was the moment, before I even stepped

onto the train, when I realized the most important thing that was happening to me. They were taking my natural feelings away, so quietly that it could have occurred without my noticing. I understood in a flash that I must keep my mind safe, whatever came next. I believe now that it was not only enormous luck that brought me this understanding the very first day, but also my habit of living closely with my own mind, alone with it while I practiced. It was the landscape in which I had always lived, toiling over its rocks and hills to find the perfect place for my music, climbing up long rows of notes in order to commit them to memory. I also believe that few of the men around me realized early enough that they would have to guard their minds, first and foremost, and not their bodies, which would be impossible to protect anyway. The man beside me, stumbling on his shredded feet, in his socks, and the man who held his other arm, were both dead forty-eight hours later.

This revelation absorbed me so deeply that I almost forgot to turn my head for a last look at the lights of the city, where Vera was—no doubt awake and terrified, perhaps sitting with her sister at the kitchen table, trying to decide what to do, whom to petition. I hoped she wouldn't go petitioning too far. I helped my staggering companion up the ramp into the train car and propped him against a wall next to me. No one spoke; no one tried to run. I fastened my gaze onto one street-light until the corrugated door slid all the way shut and extinguished it. We could hear the men from the police station bolting the door on the outside.

I didn't need to strain against the near-darkness to know what a new kind of travel this was, for me: a freight car, filled with groaning, mumbling men, not only our group but twenty others already there who must have been picked up farther west, or perhaps even in Sofia, like us. These men had apparently been sleeping on the floor of the car, with enough room to spread their limbs wide, jackets under or over them; they greeted us with muffled annoyance, putting their arms across their eyes, or tried to turn over again into oblivion. We, the newcomers, were an inconvenience, crowding them, and perhaps also further proof of the serious-ness of their situation.

Then there was a pause while the train prepared for travel, although no engineers called to one another outside, and next the hiss and pull of the wheels coming to life under our car, the lurch forward and that one reluctant lurch back to gather momentum. In this interval, none of us spoke, and I promised myself that when the train started up in earnest, I would return to my revelation and dwell on it.

The moment when the train pulled forward was terrible despite my attempt to focus beyond it, like falling off a high place; it meant we were leaving Sofia. My heart seemed to drop straight out of me, in order to stay behind with Vera, and yet I didn't know how I could travel on without it. The silence deepened over all of us. I had not wanted to return to Sofia, nine years earlier; since then, I had waited daily to leave again on some powerful beast of a train, but now I did not want this train to move. A huge desire to weep rose in my chest and throat. I felt the injured man beside me raise his sleeve and draw it heavily over his face. He was revolting to me in that moment, but I made myself put my hand out and find his shoulder, which I gripped. He moved his other hand up in the darkness and gripped my wrist in return, then dropped it; I felt the kind of hand it was, short-fingered and heavily padded, rough with calluses, a hand that had worked hard from childhood in heat and cold. We had not exchanged a single word, but I felt in his hand a history very different from my own. I had fought down my despair by befriending that hand for an instant. That was my second important realization. No— my third: the first had actually been in the police interrogation, when I'd understood that my special qualities, my talent and upbringing, far from saving me, would condemn me.

I covered myself with my jacket and adjusted my shoulders against the chilly walls, adjusted my eyes to the crack of light that flickered on and off along the top of the bolted door as we passed through the city. I made myself breathe out with the downbeat, each rumbling turn of wheels, *cha-clunk,* a deep exhale with the *clunk,* then an inhale, even if it meant breathing faster and faster for a few minutes. I tried to set the rhythm to a line from Bach—my favorite, the Chaconne from the second Partita in D minor. When we were moving steadily, the man with the wounded feet and callused hand curled up in the remaining space beside me and I addressed again that thought I'd had about my own mind, just before we'd been put in the car. I would not allow anyone into the center of myself; I would make myself a place to go, deep inside, no matter what happened.

But what should the place be? I imagined our bed, Vera asleep in the morning with her hair curling around my elbow. No. That image would break me. I would save that one for strong moments, and when these days were over and I got back to her, I would savor its reality as I had never before known how. I would tell her that I hadn't even been able to think of her, those several nightmarish days, and she would understand.

Then I imagined my favorite park in Vienna, the slide of chestnuts escaping their burrs under-foot, the drifting yellow along the avenues of poplars and beeches, the lawns in autumn light, the last few roses. I could sit down there on a bench, feel my violin in its case under my arm, which was like sitting alone with a friend, no need for words after so many years.

No. (The damaged man beside me turned and dug his knee into my thigh—he was asleep despite his pain.) Vienna was too much like a dream now, and it had never been my place, as I'd known even while I was trying to adopt it. I drew my own knees up, careful not to wake the sleeping sufferer, and rested my aching arms on them. Men breathing, muttering, piles of wool and cotton like corpses in the deadened twilight of the car.

Then I saw the place I could go, and it surprised me because it was new to me, when I'd imagined stumbling on some familiar haven.

It was a meadow, somewhere in Bulgaria, although I did not know where—somewhere outside the kind of village one passed on the train between Sofia and the northern mountains, a meadow not steep but not level, filled with scratchy sweet grasses and even-topped white flowers, not plowed or grazed, left growing wild near the edge of a river. The son I suddenly hoped to have sat in warm sunshine there, full-grown and tall, with the girl he loved sitting next to him. Their hands were interlaced on the grass, which was mashed fragrantly flat around them. They seemed to have no idea that such things could happen—that men could be put into a bolted train car in the dark and taken toward who knew what fate—and yet they were speaking of me, Stoyan. I was filled with gratitude at the thought. I walked toward their young backs and saw them turn first to each other in conversation and then, reflectively, toward the river. I raised y violin and drew my bow over the strings to serenade them.

Then darkness intervened and I was again one of those piles of clothing, beginning to smell and to snore, among many other piles; the train braked with uncomfortable suddenness and someone hit his head on the wall and swore. *A cat eat your mother's guts, you*—a villager's voice like the ones in the weekly market, and someone else had enough good spirits left to laugh in the dark. I was almost smiling, too, not because of the invisible tragicomedy but because of the place I'd found, my meadow, my future son, the sunlight there. I knew it would take practice, but I knew how to practice; that had been my life, up until yesterday. All the other benefits had been fitted richly around practicing: Vera and her family, Vienna, the orchestra concerts, my daily walks in the parks, my sweet parents with their blind belief in my future, my own blind beliefs, my books. Practicing had kept my mind from the bombings, at least for long minutes, and from the hours of hunger during the war, and from the smells of fear in the street, and later from my brief memories of slaughter at the front.

So I practiced a few more times, eagerly, to be

sure I had the outline of the new place. I walked over the grasses, feeling their warmth rising through my shoes, the legs of my trousers. I looked at the glossy heads of my son and his young love, I saw again their hands interlaced between them as they talked, I heard my name, uttered with affection, I smelled the river just beyond, I raised my instrument and drew my bow over the strings. Then I did it all one more time. When I was sure of myself, I decided to put the place away for now, in the dark, to save it in the hope that it wouldn't be needed after all.

Forty-four

The orphanage was on a dead-end street at the edge of Yambol—the perfect place for it, Alexandra thought. The street didn't so much end as peter out into a weedy field, as if the occupants didn't provide enough of a reason to continue the pavement. The orphanage itself was a large concrete building with a red-tiled roof, hemmed in by metal fences. Inside that, a huddle of peach or apricot trees with green fruit on them. Alexandra imagined the orphans picking the fruit in mid-summer; perhaps this was their biggest taste of nature, unless they were taken out on trips sometimes. She had never been to an orphanage before and thought of the word as obsolete, from a nineteenth-century novel, not part of the modern world.

Bobby tied Stoycho to a tree at the edge of the parking lot and Alexandra hugged his neck, trying to provide him with a charm against dognappers. Then they rang the electric doorbell on the outside gate and waited. Eventually a woman came out, hurrying as if she had a lot else to do. She had something on her arms that Alexandra thought at first was a rash or a tattoo but that turned out to be a lacing of blue and red paint. She looked Bobby and Alexandra over and then rushed them without a word into a court-yard and through a front door; she clearly didn't have time to think of any harm they might cause.

Inside, the halls were full of soft yellowish light. No children were visible, although Alexandra could hear a distant hum that might have been either voices or music. The walls were painted in pastel hues and decorated with dozens of bright childish artworks on curling paper. Alexandra was struck by the cleanliness of the place— shining floors, a mild aroma of disinfectant. Bobby's words had led her to imagine squalor, even horror. Instead, the building was strangely soothing, like her own rural elementary school, the same closed doors with frosted glass panes set into them, the same murmur of benign activity.

Bobby talked easily with the paint woman—she had stopped rushing and seemed to be taking them on a tour—and Alexandra could tell that he was asking about Milen Radev's niece, and maybe about the orphanage itself. Suddenly the halls were filled with children; they seemed to be going en masse to some activity. The oldest looked about seven or eight and the smallest as young as three. They wore clean, if much used, play clothes and their hair and faces shone. Bobby whispered to her that many of them were Roma, and she remembered the children at the edge of Aunt Pavlina's town, perched like birds on a fence. They put their fingers to their mouths and laughed when they saw strangers; the littlest ones, holding their teachers' hands, stared. One of the boys reached out and pulled on Alexandra's skirt as he passed her.

Bobby translated the teacher's whisper: "The children know that when someone comes to visit, they might go home to a family. It is often disappointing for them." She took Alexandra and Bobby in the opposite direction, but Alexandra turned and saw that the children at the end of the line had turned around, too, to watch them go. They were smiling, waving, one of them diligently picking his nose with the other hand.

The rest of the orphanage was also bright and clean, and it took a while for her to realize that everything they were seeing had been put together from almost nothing. The walls were nicked but painted with care and decorated with more of the children's art in cardboard frames. Alexandra noticed the portrait of a gray-haired woman badly but benignly painted in oils, perhaps an early director. The curtains were clean sheets neatly cut and sewn, and in some rooms they served to separate sleeping areas from play spaces, or hung in place of doors. A couple of women in the big open dormitory rooms were sorting shabby toys and clothing onto shelves. Rows of wooden beds sat low to the floor; on one pillow Alexandra saw an object like a ragged spider that turned out to be a relentlessly loved cloth doll. From outside the windows came the ululation of children chanting together—some song to go with calisthenics, an eerie, uneven sound.

The woman settled them in an office, where there was a large desk but no one on duty. Then she left, holding her stained arms out in front of her.

"Miss Radeva will come in a minute. She works on the other side of the building. This is nice, here, not like the orphanages I have read about," Bobby said thoughtfully.

"What are the other ones like?" Alexandra inquired, but at that moment they heard shoes tapping along clean floors and the door opened.

This brought a further surprise. Alexandra had imagined Milen Radev's niece as an aging female version of Radev himself—not in a wheelchair, of course, but with worn features and thinning gray hair and Radev's look of sunken disengagement. The woman coming toward them could have been thirty, or even twenty-six, like Alexandra. Miss Radeva was tall and slim and alert. Her smooth dark hair fell past her shoulders. Alexandra thought she had the face of a Byzantine princess —delicate, with almost unnaturally large dark eyes and olive skin. She wore a dress of lavender silk with striped collar and cuffs, more suited to a dainty lunch out than to working with children—but perhaps she did only typing and phone calls, not finger painting. She moved as if there was little to keep her tied to the ground, straight and slightly airborne, like a ballerina off duty. Alexandra and Bobby both stared at her, Bobby with unveiled admiration, and Alexandra without jealousy.

"How do you do?" Miss Radeva said in English. Her voice was quiet and musical. Alexandra remembered the ugly cement entrance to the building where this visitation apparently lived. "Madame Georgieva told me that someone might come to see me. You are Americans?"

"Only me," Alexandra said, shaking the hand Miss Radeva offered her. It was slim and cool, like the rest of her, with silky skin over the bird bones. "Bobby—Asparuh—is from Sofia."

"And you are interested in the children? I do

not quite understand why you are here." Miss Radeva frowned, a faint wrinkling of velvet. Her English was beautifully formed, the accent strong but every word clear, like her face.

"Oh, no," Alexandra said. "I mean, I love children, but we came to ask you—to talk with you about your uncle, Milen, if you wouldn't mind. We've been looking for him, or rather for the friends he's traveling with—"

"Might we close the door?" Bobby said.

When the door was shut, they explained the outlines of their search, beginning with Alexandra's meeting Milen Radev and the Lazarovi on the steps of Hotel Forest and accidentally keeping the urn. As she listened, Miss Radeva took a box of chocolates off a shelf above the desk and opened it gracefully before them, then poured water for tea from an electric pot in the corner. The chocolates tasted mainly of dust and sugar, but Alexandra ate three; they had missed lunch again. Then she showed their hostess the photograph of Neven and Vera, with a blurry Milen Radev in the back seat of the taxi. Alexandra omitted her visit to the police, and Bobby left out their lunch with the Wizard and the three episodes of graffiti. Alexandra hoped this wasn't a mistake; perhaps they could tell Miss Radeva these things later, if it became necessary.

Miss Radeva said very little until they had

finished, although when Alexandra mentioned the urn, she opened her dark eyes wide and glanced around, as if expecting to see someone else in the room. When she sat even straighter, her small dancer's breasts and lightly etched collarbone shimmered under the silk. "I see," she said.

"We don't wish to take more of your working time," Bobby amended. "We heard from Irina Georgieva that your uncle and the Lazarovi sometimes come to stay with you. Have you seen them recently? Do you know where they have gone?"

But Miss Radeva shook her head. It was true, she said, that Vera and her uncle had called her from Gorno to say they were going to bury Stoyan's ashes at last. She'd been surprised; she had assumed Stoyan had been buried soon after he died, although she did not remember hearing about a funeral. At that time, she had telephoned her uncle to give him condolences on his friend's death. When they had called from the Rhodopes, ten days ago, she had urged them to visit her, since she had not seen them in more than two years. Her uncle had said they might come to visit her sometime soon, after they buried the urn.

Bobby played with the hem of his jacket. "Did they sound unhappy on the telephone? That is—upset?"

Miss Radeva pondered this, one long finger

under her perfect chin. She wore gleaming pale polish on her fingernails, but no rings. Perhaps, thought Alexandra, angels were not permitted to marry.

"My uncle is not usually a cheerful person these days, because he is often in pain," Miss Radeva said. "But this time on the telephone I noticed that he was also rather anxious. Not in a big way. Quietly. He said that after the burial of Uncle Stoyan—and a visit to me—they would take a vacation, maybe at the sea, because Neven wanted that. But he did not sound happy about it. They have very little money—I do not know how they will manage to do this traveling. I was glad, however, because he has always loved the sea, where we all lived, and he has not been there in a long time. I asked where they would go, on the coast, and if they would visit Burgas. He said maybe not—Neven had not decided yet where to stay."

There was a knock at the door, and a gray-|haired woman put her head in, nodded to them, and addressed Miss Radeva with rapid concern.

"*Da*," said Miss Radeva. "*Nyama problem.*" The woman vanished again.

"You must go back to your job," Bobby told her apologetically. "Just one more question, if it is all right. Do you know any reason *gospodin* Lazarov could have been wanted by the police?"

Miss Radeva had gotten up, smoothing her

dress, and at this she froze. "Is my uncle in some trouble?" she asked fearfully. "Or Neven?"

"No," Bobby said. "They have not done anything illegal, that we know about. But we think that Stoyan Lazarov was in trouble, at some time, perhaps a long time ago. This might be causing trouble for them now, somehow. Did your uncle ever mention this?"

She stood very straight in front of them, as if wondering what to do.

"I'm sorry." Bobby had risen, too; he seemed about to take her hand. "I know you are close with your uncle. But we are trying to learn what we can about *gospodin* Lazarov so that we can help your uncle and *gospozha* Lazarova to give his ashes a safe—ending. You see, maybe you could help us?" His voice was gentle.

Miss Radeva's gleaming dark head drooped and she was silent for a moment. "There is something I should tell you," she said, finally. "But we cannot talk about it here." She stroked back a burnished lock of hair. "And I must return to work. I will finish as quickly as possible, so that I can leave a little before five o'clock."

"Thank you," Bobby said gravely.

Miss Radeva glanced from one of them to the other. "Please meet me in the center of the town, at the café near the mosque. I will be there in an hour."

Bobby looked wary. "Can we speak inside this

café, in private? I don't want to sit outside while we talk."

"Yes," Miss Radeva said. "It is a good place for that."

Just then, the door opened and the paint-spattered teacher came in again. She had an older woman with her, and a man with springy gray hair. For some reason, he was wearing a dark-green Tyrolean jacket, with silver buttons and embroidered flowers; he reminded Alexandra of Captain von Trapp, with his horde of children.

"My *shefs*," said Miss Radeva, and Alexandra understood this must mean her bosses.

"Are you interested to adopt a child?" asked the man in the jacket. His face was puffier than Christopher Plummer's, and sadder.

"I'm afraid not," Alexandra said, and thought suddenly of carrying one of the littlest ones away with her, a boy of four or five, maybe, as naturally as she and Bobby had carried off Stoycho. It set up an ache under her ribs.

"Too bad," said the Captain, and fell silent. Miss Radeva showed them out, then, and waved goodbye, her slender hand vanishing through the door.

Forty-five

1949

The train traveled for what seemed to me most of the day, stopping twice along the route. Each time it stopped, I thought they might open the car to let us out at our unknown destination, or to admit more men, or at least to give us water. The longing to get out of the dark and the stink began to overpower everything else, for me. Every time we stopped, some man close to the door managed to get his eye to a crack in it and report to the rest of us. At the first halt, perhaps an hour after we'd left Sofia, he told us that we were in a field, near woods, and a rumble of hope and fear went through the darkness. For a while, I felt certain that we had headed east.

"They should let us out," a man near me said. "We all got to piss." But he said it quietly, as if he didn't expect any results, and indeed there were none. The train sat until the ground began to shake, and then our car trembled briefly and frighteningly; they had let another train pass us. I wondered where on the line we had stopped, but I never knew. We all settled again to holding our bladders in the dark, but then somebody bumped into a bucket hung in the corner and

461

told the rest of us he was putting it on the floor. When we absolutely had to, we crept toward it —gripping anonymous shoulders and even the tops of heads—and relieved ourselves. Anyone who could moved away from the bucket, which smelled worse and worse as the day wore on; eventually it overflowed. It was warm for October.

We went uphill for a while, and around sharp curves, where the train's whistle blew far ahead. The second time the train stopped, the same man put his eye to the chink in the door and reported, "Mountains. Big ones, with pine trees."

Then I guessed that we had been taken on the northern line, into Stara Planina, but I couldn't estimate how far. I couldn't smell anything except the ripening urine and the man on the other side of the car who had not been allowed to clean up his pants, but somewhere out there was fresh mountain wind and the scent of fir trees under the autumn sun. I knew that region from a trip my parents had taken me on when I was small, to visit a dying great-grandmother. I couldn't recall the old woman we'd gone to say goodbye to, but I remembered the straight wall of rock, the pines crawling up it, the peak covered with snow in late spring. It was cooler up here, even in the densely packed car. For a moment, I had a strange sense that we could not be traveling through Bulgaria anymore, or that I couldn't be awake.

"It's a station," the man said. "But I can't see any sign. Maybe we get off here."

But again the train moved, and I fell asleep; I slept around the edges of an empty stomach, until thirst overcame my hunger and I woke trying to sort my tongue out from the roof of my mouth. The thought must have been on everyone's mind, because the injured man next to me began to sob for water, and someone else told him roughly to shut up. No one wanted to hear the word; I wished for a moment that I could bring the poor man a whole pitcher, and drink from it with him, and then I wished I could punch him. I moved my sore back and hips and put my arms over my ears. It already seemed to me weeks since the evening before, when I'd eaten supper with Vera, urinated in a clean W.C., drunk a glass of water at bedtime, and stretched my whole frame out on a bed.

The third time we stopped, it was for good; we could hear engineers calling up and down the tracks, someone hammering, a sound of ringing on heavy steel. Voices and hands were outside our car, shouting, unbolting, prying something off the doors, then opening it all up. We blinked and struggled, too stiff to stand, but there were men with guns in the bright opening, fitting ramps to the back of a couple of trucks. "Move!" they shouted, and somehow we moved, partly in the hope that there would be water. These were different men from the ones who'd packed us in at Sofia. I don't care to remember them. They lined us up along the ramps and counted us as we crossed into the trucks; my sleeping companion still could not walk, and it took three of us to get him on his feet. I was among the last off, and I saw the commotion at the back of the car, where the light hardly reached.

"What is it?" shouted one of the guards.

"He's dead," said an older prisoner, coming forward almost apologetically. "I don't know his name, but he got in with us yesterday, in the morning. He was bleeding."

"Move along with you," said the man. "Get on the damn truck. Son of a bitch—count him off," he added to a man with a big notebook. "You'll have to tell Vasko when we get there."

"Do we take the body with us, comrade?" the man with the notebook asked.

"Hell, we'll have to."

Three of the prisoners stayed behind to remove the dead man. I thought, *At least he's not thirsty anymore.* Then I remembered Vera and felt guilty. She would need me back alive.

The trucks were large—army transport vehicles from the war; I noticed an instruction in German along the doors as I climbed in, but saw only a few words of it: IN CASE OF—. For a moment on the ramp I caught sight of evening sky, high peaks, rocks, pines clinging to crevices, and felt

464

an unbelievably sweet, cool breeze on my face. I could also see an old train station with a tiled roof and a blue and white enameled sign. The sign said ZELENETS, apparently the name of this village. I had never heard of it. Far below the station I could see a few houses and a church.

At the entrance to the truck was a bucket of water, with a single wooden dipper. A boy in a torn jacket gave us each a gulp of it as we got on—we were not allowed to touch the dipper ourselves. As soon as I'd had a slurp of water, I began wondering when they would give us food. Troop benches lined the sides of the truck, and the first who filed in sat down there; I missed the chance to sit but was glad when I noticed that a fainting man with hugely swollen bare feet had found a place. The rest of us stood, braced together in our stink, and the men with guns shut the back doors and bolted them from the outside.

The truck climbed with a roar along the road, slipping on stones and into ruts, then moving at walking pace under its load. I hoped that if we rolled over and fell into one of the valleys, the door would break open and we'd at least die in light and air. The prisoners around me kept their heads down, exhausted, fearful. I looked cautiously at the faces I hadn't been able to see in the dark car all day—old men with white whiskers and white spittle on their lips, very young men with blue shadows under their eyes and smears of dirt or blood on their cheeks, and every kind of man in between—and I realized I was the only one looking around. Everyone else was holding on to the truck or the next man's shoulder and staring down at the swaying metal floor. We were not merely hungry, thirsty, sore, stinking, and frightened. We were too humiliated to meet one another's eyes.

The truck rode for a long time into the mountains, generally upward on winding roads, and then along a straight flat stretch for a few minutes before we halted. The back was opened again, and again the men with guns goaded us out, and they were joined by other men who had come to meet them. A few of these new guards wore real uniforms, a dark-green wool that looked hot and scratchy in the mild evening, and caps with a red star, like army officers. They were better organized, too, herding us into line down the truck ramp. It was dimmer where we got out; the sun had gone behind the slopes of a gorge, and I saw that we were on a road that followed a small river into the mountains.

Then the officers with the real uniforms ordered us all to kneel, and I thought this might be where they would shoot us. I felt oddly numb, more hungry than afraid; I regretted the idea of dying without a final meal, the last supper that condemned men in novels were always allowed to have. I decided not to think of Vera or my parents. That would make it easier. I knew I had done wrong, but not the wrong they thought they were shooting me for. I thought, *How strange to die without even knowing where you are.* Then they counted us again, swiftly, shouting; I saw that one of them had a face like that of my second-best friend from high school, with the same oversized jaw and beaky nose, and yet was not him.

Suddenly, they ordered us all to our feet and I understood we'd been kneeling not to be killed but so that we wouldn't run away while they were counting us. For some reason, this sent a spiral of hope through my gnawing belly, and I silently promised Vera that I would return.

"March, you criminals!" shouted one of the guards. "March forward! Stay together! Anyone who steps out of line or slows down will be shot! Understand? Understand?" We moved forward, heavily, rapidly, even the injured men. I kept my broken finger well away from the flailing hands of the fellow beside me. The drunk from the cell in Sofia and my companion with the swollen feet were both farther ahead in the line, and I hoped someone would help them walk. A man stumbled a few rows in front of me and at once we all stumbled, which brought a curse from the nearest guard. I decided not to look around anymore, not at the guards' faces and not at the cliffs with that beautiful last light draining off them. I could hear the little river rushing past, just under the sound of our feet in the dust. We turned up a side road and left the river behind, all that water we could have drunk in one mass of thirst. Now it was dim, almost twilight, steep woods closing in along the sides of the road. We marched, gasping, for at least five kilometers, and someone must have straggled, because the men with guns shouted and threatened behind us.

Then the road opened out again and we saw buildings, a big fence and a rough gate, a guard-house set on scaffolding. There were more men there, with guns and uniforms, and a tall alert shepherd dog hovering near them. They opened the gate and we marched through it with pathetic ardor. Before my part of the line went in, I could see the words over the gate: GLORIOUSLY FORWARD TO THE FUTURE, and another sign at the side that read HAIL TO THE SOVIET COMMUNIST PARTY. I wondered if this was a Russian camp, but the sign was in Bulgarian and the men shutting the gates behind us were speaking Bulgarian. There were no prisoners visible inside, only the open doorways of the wooden buildings, like dark squared mouths. They lined us up again, this time in rows facing forward. A man in front of me buckled suddenly and fell over. The men beside him tried to haul him to his feet.

"Leave him alone!" cried one of the officers.

"Do you want to be punished, too?" And the standing men let go. After a moment, the man who'd fallen crawled to his knees and stood again, trembling.

The officer who had spoken planted himself in front of us, where we could all see him. He had an assistant stationed at each side, but they didn't wear the same neat uniform as he did; these other two men were slovenly, in ordinary clothes caked with mud; one of them carried a heavy wooden club and looked stooped over, as if he'd beaten himself up. The officer said, "Welcome to your new home of Zelenets. You are here for a purpose. It is your duty and your privilege to work toward your own rehabilitation. Are there any questions?"

A man near the front suddenly spoke up. His voice was firm, half-pleading, and it came out loud in the silence. "Comrade, we haven't eaten since yesterday or the day before."

The officer turned and stiffened. Apparently, he hadn't expected any response. "You're hungry?"

"Yes, comrade." This time, I recognized the prisoner who had spoken up. He had helped me support the fellow with wounded feet, as we all boarded the train. He was a man with a fine big head and broad shoulders, the body of someone accustomed to working hard with his hands and arms.

The officer stopped in front of him. "Step out here and we will discuss this," he said. For the first time, I could see the officer's face. He was about forty, tall and fit in the uniform—perhaps a professional soldier, before this, decorated in the war. I wondered if running this place had been his reward for serving the Revolution as the war ended. His hair was invisible under his cap, but his face looked clean-shaven and his eyes were large and greenish, like the cap. He made a quick gesture and the two men in old clothes suddenly grabbed the big-headed prisoner who'd spoken. The younger of these two was a mere boy, but tall and strong, with a head of curly light hair. He held the prisoner fast by one arm. The other man raised his club and brought it down with unbelievable swiftness against the prisoner's shoulder. The prisoner fell forward with a scream and the stooping little man brought his club ferociously down again, this time onto the prisoner's big head. The sound was unreal, sickening—the splitting of bone and a thud into the dirt.

Four or five of us lunged forward without thinking, trying to reach our companion, to pull him to some kind of safety. The club struck another man on the side of the arm and made him stagger, the officer shouted, the young blond guard in his grubby clothes pulled out a metal stick, other guards came running. We fell back. That was it: instant death or possible survival. This was what our officer had meant when he'd asked if anyone had questions. The injured prisoner—crumpled now into the ground and twitching—was our instructor. In a minute or two he grew still, and a couple of guards came to drag his body away. I watched, nearly fainting with shock and anger, then tried not to look anymore.

Forty-six

At the center of Yambol, Alexandra was surprised to see a couple of beautifully restored buildings from the Ottoman period; they stretched upward, cool and arching, on the old square—a mosque built of rosy variegated stones and an ancient market building that now housed dress shops. The café was nearby, but they still had half an hour before they could meet Miss Radeva. Bobby bought a kilo of cherries from a fruit stand and ate them out of the plastic bag. Stoycho panted in the heavy sun and Alexandra begged in sign language for a bowl of water for him from a little grocery store. "*Voda, molya,*" Bobby coached her.

Their most important errand, which Alexandra never forgot, was a spontaneous one. On the square stood a domed church; they tied Stoycho under a tree and stepped in, out of the heat. Bobby went to a kiosk in the entrance to buy candles.

"Look what piles of them they have today," he told Alexandra. "It must be a holiday. For the celebration of Kiril and Metodii, maybe, which is very soon. That's a big one, to celebrate our alphabet. Also to celebrate teaching and literature. Just the right day for you."

"And for you," Alexandra said, smiling at him. He put his coins into the trough at the kiosk window and a woman in a blue dress handed them out four candles. Bobby gave Alexandra two of them and they walked together into the apse, hand in hand for a moment—the way she might have with Jack, Alexandra thought, if he'd been here.

But as they were leaving the church, a figure at the end of the steps turned and came toward them with a weirdly uneven gait. Stoycho, tied up nearby, got to his feet, watching. Alexandra drew back, shading her eyes in the glare, but Bobby stepped forward. The figure was an elderly woman, her back bent almost parallel to the ground, her head covered with a scarf that left her face a tunnel of darkness. Over one arm she had hung a pile of crocheted doilies and over the other several heavy old necklaces. She couldn't raise her head far enough to look at them, but she held out her arms and said something in a soft, cracked voice.

"Is she selling these things?" Alexandra asked.

"I think so," said Bobby. "I can't quite understand her. They probably belonged to her family. I guess she has nothing else left."

With great effort, the woman held her arms

higher, closer to their faces. A smell like rotting vegetables rose off her clothing.

"Shouldn't we buy something?" Alexandra whispered.

"I could give her a few coins," Bobby said doubtfully.

"She's not begging," said Alexandra.

The woman stood near them with terrible patience, not even lowering her arms, which trembled. She didn't speak again, as if she now knew that they wouldn't understand.

"I'll buy you a necklace," Bobby said suddenly.

They were strange and beautiful, tarnished brass, with large reddish beads that looked like carnelian. One of them had a row of old coins fastened to it.

"Oh, please don't," she said. "They might be expensive."

"I'm sure they're not, and I want to." He spoke to the old woman. They seemed to come to an agreement; Bobby pulled several bills from his pocket.

"You choose," he told Alexandra.

She hesitated. "I'd rather you chose," she said. She was afraid the old woman must be exhausted just from holding them up, and she wished they could see her face, could know if the woman was pleased about the sale or sad about losing something that might be an heirloom. Surely whatever Bobby had offered was a pittance for such a treasure. Perhaps, Alexandra thought, they shouldn't even buy one—she shouldn't take it out of Bulgaria.

Bobby reached down and drew the second necklace gently off the woman's sleeve, threading it over her misshapen hand. She lowered her arms at once and put the rest of her wares into a deep pocket. Alexandra thought she might limp away, but she stood looking at their feet from the darkness inside her scarf. Bobby handed Alexandra the necklace. It was surprisingly weighty, clean but discolored with age, with ornate links of silvery brass, globes of amber like honey, and a pendant of softly red carnelian set in more brass. It had an Eastern look, Byzantine, like the inside of the church itself—an aesthetic long predating this world of cars and cell phones. Maybe, she thought with a twinge of wonder, it really was from Ottoman times, which would make it at least a hundred and thirty years old.

"You never know, here," Bobby muttered when she asked him. "People sell all kinds of stuff. It could be imported from India."

The old woman raised her hand and waved a finger at them. She said something, but slowly, for the children to comprehend.

"She says *not* India." Bobby shook his head. "From her village, very old. Her great-grandmother."

"I hope that's not true," Alexandra murmured,

but the brass was already warming sweetly in her hand. Bobby unclasped it and put it around her neck, where it descended to her breastbone.

"Thank you, Bobby," she said. Stoycho was whining for them now. The necklace hung heavy on her heart.

"Come on," said Bobby. "Let's go to the café. We can tie Stoycho just outside."

A few minutes later Miss Radeva appeared, walking lightly toward their table. Alexandra wished they could have seen the inside of her apartment at the housing complex; she imagined it very simple, entirely furnished in white, a swan's nest. Miss Radeva smiled briefly at them as she sat down. She seemed a little tired now, with the first signs of age around her eyes. Alexandra thought this gave her the air of a saint in an icon, weary from the persistent evil of the world, although it would have made most people look merely run-down. Miss Radeva had braided her long hair into a complicated knot at the back of her head. What would it have been like, Alexandra wondered, to grow up with some peerless older sister, so that when Jack was gone they could have comforted each other, traveled together?

Bobby was scanning the café, which was only half full, and ordering coffee for all of them. Miss Radeva poured an extra helping of sugar into hers and leaned back in her chair.

Bobby regarded her. "Have you lived very long in Yambol?"

"Yes," she said. "I came here to work when I was twenty-three. About twenty-three years ago, in fact. I grew up at the sea."

They both stared at Miss Radeva; it seemed impossible that she was in her mid-forties. She did not appear to notice. "All of our family was from Sofia, like the Lazarovi, and we lived there until I was five. Then we went to Burgas. By then, Uncle Milen had been working in Burgas a long time. He is my father's older brother. He found my father a job in the petrochemical plant, which was very big in those days." She stirred her coffee, too many times. "The Lazarovi went there to live, also. Uncle Stoyan was sometimes playing in the orchestra in Burgas, and in the opera, but he mostly worked at a food-processing factory. I always called them my uncle and aunt—Uncle Stoyan and Aunt Vera. Neven was like my cousin, too, or a big brother, because I did not have one."

Bobby put his spoon down. "Do your parents still live there?"

She shook her head and her fine features sank a little. "My parents are dead. They died together in an accident on a boat while I was in my high school." She picked up her cup.

Jack, Alexandra thought. All these shades and shadows who had gone to join him, or whom he had gone to join, from every side of the globe. Some favorite lines from her college Milton course suddenly came to her: ... *thousands at his bidding speed / And post o'er land and ocean without rest.* At that moment Alexandra realized she would someday be teaching other readers, other young people, about those words that had the power to still the shaking of her hands.

"I'm so sorry," she said, trying to raise her voice from an inaudible place.

"And I am," Bobby said.

Alexandra felt he had heard the quiver in her tone—that knowledge, with the Milton, somehow reduced the pulsation of the café around her. She thought suddenly, "Miss Radeva is an orphan," and turned to ask her if this had been the reason for her choice of work, then stopped herself. Instead she said, "What about *gospodin* Lazarov? Did you know him well?"

Miss Radeva put her cup down and sat lacing and unlacing her delicate fingers. "Not so very well," she said. "He was always there, but he was much quieter than Aunt Vera. He didn't seem very—interested—in children, except in his son, Neven. He was very proud of Neven."

Bobby set down his coffee, too. "Are you still close to Neven?"

Miss Radeva shook her head. "I do think of him as a brother," she said, "but unfortunately we have lived not near each other in many years. I think he is also more quiet now than he was when we were children and having fun. Maybe he is harder to know. He works for some online accounting company from the old apartment in Burgas where his parents used to live. It is a very small apartment, not very nice, especially now. I think he often works long hours—that must be lonely for him, although he told me his job allows him to go sometimes and stay with his mother. And Uncle Milen and Aunt Vera looked very old, when I saw them the last time." She shook her head.

Then, as if to change the subject for a minute, she asked Alexandra where she came from in the United States and whether there were discos in her town. Alexandra, who spent most of her time at the library or in the mountains, had to think hard. "Yes, there is one. I'm not sure what it's like."

"I thought an American town would have lots of discos." Miss Radeva puzzled over this. "We have at least four discos here, and I go every weekend. I love to dance."

"So," said Bobby, putting his fork down. "You know we are very worried about how to find your uncle and the Lazarovi. But, as I said, we wonder if there is something about *gospodin* Lazarov that we don't know and that might help us."

"Yes," Miss Radeva said. "And now I am worried, also." She sighed. "I have never heard my uncle so—strange and serious like he was on the phone. He is usually a little more calm. He said they couldn't tell me where they were going on vacation or when they would go, or exactly when they would come to see me. I think he was saying he did not want to tell me. I felt hurt by this, because he is my closest relative, and I also was afraid that his mind was maybe going bad. I even had for a moment the idea that they would leave Bulgaria on a longer trip, if he had some money I do not know about."

Alexandra felt a rawness in her stomach. She had never before considered the possibility that the Lazarovi might leave the country. Would they do that, if any of them knew what had been hidden in the urn? And was this an indication that they did know they were in some danger? On the other hand, Milen had talked with Miss Radeva before they'd lost the urn. Had Neven himself hidden Stoyan's confession inside it, with Nasko Angelov's help? Was he frantic to retrieve it, or had something happened since then to make them flee Bulgaria? She imagined Neven at the railing of a ship, growing more distant every moment, until she could see only his black and white clothes. Maybe she herself had caused all this, by taking the urn, so that he would never get it back, never be able to bury his father, perhaps never be able to return safely to his country. She had thought she could do that much right—give back what belonged to one family, at least, and to the earth. She squeezed her hands together in her lap, to keep the right one from creeping inside her left sleeve.

"Do you think"—Bobby was asking for both of them—"do you think that they felt afraid enough about something to seriously consider leaving Bulgaria?"

"I would never have said that." Miss Radeva stroked her hair off her shoulders. "But now I am not sure. The whole conversation was a little not right. And because you came today and asked if I thought that Uncle Stoyan had been in trouble with the police, I am feeling suddenly more anxious. Uncle Milen has always been nervous about the police, but I thought that was only because of the time in which he was a young man, under the early socialism."

"Was he ever in trouble himself, in those times?" Bobby leaned forward.

Miss Radeva was thoughtful, her large eyes clear. "I don't think so. Maybe Uncle Stoyan's experience made Milen nervous. Anyone could be arrested, in those days."

Still can, Alexandra thought, looking at Bobby. *A poet, for example.*

Bobby was clearly not dwelling on his own situation, however. "Uncle Stoyan's experience?" he asked. "What was that?"

Miss Radeva looked uncomfortable. "That is

what I feel I should tell you. Uncle Stoyan did not ever talk about it, but I know that he was arrested by the state security, and maybe more than once. Aunt Vera did not talk about it either. One night, a few months after my parents died, Uncle Milen took me to dinner in Burgas, and he drank very much. I think he wanted to speak to me about my parents, but he was too sad, and instead he told me about Stoyan, almost by accident."

"That must have been very sad for you, too," said Bobby.

Alexandra, looking at him, thought suddenly: *You could get a stone to talk.*

Forty-seven

We were sitting at an outdoor restaurant in Burgas, Miss Radeva said. *It's in the old Sea Park, the Morska Gradina.* If you go to Burgas, you will see it—a lovely place above the beach, although not as nice now as it once was. It had tables outside, on a terrace with a big stone *balyustrada* and a huge view of the water and sky. I was seventeen, and I had not been to the park since a day two months before when I was called to the hospital to hear that my parents had been brought there dead, and to receive their wet clothing in a bag. I had not been even to the beach since then. When I saw the outdoor restaurant again, with the evening sun over the big bay, the tables shining, and the stretch of blue water, I thought that I really did not want to sit down there. But my uncle seemed determined we would do it and I followed him. He held my chair, which he had always done for my mother but never before for me. That made me sad right away.

Uncle Milen ordered me a glass of wine, although I was too young and he didn't like to watch women drink. He ordered *rakiya* for himself and wished me health in a shaky voice. I could suddenly see that his straight dark hair, which was so thick when he was young, had begun to look frosty and thin. His eyes were red around the edges, maybe not from tears so much as from exhaustion. I had worn my favorite green dress and some shoes I liked with it, to thank him for taking me out, and he complimented me on my appearance. I had always felt I was his child, his favorite, because he had no children of his own and had not even married. He had told me once that he'd given his heart when he was young to a woman who couldn't really love him, but that he had never regretted it.

We sat eating and talking about unimportant things in the warm evening, and for a while I could believe that we were just out to dinner, uncle and niece, and that he would take me home to my parents later instead of to my grandmother's apartment, where I had been living since their deaths. The trees were fully green, the best time of year, and there was a wonderful saltiness in the air instead of the stink of the refinery plant. I had thought many times since that day at the hospital that the beautiful weather was very strange—the sky had stayed blue and the sun kept coming up over the sea in the morning and going down behind our backs every evening. It had been a lovely day when they drowned, just very windy.

Uncle Milen spoke for a while about his work, which had not been going very well, and asked me a little awkwardly how things were at my grandmother's. He asked me if he could do anything for me, and to spare him from hearing the truth aloud, I said that he could take me out again to dinner in the Sea Park now and then. That made him smile—we always have known how to laugh and smile together, although he is also a serious and sometimes even grumpy man—and he said that with such good company he would want to come back often. He kept ordering small glasses of *rakiya*, and we ate the good food, and eventually I realized that he was a little bit drunk, or more than a little, since he stays calm and polite if he drinks. I was feeling somewhat off from the wine, myself, because I had rarely had a full glass and now I'd finished almost two.

I thought about asking him what my mother had been like at my age, because I was hungry to know everything I could about my parents, now that they were gone. Instead I asked how the Lazarovi were, since we had often been at their place over the years and they were our great friends, almost like family. I knew that they must miss my parents, also. Neven was still living with them, studying at the chemical institute. "I suppose Stoyan will be disappointed to get an engineer instead of a musician," my uncle had said to me once. Stoyan had tried for years to teach his son to play the violin, with no particular luck. Neven could play lots of pieces, but slowly and without expression. When we were children together, we both dreaded the end of each afternoon, when Neven would be called in from the street to practice his violin. He very much preferred playing ball, and we also had a large secret collection of foil wrappers—you know, from candies and other things. We spent hours smoothing them out, which makes them even shinier, until they get too fragile and crack.

In any case, my uncle said that Vera and Stoyan were all right, but he thought Stoyan was a little ill. Not ill in body, he said, but in heart. Sad. "He gets this way now and then, in spite of his music." My uncle sipped his *rakiya*. "You should have seen him before his arrest. So lively— not a noisy person, but full of life from his head to his shoes. Completely energetic."

I had never heard before that Stoyan had been

arrested, and my uncle didn't seem to notice my surprise, so I stayed quiet and let him talk. He was sitting back with his arms folded over his stomach, shaking his head. He said, "Stoyan was not the same after. I remember the time they came for him in Burgas. I was actually there, God help me."

He drank off some more, and again I didn't try to stop him from speaking—or drinking.

"Well, you know," he said, "it was many years ago and we were all still more or less young, when they first moved to Burgas. I went to have dinner with Stoyan and Vera one evening, as I often did. I brought them some jars of pickles I had received from my grandmother in the village that week. It was an evening when Stoyan did not have to play in the orchestra, and we were all sitting at home in their front room. They had a section of an apartment, with an old couple living in the back room, hardly enough space for a young family. Vera had made it nice, with curtains she had sewn from some bright-colored material. After dinner we sat around talking. Stoyan said he would play for us, which he rarely did at home, and I remember that he played some of that Italian he liked so much, from memory, sounds like a—I don't know how to describe it, very numerical and neat but also like water running down a slope. I can't remember the composer's name, just now, but I will think of it. Fantastic. I suppose I need a little more *rakiya*. Vera looked incredibly beautiful, sitting on their divan in the light from the lamp. Little Neven was away with his grand-parents and it was like old times.

"After Stoyan played, we sat talking some more and I began to think about getting home in time for the curfew, although I never liked to leave, and my own apartment seemed bare to me whenever I had been with them. But then there was a strong knock at the door. Their apartment was on the first floor, in an old building. That was a little strange already, because it was past eleven o'clock and the street had been quiet for a while. Vera got up to answer, looking worried. Stoyan sat with his face set and still, as if the sound had frozen him. He said, quietly: *Pak*. Again.

"Then he lifted his violin, which he had been holding across his knees, and put it into the case with its bow, and swiftly put the whole case behind the divan before Vera even opened the door. When she turned from the person at the door her face was white. She and Stoyan looked at each other, and I felt as if I was not in the room. She stepped aside, and an officer in a plain uniform came in without speaking. Stoyan and I both stood up. For a minute I understood that this was some kind of summons but thought it might actually be for me, possibly something I had done wrong at work without knowing it.

"Then Stoyan stepped forward. The officer took

out some papers but still he didn't even have to speak. I tell you, Stoyan went forward as if drawn toward him by a rope. The man put a hand on the gun at his belt, actually a bulge under the jacket, just for a second. I almost missed it, that gesture. Then he turned back to the door and Stoyan followed him. Vera was clenching her hands together and I knew she wanted to run to him. Stoyan turned around, and without looking at Vera at all, he said to me, *Take care of her.*"

When my uncle reached this point in the story, he pinched the top of his nose with his thumb and forefinger and didn't speak for a moment. "And I swear I did try," he said. His voice wobbled. "I did try to do that. I admired him more than anyone I ever knew."

"What was he arrested for?" I asked him, hesitantly, because I had never thought of Uncle Stoyan as someone who could be in trouble. He had always seemed to me just a quiet person, a musician, hardworking, not many smiles but not any harsh words, either. He was not my idea of a criminal, but I knew that in earlier days people were sometimes arrested even when they were not criminals.

Uncle Milen didn't answer. His nose looked red. Instead he said, "I should not have told you this. I know I should not. You must never tell anyone."

"I won't," I said. "But Aunt Vera must have been glad to have him back safely."

That appeared to reassure him a little. He knew I would not speak about it outside our family. "Yes, she was very glad, when he came home." And he ordered coffee for himself, and pancakes with cherry jam for me. That's all I remember.

Forty-eight

Bobby sat with his arms folded, face thoughtful. "And he never told you anything else about Stoyan?"

Miss Radeva shook her head. "No. Not about his being in trouble with the police. It must not have been bad trouble, because I didn't hear any more about it. I would have been six or seven when it happened, and I remember only that Uncle Stoyan was away from home for a while. Of course, Uncle Milen told me some ordinary things about Stoyan, over the years, too—like that they had studied in Sofia at the same *gimnasium*, although my uncle was younger and they had not met then. They became acquainted later, when Stoyan returned from studying in Vienna and before Uncle Stoyan and Aunt Vera got married."

Miss Radeva was playing with a wisp of her dark hair that had escaped from the knot. "My uncle knew Aunt Vera's family for years, too, because they lived in the same neighborhood in Sofia. They all loved music. And he told me that

Stoyan liked to nap at lunchtime, so Neven and I should not be noisy at their apartment if we played there then."

Alexandra took a last sip of her coffee, thinking about Stoyan Lazarov, a musician who napped during his lunch hour and had been called away from his beautiful wife to the police station more than once. She imagined him coming back the next morning, dirty and tired, maybe even with a bruise on his face. Or had he been away for months, that time? Years?

"Why did he say that—'*Again*'?" Bobby asked.

"Again?" Miss Radeva frowned.

"Yes," Bobby said. "Do you know why *gospodin* Lazarov said '*Pak*' when they arrested him, in your uncle's story?"

Miss Radeva shrugged. "Nobody talked about these things. But I have heard that in those days if a person was arrested once, he was often arrested again, because he was under suspicion for the rest of his life. Now that I am thinking more about it, I remember that Uncle Stoyan was actually away several times while we were children and teenagers—one time for two years. Aunt Vera always said he was working in another part of the country."

Bobby and Alexandra glanced at each other. "We actually know," Bobby said, "that he was arrested and sent to a labor camp, before Neven was born."

She shook her head, slowly. "They never told me that. But it explains a great deal."

Bobby hesitated. "We came here as quietly as we could, but we must tell you a little more now. We have been followed recently, and threatened with graffiti—or perhaps it is the Lazarovi and your uncle who are being threatened." He told Miss Radeva everything else about the events of the previous five days. She looked increasingly distressed, twirling the lock of hair around her finger.

"We're sorry to involve you," Alexandra said. "Please be careful. If you see anything that makes you nervous, call Bobby right away."

"Or if you remember anything else about Stoyan Lazarov that you think we should know," Bobby added.

"I will do that. But please, please—let me know, too, if you hear anything about my uncle, or any of them." Miss Radeva stood, still graceful. Bobby and Alexandra got up, too, to tell her good-bye.

"*Blagodarya.*" Bobby kissed her on both cheeks. "Of course we will call your mobile immediately if we hear something."

"Thank you," Miss Radeva said.

Alexandra put her arms around Miss Radeva's slender shoulders and clung to her for a moment, although she knew this wasn't the thing to do. Miss Radeva lifted Alexandra's long hair gently in her hand and then let it drop. "Please drive carefully," she said.

Bobby and Alexandra watched her walking out the door, graceful in her heels. They sat down again for a moment while Bobby counted out money for the coffee and put it in a pile in the middle of the table. Just as he set the last coin on top, his phone rang.

"It's Irina," he said. Alexandra could hear the old lady telling him something in Bulgarian, agitated. Bobby was alert at once, and when he hung up, he turned to Alexandra.

"Bad news," he said softly. "Very bad. Atanas Angelov has been found dead, in Irkad. She heard about it only a few minutes ago, from his son."

Alexandra could not make sense of this. "You mean *gospodin*—Irina's artist? From yesterday? Oh, no," she said. "Oh, no, no."

Bobby clenched his hands on the table. "Yes. He was found this morning in the forest near Irkad. It looks as if he went there by himself to meet someone after we left—his son did not see him all night and was very worried. A man from the village found him."

"He went to meet someone?" Alexandra said stupidly.

Bobby squeezed his hands together. "Someone who cut his throat."

"Oh, my God," Alexandra said. Her breathing

seemed to have shut down. She felt she was looking again at that quiet brown face, the tears trickling along its wrinkles but falling now into a wicked gash.

"This is because of the urn," Bobby said harshly. "It must be."

"Oh, no—it's me," Alexandra said, and she began to cry. "None of this would have happened if I hadn't taken it to the police and tried to find all these people. Or if I hadn't kept it to begin with. This is the way I mess things up."

Bobby turned suddenly and, reaching out, shook her by the shoulders. "Stop that," he said. She could see the fear in his face; she remembered how Angelov had been saddened by the fate he'd read there. "Stop that or I will slap you, Bird."

"What?" Alexandra said, outraged, but his tone was so angry, so affectionate, that she dried her eyes.

He put his forehead against hers for a moment, right in the middle of the café, then straightened. "Irina is very upset and I am even more afraid for her safety, and Lenka's as well. I told her we will go back to her right away."

Forty-nine

1949

We were divided into three groups and assigned to men they called our brigade chiefs. The brigade chiefs looked to me more like prisoners, in their torn garments and ill-fitting shoes, and I soon learned that they were just that: prisoners who had been promoted. They carried clubs, which they did not need just then; we went quietly with them to the cement washroom in our new divisions. Among the men with me, I knew the drunk from Sofia, who was dazed beyond speech. I also recognized from somewhere, but by face only, a gentle-looking young man with a brown beard and soft brown eyes. He moved quietly and gave me a glance so full of dignity, pain, and outrage that I felt we'd had an entire conversation. We might have met, in the old days, in a café or library in Sofia, where we would simply have nodded to each other.

In the washroom, we were ordered to strip. I saw welts on the bearded man's back, scabbing over like garnets. Our brigade chief looked so elderly that I wondered if he would be able to keep order among us, and also how he'd survived the horrors of this situation. Then I realized that he was not old but had simply lost almost all his teeth, so that his face had shrunk into itself and his eyes had drooped toward his cheeks. He told us that his name was Vanyo, but nothing more. He searched us while we were naked, in a businesslike way, taking a wristwatch from one man and an icon on a chain from another. He stuffed the watch into his pocket and dropped the icon into a slop bucket in the corner.

Next he ordered another prisoner to help us shave our heads, which was painful, and check for lice; this they accomplished with old razors, buckets of cold water, and coarse lye soap in wooden trays. I never saw my clothes again. They gave us piles of shirts and undergarments and trousers to choose from and watched as we traded feebly for anything that might fit: *dead men's clothing,* we were all thinking, although it was at least relatively clean when we received it. There were some odd socks and shoes, not enough for all; some of the men with larger feet remained barefoot the first night. I found a pair of torn leather street shoes that stayed on if I tied the laces tightly.

Our new brigade leader took us out into the yard again and distributed pans of bread and a pot of bean soup among us; it was foul, especially the soup, but we ate hungrily. He told us we would work and sleep together and that we must be ready to join our barracks, because the workers were returning soon. He did not say what work. Twilight had settled into darkness now and some of the guards switched on electric lights in the guardhouse; the rest carried lanterns, setting one outside each barrack door.

Then we heard shouts, tramping steps, and a weird sort of horn, like a muffled army bugle, and the workers were coming through the gate, guarded with guns and clubs. I could hardly believe my eyes. The figures that moved into the light of the yard did not look like men but living skeletons—eyes hollowed out as if by giant spoons; heads patchily bald; clothing falling from their bodies and covered with soot, rock dust, machine grease, so that it no longer resembled fabric. And yet these figures moved forward, toward the pans of bread and pots of reeking soup; they pulled battered tin cups and bowls from under their rags and fed themselves ravenously.

With a surge of horror, I remembered the etchings in my grandfather's book of Dante, the masses of dead souls in the halls of the Underworld. These men did not glance at us. I had thought we looked disheveled and broken, but compared with these apparitions we were well and whole. I saw with fresh dismay how damaged their hands were, too—many of them wore grimy or bloodstained bandages, or were missing digits. How long had they been here? I put away, care-fully, my belief that I would return to Vera in a matter of days; I didn't want even to glance at it anymore.

The old prisoners hardly had time to cram their bread into the hollows of their mouths before the bugle blew again, close by, and we were all lined up together for roll call, each by his full name, the newcomers last. The names seemed to go on forever, while the workers swayed and twitched, dead on their feet; I watched with amazement as one skeleton responded—*Ivan Genev!—Here!*—and then fell instantly asleep standing up, as if he'd been waiting for that moment. Sometimes there was confusion about a name or a response, and then the guard with the roll call would back up many names and go through them again, all the first names I'd ever known or heard of, and some that were even new to me, but clearly Bulgarian. Once or twice I heard what sounded like a German or Romanian or Hungarian name, but could not be sure.

At last we were dismissed, and I took advantage of the momentary confusion to ask a cadaverous man standing near me what work they did.

"Quarry," he said, as if extra words were too expensive to be wasted. "Mines. And a few to the timbering." He kept his voice low and did not try to meet my eyes. Then he shuffled away from me.

I had assumed we would sleep in the two large

wooden buildings, but those appeared to be full already. My new brigade was directed to a barrack near the back of the yard, a structure so low that the door seemed to lead into the ground—which it actually did. It was not a real building but rather a huge dugout in the mountain earth, and when we ducked down to get inside, the smell hit me so that I would have turned and gone back out to vomit if there hadn't been another man crawling in just behind me. It was a smell like meat left out too long, but infinitely stranger than that. I put the sleeve of my dead man's shirt over my nose and kept it tight. There were men already going to sleep, lying on the wooden bunks and even the floor. Our brigade leader, toothless Vanyo, pointed out empty bunks; because we were new, we would sleep near the slop bucket. The bucket accounted for some of the smell, but only some of it. Each bunk was covered with shreds of material that might once have been matting, and each of us had a decaying blanket from the war. There was one lantern to light all this—one lantern, one slop bucket, one doorway, and at least eighty men, once we were all in.

Now the skeleton workers were putting their shoes under their heads, for pillows. Some of them also had nests of things other than blankets —rotting jackets and rags from torn trousers. Someone was bolting the wooden door from the outside. If the lantern fell over, we would all roast, trapped. The smell hung in the air like something solid. A man in the bunk just above mine leaned down for a minute when I crawled in. His face was a skull like the rest. But I saw suddenly, as I would see over and over with other prisoners, that it was still a face, had once been normal and maybe even handsome. He almost smiled. "New," he said—it couldn't be a question.

"Stoyan Lazarov," I said. I decided not to add that I was from Sofia.

He reached a bundle of bones down toward me and shook my hand. "Petar, from Haskovo," he whispered.

"What is it?" I said. "The smell?" Someone blew out the lantern near the doorway.

Petar's voice came again. "It's the wounds. Our wounds. They get infected. Try not to notice, son," he said, not unkindly. "And try to keep clean. Let's sleep." He retreated into the darkness above me. Someone else was hushing us, angrily. I tore a little cloth from my bedding and bound my aching finger with it, hoping that would help the bone heal straight. I knew I should sleep, too.

But I lay awake, most of that first night. Once the men were breathing quietly around me, or whimpering a little in their sleep, I began to hear the millions of bugs that lived in the walls, in the ceiling of woven branches and earth, in our bedding, in our clothes. I began to feel them on my skin, inside the dead stranger's clothes, and I trembled and scratched myself with my good hand. I considered allowing my thoughts to return to that wonderful field, by the river, where my son sat, and then drew back. I wanted to save that, still—to look forward to it. Instead I said a short prayer for Vera and my parents, although I had not prayed since childhood and had no idea how to address it. It went out from me like a letter with no stamp.

Lying there, trying not to think about the itching or my hunger, I made myself a second promise. I had caused something terrible to happen, back in Sofia. These thugs could punish me for their own purposes, but only I had the right to punish myself for what I had really done. When I got home again, I would somehow attend to my real penance.

At last the sound of insect movements, their chewing and shredding, became my lullaby. I slept, briefly. Then the bugle blew, before dawn.

Fifty

1949

I woke exhausted but painfully alert, knowing before I left my dreams that I was not in the right place. I felt the griping emptiness in my stomach and sensed the men moving around me. I saw a rectangle made of light, which was the opening of the dugout with a lantern sitting just outside. Someone had unbolted our barracks and opened the door, but the dark cool morning could not reach us in that stink. My ears suddenly remembered the call of the bugle—without it, I would have slept forever. In fact, I had no desire to wake up at all. I ached from head to toe. I wished for a moment that they had pulled me from the train car and shot me instead.

"Get up," someone was hissing, and I climbed down and put on my ill-fitting shoes. My head itched where they had made me shave, and now there were rough places on my skin, under the worn-out shirt, either from the bugs or from the sheer filth. I told myself not to scratch them into open sores, remembering what Petar from Haskovo had said the night before, about infections. He wasn't in sight, in the bunk above—half the place had emptied already, in a silent rush. I scrambled out of the dugout and limped toward the wash-house, taking long breaths of that normal air, wanting to eat it. It was still quite dark, apart from an electric light that burned on the other side of the yard. A moment later, two guards rushed past me to the doorway; when I turned, I saw that the next prisoners to climb out, the stragglers, had caught blows from their clubs and were ducking and yelping. One fell to the ground and a guard kicked him. I thought, *On the street, in Sofia, I would have run to save the man on the ground.*

Yes, I would have been afraid for my hands, as every violinist is when a fight breaks out, but I would have helped.

At the washhouse, we stood in long lines for a row of eight toilet holes. The odor was terrible, a different terrible from the smell in the barrack. A few of the prisoners pushed to the front—hard-faced, rail-thin survivors—and everyone else let them barge ahead. It was the same at the basins, eight rusted metal bowls for hundreds of men. Each of us had a second or two at one bowl. I washed in gray slop from the faces of thirty or forty, not daring to take fresh water from the pitchers nearby, if it even was fresh. I didn't know the rules here; I would have to watch everything carefully, as one did in a new orchestra, with a brutal new conductor. No one spoke, except to mutter at any man who was slow at the latrines.

Breakfast, which was given to us in the yard, was tea with a smear of jam on the lip of the cup. We drank it standing up. At first I did not understand that this was all we would get, nor that the tin cup I'd been given was mine to keep.

"You're a lucky one," said the man next to me. "But you'll have to share. One in ten gets them." The cups, he meant, although it looked to me as if many of the men had similar tin cups; they hung them up somewhere inside their clothes when they'd finished drinking. "Watch out or someone will take it from you," growled the man.

I wondered suddenly if he intended to steal my cup himself, and I tied it hard to the belt-loop of my trousers, using a shred of fabric from the end of my shirt.

Then we had to line up in our brigade groups again to be counted. While I stood there, the long list of names pouring over my head, I looked cautiously up at the night sky. It was rustling with stars. I had not noticed them, the evening before, or perhaps they were brighter toward morning, even with the watchtower light on. It had been years since I'd really looked up at the stars; in Vienna, I'd sometimes seen a cold arch of them from my favorite park, when I was walking back to my room late at night.

Now I could trace long clear patterns, constellations whose names I wished I still knew. At the edge of the black sky, away from the lights of the watchtowers, one star stood by itself, as if it had fallen off the nearest constellation and drifted alone toward the horizon. I understood—from having seen sunset the evening before—that it was in the northeast, toward the faraway Black Sea, the Danube, the border with Romania. That star lingered by itself above a peak studded with fir trees; the trees looked blacker than the sky, as if their shapes opened onto an unthinkable dark-ness. I decided to call the star Beta-49, the most anonymous name I could think of, for the year in which I had discovered it.

When I turned my head toward the shouting, the guards we'd seen the night before—those three who'd beaten the man who'd spoken up—were standing in front of us. "New workers!" called the only one who had a uniform. "Does anyone have complaints this morning?"

We were silent, and the skeletons shuffled their feet like leaves, as if to warn the rest of us.

"Very well," he said. "Let me show you what happens to complainers. Also to those who fall out of line, and to anyone, anyone at all, who tries to leave his work site. Momo!" He made a quick movement of his hand, and his assistant, the light-haired young man who'd held the prisoner for him to beat the night before, stepped forward. "Which one, Momo?"

Momo smiled at us. I saw with creeping horror that he looked like a little boy, the innocent face of seven years old, with a broad gap between his top front teeth. But this child was perhaps sixteen or seventeen. His name struck me as ridiculous; in Vienna or Paris it would have been the name of a clown, or a street magician. He scratched the back of his head and rumpled his angelic hair. I thought he might be German, or Russian, or Czech, with that curly yellow hair and the purity of his face, but his voice was Bulgarian when he spoke. "Don't know, Chief. Maybe that one." His hand darted out and he pointed at a man near the front of the line, not one of us new men, but a worn-down fellow with graying stubble on his shaved head.

"Well, then." The Chief handed Momo his own club, and although the prisoner ducked quickly, it struck him on the side of the face and an animal sound of pain rose out of him. He bent over, shielding his head with both arms.

"He's good for nothing," the Chief said in a loud voice. "Be sure the rest of you are good for something." He made another rapid gesture—the guards seemed to have a sort of sign language among them for all their rituals—and the boy Momo reached into a wheelbarrow that stood nearby and handed the cringing man a big empty sack.

"No," said the man. "Please. I beg you."

"You'll have to carry it, you know," Momo said. The prisoners were all stock-still, no one looking at anyone else.

"Please," said the man. "I have a family at home, two children."

"Well, we all have families," the Chief said reasonably. "But we can't keep bad examples here. Is that understood?" His voice rose to a sudden shout. Momo stepped back, smiling, as if his work was finished, and had been done well.

"Yes," the men muttered, but it was like wind among old trees, no real sound. I didn't know why the man who'd been given the sack was in despair—it was empty, light to carry; it couldn't be any burden to him. But when we were ordered to march forward, we rounded the corner of the washhouse; huddled against the base of one wall was a similar sack, full of something lumpy, the shapes of a head and limbs, a dead weight. I realized it must be—it had to be—the man they'd beaten the night before, unless someone else had died during the night. My stomach twisted inside me and I thought for a moment I would have to lean out of the line to vomit up my breakfast of tea.

Then the bugle blew, and we marched out of the gates, as if we were heading back into freedom. I could see the gentle-looking, brown-bearded man—now minus his beard—who belonged in a Sofia café, and also the drunken man from my cell, both of them ahead of me. They were still part of my brigade, and I hoped to speak with the gentle-faced man, if there was a chance, later on.

I walked with my brigade that first morning up a road that wound behind the camp area and into the mountains, perhaps two kilometers. The road unfolded along a railroad bed, although I hadn't heard any trains pass the camp. I wondered if this rail line was the same one that had brought us to the village of Zelenets, and whether anyone ever tried to jump onto the side of a train to get away. There was no place to run to, even if we'd wanted to dare the guards to catch us; the mountainside rose steeply on our left, just beyond the railroad—exposed rock with sickly trees clinging to it. To our right, the land fell away among shrubs, so that anyone sliding down into the abyss would either tumble to his death in a few minutes or be shot easily from above. I wondered who had built such a road around the edge of a mountain—perhaps other damned souls like us.

The walk to our destination would have been easy for me a few days before; now, hungry and faint, I found myself gasping on the slightest rise. The guns prodded us along, and I noted that a couple of the younger guards, including the cherubic-looking Momo, cradled clubs in their arms as they marched beside us.

Around a curve in the road, the mountainside opened into a flat area with a huge pit in the middle, perhaps two hundred feet deep. I could see the zigzag of ramps leading up to the edge of the pit from shelves of earth inside, and wheelbarrows sitting nearby. Piles of half-split rock lay strewn around the open area. The railroad ran directly beside it, with a long spur for trains to stop on.

"Quarry!" shouted one of the guards, and half the brigades, including mine, fell out of our long line and walked with him toward the pit. The rest of the men, skeletons and newcomers, went on up the road without us, and I saw the small stooped man with the club walking behind them, as well as two guards in uniform. Momo had come with us to the edge of the quarry. When I turned around and took note of his presence, he caught my eye with a look I did not like at all, although I couldn't have said what it meant. I had noted his face, earlier, but now I saw how strong his frame was, with broad shoulders and massively thick arms. His clothes were nearly as shabby as my own; but he, like the other guards, seemed to be getting enough to eat.

I was assigned to a plateau partway down the pit, where we would break quarried stones into rocks small enough to load on the wheelbarrows. The wheelbarrows were built to fit onto narrow tracks and be pushed up the ramps. Three or four of the men from my brigade were also sent to this plateau, including the gentle-looking man and an old fellow with tufts of white hair at each temple. The old man's hands shook and I wondered if he would last the day. As it turned out, he had worked on construction sites all his life, and he picked up pieces of rock faster than I could.

At first we all did the same thing, each in turn breaking stones with a pickax, loading them on a barrow, and pushing the barrow up the slope on the rails to where another brigade took it away and hauled it toward the railroad line. Before long, however, we'd figured out that it made sense to divide the labor. The gentle man and a middle-aged fellow who said he was from Pirin broke the rock with pickaxes, straightening up frequently to relieve their backs. The old man volunteered to keep lifting rocks with his strong, shaking grip. I was grateful to be able to push the barrow; this was hard on my hands, especially since I had to keep my swollen little finger off the handles as much as possible, but it was not as damaging as the rocks or ax would have been. It was only a matter of time, I knew, before I would develop blisters and then wounds.

It seemed to me that the sun had barely risen before we were already tired enough to stop for the rest of the day. The guards noticed, because suddenly several of them were climbing down into the pit to shout at us about our laziness. Momo stopped at our plateau and swung his club in the air near the old man's head. "What are you slowing down for?" he cried.

The old man said nothing, but his strong shoulders and arms swung a little faster between the rock piles and the wheelbarrow. I held the barrow as steady as I could for him to drop in the rocks. I could see his hands were reddened and cut already; I decided that as soon as Momo left I would offer to relieve the old man of this work, or help him wrap them. Anger surged up inside me; this was a terrible dream, a piece of nonsense, a sickening joke. I looked carefully away from Momo, but he seemed to smell my emotion, like a dog, and he stepped closer. "Why don't you take a turn with the rocks?" he said.

"This fellow is a violinist," the old man said proudly. I wondered how he'd found this out, and then remembered I'd told him myself during our first and only exchange. A peasant from Pirin, a construction worker, a violinist. The gentle-looking man had said nothing about himself.

"A violinist?" Momo looked at me with curiosity. His face had the peculiar blankness of beauty stretched over a void; he didn't seem so much unaware of his own good looks as unaware of even being alive, in this place where no kind of beauty counted, anyway. I thought he was like a dangerous animal, a lion pacing a zoo enclosure, without self-consciousness, out of place. "You play the *tsigulka*?"

"Yes," I said. I told myself not to let even the smell of my anger seep out again, but he was already toying with me.

"Oh," he said. "Did you bring your *tsigulka* with you?" He laughed, as if he'd found his way to hilarity and was proud of getting there all by himself. I wondered if he was right in the head—but would anyone do his job who was right in the head, or remain sane while doing it?

"No, I didn't bring it," I said evenly, and steadied the barrow to push it uphill. He might be trying to see if he could get me to pause in my work, so he could punish me for it.

Momo turned his golden head around. The sun was up, above the mountain slopes; it came down into the quarry in a dome of light, catching the color of his mane and the transparency of his eyes. His neck was grimy but muscular, as large and perfect as Michelangelo could have made it. "You are not supposed to talk while you work," he said petulantly. "Now I have to punish you for it or the guards will be angry."

I had supposed he counted himself among the guards.

"Well?" he said, looking at me. The gentle man and the man from Pirin worked with their heads down. "Should I punish you or him?" He pointed with his club to the old man, who was lifting another rock and tipping it into the barrow.

"Oh, punish me," I said. I could hear Vera telling me to keep quiet and come safely home to her. The anger had welled up in me anyway, just as he'd wanted it to. The old man dropped his rock into the barrow and was watching, frightened of us both. I put the barrow carefully down and turned my shoulder toward Momo, keeping my hands more or less out of the way. If he hit me, I would try not to let it break my hands. He swung his club hard and then stayed it at the last instant, so that it grazed my shoulder and made me stumble, without really hurting me. My heart was pounding.

Momo laughed. "I missed," he said. "But only this time." When he laughed with his mouth open, I saw that several of his molars were gone and the remaining ones were dark brown, like peach pits. "Get back to work. You cunts," he added. He climbed down the next ramp into the quarry pit and was soon out of sight.

When Momo had gone, I saw the gentle, brown-haired man trembling, about to faint. I caught his arm, glancing around to make sure there was no guard just above us.

"Look, we're not hurt," I said. "Just take a breath. He didn't hurt me. We're all still here."

"Thank you," he said. It was the first time he'd spoken in my presence.

"What's your name?" I whispered, picking up the barrow handles again, to look busy.

"Nasko," he said softly. "I'm from Sofia, like you. I've heard you play once. A chamber music concert. You were wonderful."

"What did I play?"

"Beethoven. Then Tchaikovsky."

We smiled at each other and it was the first time there I'd felt human. I gave him my hand, for an instant, and then he took the pickax up again.

"What do you do in Sofia?" I asked him. I almost said, *What* did *you do in Sofia,* as if we were already dead.

"I'm a painter and sculptor," he said. "I came to Sofia from the Rhodopes when I was eighteen, because I wanted to paint."

"You should be saving your hands, too," I whispered.

511

"Hands!" He wagged his head.

"I'll help you wrap them up, later. We can use part of our shirts."

"All right," he said. His eyes went on smiling for a moment.

That was the only conversation I had that day.

Fifty-one

Two hours later they were driving up the hill toward Irina's street. The gate in the wall was unlocked, but there was no answer at the door of the small reddish house. Alexandra stood holding Stoycho's leash; the bag with the urn was firmly over Bobby's shoulder. Bobby knocked again, and Alexandra noticed that he scanned the upper windows for a moment as they waited. "I'll check the garden, too," he said.

He was gone briefly and returned with the calm face that Alexandra had learned to pay attention to.

"Here—take the bag. Go back to the car," he told her. He gave her his keys so quickly she didn't know it had happened until she felt them against her hand. "Lock the doors and if there is any problem drive all the way down to the town center and park there somewhere on a main street."

He smiled at her, as if discussing something

trivial, and she turned mutely and did as he'd instructed, shutting the gate in the museum wall behind her. She sat in the car with Stoycho, the doors locked. She remembered this kind of fear, her heartbeat rising in slow insistence. It was a dread sufficient to distract her from the situation at hand; it had a life of its own. She watched the gate in the wall. Behind that wall Bobby would be walking carefully around the outside of Irina's house, perhaps picking the lock on the kitchen door. The table where they'd sat in the moonlight would be empty, wiped down, unused. Or, worse, scattered with uncleared dishes, ants crawling into the last crumbs of the white cheese Irina and Lenka loved.

Or worse than that—but she tried not to imagine that they were there and no longer able to call for help. She thought she might not have enough patience to wait for Bobby's return; she sat on one sweaty hand and touched the key in the ignition with the other. Stoycho panted audibly in the back. It was too hot—Alexandra rolled down her window and thought for the tenth time that it had been years since she'd been in a car like this, with handles instead of automatic window buttons. The waiting was—sometimes—the worst part. She remembered that, too. But she also remem-bered that it was the outcome of the waiting that later determined whether it really had been the worst part or not.

At last the gate in the wall opened and Bobby stepped out. The sight of him—hair hanging into his eyes, his runner's legs lithe in the worn black jeans—hit her with a force beyond love. He was alive and real and tied to her until the moment she died, or the moment he did. She swore it to herself, fighting down a little voice that reminded her that people often feel this way about friends they make on trips and that sooner or later she would leave this country. She unlocked the driver's door and clambered across to the passenger seat so that Bobby could slide in behind the wheel, and when he was settled she gripped his arm. He nodded and drove away.

"They weren't home?" she said fearfully.

"No. I knew that at once, from the way the garden looked." He was driving with casual grace, as if they'd come up here just to see the old streets. No screeching of tires for Bobby. "The doors were locked, but I went in—I broke in—and looked everywhere. When they left, they must have left quickly. The beds were not neat and there were some clothes on the floor. Their bags from our trip were still there, open but not completely unpacked—they did not take anything with them, I think. They locked both of the doors as they left, so at least they had time to do that. But I found this on the floor." He steered with one hand, drew a piece of paper from his jacket pocket, handed it to her.

Unfolding it, she saw the untidy Cyrillic words. "What does it mean?"

Bobby's face was tight. "It says, *You will be the next ones*."

"Oh, what's happened to them?" cried Alexandra.

"If they're wise, they've disappeared for a few days," Bobby told her firmly. "The question is whether they left because they found this note, or whether someone left it afterward, maybe for us, and locked the doors again."

"Irina is so fragile," Alexandra whispered. She found the pack of American tissues in her purse, an artifact that already looked unfamiliar to her, and quickly wiped her eyes and cheeks.

"I don't think Irina and Lenka would have locked the doors like that if they had to actually run away from something," said Bobby. "In fact, Irina could not run away. Maybe someone came to see them—but if that happened, whoever it was did not hurt anything there. I also asked the guide at the museum if they saw Irina today, but they were closed for a long time this morning, for some meetings. She didn't remember seeing Irina or Lenka outside at all. I called Lenka's phone three times. No answer, and it rang only once each time."

"So maybe somebody took them?" Alexandra could hardly bring herself to say this aloud.

"Well, that is the other question, of course," said Bobby reluctantly. "Someone might have taken them and left this note in their place."

He had pulled down into the main streets of the city now, and Alexandra recognized the outdoor cafés, the big hotel signs and ice-cream stands. None of it looked festive anymore. "Oh, no, no—I hope not," Alexandra said. She was thinking of Atanas Angelov lying in the woods, the grinning wound. Or had someone left him face down in the dirt?

"I'm not sure that anyone took them," Bobby said quickly. "I would have found some sign of a fight." He shook his head.

"Maybe," Alexandra said. She tightened her feet around the bag with the urn, feeling the solid wood inside. "Although if they went against their will—but without any struggle—it would look the same as if they had left by themselves, right? Maybe someone even made them lock the doors behind them."

Bobby glanced at her thoughtfully, slowed for a red light. "I think that Irina would have left some sign, or Lenka would have fought for her."

Alexandra wiped her face again and looked out the window. An old woman was selling wilted flowers, approaching the stopped cars. Bobby rolled up his window and shook a finger at her as she approached, and the woman turned away.

"From cemeteries," he explained.

"What?" said Alexandra.

"The flowers—she is trying to make a living, not to beg but to sell something instead. But the flowers are from cemeteries. People steal them to sell."

Alexandra wondered if someone would take flowers away from Stoyan Lazarov's grave. First he would have to have one.

Bobby shook her arm. "Don't cry again, please. We must decide where to go now."

"But we don't even know where Irina is." *Or if she is dead already, like her friend Nasko.*

"I will call Miss Radeva to see if she has heard anything. And Neven—and the mountain house, just in case." He dialed several numbers, reaching only Miss Radeva, with whom he spoke quickly. After he hung up, he said, "She has not heard anything and she is even more distressed now. I told her to be very careful at her apartment and to think about staying with someone else for a few days."

"But where can we go?" Alexandra tried to keep her voice steady. "We don't even know where to start, now."

Bobby sat still for a few minutes, with the absorbed look she recognized as his deepest thought. "Bovech," he said firmly.

"To look for Irina and Lenka?"

"To look for—whatever we find. We could have missed something the first time, because we knew even less then. Always go back. I mean, always go back to the site where something happened, or the place where somebody lived."

He said this last like a line from a textbook and she wondered if it had been part of his professional training. She knew, watching the moles quiver near the corner of his mouth, that she would have to wait for the rest.

He turned to her. "Look, we must go to a hotel tonight. I am too tired to drive very late again, and I cannot risk staying at my aunt's, or with any friends. And I think we should find a small place, away from the city."

"I have money," she assured him.

"We might need to pay extra for a room," he said. "Because of Stoycho." She moved her shoulder closer to his. Perhaps they should just stop at the side of the highway, open the door, and set the urn down in a field. But would that save any of them, at this point? She remembered her dream about Neven—she had thrown herself at his feet and he had lifted her up and kissed her.

Fifty-two

1949

The second morning, just before I awoke, I dreamed for the first time about Vivaldi. He was a little older than I, red-haired and in the long frock of a priest, and he was unlocking the small side door of a church as the sun rose; he glanced up at the light on the water, which was divided into thousands of Adriatic crystals. I could hear the slop of water above the rattle of big rusty keys, but he seemed so accustomed to that sound that it made no impression on him. I saw his hands fumble with the lock and then unlatch the wooden door. Inside, the church was cold as an under-ground passage, and its ceiling rose like a voice above him. For some reason, a pink-and-white cat sat licking itself in the aisle, but no one else was there yet. To one side of the nave stood a screen of gilt-laden wood—shining branches and leaves through which a thousand small eyes might be peering.

Vivaldi went to the altar. He arranged chairs, benches, music stands unlike any I'd ever seen, although I could easily tell what they were. He set freshly copied scores on the stands with his long hands, enough for twenty musicians. I waited for him to get his violin; in fact, why wasn't he carrying it with him? Did he keep it in the church? Was that safe? Had he left it somewhere? I was suddenly in a panic, on his behalf. What if his violin had been stolen?

When the bugle blew, I woke startled, and found that I was lying on the shredded mats and old clothes of my bunk.

On my third day at Zelenets, I began to practice again. I made myself wait until I'd seen my star,

Beta-49, during our morning roll call, and had answered to my name. As soon as I'd accomplished both those things, I set off in my head: my Bach Partitas, which I had always used to warm up. I played them more slowly than usual. At first I thought I would only be able to hear the notes in my head, but after a few minutes I found I could see some of the fingerings as well. Sometimes I missed a note and made myself start the whole exercise over.

Then I decided to work on the Unaccompanied Partitas, all the ones I had by heart, beginning with the second Partita in D minor. I started on the first movement, the Allemande, and worked up to the sublime Chaconne. I found it difficult to hear, in that terrible place, but I made myself press forward. The D minor took so much time that we were at the quarry by the time I finished all the movements correctly. I settled into work on the shelf of the pit, exchanged a few quick words with my companions there, and helped the muscular old man wrap up his hands the way I had my own, to shield them a little from the sharp edges of the rocks. I could see that the rocks would cut through his wraps, too, by the end of the day; we would have to look for more cloth.

Later that morning, I practiced Franck's violin sonata, in the key of A major, which I had learned my first year in Vienna. I was glad now that I had made myself memorize it. My back and legs were

terribly sore from pushing the wheelbarrow, but I went through each movement several times, hearing in my head the piano part intertwining with my own. If there was an interruption—a guard coming down to harangue us into working faster, for example—I started that movement from the beginning again. And when we had to work faster, I was careful not to increase my tempo inappropriately. If I accidentally sped up the music, I made myself begin that movement over again, too.

In the middle of the morning a train came through, passing close to the quarry on the tracks I'd observed the first day. When we heard it coming, all the skeletons shouldered their tools at the same time, like guns, and I thought for a moment that they were going to run toward the train to beg for freedom, or to try to jump on. To my amazement, they stood facing the track until it was actually passing, and then they waved. There were several passengers, with faces staring from the windows, and a hand or two waved back.

After it had passed, everyone hurried back to work and the guards walked around to harangue those of us who hadn't known what to do. "Next time, wave!" one shouted. "Anyone who doesn't wave will pay for it!" yelled another.

I had not finished the Franck when we broke for lunch. During our lunch, one of the skeletons went mad, suddenly getting down on all fours

and scuttling around the edge of the pit until he ran straight off it. The guards cursed and shouted—now there would be a late start back to work. One of the younger skeletons, the man's son, threw himself toward the edge of the pit after his father; the guards caught the young one and beat him until he was quiet. He lived through it to start work again two days later.

On the fourth and fifth days, I discovered something important from watching the other men: if I always had two sets of wrappings for my hands and rinsed one set in water from the washhouse pitchers at bedtime, I could have a fairly clean pair for work each day, while the other pair was still drying. In this way, my hands stayed slightly less raw. My little finger was healing despite the misery of the wheelbarrow, and I hoped to postpone infections as long as I could. I scavenged my own clothes and my bed for lightweight rags to tear into strips, washed them and hung them at the edge of the bunk. Many| men did the same to make foot wraps, since few of us owned socks, although I was lucky enough to have gotten two good ones. I kept my socks on my feet, or care-fully hidden, at all times. I also traded one of the prisoners in the next row of bunks four thick pieces of wood I'd found under my bed mats—he gave me the whole back of a cotton shirt for them, which would see me

in clean hand wraps for quite a while. He wanted the wood because he liked to whittle figures of naked women, using a sharp stone. I tore the fabric up into neat strips and carried them in a pocket inside my jacket, so that no one could steal them while I was out of the barrack.

Each afternoon, pushing the wheelbarrow, I worked on a concerto. I had quite a few by heart, or mostly by heart. I began with my favorites— the Brahms, Bruch's first concerto in G minor, the Mendelssohn, and the Tchaikovsky—and then a fifth, Sibelius. I chose the Mendelssohn for that first day because I knew it best of all. It took me most of the afternoon to get it running smoothly. When I came to the third movement, I had to begin it eight or ten times over, because my memory seemed about to fail me. My hunger made it more difficult for me to think, and I wondered if I would get used to this. Sometimes I moved my fingers on the splintering handles of the wheelbarrow, to help me remember notes, until I found that simply increased the pain and fatigue. There was plenty of time to work at it. Even the trains didn't interrupt me often; I'd learned that they passed only a couple of times a week. They were usually freight trains, and for those we didn't have to shoulder our tools and wave, although some of the skeletons did that automatically.

I also discovered that my companions at the pit

didn't mind if I hummed. Nasko whispered to me that he liked it. I wondered if he tried painting, in his mind, but didn't ask him in front of the others. And if a guard appeared on the rim of the pit, we fell silent. Mostly we did not talk, anyway. They had told us already to watch one another for poor work.

But for a few seconds, under the late-afternoon October sun, my hands bleeding and my back aching severely from the weight of the wheelbarrow, I heard the Mendelssohn aloud. The first movement, which I'd always loved plunging into. It was the sound of rapture.

The sacks did not disappear until there were seven or eight of them, by which time we turned away our noses as well as our eyes if we had to pass the side of the washhouse. I made a bargain with my own mind: whenever I imagined myself in a sack, I would immediately think of something else. I would not think of Vera—I saved her, and my parents, for my nightly prayer into the stinking, coughing, unlistening dark of the barracks. I would not think of my son, sitting on the sunlit grass of the field; that was for even worse moments.

When I imagined myself in a sack, I thought instead of Venice, which I had meant to visit years earlier. I thought of Vivaldi, unlocking his church door for rehearsal in the early morning, and the way the air might feel coming over the salty lagoons and the waves of the Adriatic. I thought of the piece I had not let myself practice since my arrival, although I knew it better even than my Bach. I would have to be careful, though, not to forget it.

Vivaldi had died at sixty-three, poor, his music no longer in fashion. I had read somewhere that he had probably been buried in a pauper's grave in Vienna. Perhaps he had been put in a sack, too. But not by thugs and criminals, and not before he had composed music like the moon above islands that bristled with churches.

Fifty-three

1949

One evening, a miner was brought back to the camp with his hand missing. Two other men supported him as he walked. He held the shredded stump of his sleeve tightly with his remaining hand, to slow the blood. Some rocks had fallen inside the mine and pinned him to the floor of the chamber; his workmates had tied the crushed arm off, elevated it, and saved him from bleeding to death. I wondered why the guards at the mine had allowed anyone to help the man, but they had. He had been unconscious for hours before they brought him back to the camp, and was still hardly awake. He was taken to the big shed used as an infirmary; from what little I had heard, so far, very few left the infirmary except in sacks. After he was carried in there, we had roll call in the yard, and no dinner. The uniformed guard, the one the others called the Chief, shouted at us during the count. He told us that the kind of carelessness we had witnessed was its own punishment, as we could see, but he wanted us to remember it well. When someone failed to respond in the roll call, the Chief started over, from the very beginning.

In the morning, we could hardly walk or work, on our breakfast of tea and that shit-like smear of jam. I thought even more about the man's missing hand than about the pain in my stomach. Was it still lying under a pile of rock, up in the mines? It had been his left hand—the note-producing hand, if you were a violinist. I forgot to practice, that morning. Instead, I thought over and over about my son and his love, sitting by the river. I did not try to serenade them; I simply walked down to the river and stood quietly behind them, looking at the sunlight on their glossy hair. My own hair was just beginning to fall out. I was grateful that they didn't know I was there, couldn't turn around to see me.

On a sunny morning about three weeks after my arrival at Zelenets, my hands were so swollen that

I found I could not play, even in my mind. The blisters had broken many times, of course, but now my hands had become hot and red all over, not only in the damaged places. The only good thing about my burning hands was that they made me feel a little less of the pain in my stomach. I cleaned and wrapped them and tried to think of some other way to spend the work hours. It was then that I began to wonder more about my son. I had not thought about him except as that dark-haired figure on the riverbank, with his clean white shirt and black vest, his broad shoulders. He looked like a dignified man, neat and sober, perhaps a quiet person. Had I raised him well? Was he a musician? A scholar? Of course, Vera would have been an excellent mother. I wondered if he had brothers and sisters, but decided against it. There would never have been enough money for them, not in this new world of cramped apartments, where musicians were assigned to factory marching bands. I decided he would be an only child, conceived in love and on purpose, but alone with us after that.

During the march to the quarry, I let myself think about his conception.

It would have been an unbearable pleasure, different even from all other pleasurable times. Out in broad daylight, I let myself think of Vera's body, and then of the exquisite suddenness that would create our son. I looked at the ground as I thought about this, so that I would not see any of what was actually around me. For a moment it was only the two of us, on a different kind of day.

Then Vera, subtly changed, in her worn cotton nightdress, coiling her hair up in the mornings before she cooked our breakfast. She would go to her job at a factory canteen looking radiant, her waistband beginning to press a little, her skin beautiful, and one evening she would say she had finally been to see a doctor and it was true, what we'd thought. She would look away, awkward but overjoyed. I would come around the table to stroke her braided head and we would both laugh so that we didn't cry. She would assure me she was healthy as a farm animal, no worries. The next day, at the orchestra rehearsal, I would keep forgetting—and then remembering in a burst— the coming change. It would make my hands shake with happiness as I lit my single cigarette during the morning break.

That was all I could manage for one day. But when we reached the quarry, I asked Nasko to push the barrow while I relieved him of the job of splitting rock and lifting it, although he protested in a whisper that it would hurt my hands even more. I wanted to do it for him. After all, I'd had good news.

This joy did not last—no joy could last in such a place. The next day, I was so sad that I told myself

I would not let myself think about my son again for three days. First, I would practice for a day, even if my hands could hardly bear it. Then I would spend a day thinking only about Vivaldi and his rehearsals with his orchestra. The third day, I would practice again—exercises, sonatas, a concerto. On the fourth day, I would finally begin to raise my son. If anything appalling happened in the meantime, I could visit him and his love at the river until it was over. It was always early summer there; that river was never slimed with gray-green ice, like the one we marched along to the quarry.

In this way, I began to make a deeper pattern. When I'd completed these four days, I would begin again, with a day of pure practice. I thought about telling Nasko how I was spending my time; often, I saw a faraway look on his face while we worked, and I wondered what he was dreaming about. I was sure he would never report me for "poor effort." But I was afraid that if I told any-one at all about my days, they would cease to have the same effect.

By then, my hair had fallen out across the top of my forehead, and I could feel my ribs against my dead-man's shirt. We'd had only two baths since the first lice killing, and there were insects living on me and in my clothes all the time, not only in my bed.

One morning, the angelic-looking brute Momo paused in front of me and gazed into my eyes for a moment. He had an empty sack in one hand; he raised both hands and played an invisible violin for a moment, so that the sack swung around in the air. Then he suddenly handed the sack to the man next to me. The next morning, Momo did this again, eyeing me humorously for an instant before he chose someone else. I stayed as still as I could, trying not to appear frightened, unable to look at the doomed man. That day was normally a Vivaldi day, but I allowed myself to skip ahead to a day with my son, in case it proved to be my last.

Fifty-four

1949

Of course, before I could begin to raise my son, on that first fourth day, he had to be born. It was a miraculously easy labor, as I couldn't bear to know Vera was suffering. I decided it would happen during the afternoon, suddenly, when she was large and ripe as a peach. That morning, before I went to my rehearsal, she told me that the small of her back ached more than usual and I rubbed it for her, the animal curve that still looked as graceful as the midsection of a cello. Her skin was warm under my hands and she said she felt better, that her mother was

530

coming to see her and they would do some extra baking together in case the baby arrived soon. I was so startled to think of this that I let the wheelbarrow slip for a second, and it hit the top of my foot and bruised it badly; I would be hiding a limp for the rest of the day.

Vera smiled as she closed the door on me, her face tired but rosy, and the next thing I knew her father was summoning me from the rehearsal during our break—so that I wouldn't have to interrupt our work and possibly anger the conductor—and we were hurrying to the hospital, the old one where I'd been born myself, now with a red star above the front entrance. I ran up the stairs and begged the nurses to let me go in, although I had no idea if that was allowed. Vera lay in a narrow, clean bed on the top floor, with my mother-in-law hovering over her. I kissed her and stroked her hair; she smiled at me again, radiant, proud, but also very tired. The baby was in a big room with other babies, and the nurse pointed him out to me. He was wrapped tightly in white flannel, his face soft and sleepy, his eyes shut. Tears sprang to my own eyes at the sight of him, and I had to set the wheelbarrow down for a moment and wipe them with my sleeves. I wondered if I might hold him, and then if I would be able to hold him safely. A nurse showed me how and put him in my arms, which made him open his eyes and look up at me. His weight was terribly slight, but warm, resting on my arm.

I went back in to see Vera. "I would like to call him Neven," she said drowsily. "I dreamed that that was his name." I thought about this; Neven was really more a woman's name—Nevena, or Nevyana, *marigold*—and I had thought we would name him for my father, the traditional way. But he really was like a marigold, with his round, tawny face and unfocused golden eyes.

"We must name him for my father," I said softly, "but we could call him Neven ourselves."

She was already sleeping. I kissed her forehead and went downstairs to my father-in-law.

"A very fine boy," I told him. We stopped by a tavern and had a stinging, marvelous glass of *rakiya* before I returned to my rehearsal.

Lunch that day was something different, as if they had run out of beans: a kind of stewed turnip, almost not food, tasting of dirt. I hoped this was a temporary change. For a moment, I thought to myself that this would be bad for Vera while she was nursing the baby; she must have real food, and plenty of it. Then I realized what I'd just been considering, and it gave me a shock. I would have to guard my mind in a second way, not only against this place but also against itself. I gave myself strict orders: if I ever again felt the line blurring between my mind's work and this terrible reality, I would assign myself an entire day of scales. No concerti, no Bach, no Venice, no Vera, no Neven—just scales, until I made it right again.

On the next fourth day, I began to get to know my son. Neven proved a tranquil baby, who smiled and laughed early, although we did have some sleepless nights the first months. Vera worried that our neighbors in the apartment, with its thin partition walls, would be annoyed when he cried. But they were mostly patient with us and him. The old woman who lived on the right side, in what had once been part of the same apartment as urs, took a great liking to him and helped us with him sometimes. Vera was a happy mother, cuddling and rocking him, watching him sleep, and her own mother came constantly to look after them both.

They say fathers become impatient, like neighbors, but I could never hold him enough, and I grew to love the smell of milk, and even the reek of diapers boiling in their soap on the stove. Vera read my small library of books while he napped, or she cleaned the apartment, or slept herself. She wanted to keep her German and French going. Once I thought confusedly that she must be having a hard time caring for the baby alone while I was far away in this hell-hole. The next day I played scales, all day, in every key.

That was a hard day; scales did not keep my mind far enough from the pit and the pain in my hands and legs and back. At the end of the afternoon, instead of marching us home, the guard and Momo and a couple of other assistants lined us up and pulled two skeletons from the line and shot them, as an example. I hadn't known they ever used their guns except to guard us; they all seemed to prefer clubs. Momo was allowed to shoot one of the men himself; he handled the gun like an amateur, or a boy with a plaything, so that we were all ducking and flinching as he waved it toward us. Then I saw he knew exactly what he was doing but had once again simply enjoyed frightening us. They shot the two skeletons right in front of us, but in the backs of their heads, as if they'd been targets with bull's-eyes. The sound ricocheted off the mountain wall beyond our pit.

In other words, the Chief let Momo shoot a man, but I did not let myself think about my son, or walk down to the river to serenade him; I didn't let myself consider Vivaldi's stroll home across the Piazza, or vow to get back alive to Vera. Instead, I made myself watch as each man leapt into the air and fell forward. I told each one silently that I was watching for him to the very end, that I would never forget, and I thought of each one as a baby, sometime long before, opening sleepy eyes.

• • •

Every third day, I practiced, and it seemed to me that I had now gone at least twice through all the repertoire I'd ever learned. I selected a piece or two to focus on, beginning always with Bach in the morning and then working on my chosen pieces all afternoon. I wondered if it was possible I was improving; I thought sometimes that my memory of a work had gotten better, and that I was hearing my phrasing improve, especially in a Dvořák symphony, his third, which I'd always loved. More and more, I could hear the other parts in my head. The academy orchestra had played that repeatedly in Vienna, and once in Prague as well. We were very good that night. The Prague audience had given us a whistling, stamping, cheering ovation—they who thought of the composer as their private property. That symphony did seem to be improving, at least in my mind, and the swell, the sweetness of it filled the pit for me, some days.

One afternoon Nasko leaned forward from his miserable rock splitting to whisper, "What is it today?"

I was startled, wary for a moment, and then I thought, *Why not?*

"Dvořák's third symphony," I said softly.

A smile brushed his lips and he bowed his head, deeply pleased, and lifted the pickax again. His cheeks were hollow and his brown hair was threaded with white now. In the purple below his soft eyes, I saw a shadow that I hoped was not death. I knew it lay across all our faces, a warning. Sometimes it claimed men quietly, in the night. We lived just under its wing.

Then Nasko lowered the ax again. "I finished a big canvas yesterday," he whispered. "A man on horseback, with white fur boots. The horse was quite difficult." There was no death in his eyes now, and I saw no madness, either.

"Good," I said. I knew that he knew I meant, *Good—we might see each other out of here alive.*

We didn't talk more about it, but after that he gave me a nod before we started work every morning, and I nodded back, very slightly, hoping we would not be reported for conspiracy. When the man from Pirin disappeared one night and was not there to work with us on the ledge the next morning, I felt terrible, guilty, as if we should have helped him, too, with our friendship.

The days I spent with Vivaldi, I often helped him rehearse his chamber orchestra. I tried only not to think about what he might be eating for his midday meal. One morning I watched him rehearsing his young choir in a new oratorio and I saw the concentration, excitement, and impatience with which he instructed them. I wondered how he himself would have played the piece I was saving in secret, but I never asked him to play it for me.

More than anything, I looked forward to every fourth day, when I would see Neven growing up. He was a toddler now, square-shouldered and solid, taking a step or two with his hands hooked over Vera's guiding forefingers; they practiced in the tiny apartment but also in the park, with her father walking next to them in his discreetly patched jacket, or her mother carrying a folded blanket over her arm. Vera's sister, Irina, weary from long hours of painting murals and portraits of factory workers, found Neven more interesting now that he knew who she was. Whenever she appeared, he lit up and began to laugh, which made everyone around them laugh. His hair was the color of new brass but already darkening into tarnished curls.

I spent a great deal of time considering when to present him with an instrument, and what it might be, and how we would find one, and how we could afford it; Vera said it was nonsense, that he would only break anything we gave him, and I agreed to wait until he was three. "Four," said Vera. I agreed to that, too. She had gone back to her canteen job and she looked tired, which worried me and made me say yes to her at every opportunity.

I wondered if we might have another child, and then remembered that I had already decided to imagine only one, since the apartment was so small. Besides, when the country opened up again,

I would probably have to travel for my music, first back to Vienna and then to competitions again, and ultimately to tour Europe. It would be hard for Vera, who would have to stay and work until I became successful again; she would have her hands full even with only Neven at home. I didn't think they would be able to come with me, at least not until Neven was much older, and then maybe we would perform together. I pictured Herr Mozart and his stiff little boy and girl, visiting the great cities of Europe, playing for heads of state.

Sometimes, looking up from the wheelbarrow, I wondered if the guards had hopes for themselves, too—things they imagined for the future. Did the boy Momo hope to be chief someday, if the Chief fell into the pit accidentally or died of influenza? Did the Chief hope to be sent to sit behind a desk in Sofia, with a nicer job and a bigger salary and city clothes for his wife? Did he even have a wife? Did the prisoners around me still hope to die in their beds at home?

I made myself think instead about Neven, getting steadier on his feet now, walking toward me, his face alight as I knelt in front of him—a little farther, a little farther—and then falling into my arms with a scream of laughter.

It was fortunate that little Neven was doing so well, because I knew that my strength was beginning to ebb in a new way. I wasn't sick, thank

God, although I sometimes felt that the line between sickness and health didn't exist in this place. The wounds on my hands oozed pus in the evenings, but often I scrubbed them until they bled—I came to welcome the cleansing, fresh blood, even the pain. My shins became infected where they constantly grazed the metal brace of the wheelbarrow. I struggled not to scratch my torso when the bug bites turned into infected welts. I sometimes fought fever in the evenings, which I knew was from all those small infections; there were too many of them. I willed myself not to get really ill. A man in the barrack sold me a second shirt in exchange for part of my bedding, so that I could wash or at least air out one shirt at a time. It was growing cold outside now, and the nights felt like winter, but I still had a blanket to cover me.

One evening, a new group of men was brought in; we saw their stunned faces in the lights of the yard when we returned from work in the dark. I realized that I must look like what I'd seen my own first evening—gaunt, hollow-eyed, ragged.I was not yet skeletal, but that wouldn't take much longer. The new men, young and old, filled the last half-empty barrack in camp; I wondered if the Revolution would make us build more barracks, to house more of us, and more, and more. We didn't ask them why they were there, although one man told me on our way to the quarry that he didn't even know, for himself. He was black-haired, barely in his twenties, still healthy-looking.

"Everyone else was accused of something," he whispered, as if he had to say it aloud; I didn't understand why he'd chosen me to talk to. "But I wasn't. I've tried and tried to guess what it could have been, but I can't think of anything I did wrong, and they didn't say." He threw his arm wide toward the men around us, his face working. "All of them—at least they know why they're here."

"No, we don't," I said harshly. "Even if they told us, we don't know." The stooped guard with the club sidled toward us and we stopped talking. Then I thought of Neven and I wished I'd whis-pered something to comfort the young man, but it was too late. I didn't have the energy left to comfort anyone but myself, even when the guards weren't watching.

Fifty-five

Bobby found a roadside hotel northwest of Plovdiv, an hour from the main highway. The front gate displayed three stars on a sign that was partly in English; Alexandra hoped this meant it would be a decent place.

"I will talk," Bobby said, and they left Stoycho in the car. There was a little swimming pool out front, sunk into a terrace and lit with underwater lights—the night was very dark now, with a thick scattering of stars. Bobby conversed genially with the man at the front desk while Alexandra held Bobby's hand and hoped they looked like a family.

"*Kuche*," Bobby said eventually, and the man glanced up, startled. More chat, until Alexandra understood that the man was going to put them in a room at the back of the building and that the dog—he raised his hands as if in disclaimer to some other party—the dog would need to be invisible. She counted out a pile of ten-*leva* bills, more than she'd imagined spending all at once, and they drove around back. The room they'd been assigned contained a double bed and was entirely brown—brown carpet, shiny brown bedspread, brown curtains, as if some earlier dreariness had simply been updated with fresh fabrics.

The restaurant near the lobby ate up some more *leva*, but Alexandra thought it was good. In the pool, she wore her bra and underpants; she floated in the lights and hoped the mustached manager wasn't watching. Bobby was pacing the terrace, talking quietly on his cell phone. When he hung up, he reported to her that Miss Radeva had still heard nothing. He'd called Lenka's phone, too, but again it had rung only once, as if it had been turned off. There was no answer at the mountain house.

Alexandra slept that night with the urn close to her side of the double bed, Bobby rolling over with a snore so that his arm touched her back, Stoycho breathing softly in the corner. When she woke, briefly, during the night, she pulled the shared blanket over Bobby, in case he was chilled.

Fifty-six
1949–50

Real winter came and the cold added to our miseries. I began to work on my Bach again, all the Bach I knew, even the violin parts of the masses, to keep warm. One morning before dawn the world seemed strangely brightened outside the door to the dugout; snow stretched as far as we could see, and when the sun rose at the quarry it turned the world lavender and gold.

After that it snowed every few days. I had hated being assigned to the stinking dugout, but now I learned that it was far warmer than the wooden buildings, where a sick man could die twice as fast. Everyone was cold in the quarry, of course, and the men in the mines were never warm even in summer. Cold became our constant companion, rivaling our hunger. Some of the men from my barrack disappeared to the infirmary, their toes or fingers or whole feet frozen dead-purple after the workday, and did not come back. The nurse ventured out among us for the first time, telling us to wrap ourselves more warmly—as if we had garments in which to do that. He was a man of forty with black eyes like pebbles in a withered face, his clothes only a little better than ours but his flesh still reasonably well fed. The guards referred to him as Nurse Ivan. After he spoke to us, in a gravelly baritone, his eyes averted from our emaciated mass, the Chief sent him away and repeated what he had said, but with threats.

We tried hard to stay warmer. We wrapped our feet in many layers of old cloth. My socks had disintegrated now and I made long bandages to wear inside my shoes. I was frantic to protect my hands, which were swollen all the time now, crusted and scarred all over the skin; I tried in vain to find strips of wool to wrap them in, instead of the usual curls of dirty cotton. My fingers burned terribly whenever they warmed up a little. A few men had an odd glove or two; on our ledge in the quarry, we gave those to whoever was lifting icy rocks. One morning in January, to my amazement, Nasko gave me an actual pair of gloves, pulling them out of his pocket as soon as we reached the edge of the quarry. They had a few holes in the fingers, but I knew I could find a way to sew those up. I had no idea how he'd gotten them and wasn't sure I wanted to know.

"But you—" I said. His own palms were in

shreds from holding the pickax and sometimes lifting rock.

"Nonsense," he whispered. "I want you to have them. You must."

I knew he meant, *I want you to play again, if we ever get out of this fucking hell.* I was cold to the core, but my heart hadn't frozen, and neither had his; our tears were warm on our faces.

Some ancient army coats were distributed among the barracks one evening. There were not enough for even a quarter of the camp, and those who felt they needed them most traded desperately for them. Fights broke out over those coats, the next few days. The hard-faced men I'd seen the first morning pushing to the front of the toilet lines—true criminals swept into camp with the rest of us—often won a coat by fighting, or even by simply demanding one. I didn't have a coat, myself, only a heavy sweater that had been among the garments I had originally been given.

There were episodes of strange kindness, too. I saw a well-built newcomer of thirty—with a stubble of gray hair on his shaved head—give his coat to the old man who slept in one corner. The old man promised to leave it to the younger man when he died.

"Do you hear?" he hissed to the silent barrack at bedtime. "This is my will and testament. Do you hear? I leave it to him, the young one, this good boy. Nobody dare take it from him or I will haunt them."

We all turned our faces away, repulsed but a little awed, too, by his vehemence. But a few weeks into winter, the old man slipped near the edge of the quarry and fell in. The coat went down with him. We never knew what happened to it, or to his body.

Winter brought clouds as well as snow and cold, and one morning I realized that I hadn't seen my star, Beta-49, in more than two weeks, although it seemed to me the sky had sometimes been clear. A numbness slithered across my heart. Things were being taken away—my star, my ability to keep warm, and, worst of all, the clarity of my memories. Sometime in that stretch of winter, I realized that I could not picture Vera's face as clearly as I had months before. There were days when the snow seemed to silence me inside, so that I lost concentration and drifted and didn't practice for most of an afternoon. Soon there were days or maybe even weeks of silence. I couldn't play; I couldn't pretend. I didn't want little Neven with me, there, in the cold, where he might easily fall ill. If I thought of Vivaldi, I became jealous of his undamaged hands. It was more difficult for me to imagine Venice than it had been before, because it must be warmer in Venice; I no longer bothered thinking about whether I would live to see the city myself someday. I felt that as long as my mind did not cave inward, I could afford to be silent. I was too tired to think even about my concerti, and so I stayed in the silence for a while. The silence was white, like snow, a blank page.

We dragged ourselves to the quarry. We dragged ourselves back in the evening. The mountains, magnificent above us, were so completely unmoved by what was happening at their feet, by our cold and our impossible labor and our numbing fear, that I began to hate them. The guards were constantly irritable; they, too, disliked the cold, although they all had real boots, if old ones; and they disliked the increased number of deaths, which made more work for them. Some men seemed to give up and sicken, spontaneously. A few crawled away from the quarry and died in the snow, or were shot there if they crawled too fast and attracted attention. I thought they must have decided they wanted to die in open air, at least, under the sky. There was a rumor in the barrack that it was good to get sick and go to the infirmary for a few days, if they would let you, because Nurse Ivan kept a fire burning there in a little stove. Some of the wooden barracks had stoves, too, which the men stoked every night. They did this with sticks they collected on their way back from work, especially the men who were sent out timbering. I didn't know any of them, but I'd heard they went in small groups with a special guard and provided wood, less for the camp—for building and burning—than for export on the trains that stopped at the mines. That, I'd realized, must also be the source of wood for the guards' clubs, always in fresh supply.

One morning in February the clouds cleared for the first time in many days and I saw Beta-49 brighter than I ever had, in the crystal-cold sky. It was higher than it had been a few months ago, and it shone directly at me from its lonely perch above the mountain; it shone over all of Stara Planina, Bulgaria, the Danube, the long curve of Europe, the Alps, over Vienna and Venice. I caught its eye for a second and made myself a promise: I would live through the rest of the winter, and if I could live through this winter, I could survive anything else. I didn't dare promise Vera; she probably thought by now that I was dead. It wasn't the first time I'd considered that, but it was the first time I'd felt it might be better this way, for her to stop hoping. While she stopped hoping, I would start simply surviving, and then I would come home to surprise her into joy and relief.

To celebrate this decision, I canceled my usual routine and let myself spend three days in a row just raising Neven, who was now a sturdy four-year-old. I wondered if I should let him grow up so quickly, but I was afraid that I might not live long enough to see him do it, otherwise. In fact, the morning I saw Beta-49 again, I allowed myself to give Neven his first violin. I intended for him to play the cello, eventually, but that would come in a few years, when he was taller. I brought the violin home from a store at the outskirts of Sofia where an old friend of mine made and repaired instruments for all the orchestras. Never mind that he'd been arrested just at the end of the war. I imagined him still there. He sold me a tiny violin, the only one at the shop, and I wrapped it in a jacket and took it carefully home in my bag of scores.

Neven was playing with his red train under the kitchen table. Vera looked around from cooking and I showed her, in pantomime, what I'd brought, and she laughed and shook her head— the inevitable violin. I coaxed Neven out and told him to sit on the edge of a kitchen chair, and showed him the precious thing he must never let slip from his hands or drop on the floor. He recognized it right away, from seeing me practice, and from watching me play in a concert or two. He nodded, serious. I told him that it made music like my violin, but I didn't play it for him; I was determined that he should sound the first notes on it.

Then I settled the violin in his hands and under his soft chin and crouched behind the chair, holding my fingers over his and helping him draw the bow across the strings. He cried out with pleasure and surprise at the sound; I had to stop him from dropping the instrument. I put it back under his chin and supported just the neck of the violin with my hand. He tried again, alone this time, drawing the bow carefully away from his nose so that the strings squawked. I took the violin gently from him and came around the chair to study his face. He smiled and raised golden eyes to me, and I kissed and hugged him. I didn't need him to be a child prodigy, on the first day—besides, I knew that prodigies are made, not simply born.

Fifty-seven

Alexandra and Bobby overslept and found themselves rushing through showers, taking Stoycho out to the field beyond the hotel, then hurrying to collect their belongings. Breakfast, in the hotel restaurant, was an array of cheese and too-pink sliced meats, white bread, tomatoes, hard-boiled eggs. A young woman with a green flower pinned to her hair was setting out fresh teacups. Bobby wrapped a pile of salami in a napkin and they fed Stoycho next to the car. The road looked so bright, with trees on either side and chicory blooming purple—not blue like at home—that Alexandra felt for a few minutes that nothing else could turn out badly. As long as she didn't think about Irina and Lenka.

Away from the hotel, Bobby drove hard on back roads for more than an hour. Alexandra noticed that he frequently glanced at his rearview mirror. Once he stopped to make a call, and Alexandra let Stoycho wander around the edge of what at home might have been a rest area, but here was a cracked parking lot with movable cement barriers fencing it from the road. Midmorning, Bobby took another turn into a town whose name Alexandra missed. It would have looked much like the other small towns Alexandra had seen, except that there was an enormous monument in the center. He pulled up at the curb near the main square.

"What are we doing here?"

"Getting something," said Bobby. "It won't take long. But I have to wait for a call."

They climbed out, leaving the windows open for Stoycho, and stood looking around. Alexandra could hear children playing somewhere just out of sight. The main square was small, with a dingily domed church at one side and a modern bell tower next to that, and people walking around on errands. The air was hazy. At first the monument looked like a pile of rubble; at second glance, it seemed to be a gigantic rusted-out robot.

Bobby leaned back against the car, assessing. "That is in honor of the Red Army," he said at last. "Do you see the words across the bottom?

It says, *Glory to the Liberators of 1944 from the grateful generations.* The Russian Army came in 1944 to liberate us from the things we thought we wanted, like democracy and having our own farms." He clasped his hands on one knee. "It looks as if someone else did not agree," he added drily.

Alexandra could see what he meant. The monument, abstract at first glance, was actually the statue of a huge, angular soldier, planting his feet in the middle of the square. His arm towered above her head. Apparently, he had once held a flagpole in his gargantuan fist, but that was long since gone, as was the fluttering tail of his coat, which seemed to have been sawn off. Part of what made him hard to recognize as a human figure was the paint sprayed all over his body. Somebody had spritzed him with streams of red, which were turning brown like real blood, and put ghoulish white circles around his eyes. He wore painted yellow gloves and his sleeve was ornamented with a green peace sign like a symbol of rank. He looked like a figure from a nightmare, Alexandra thought, and she dreaded the moment when he might suddenly stand and shake himself, offended, outraged, enormous. She backed up to the car and glanced in; Stoycho was awake and gazing at her but hadn't moved. She reached for him and stroked his black muzzle.

"There you are, Bird," said Bobby. "In your

country you don't care about history, and in my country we cannot recover from it."

"How do you know that about my country?" Alexandra said, but his cell phone was vibrating and he checked a text on it. At once he climbed back into the driver's seat. Alexandra got quickly in beside him. He drove slowly to the edge of town, stopped, and put a map on the steering wheel. Then he turned a corner.

"Here's our street," he said. "The garage will be number 61." They found it at the end of the block. The garage was really a large mechanic's shop, and Bobby drove straight into it. A young man came out of the back of the shop wiping his hands on a grease-blackened rag. He was very muscular, with another rag hanging out of the back of his jeans like a tail. He and Bobby clasped hands with an audible slap and he nodded to Alexandra but kept his stained grip carefully away from her.

"This is Rumen," Bobby said, and the young man smiled. Alexandra liked his smile, the way his teeth were crooked in the middle. "He has a car for us."

Alexandra knew the routine; they switched everything out of Kiril's green car and into a black Ford that looked as if it had seen better days. Rumen squeezed Bobby's shoulder and flicked Bobby's cheekbone with thumb and forefinger in a kind of parting caress.

"How will Kiril get his car back?" Alexandra said.

"Oh, they know each other. They'll arrange it." Bobby was backing the Ford carefully into the street.

"Which one of them is your boyfriend?" Alexandra said.

Bobby laughed. "Neither—anymore. Rumen is a great guy. A novelist."

"Of course," Alexandra said. "What about Kiril?"

"No, Kiril works for a real estate company in Sofia."

Alexandra shook her head.

In the back seat, Stoycho lay down again and groaned, once.

"Now what?" Alexandra said.

Bobby sighed. "Now what, now what. So American," he said.

Alexandra was hurt. "What is that supposed to mean?"

"Never mind," said Bobby. "What I'd like is to find Stoycho some water—and us some food, quickly—and I would like a cold beer."

But instead of stopping at the little café in the park, he drove straight out of town and back onto the highway.

It had begun to seem to Alexandra that she was going in circles now, in Bulgaria; they had started returning to places they'd been before.

There was something eerie about that, and she suddenly wondered if they'd end up back at Velin Monastery, to bury the urn themselves. Then she remembered that their first trouble had appeared there.

But Bovech did not look familiar to her as they drove into town—this time they were approaching it from the east. In the first neighborhood, she saw a weedy deserted piazza occupied by the sculpture of a man, larger than life, his granite peasant garb falling in angles around him and a huge stork nest—a real one— on his head. Standing in the nest was the stork, which made the figure even taller, like someone wearing a preposterous hat. A pack of street dogs slept at his feet, too lazy even to raise their heads from the dust; Alexandra was glad that Stoycho was safely in the back seat of the car.

"Another monument," Bobby muttered, in answer to her silent question. "All right—this one says *1923* because it marks the first big communist uprising in Bulgaria. It was suppressed very brutally, out in the countryside." As they watched, the stork raised its wings and flapped, then settled onto the nest.

The Lazarovi house when they found it again was a shock to her, as if she'd been there many times before instead of once. They found the pretty neighbor crocheting under a tree while her two children played with plastic trucks on the front walk. At first she seemed not to remember Bobby and Alexandra; then she greeted them with the warmth of boredom, until she spotted Stoycho. She looked hard at him and backed away. She told them that only one person had come to see the house next door since their visit, right after them—a young man who didn't want to buy it for his parents after all. (The Wizard's detective, thought Alexandra.) Good thing for the Lazarovi that this nice young couple was interested enough to look again—she would get the key. She seemed to consider them trustworthy this time, or couldn't be bothered with another tour, and they entered the house alone.

The smell inside was the same, smoky and clean and musty all at once, and the light filtering through the cheap curtains was just as Alexandra remembered. What was different this time was her sense of Stoyan's presence—that he'd lived a whole life, and for a while had lived it here, and had perhaps died here as well. Or had he died at a hospital nearby? She wished she'd asked Miss Radeva, or Irina.

Nothing had been disturbed in their absence, even by the police officer who had lied about his parents. "At least that's good," Bobby said, as if other things might well not be. He paused in the middle of the kitchen and looked around very slowly. There were a few handwritten notes taped to the side of a cupboard. "Those were here before." He translated for Alexandra: *Fix 2 chairs, take shoes and tomatoes to P, fabric, call Irina.* Old paper, yellowed, a reminder of tasks long since done, or not done. She wondered whose handwriting it was—probably Vera's, since it looked somehow like feminine Cyrillic, and not like the writing in Stoyan's confession. Besides, a woman would be more likely to make such a list.

The kitchen bed sat mute—as did the wood-stove lid with its handle sticking up like the handle of a pie-server, the plants alive still on one windowsill, the fossilized rag over the faucet. This time Alexandra felt the presence of real people, an old lady who had cooked here a thousand times and cleaned the counters bone-bare, an old man who had probably stopped playing his violin only when his hands got too arthritic; he had sat at that table, defeated, reading a newspaper full of unimaginable political change. And, at some point, the second old man —Milen Radev, who had been their best friend and perhaps had no other place to go after his retirement, had come here to live—and then to care for the old woman just as Stoyan had once commanded him to, when she became a widow. Now the kitchen was full, for Alexandra, not empty.

She followed Bobby into the sitting room; he seemed to scan it all with new attention, but this time he touched nothing. He bent to look at the top of the antiquated television; the neighbor had done her job and there was not even any dust. Alexandra pictured Stoyan seated on the divan in front of the evening broadcast, his hands in his lap—listening, maybe, to stories about young people who were no longer required to work only where the government sent them, or prevented from studying abroad. By then, he would have been too old to be sent anywhere, anyway.

They went upstairs. "What are we looking for?" she asked Bobby.

"Whatever we can find," he said, maddeningly, but now he pulled thin gloves from his pockets. He was so thorough, opening drawers again and searching closets, that Alexandra found herself listening hard for the sound of the neighbor coming to the door, or the police to the curb. In the bedroom, under the neatly made double bed, he found a tin of dried shoe polish and some stained rags folded in newspaper. "For black shoes," Bobby noted.

"Orchestra shoes?" Alexandra said automatically.

He unfolded the newspaper. "1987. *The July meeting of the Miners' Trade Union began today in the capital and will continue until August 1.* Okay." In a drawer of the stand by the bed, he found a loose photograph—the black-and-white image of a young man in his late teens or early twenties, his dark hair unbecomingly shaggy, his sweater knitted in diamond patterns, his long fingers restless on one knee. Sitting on a bench or wall, the badly faded sea behind him.

"That's Neven," Alexandra said, taking it carefully in her hand. It was worn at the edges, as if someone had held it many times. Opening the drawer by the bed, picking it up, looking at it. *Every night, before sleep.*

"How do you know?"

But she knew. She knew the shape of his head and the fine planes of his face, the way the thick hair would someday be cropped short, the long quiet body, the magnificent hands, the look of curiosity curbed into diffidence but not tamed— the directness of the eyes, even blurred in a bad photo. She had stood right next to him, in his shadow, and looked up at his face above her. In life, his physique had thickened and perhaps also grown stronger, but here he was. No writing on the reverse, no date. When Bobby turned to another part of the room, Alexandra put the dog-eared photo into her purse. She would give it back with the urn, if that ever happened, and confess all then.

The photographs on the walls held them for a moment; Alexandra looked hard at Vera in her Hollywood pearls, wishing she could ask the woman in the photograph where she was now. And also tell her that she, Alexandra, knew at least some of what had happened to Stoyan to make him sad and silent for the rest of his life.

But there was nothing else new, and Bobby

turned from the bedrooms with a grunt of frustration. In the living room Alexandra paused before the bookshelf: Italy, Hemingway, music history, all those titles in Cyrillic, a few in other languages. Dictionaries. Below them, half-obscured by the small television, was the shelf of bound sheet music, some of it worn at the edges like the photograph in her purse, perhaps also loved, pages turned again and again in rehearsal.

"His music," she said aloud, and stood there in front of it. This had been his vocation, even if he'd never been able to return to study in Vienna or play in front of grand audiences around the world. She thought about how a person's life could be distilled into so little—the person in ashes, the work a shelf of melodies dead to the air.

"Bobby," she said. *"The story of my life."*

Bobby turned from pulling out sofa cushions and looked at her, frowning, confused.

Alexandra pointed. "Remember? He said that the story of his life was in his music. He told that to—who?—Irina. And *gospodin* Angelov." She faltered, thinking of the artist, the way he had suddenly kissed her forehead. "This is where we found the box with the bandage things, too."

Bobby was beside her at once, carefully moving the television and the table it sat on. She thought he might start pulling out the row of bound music. Instead, he stood staring at it for a moment, as she had.

Fifty-eight

1950

Into the early spring, I pursued Neven's musical education, with snow still on the ground and the cold still hounding us, and one night I dreamed again of Vivaldi. It had snowed in Venice, too, and the Red Priest was hurrying alone to the printer's with new scores, his long wool coat with its shoulder-cape flapping around him. He wore a triangular blue hat on his pale wig, no gloves; perhaps he didn't need gloves, if Venice was seldom very cold. His boots took him swiftly across a square I didn't recognize—not San Marco, but still a rather large one—and they added footprints to all the others crossing the snow in every direction. It was morning, not early; the sun had crested the buildings that shadowed the square. He passed a woman with rosy jowls inside her head-shawl, a basket on her arm. I felt afraid, for some reason, and frustrated; he was in danger and I was supposed to tell him but couldn't make my presence known.

In fact, I seemed to be invisible, or even not there at all. I couldn't see his face, but I knew it must be lined with worry. I watched his long coat move across the square, as if I had a bird's perch in the buildings and couldn't screech loudly enough to get his attention. He was quick, and he seemed to be talking to himself. Work weighed on him; I knew that kind of hurry myself, when I'd tried to fit some errand in before the inevitable rehearsal.

Church bells were ringing now, and I wanted to count them—this was also important—but I lost count at four, although I knew that it must be at least nine in the morning. He passed out of the edge of the square into an alley at the far corner, and I watched him disappear without being able to follow him. Then I realized that he'd dropped a score from his bundle—a thick handwritten sheaf—and I attempted to fly down to pick it up, but I couldn't. I knew the ink would melt and smudge in the snow, and that perhaps other people would come along to steal it, or perhaps, not noticing, would trample it. Then I understood that it contained a message for me, which I would not be able to retrieve.

Spring brought an end to the searing, terrible cold, and summer brought warmth and then heat to replace it. For me, the cold was also replaced by a mental misery I could hardly describe even to myself. Then even this was replaced by a fever. My frame, after surviving the bitterest cold workdays, seemed suddenly weak in every joint; one morning I could hardly stand up. I could not walk all the way to the latrines; I collapsed in the yard. My first thought was to tell Vera and Neven and my violin goodbye, since I would probably be shot in the dust there, a useless old horse. But the Chief sent Momo to me, with a great show of irritation, and made the younger man hoist me over his shoulder—I was lighter, of course, than I'd ever been—and carry me to the infirmary. The ground looked distant and the sky yellow, the mountains wavering and shrinking above the camp. Even in my mounting delirium I didn't want Momo to touch me and I didn't want to go to the infirmary, from which so many returned in tightly tied sacks. But I couldn't struggle. The Chief must have felt I was somehow worth saving, and also not too sick to save—or perhaps he simply didn't want me to infect the other men.

Momo carried me to the infirmary without speaking; when we arrived, he dropped me almost absentmindedly on the bed nearest the door, one of the few that was empty. Then he seemed to remember me and turned back. I saw him loom over me—the heat in my head made him look even larger and more angelic than usual—and he swatted me across the face, but casually, as if his heart wasn't in it. It hurt terribly, more because my head was swollen and fiery already than because there was any force in the blow.

"Aw, get up, get back to work, faker," he said,

but as if practicing, a boy imitating more authoritative elders. I felt my contempt for him oozing up through the misery of fever. I tried to turn my head away but was too weak even for that. He was gone suddenly, as if snatched out of my vision by magic. A man I thought must be Nurse Ivan had come over to talk to me; I seemed to have been there hours already, and the nurse was putting cloths soaked in terribly cold water on my face. Cold water dripped into my ears and clothing. I understood that the pain of the cold water just might undo the pain of fever: a trade. It seemed to be winter again, possibly spring, then a scorching summer afternoon, then Vienna in the parks—autumn—red leaves in a whirl like music on the pavements.

I remembered Vera and decided that I would simply stay very close to her until the end came. It seemed to me we had a son, whom I loved, but I was having trouble remembering the unusual name by which we called him. Vera sat next to me stroking my forehead, a treatment that felt infinitely better than the smelly cold rags I'd imagined there a moment before. She sat caressing my head and face with her cool hand for three or four days. I realized once that I should be practicing; or teaching my little son—what was his name?—to play his *tsigulka*; or following Vivaldi around Venice for his rehearsals. But it also occurred to me that the Red Priest might be too busy composing, might not want me interrupting him in his rooms while he worked, and that I had lost track of which day it was anyway. I struggled to sit up and go back to work—they would shoot me if I didn't get to the quarry, and then I would never be able to take the train back to Vera. Someone pushed me down; it was no use. I waited to die, keeping Vera's name in my bloodstream, where it pulsed.

And then I woke one morning, exhausted and half-alive, but no longer on fire. My mind was stunned but clear. I looked around in the early light and saw that I was still in a building that must be the infirmary. I had the strange feeling of having been out of camp for a while, free for the first time since I'd arrived, not a prisoner. Now I was enslaved again and Vera was not there. Water welled up in my eyes and ran down the sides of my face, but my hands were too weak to reach it. Daylight was pouring in through four tall windows, which must be nailed shut. The room was warm.

Turning my head a little, I could see men's bodies, dead or alive, in several other beds, one heap to a bed, unmoving. If it was daylight, all who could stand on their feet were at work already, in the quarry or the mines. I wondered how Nasko was, whether he was living, whether he had missed me, and then how long I had been away, or asleep with fever. I remembered that if I was alive, even in camp, there was a chance I would be released one day to see Vera and my son Neven and to play music again with my own hands. Next I remembered that my son had not yet been born, that my hands might never heal enough, and that perhaps Vera had already given me up for dead.

Nurse Ivan came to my bedside, a blurry figure still, and bent over me with a cup of water, then a cup of the usual thin soup. I couldn't hold on to anything, and when I tried to drink I coughed it back up on his arms and hands and he wiped them on my bedclothes. That was when I realized there were sheets and a real blanket—I hadn't felt such things against my hands for so long that I could hardly recognize them. They were rough sheets and probably dirty, but thcy were like messengers from another world.

Nurse Ivan said, "You've had the bad one, but you lived." He didn't shout at me or threaten me; it had been a long time since any camp official had spoken to me in a normal voice, if it had ever happened before at all. "Five others didn't. And, see, those men over there are still recovering." He didn't sound much interested, and I remembered that people said he was not a real nurse.

"How long was I sick?" I said. "I can't remember."

"Several days, I suppose," said Nurse Ivan. "You better rcst more."

I reflected that I had no choice; I could hardly move. He went away and didn't come near me again for hours, until I was calling for water. I drank greedily this time; the fever had left me as dry as dirt.

The next morning I could eat a little more soup, but still couldn't sit up. I had learned by then to urinate into a jar if the nurse held it, which he did with barely controlled distaste—I probably smelled as bad as any of them. He took away my urine-stained sheet, too, and brought me a cleaner one. I lay looking at the light on the other side of the dusty windows, and the shapes of trees, which sometimes moved in the breeze. It was apparently summer out there; that was why it grew hot in the infirmary as the day progressed. I wished they could open the windows but knew better than to ask. I thought that I should get better as slowly as I could so that I would not have to return to the quarry a moment earlier than necessary—if they sent me back too early, the work would probably kill me. Simply resting, floating horizontal, was such a novelty for me that I kept feeling I must be dreaming. A man in another bed began to moan over and over and I realized I had heard that sound often during the previous days without being able to place it. I hoped Nurse Ivan would come to the poor man's aid; I didn't see him anywhere in the room.

I tried to think about Venice, but my mind was

too weak to imagine anything from a painting or an engraving. I decided in a rambling way that if I got out of the infirmary and then out of the camp, I would somehow, sometime, go to Venice. In a few more years, with the new society confidently in place, or perhaps failed and behind us, the borders would reopen. Venice was the first destination to which Vera and I would travel, even before I went back to my studies and performances and competitions. We would take Neven. We would stand on the Piazza and I would realize I had imagined it all correctly.

I must have slept through this travel, because suddenly it was evening, the light low across the floor, and I had a visitor.

Fifty-nine

It took Alexandra and Bobby at least half an hour to remove each score from the music shelf and look through all the pages. He showed her how to keep them in the order in which they'd found them. Alexandra strained her ears, listening for the neighbor's return, worrying about Stoycho tied up in the meager shade of the yard. But while she listened she worked, swiftly, turning pages of sheet music until the notes ran together under her eyes. There were volumes of solo music—Bach Partitas, Paganini—and piles of orchestral scores—Beethoven, Tchaikovsky, Rimsky-Korsakov, their covers mainly in Cyrillic. Stoyan's orchestras seemed to have favored Russian composers. There were genuine antiques among these volumes, she felt sure; the very oldest were brittle and dark yellow. The tin candy box was still on the shelf, behind them, and Bobby set it on the table with half a smile.

"Dimchov's man was not so good after all," he said, modestly. "Or maybe he was looking only for people, not treasure boxes."

They turned through page after page, but there was nothing except music—it filled the room, silently. *Where was Stoyan's violin now?* Alexandra wondered for the first time. Had it been the one Baba Yana had heard him play in the village, music under the stars or coming out the chimney? At last all of Stoyan's scores sat in piles on the floor, their order carefully preserved, his life's work.

"Maybe I was wrong," Alexandra said.

"Or maybe he meant this—whatever those things are, inside." Bobby reached out and opened the tin box on the table, so that they could see the stained curl of fabric inside. "And we have looked at all his music."

"No," Alexandra said slowly. "We haven't. There was no Vivaldi."

Bobby regarded her in silence.

She sat back on her heels. "Irina said he played

Vivaldi, and Milen Radev told his niece something like that, too—that Stoyan loved the music of some Italian. And—Nasko Angelov. He said he knew that Stoyan was feeling better whenever he played Vivaldi. But there isn't any Vivaldi here."

She was thinking about something else, too: a young brother and littler sister, lying under the dining room table at the farmhouse, their parents' LP of *The Four Seasons* revolving on an already dated stereo with a diamond needle. They loved the idea of a diamond needle, because it was the only jewel in the house; even their mother wore only a plain gold wedding band. Alexandra liked to listen to "Spring," which made her think of fountains and gazelles. Jack preferred "Autumn," which he said sounded like tornadoes, and she, too, could see the red leaves caught up in a whirlwind. They flipped a coin about where to put the needle of the record player, until their mother came down from cleaning the attic and reminded them that this was bad for the record, they might scratch it, that they must always start from the beginning.

"And let the year run its course," said their mother, smiling, with a big cobweb on her shirtsleeve. It was the first time Alexandra had heard the expression "run its course," and for years afterward that phrase meant to her letting a record play all the way through, and something about a cobweb. At least Jack had died during his favorite season. She would never stop missing him, but now it seemed that worse things sometimes happened to people—men moaning on the floor of a train car, which telescoped away from her into darkness.

"Bird," Bobby said, stroking her forehead, and then her stomach came back up to the right level. "You fainted."

She could feel his hand on her hair. She was lying on the living room floor, looking at the ceiling. She thought she must have fallen gently, and not far from her kneeling place by the table. Then she realized that Bobby had caught her, so she hadn't really fallen.

"Sweet girl," Bobby said, and Alexandra knew he meant her. He helped her sit up and cradled her head against his shoulder with his gloved hand. "What happened?"

"My brother," Alexandra said. She found she was sobbing, but quietly. "He died so long ago already, and we used to listen to music together."

"I'm sorry," Bobby said, and she knew he really was, although they had met only six days earlier.

Alexandra reached for her purse, which she had set on the sofa. She took out her wallet, carefully avoiding the stolen photograph of Neven.

"Here he is," she said. Her voice broke again. *Maybe I should go home,* she thought. *I shouldn't have left my parents alone there, without either of us.*

Bobby took the picture with tender respect. This was her favorite, worn around the corners like the one of Neven. She kept it in a plastic sleeve in each new wallet she got: a copy of a school photo taken weeks before their hike and delivered personally to her family by a regretful high school principal, months afterward. It showed a boy, insouciantly adolescent, blond-red hair standing up in his usual buzz cut, his gaze careless, fixing the viewer with some amusement. He was beauti-ful, and she had the bittersweet pleasure of watching Bobby's eyes widen briefly in admiration. Bobby bowed his head over the picture for several seconds, then handed it back to her.

"So young," he said. "Thank you for showing him to me." She thought of the losses he must have known, too. No one escaped. Bobby was combing his hair back with thin fingers, that nervous gesture. "He was—how old?"

"Sixteen," she said. "And a day."

Bobby was silent, his gaze moving back and forth over her face, wondering. "You don't look very much like him. But in the smile," he said.

"Thank you." She put the picture back in its wallet sleeve and wiped her cheeks. She wouldn't start crying again.

"It must have been terrible for you after he died," said Bobby.

She sat looking at him, feeling her cheeks stiff

with salt, her eyes gumming shut. Then she slowly rolled up the sleeve of her cotton blouse. The long scar was pale now, not the pink it had been for months after, although there was still a jagged place where she'd lost courage for a moment. Without comment, she held her arm up under his gaze. He bent down suddenly and kissed the scar, and her eyes spilled over.

"What does that make us?" Her voice felt thick.

Bobby took her wrist and lowered the arm gently, as if it were broken. "Blood brothers," he said.

Leaning forward, she hugged her taxi driver fiercely. Then she rubbed her other sleeve over her face. There was something she must do now, even if she could never save Jack. It had been at the edge of her mind before she'd fainted.

"Vivaldi—we didn't find any," she said.

"What?" He turned back to the music and looked around, but absently, as if still gripped by her pain. "That's right. No Vivaldi."

"How about somewhere else in the house?"

"We've looked everywhere," he said. "The shelf is empty."

"I know. But Vivaldi was his favorite. Where would you keep your favorite music?"

Bobby shrugged, but he was still staring at her. "I am not a musician."

"Your favorite book of poetry, then."

He nodded. "Under my bed, where I can reach

it when I wake up. But we looked under the beds, and I looked under the mattresses."

She groaned. What could they do?

"Time to leave," Bobby said. "We must put all this back. We have been here too long."

They had, Alexandra knew, and the neighbor must be suspicious by now. "But Vivaldi— maybe Stoyan even had many scores by him, if he loved him so much."

"Or maybe he memorized the music and didn't need scores anymore," Bobby pointed out. "Maybe he gave them away. Maybe he kept them at the house in the mountains. We did not look in every corner there, you know. Usually when something is hidden, there is a sign, something else not quite right. But every little thing in this house is right. They cleaned it out, except for the photographs."

Spring, thought Alexandra, and Jack's Autumn. All the seasons that had passed, unmarked. She looked at the shriveled brown curls of fabric Stoyan had left them instead.

"There is one thing not right," she said. She went quickly back up the stairs and into the bedroom with the photographs, Bobby at her heels.

The calendar hung on the wall where they had seen it both times: June 2006, almost two years ago, the month Stoyan Lazarov had died, with the maidens in their red-and-white costumes dancing around a well. She lifted it down. The wall showed only a shadowed peach color where the paint had faded less. But June 2006 felt heavier in her hand than the months that had preceded it; taped to the back of the page, where the maidens danced in the other direction through the paper, was not a musical score but an envelope.

They knew the fine handwriting on the front of it. Bobby translated for Alexandra: *The last part. Never for publication.*

Sixty-

1950

My visitor was Momo. I didn't see him until he was standing close by, then sitting in a wooden chair he'd pulled up to the bed. He leaned over me and shook me by the shoulder. The chair was ramshackle, canting to one side, and I thought surely his big muscular body would splinter it. But he perched there and smiled at me with his gapped front teeth, like a little boy. I hoped I was dreaming his presence, too, but he did not disappear. His strong hands, which had killed so many, had no club in them; they lay neatly covering his knees. He seemed incapable of uttering any normal greeting, but after a minute or two he addressed me. "I carried you in like a sack of potatoes," he said.

He seemed to be considering the possibility that I would say something, so after a moment I replied. "Yes."

"A sack of potatoes," he said, smiling, as if well pleased with the image.

"Yes," I said, hoping this would make him go away. I wondered if he'd come to visit me in order to congratulate himself on having saved me, which made no sense. Maybe he was seeing himself in an unusual light, as savior rather than murderer, and found it interesting. I wondered also how he had the leisure to come to see me, when the prisoners would soon be returning from the workday, some of them perhaps needing to be killed. Had the Chief given him an hour off?

He adjusted his frame in the rickety chair. "You are the smart one, aren't you? The musician?"

I lay still and studied what I could of his face, which was as empty as a plate, but with clever eyes, especially when he wasn't smiling. "Well, at home I was a musician," I said, as indifferently as I could.

"I have to do something for the Chief," he said, "and I need somebody smart."

"I'm not that smart," I said quietly. "Do you think I would be here if I were?"

He considered this for a little but didn't seem to be able to sort it out, although again I suspected, from the flicker in his eyes, that this stupidity was at least partly a ruse. He wiped his nose with his hand. "But you are smart, aren't you? The other men said that you are a famous musician and it was too bad you were sick."

I wondered who'd said this—certainly not Nasko, who would never have spoken so foolishly. But there seemed to be no secrets in camp.

"I'm no smarter than other men," I said.

"Well, they said you were." He looked obstinate and folded his arms across his bulky chest. "So I guess you are. I need somebody to go with me to the town, a smart prisoner, to tell a somebody there that we run this place good." Again, I had the strange sense that he wasn't as dumb as he certainly looked. Perhaps he had an impeccable ability to adapt?

"Why doesn't the Chief go?" I said, but immediately regretted it. Momo puffed up like a frog, indignant.

"The Chief has to stay here. He is a busy man. He is the Chief! It would be dangerous for him to leave someone else in charge, even me."

This was the most coherent thing I'd heard from him, ever. The man in the next bed, sticky-faced with fever, turned over, restless; probably we were a part of his dreams.

"Why are you telling me this?" I said. My voice felt very weak, still.

"Well, the Chief said I could take a smart prisoner along to tell them, and then if that prisoner was smart enough to stay quiet after ward—" He seemed to get stuck there, or to pretend to. He was silent for a couple of seconds.

"If he was smart enough to stay quiet?" I prompted.

"Well, if he was that clever, and he knew we would always have an eye on him ever after, we might let him go home."

There was a long silence in the room, filled with Momo's last word, until the man in the next bed turned toward us again. Clearly Momo thought him as good as dead.

"What would this prisoner need to tell them, exactly?" I found it hard to keep my voice steady.

Momo pondered this. He had the kind of eyes one sees in marble statues, wide open but consciously empty, marked in the stone by contour rather than color. "I guess the prisoner would need to tell the Commissioner from Sofia who is visiting the town that things are going well in our camp. Otherwise, the Commissioner might visit for himself, and that makes some work for the Chief. You know how it is," he added confidingly.

"Tell him that things are going well?"

"You know, for the prisoners. They are workers. They work hard and eat and sleep and we help them to be rehabilitated. We keep things organized here. They do well."

"You mean," I said with care, wishing I could sit up and look more easily at him, "you mean that we are well treated."

"Yes!" He smiled again at last, the gap showing broadly between his front teeth. "That is what they would like to know."

I thought about Vera, and her joy at my return; I thought about the son we would have. I thought about my hands, someday healed, drawing the bow over the strings. Then I thought about Nasko and the others. Who had been pushing the wheelbarrow for Nasko since I'd fallen ill? Perhaps he'd been doing it himself, the turn I'd often urged him to take, to save his own hands. I remembered what I had actually done, which was not the thing I was being punished for.

"I'm sorry," I said. "Unfortunately, I am not that smart."

His smile faded. "You are not?"

"No," I said. "I am a good musician, but you need someone very smart—very, very smart—to be able to tell the Commissioner properly."

He sat looking glumly at his knees; his good idea, or at least what he'd been asked to do, had failed. Or—was it possible?—he couldn't show his hand to me now; he had to remain stupid.

"Too bad," he said. "I thought it would be you. Wouldn't you like to go home?"

"Of course I would," I said. Now that it was over, my mind swam with grief, and I could hardly keep my eyes open. I wished Nurse Ivan would come interrupt us. "Wouldn't you like to go home, too?" I turned my head and looked carefully at him.

He shrugged. "I guess I would. But I don't really have anybody." He was still studying his knees. "My parents died before the war—they were *partizani*, fighting in the mountains. They were fighting the fascist government. My father got caught by the King's police. They cut off his head, you know, and then they killed my mother and sisters, for helping him. First they raped them."

He seemed to have forgotten that he was supposed to be dull, to speak slowly. He glared at me, as if I had contradicted him. "That is what they did to good communists. You know that? They cut off their heads and raped their women. Then my grandpa I lived with died, and my cousins moved somewhere else—I don't know where. Maybe to Sofia where there is a lot of work now. So I guess I don't know where I would go."

He leaned back, angry, wistful. "Most of the people I know are here. I came here when I was only fourteen, three years ago. The Chief took care of me and gave me this job."

I thought it was good that his parents, whoever they'd been, had not lived to see their son grow up. Certainly they had believed in what they were fighting for, but I wondered if Momo believed in anything at all, apart from his own animal intelligence. It puzzled me that he didn't simply offer to beat me into fulfilling his request, or kill me for refusing it.

But he was still contemplating his life. "Someday, you know, I'm going to get married to a beautiful woman, a good communist, like the ones in the moving pictures, and we are going to have kids. And I will be a general." He didn't smile; it was too earnest a desire. This might, I thought, be the real Momo at last. Then he looked quickly at me. "You won't tell the Chief?"

I thought at once that this strange scene would now indeed be the death of me; I had heard Momo say he wanted to be a general and he would probably never forgive me for that, even if it had been playacting. My limbs began to tremble from sheer weakness under the blanket, but I tried to keep my mind clear.

"No," I said. "I won't tell him, if you won't tell him that I am not as smart as you'd hoped. In fact, you don't have to tell him you talked to me, since I turned out to be the wrong person."

He looked fixedly at me. "I don't have to tell him."

"No," I said. "You don't have to tell him, since I turned out to be a disappointment."

He flexed his hands on his knees, still thinking. "All right," he said. "But I don't know where I am going to find somebody else, somebody smart."

"This place is full of smart men. Or perhaps the Chief will go tell the Commissioner himself, after all," I said. I was becoming faint. To my acute relief, Momo stood up suddenly and walked out, as if we had not been talking. He vanished at once from my blurred view.

Then he reappeared, and I feared for a moment that he had come back to kill me in my bed. But he merely looked around the floor and under the chair he'd been sitting in. "I thought I dropped something," he said. "Maybe some-where else."

He went out again. I heard him unlocking the door from the inside and locking it from the out-side.

I couldn't help it; I slept, on the instant. When I awoke, minutes or hours later, I found in my rumpled bedclothes what he had lost. I didn't return it. Instead, I slid it carefully into a crack in the wall beside me, where I could get it back if I ever recovered, and where the nurse would never find it.

By the end of another two weeks, I could walk well enough to work—in fact, I could have tried earlier, but I was careful to feign unsteadiness on my feet for longer than it really persisted. Nurse Ivan released me at last to the hell of the dugout barrack and I slept again on shreds of wool and roiling bedbugs; I'd been in the infirmary just long enough to make this a fresh misery, although I don't think the bedbugs had ever quite left me, or the lice. The next morning I was lining up for work with the rest. Momo marched with us all to the pit but paid me no particular attention—nor, I was glad to see, did the Chief.

Nasko was near the back of the line; I didn't get to speak with him until we were on the ledge, where two new men were working with us. There, he grasped my hand, quickly, and I saw the pleasure in his face, as plain as words: *You're alive.* My heart had been twisting in me all morning, along with my sickened stomach and weak limbs. I was relieved that he was still there and glad to be able to look him in the eye. It was hot, even in the shadow of the pit and the deeper shade of the mountains.

Nasko had been lifting rocks and someone else had pushed the wheelbarrow; now I took back my old job, straining up the slope. I was so weak that every trip took me three times longer than it had before my illness. Nasko slowed his dumping of rock into the barrow just enough to give me some relief, but not enough to get caught. My head buzzed so that I couldn't hear even the shouts of the guards or the sounds of the birds. It was deep summer; I had been sick longer than I'd realized. I decided I would arrange my schedule again tomorrow, beginning with a day of practice. This first morning, I simply kept a name close to my ear: *Vera.* When I'd said it many times over, I varied it: *Neven.*

Sixty-one

They took the envelope with them, tucked inside Bobby's jacket. They replaced the musical scores quickly and in order—Alexandra felt a surge of regret as she fitted all the Bach onto the shelf. Bobby moved the television back to its forlorn spot. At the last moment, he took the tin box and put it into his jacket with the envelope.

Outside, it was already getting dark. They returned the key to the neighbor. "I told her we thought carefully about where we would put our furniture, but that we decided the house is too small for all our books," Bobby said afterward, shaking his head. They retrieved Stoycho, who had fallen asleep on his side, near the front gate.

In the car, Bobby checked his cell phone.

"Shit. There's a voice message," he said. It was the first time Alexandra had heard him swear in English. "It didn't ring before, somehow. It's Lenka's number."

"Thank God," said Alexandra. But as Bobby listened, she saw his face grow dark. The message was very short; she could hear the voice leaking out—nervous, hushed, hurried. Bobby listened twice. He turned to her.

Alexandra's fingers had already begun to tremble. "What?"

"She says"—he paused. "She says, *They took us. Neven might know where. He called Irina in Plovdiv. He is at—* Then she gives an address in the town of Morsko. That's near Burgas, on the sea. Then she rings off very fast." He played it again. "She sounds really frightened, or upset, and she is trying to speak in a whisper."

"I could hear that," Alexandra said, clenching her hands. "Who took them? Dimchov? The police? Why to the sea? Bobby, let's go now, right away."

Bobby didn't move. "This might be a trick." He put his hand in his hair. "Maybe whoever wants the urn hid Irina and Lenka somewhere and made Lenka call us. We will be frightened because Irina and Lenka are hostages, and we will try to go to Neven with the urn." Bobby's voice shook a little. "Then they are waiting for us at that address in Morsko. Or they don't know the address yet because Lenka has not told them, but if we go there they will follow us. Why didn't Lenka tell us in the message where she and Irina are?"

Alexandra tried to keep herself calm enough to speak. "Maybe she didn't dare. Or she didn't know, if they were taken there at night. Or maybe she wants us to come with Neven, not by ourselves, for some reason."

"Possibly," Bobby said.

"Listen," said Alexandra. "We don't know

anywhere else to go. If Neven really is there, he might be able to help them." She had almost ceased to believe that Neven existed; he had become for her part of a story, a battered photograph, a longing under her ribs. "Please, we have to go now."

"I know," Bobby said. "But it's a long drive, and I want to travel late at night, when there are fewer police on the roads. I will have to be careful not to speed, not to get us any attention."

Stoycho sat up and shook himself.

Alexandra touched Bobby's arm. "Can you drive safely? We could take turns, if you want." She wondered whether she would be able to navigate alone, if he fell asleep.

"Of course I can. We slept last night. Let me sleep in the car for a couple of hours, away from the highway, and then get some coffee."

He started up the Ford. Alexandra reached out and put one hand on Stoycho, in the back, and watched the gritty outskirts of Bovech rush past them.

Sixty-two

1950

My misery took new forms. A few months after I recovered, if you could call it recovery, Momo suddenly approached me during evening roll call. I was in the front row, half-collapsing from the day's work under an autumn sun. As the Chief paced and lectured in front of us—he had good boots from somewhere, and seemed to enjoy striding up and down in them—Momo wandered about, looking first at one prisoner, then at another, each man no doubt praying he would not be selected for sacrifice. Then he paused in front of me. He made a show of standing up very straight, with his hands behind his back, the way the Chief did, examining me. "Well, do you think you are so smart?" he said, in a low voice.

"No," I answered, my heart sinking. Although I was trying not to look at him, I had already caught the almost hopeful expression on his face, which belied his aggressive stance. Apparently he hadn't found anyone else to perform his mission for the Chief. Or perhaps the need for the mission had disappeared, and he wanted to be sure I remained afraid of him.

"Are you sure?" he whispered.

"Yes," I said, as quietly as I could. I had no idea what the exhausted men around us made of this, except that it was causing a further delay of our supper. He turned away, as if he couldn't find anything else to ask me, and the Chief dismissed us all.

After that, Momo looked up whenever my name was called from the list, and stared hard at me. Sometimes it was a look of approval, almost of complicity, as if his having saved me by carrying me to the infirmary, and my having turned out to be interesting, had produced for him a new pride in himself. This added a wretched theme of alertness to my days. The fact that he was watching me made me watch him, inevitably, so that a glimpse of his big frame and curly head at the rim of the pit while we worked could make my stomach turn over. It meant, too, that I had to be alert enough to prevent him from seeing that I was alert. And had I been correct in my glimpse of something clever, discerning, under his idiocy? What would be more dangerous to me, an idiot or a subtle man pretending to be an idiot? In a place like this, perhaps it didn't even matter.

I burrowed into my routine again, rehearsing the Tchaikovsky concerto, trying out the Sibelius, working my way through my orchestral repertoire, or at least the swaths of it that had lasted in my memory. I made a new rule for myself that if I saw Momo, or even thought of his disquieting offer, I had to start a movement over. If I was angry enough at myself, I would make myself begin the whole piece again.

The day I watched Momo and his companions beat a newcomer until the bone in the man's cheek showed, I went somewhere I hadn't been in a long time. I'd become so attached to Neven the baby, the small child, that I had nearly forgotten to believe in him as a man. But that day I visited him again at the river, walking down the gradual slope to where he sat with a young woman beside him. I watched the sun play on the surface of the water, the gleam of their heads as they talked —his hair dark, almost black, in soft short waves but shaved close at the neck so that his skin looked white there; hers chestnut, with red glints like the coat of a horse. She had absently braided a heavy section of it over one shoulder. I stood smiling at their backs and then I raised my violin and tucked it under my chin. With my supple, strong, smooth hands, I drew the bow across my strings to serenade them. Even the stiffness from my war wound was gone.

On the other days, I walked through Venice with the Red Priest, or I gave Neven—now a slender, large-eyed eight-year-old—his daily violin lesson. He didn't always want to practice; but then, as I told him, discipline is the first thing a musician has to learn, and it would serve him well in any situation. By the time the dreaded cold weather came to the quarry again, Neven was an affectionate, if reserved, twelve-year-old, his pretty voice just beginning to break at the dinner table. I thought he was ready for competition; if anything, we were beginning late. The only problem was that I didn't know how this would work, under the auspices of our glorious revolution. Everything would be different now, probably, for a gifted child musician. On the worst days, I had my doubts about whether I could find a competition in which to enter him—Neven, the son of a convict.

That winter I was weaker than I'd been the first one, and in an odd, slight way stronger, too, accustomed to certain hardships even while my body declined. I imagined dying and living on in my own story as a ghost; maybe then, I would go tell the Commissioner how things were in Zelenets, but I would tell him the truth. Momo didn't leave the camp, even briefly, so perhaps he had never made his errand to town. Probably the Chief had taken care of it himself, or sent someone else. It occurred to me that maybe Momo had only imagined that the Chief wanted him to do it—or that he had invented the story to torment me.

One more group of newcomers arrived before the first snow, and I read in the eyes of the young ones when they glanced at me—at all of us—that

I had indeed become what I'd seen here the first day. I was a skeleton, not quite among the walking dead yet, but edging ever closer. I felt I might be able to eat air one day, or to float without a struggle into the pit—there was plenty of room, of course, to dive—die—from our ledge. Our original shelf was long since exhausted of stone, in fact, and Nasko and our companions and I had been sent to a larger outcropping already loaded with quarried cubes, to break and haul rock there. I savored every day I saw Nasko now, and when one of our fellow ledge-dwellers died in the night, I chided myself for thanking heaven that it had not been my only real friend.

At least sixty men died that winter, if I counted correctly. The camp was terribly crowded, since newcomers had been pushed into barracks already full. Increasingly, it puzzled me that I was alive. A few of my fellow skeletons went mad, no longer marching to work even under threat of being beaten or shot. Instead they scrabbled for food scraps around the kitchen door until they collapsed and died in the snow. The cooks, prisoners who ate only a little better than the rest of us—although they could at least grab scraps without being seen—tried to drive the mad skeletons away, but without success. Frequently, now, my prayer to nothing was that my death would contain a little dignity when it came to me. I hoped most of all that I would go to sleep one night among the men and the bugs, dreaming of Vera, and never wake up.

I tried to push such thoughts down, as I pushed away my eternal awareness of Momo's offer, his continued scrutiny. Had I been foolish to refuse that chance? Would there be another?

Sometimes I imagined what it would have been like for me to go meet the Commissioner. Did Momo watch me because he had some other offer to make, and if he made one, what would I say? After all, I had decided my first night in camp that they had no right to punish me for the wrong thing. Now doubt began to work on my brain, an additional torment; if I'd accepted what Momo had proposed, I might be home with Vera. She would never know what had become of me, where I'd lived and worked and died, and I had denied her the last possible chance. These doubts mingled with my hatred of Momo every time I saw him. Shadowing my doubts and my hatred was the knowledge that he would never offer to send me out, at this point—how could a skeleton show up in town to assert he'd been well treated back at the camp? Although surely I had already looked too ill and unpresentable when he had asked me.

By spring I had taken Neven to four or five competitions—his tone was celestial, throbbing but restrained, and his technique was as good as I could help him make it. I tried to imagine the competitions, where and how they were held and who judged them these days, but all that was a blur. Instead, I saw my boy on stage, his thick dark curls moving with the emphatic tug of his bow across the strings. The applause of the little group of judges, whoever they were, the conference among them afterward, their heads bowed together. He was young, but he was meticulous, and he was passionate. At thirteen, he soloed with the Sofia Philharmonic. At fifteen, he lost two competitions but won a more important one, and if we'd been able to travel out of the country he would have placed in Europe as well. He practiced now without any prompting; his school hours had been shortened to accommodate his music. On alternate days, in the quarry, we practiced together, sometimes playing a concerto in unison, sometimes working on duets. My mind was clouding as the warm weeks went on, and that dark wing brushed it more caressingly. I was determined to see him to manhood before I died.

One day in the late summer, a day I usually spent with Vivaldi, playing in the churches while he conducted, I took a formal vow, the third since my arrest. In life, or—if necessary—in death, Neven and I would travel to Venice together.

Sixty-three

Alexandra must have slept, too; she woke in time to catch a faint brightening of the sky along flat roads, lit-up factories in the marshes, and then a gleam beyond them that Bobby said was the Black Sea. She had thought she would get her first glimpse of the sea very differently— from a train, with her backpack and book. Now she craned to look out the car window and reached back a hand for Stoycho. He stirred and woke and they all regarded their passage through a twilit city, housing complexes and empty streets, a clock tower at a port, and finally a highway out of town. Dawn would come soon.

"Burgas," Bobby said. "This is where the Lazarovi lived, and Miss Radeva's family." When Alexandra lowered the car window she breathed salt air and a swampy, industrial murk. Bobby had put on one of his Dylan CDs, turned low. Alexandra thought—out of her skimpy knowledge —of the Delta, home of the blues; it must smell something like this. *"You ain't goin' nowhere,"* Dylan muttered. The highway wound through sloping fields and patches of flat brush, with a hotel here and there at the edge of the road, and honeycombed stretches of housing like prefabricated ruins, roofless under the first light. The distant sheen of water had vanished.

"People are building like mad here," Bobby said. "Everyone wants to be near the sea, including many foreigners. Some people start to build but they cannot afford to finish."

Soon the sky was softly yellow and pink, the sun beginning to rise; they came around one last curve and Bobby pointed to their destination— Morsko, a red-roofed old town on a high peninsula edged with cliffs. They were approaching it on an even higher road, and she could see gray water breaking around the feet of the town. Bobby drove carefully in—near the entrance to the peninsula a police car was parked, lights and motor off, a dim figure at the wheel. Two men were setting out vegetables on a wooden stall next to the sidewalk, and a lone tourist padded past them in bathing suit and sandals, a towel folded over his shoulder. On the roof ridge of a house nearby, gulls complained to each other out of the silence, startling, acerbic.

Bobby drove along a wide paved port where boats bumped together in the waves. Just out to sea, Alexandra saw an island with a lighthouse, and then horizons of colorless water—a few boats drifted there, too, with their lights still on in the dawn and their nets trailing behind them. Then Bobby was saying something about the address; he'd been to Morsko before, he told her, in child-hood and once after, but didn't know the town well. The car wound up steeply cobbled streets and Bobby wrestled with corners and gears.

Alexandra had never seen houses like these. They were wooden, or sometimes elaborately patterned old stone. The wooden ones were stained a dark chocolate from the salt wind and wet, their shutters still closed against the night, balconies writhing with bright-colored flowers in pots, laundry hanging on lines, roofs almost touching above narrow streets, walls and fences shielding front courtyards from the sidewalk.

At the top of the town, Bobby parked not quite in front of a house of aged wood panels with a balcony and green shutters, sheltered by a high wall with a door in it. Along the top of the wall ran a roof that matched the roof of the house; the ceramic of the tiles on both had faded to variegated browns, like autumn leaves. Bobby pulled the parking brake and Stoycho stretched, hitting the back of the seat with his nails and then drooping again. When they got out, Bobby scanned the wall and the front of the house, walked to the corner of the block. Then he rang the bell.

The man who answered the door was a stranger. He wore green flip-flops on his feet and held a trowel in one hand, as if preparing to defend the house with it. It surprised Alexandra that anyone else was up so early. Bobby spoke to the man in quick Bulgarian and gestured toward Alexandra; the man looked them over—the Bulgarian stranger, the young foreign woman with a black bag in her arms, and the self-contained dog. He asked Bobby a few sharp questions. Then, as if satisfied with the answers, he gestured them in with his trowel.

"His family are old friends of the Lazarovi, from Burgas," Bobby told Alexandra. "I think Neven came here for safety." Without warning, Alexandra's heart began to pound harder. "I told him what we've brought," said Bobby.

Inside, there was a rectangular courtyard completely hidden from the street—a kind of outdoor room, Alexandra thought, observing the long table and chairs, the porous roof of vines, the pink geraniums in pots, the open cupboard full of gardening tools and cans of paint. There was no sign of disruption—no police officers, no thugs waiting for them, no Irina or Lenka. No Neven. The man with the trowel had been digging in a vegetable bed along one wall, where potato plants sprouted leafy green. A door into the house stood open, with a small kitchen visible just inside.

In the middle of this greenery sat an ancient figure, more like a sack than a person. Alexandra knew him at once: it was Milen Radev, asleep in his wheelchair. Alexandra went closer and stood gazing at him, holding the urn in its bag. His skin looked gray and patchy as old cement. His hands were in his lap, where someone had spread a knitted afghan. He wore the clothes Alexandra remembered, the rusty dark jacket and trousers, all a little too big, as if he were gradually disappearing inside them.

She had looked at him so many times in her photograph, where he sat blurry in the depths of the taxi, that it surprised her to find him distinct and made up of actual skin, hair, worn fabric. His cheeks hung in folds on each side of his jaw; a ripe smell rose from him, like the rind of a cheese. Alexandra had just decided not to wake him when he opened his eyes and stared at her with a baby's gaze, unfocused. Then his face collected itself and drew together and he sat up a little straighter in the wheelchair. Alexandra put out her free hand.

"*Gospodin* Radev," she said.

Sixty-four
1952

Sometimes as I watched the guards with their guns during roll call, that next year, I imagined there was a gun in my own hand, a long heavy one, and that I was going to shoot a guard with it. Then I would remember what I had seen the day I was arrested. It had been more than two years already. The giant sores made my hands throb and the boundless hunger made my stomach float up and out of my throat. Even with a gun in my hand, I could not have shot a guard, because I wouldn't have cared enough.

Sixty-five
1952

I reminded myself that this must still be happening to me, since I was still alive.

Sixty-six

The old man in the wheelchair took her hand and held it, not firmly, and gazed at her, waiting for an explanation. She couldn't tell whether he needed just an explanation of who she was or an explana-tion of everything around him, of what he had woken to.

She said, "I'm Alexandra Boyd."

Then Bobby came to her rescue. Radev dropped Alexandra's hand and shook Bobby's, holding it for a few seconds and looking at Bobby with new sharpness. His eyes were dark, the whites yellow. Once you got used to those eyes, you could see that his face had been a pleasant and shrewd one and was still both. Bobby began to speak with him; the man with the trowel pulled out two chairs and went into the kitchen, where they heard him rattling around as if making coffee or breakfast.

Bobby pointed to Alexandra, but Radev nodded

and clicked his tongue—*no*—and told Bobby something very slowly, searching with his hands for the words.

"He doesn't remember you," Bobby said. "He doesn't remember you taking their picture in Sofia, although he knows that they were in Sofia. I don't think he understands what happened there. He also does not seem to remember who Irina and Lenka are."

Alexandra set the black bag gently onto the table. She wondered at what moment she would be called upon to present the urn to him, or if they should wait until Vera and Neven could be found as well. Now that the moment was almost here, she wanted only to run away. Stoycho gave a sharp whine behind her—they had left him tied up just outside the door to the courtyard and now Bobby went to bring him in. The dog pulled at his leash, twisting toward Radev. Perhaps, thought Alexandra, he'd never seen anyone in a wheel-chair.

"Stoycho," she said. "Don't be rude." Then she saw Radev's face tip toward them, wide awake. Suddenly the old man put a hand up and pointed at the dog, as if he had not noticed him earlier.

"*Ela!*" he said. He groped without success for the wheels of his chair, then beckoned Bobby closer. His eyes were large and bright now, and he stretched out one arm.

"Careful," said Alexandra. Radev reached forward, muttering something, and Stoycho began to lick his hands—wriggling, frantic.

Bobby turned to Alexandra, astonished. "He says that this was Stoyan's dog."

They stood watching while Radev's mottled hands rubbed the dog's head, smoothed his ears. Stoycho's sides were quivering and his tail whacked the flagstones of the courtyard, but he was careful not to jump on the beloved figure. Radev spoke to the dog; he spoke rapidly to Bobby.

Bobby shook his head. "This dog lived with them during the year before Stoyan Lazarov died," he told Alexandra. "They all loved him, and when Stoyan died the dog ran away. They thought he had run away because of a broken heart, or perhaps was stolen. I just explained how we met him. *Gospodin* Radev says that someone else must have fed him, maybe in another part of the town, all this time."

Alexandra couldn't take her eyes off the man, the ecstatic dog. "That's why Irina Georgieva didn't recognize Stoycho—she hadn't been to visit them in Bovech for a long time before *gospodin* Lazarov died. But I think she felt something strange about Stoycho—remember? She liked him right away, and he liked her."

Stoycho posted himself next to the wheelchair and leaned against the old man's knees, but only for a moment; just then an elderly woman stepped out of the kitchen into the courtyard, carrying a plate of cheese and salami and bread. Stoycho bounded forward to meet her, whimpering again, although he was careful with her, too, not to jump.

Alexandra got to her feet. As she stood there, she suddenly thought of a time when she had been only six or seven years old, and had had a high fever. Her family had been living out on the mountain, Jack hovering in the background while their parents decided whether or not to take her to the hospital, an hour's drive. "Let's try one more thing," said her father. Alexandra remembered the feeling of being stripped down, clothes coming off over her head, and the cold, cold water in the bathtub. For a long minute she had struggled to get away. Then she'd understood: this pain would reduce the other, greater pain— a trade. She had sat enduring it while her parents took turns squeezing the bitter washcloth down her back.

The old lady coming out into the courtyard wore a dark skirt and blouse; her hair gleamed discordant red, with that gray streak down the center, and her legs were bowed but strong. She looked alert and also unaware; she seemed only to be bringing refreshment for whoever had arrived to visit, as if the man with the trowel had told her nothing. Her face was deeply lined, her eyes bloodshot and wide set and still luminous, her nose long and fine. Alexandra felt a repeat of her earlier shock; this was the reality of a person, not an idea or a photograph.

This time the surprise was mutual—the old lady's expression changed to alarm; her gaze widened under scrubbed-off brows. Her mouth opened and Alexandra could see the unnatural evenness of her dentures. She gazed down at Stoycho, who was pushing up under her hand. She stared at Alexandra, then put the plate slowly on the table. *This is it,* Alexandra thought. *She is furious. Or bereft all over again.*

But the old lady did not seem to recognize the bag with the urn, although she'd set her plate next to it.

Alexandra made herself step forward. Bobby had turned and come to her side. The old woman took Alexandra's hand, still staring at her. Alexandra felt herself about to cry, in spite of her effort not to. She bent over and put her arms around the woman's neck.

"I know you are Vera," she said. "I'm Alexandra Boyd. I'm sorry I took it. I didn't mean to."

Vera Lazarova stood frozen in her embrace. Alexandra drew away, ashamed: she had done the wrong thing, and she spoke the wrong language. She pointed to the black bag—she did not dare hand it to the old woman; if Vera didn't drop it in her surprise, Alexandra would surely do that herself. Vera was looking at the bag in silence. She touched the top of it with a gentle hand, then turned to Alexandra. Tears wobbled in Vera's eyes, jeweled, and for a moment Alexandra saw the younger woman she had been, the translucent beauty. Then Vera reached up and kissed Alexandra on each cheek. Her breath smelled like garlic and also something sweeter. She took Alexandra's arm and drew her to a chair and pressed her down into it. She called over her shoulder, so that the man in the kitchen came out with a tray of coffee cups instead of his trowel. She spoke to Milen, pointing to the bag. Her voice was strong, a little raspy. The old man seemed to come to life, throwing one arm weakly wide and then covering his face with a veined hand. He wheeled his chair forward and Stoycho walked with him as if to help.

They all sat down together, with the urn at the center of the table. It wasn't until they were seated there, and their host was pouring coffee, that Alexandra remembered Neven was still not there. Neither were Irina and Lenka.

Sixty-seven

1953

When spring came around again, there were changes. Two new guards appeared in the camp, and the small stooping man who had been one of the Chief's favorites disappeared. The new guards were young and confident, professional-looking. I had a sense that they watched the Chief as well as obeyed him—perhaps they'd been sent for that purpose. Nasko fell ill with dysentery and went to the infirmary after supper one night; I saw him carried by on a stretcher and ran to grasp his hand until the guards shouted at me to get away. He moved his eyes weakly in my direction and tried to smile. I felt sure that I would never see him again.

I wept, then, standing in the yard, until Momo came up to me. "Something wrong? Nothing a good beating wouldn't fix, right?" He spoke heartily, as if we were friends.

I turned away to keep myself from striking him with my skeleton's hand—he was probably inviting me into suicide. I made myself walk toward the barrack, to go to bed even earlier than usual, without speaking over my shoulder. I lay there thinking through everything I knew about Nasko, which was not as much as I would have liked. I lay in my bunk painting for him: a big diptych with the Holy Virgin on one panel, bowing her head, and the angel on the other, in a flaming orange robe. The angel was dark-haired and looked very much like Vera; I put a tumble of cubist quarry rocks behind the two of them, as if the angel were delivering good news out in the desert. I considered praying to Sveta Bogoroditsa that I would not wake up in the morning, not survive after all, and then I asked the angel to forgive me for this thought.

Nasko didn't appear the next morning, of course, at roll call, and not the next week, or the next, or ever. I watched the sacks against the wall of the latrines come and go—they were removed at least a little more quickly now that it was spring—and guessed that he must be in one of them. It no longer mattered which, so I bade them each farewell as I passed. A newcomer worked Nasko's job in the quarry, a man of forty with a big mole on his cheek, and we did not speak to each other. I pushed the wheelbarrow only with the greatest effort. I tried to stay in my routine of practice, although the notes were becoming difficult for me to hear and I had an increasing sense of them as mere patterns in the air. I tried to think about Vivaldi, and to walk through Venice, on the right days; I had begun to see not a city but a panoply of separate images like sketches in an encyclopedia.

Only Neven was true to me, always vivid: he was eighteen now, handsome and affectionate, a consummate musician, studying and practicing independently, his sound unbelievably mature. Sometimes we worked together on duets. As he played, he glanced over the bridge at me with his golden eyes and suppressed a smile. When he came into the little kitchen after school he kissed not only his mama, who hadn't aged a day, but also me, his skeletal Tatko, the nearly dead. It was clear to me that of the two of us, Neven would be the greater musician. He would surpass me even after my hands healed and I could rebuild my technique—and I discovered joy in that thought. Something else troubled me, however: I still didn't know if the government was allowing people to travel, although the war had ended years ago. If they didn't, how would Neven go to study in Vienna? How would we visit Venice together? Or was I confusing this with some other problem?

On my one thousand and sixtieth day of camp, not counting my days in the infirmary, I was standing in the front row of evening roll call, half-fainting with hunger and weakness, when the Chief announced that he had noted poor work for several days.

"We are behind on our goals," he said, facing us angrily. Momo prowled behind him, ogling us from a distance. He had not shown much interest in me since Nasko's disappearance a few weeks before, although the two facts were probably not related.

"You are behind on your achievement," shouted the Chief. "How will you become decent members of society again if you cannot work?"

We shuffled our feet, all ghosts already.

He turned to Momo and made a gesture of exasperation, as if Momo had shirked his work, too. Momo sprang toward us and paced along the front row, staring each of us in the face. He wore his gap-toothed smile, but I noted wearily that he seemed unsure what the Chief wanted of him. He paused before me. I could hardly care even about this. Either he would murder me or I would die, one of these nights, in the barrack or under the sun at the quarry. I wished only that I had figured out what to do for Neven, where to send him, now that he was a man and a musician, with the borders closed.

Momo leaned in a little, trying to catch my eye. I looked away.

"You," he said. "Do you still feel you are not so smart?"

I said nothing. He might as well kill me for being silent as for speaking—in fact, I held on to that idea as a last piece of will. I would not speak.

"If you are not so smart, what about him?" He pointed at the man next to me, and I turned a little, involuntarily, to glance at the poor fellow. A corpse, like me, one I barely knew by sight, and not one of my barrack-mates—probably a miner, from the look of his black and stiffened rags. I caught a glimpse of trousers torn off below the knee, showing a shin brilliantly red but crusted over with large darker spots. It was hard to tell what color his hair had been, since he had none, or what shape his face.

"Well," said Momo. "Is *he* smart—your friend, here?" He was leaning closer to me, his golden outline filling my vision. As I often had before, I had the sense of seeing a clever man duck out of sight. I vowed to hold on to my notion of saying nothing, at least until I fainted.

The man beside me bowed his head, as if he, too, hoped this would all disappear.

Momo paused and stepped back, apparently at a loss. I could see the Chief watching us now, his arms folded. Perhaps he was giving Momo new freedoms? Or was he asking himself if Momo was worth keeping on?

Momo pointed at my neighbor with his club. "Step out and tell me how smart you are, since the *tsigulka* player won't." The man shuffled forward.

"No!" I screamed, a wispy sound, too late. Momo brought his club heavily down on the miner's skull and the man fell forward onto his knees. The other guards did not bother to help; it was over in another second. None of them even glanced at me; no hand dragged me out of line for my turn. It seemed that Momo had not heard my protest. Had I even uttered it? I began to doubt that any sound had come out, or that I had even opened my mouth to protest, although I still felt the scrape of the noise in my throat.

We were dismissed, brusquely, but the miner's body was left in the yard until morning, where we saw it again in the electric lights of the early roll call—a dark shape on its side, no longer particularly human. It was gone in the evening, but there was a patch in the dirt where his blood had spilled instead of mine.

After that day, I did not try to practice anymore, or to follow the Red Priest around. I could not see even Neven's face. There was only silence. People seem to believe that despair is the same as anguish, but it is not. It's true that despair is surrounded by anguish, but at its core, despair is silent, a blank page.

Sixty-eight

Neven, Vera told them, had gone the evening before to check on Irina and Lenka in Plovdiv and had not yet returned—for some reason, he had seemed worried about them, perhaps because he hadn't been able to reach them by telephone for a couple of days. She clung to Alexandra's hand while she talked, and Alexandra reflected that Vera and Irina, sisters, had more in common than people seemed to think. Stoycho sat with his cheek against the old woman's leg. Vera's smile was still beautiful, and there was a slow grace in the way she turned her head above her wattled neck. Alexandra had seen none of that on the hotel steps in Sofia, but she had not known Vera Lazarova, then.

Bobby made Alexandra get out her camera and show Vera the photo. She nodded, sober, and spoke in her turn, with Bobby translating. She and Neven had not understood the bag was gone until partway to Velin Monastery, and then Vera had suddenly noticed that neither of them had it. At her insistence, Neven had made their taxi return to the hotel in Sofia, but they hadn't found any sign of Alexandra or the bag there. Vera said she had been distraught and wanted to go to the police, but Neven had persuaded her that they should not. He said his father had hated the police and would not have wanted their help.

In fact, Neven had had a quarrel with someone in the hotel restaurant, even before they'd lost the urn—he had already been in a bad mood, upset and agitated. She and Milen had not heard what the quarrel was about. In the end, they'd returned to the hotel and had left a note at the desk with Neven's name and number on it. Since they couldn't stay in Sofia, Vera had wanted to visit Irina and then return to the mountain house in

Gorno to wait for news. But Neven had insisted on bringing them straight to the sea. And he would not allow her to call the police or Irina or even to answer the phone.

Bobby said to Alexandra, "I didn't tell her anything that would frighten her. They clearly have no information about where her sister is, and she already thinks something is wrong with Neven—she says he has been angry and nervous all week. But she believes it is because his father's ashes were lost."

"And you don't think so," Alexandra guessed.

"I think it is more than that," said Bobby. "I think he is protecting the old people from his real worries, whatever they are. He must have known they were being pursued."

"No one followed them on their way here, right?" Alexandra scanned the terrace again, hopelessly.

"It does not seem that she noticed anyone," said Bobby. "And, after all, she and Milen didn't have the urn. Unless someone thought they did, or was trying to get them out of the way."

"You mean for good?" She tightened her hand on Vera's. The old woman looked tranquil now, ignorant of both the English they spoke and the threat that hung over them all.

"But now they do have the urn," said Alexandra. "Bobby? You don't think that Neven took Irina and Lenka with him before we got there?" Her throat closed painfully.

"You mean he might have kidnapped them himself and left that note? It is not possible—he left Morsko too late to arrive in Plovdiv before we did."

Alexandra drew a long breath and kept Vera's hand in hers.

After breakfast was cleared away, Alexandra helped Vera carry the urn into the sitting room of the little house. She wondered if they should hide it instead, but didn't think she could suggest that. She wondered, too, if Neven would be as angry with her as she had sometimes imagined, in contrast with Vera's kindness, especially if he was already worried. Her stomach dropped when she thought of seeing him again; he would become as real then as Milen and Vera, of course. But the most important thing was to find Irina, and how could they do that without more information?

Then another old woman appeared—Vera's friend, apparently also the mother of the gardener who'd opened the door to them. She had been out buying vegetables. She was squarely built, vigorous, with short gray hair that stood on end. Vera explained that this was Baba Vanka; they had been schoolmates in Sofia and had found each other again fifteen years ago. Vera and Vanka had work to do in the house. They settled the urn with a pot of flowers on each side—grief itself seemed forgotten in Vera's relief at having

Stoyan's ashes returned—and went up the stairs, Vera with her arm tucked under Vanka's round strong one. When the two women had disappeared, Alexandra and Bobby returned to Milen.

"I want to ask him about Stoyan's police record and why he was anxious, himself, when he talked with his niece," Bobby said in a low voice.

Milen Radev sat with his elbows resting on the arms of the wheelchair. He had taken out a big blue handkerchief and was wiping his eyes with it, not as if he were crying but as if they leaked. Alexandra remembered what Miss Radeva had said about his former strength and liveliness.

"Tell him that we met Miss Radeva and fell in love with her," Alexandra said.

Bobby conveyed this, and Milen Radev's face lit for a moment. There was the young man again, Alexandra thought—the energetic scientist, the music lover who had followed Stoyan Lazarov's performances and admired his genius. His eyebrows were gray and black and his yellowed eyes were gentle, forgetful. Four or five wiry hairs stood straight out of the middle of his forehead, like the strong whiskers of a walrus or the hairs on the back of an elephant—she suddenly thought of Irina Georgieva's animals. He must have loved Stoyan and Vera very much to have stayed with them in old age; for all his current feebleness, Milen Radev had somehow watched over this stranded family. Now he seemed to be falling asleep, his tea steaming in his cup and his slice of bread with marmalade only half-eaten. They had not cleared his breakfast, because he ate so slowly.

"*Gospodin* Radev," Bobby said in a soft voice. The old man's eyes unhooded with a look of surprise, as if he had not expected to be called upon ever again. Alexandra thought it was like telling a mountain to sit up straighter. Bobby reached into his backpack and brought out the battered candy tin. He spread a clean paper napkin beside Radev's plate and set on it the two rolled rags, which looked dirtier and more fossilized than ever.

"*Gospodin* Radev," said Bobby.

Milen Radev opened his eyes a little further and raised his handkerchief toward them, then lowered it. He bent closer and put out a finger, touched one of the curling stiff rolls. His words, when they came, trembled like his finger.

"He says," Bobby told her, "that he has seen these before. Stoyan showed them to him many years ago, and he told Milen what they were and where he got them."

"He knows about the camp?" Alexandra said. Her heart was thudding uncomfortably because Milen Radev's eyes had begun to water again; this time his handkerchief was forgotten. Stoycho crept to the side of her chair and lay down.

Bobby watched the old man for a moment. "He says Stoyan revealed it to him, about thirty years ago, when they were drinking together. He says that Stoyan was arrested two more times and sent to work far away from Burgas. I think one of those arrests was the one Milen witnessed and told his niece about. Milen has never talked to anyone, even Vera, about this, because Stoyan did not want her to suffer more. Vera knew what had happened, of course, because she saw Stoyan taken away and then returned broken three times, but he refused to tell her the details. Milen believes that Stoyan told him everything in order to punish him, the only punishment Stoyan ever gave him."

"To punish him? What did he do? I thought Stoyan was the one who punished himself."

Bobby looked thoughtful. "He doesn't seem to want to say more. But I will ask him now what Stoyan might have meant when he wrote that only Milen Radev knew."

He spoke to Radev, who wiped his forehead with his hand, clumsily, before answering.

"He says," reported Bobby, "that he thinks Stoyan wrote something about his life but he doesn't know where the manuscript is now. He believes Stoyan gave it to Nasko Angelov. And we know that is true."

"And these things that *gospodin* Lazarov saved behind his music?" Alexandra asked.

Bobby spoke to Milen Radev, gently indicating the curls of dirty fabric.

But Radev did not seem to hear him; he rolled his chair backward a few centimeters and fell asleep.

Sixty-nine
1953

1953

No.

1953

1953

Then something changed, but at first I did not
know what it was.

Seventy

They sat for a moment, watching Milen sleep, until the phone rang in the kitchen. The trowel man came out to ask someone to take it. It was Neven Lazarov, he said.

We won't be able to understand each other, Alexandra thought, panicked, although of course Neven had spoken some English to her.

But Bobby went in to take the call, to explain who they were and why they were there. When he returned, his face was set, wary. "Neven wants us to come speak with him in a village near here. He gave me the location of a café. I asked him if he knows anything about Irina and Lenka, but he wouldn't talk about them on the phone. He only said that he found their house empty—as we did. The drive to this village is more than an hour. I don't know why he is there, or why he wants to meet us there, but he was very definite about it. He says he will wait for us."

Alexandra thought, *He suspects this is a trap, too.* She studied his face. "And you told him about the urn?"

"Yes. He said that he will thank you when he sees you. But he sounded very anxious about Irina and Lenka."

"Oh, I hope he knows something about them,"

Alexandra said. "And there's Stoycho—can we leave him here?" She looked at the dog and he raised his head; his brown eyes were serious in the black velvet face that didn't match the rest of him.

Bobby looked at Stoycho, too. "We'll take him," he said.

Late morning had risen in a dome of sun, not yet hot, over the town. As they drove down the steep street, Alexandra saw the sea at its foot, an expanse that glittered all the way out to a lapidarian horizon. A thread of shivering had risen inside her, something that seemed immune to the beauty of the place and the day. A few minutes later they pulled past the last old walls of the town and onto the winding coast road. Bobby came around a sharp curve, swerved, and swore in two languages.

"What?" gasped Alexandra. Then she saw that there were two men standing in the road. They had been completely hidden by the bend of road and the trees; Bobby had come within a split second of hitting them. She turned to look. One of the men stood with his hands on his hips and the other was talking with him, as if they were relaxing on an empty sidewalk or in an open field, instead of on the road. They were gazing at something—their own handiwork, apparently. She saw a metal cross freshly decorated with ribbons and artificial flowers, at the side of the road, where someone else had been killed driving in that same tight curve. *Or standing in it,* thought Alexandra.

Bobby pulled off the main road onto a smaller one, which took them away from the sea. In an hour she would see Neven again.

Seventy-one

1953

Something had stirred far away, in fact, first in the great Soviet state, where Stalin had died, and then in Sofia. The change reached all the way to us, the silent skeletons in camp. When we returned from the quarry that evening, there was a strange truck at the gates, and men in newer, cleaner uniforms than our guards wore. Some of them looked at us and walked around us, although they did not speak to any of us, as far as I know. They went into the barracks and latrines; all usual activities were suspended. Some wrote in notebooks. We saw them speaking with the Chief, and we saw that the Chief was afraid of them. The cooks forgot to serve us our beans. Most of the younger guards hung back in corners, but Momo saluted the visitors and strolled around showing them the sights, even daring to joke with them.

It seemed that, although Momo hadn't found a

prisoner to go to the Commission, it had finally come to us.

They left. A day or two later, or three days, bigger trucks arrived. Men with bigger stars on their caps and better guns at their belts lined us up and read us declarations. They declared that because we had served our sentences—many of us had never been given sentences, but no one mentioned that—we would be moved back to Sofia and processed for work in society, where we could expect to do well as long as we never descended again into criminality or spoke lies about our rehabilitation here in camp. Those who had not finished their sentences would be taken to a more modern camp elsewhere to complete them—they did not say where.

A rustle of surprise and confusion and feeble interest went through our ranks. I think most of us could not really understand what the big men were saying. I knew instinctively that I would be among those sent on to the "more modern camp," but when the men from the trucks began to divide us into two lines, they pushed me into the line for release, or at least transport back to Sofia. I did not yet believe in any release. I felt the tears running down my face, but hope had become such an unfamiliar sensation for me that I actually wondered what was wrong with my eyes. Momo was nowhere to be seen, now, and I wished I knew at least where they must have buried Nasko, in what pit in the woods.

They gave us an extra meal, which had never happened before. We were sent to wash—although it was still a week away from the usual bathing day—and then handed piles of old but whole and reasonably clean clothes to put on, as if we were newcomers all over again. I had nothing of my own to keep, unless you counted the tin cup; but I left that in the washhouse for whoever might need it. At the last second, I took the curls of dirty bandages I had removed from my hands and rolled them up tightly in my pocket while none of the guards was watching. After all, they—and all the others like them I'd made for myself—had protected my hands for more than four years.

Then they herded us toward the trucks. It occurred to me belatedly that this was a trick; the camp had become too crowded and these new guards were taking us out to the mountains to shoot us. But I reasoned with whatever was left of my mind that if that were the case, they would not be wasting good clothes on us, or extra food. They must want us to look better than we actually did when they drove us through the village. One of the men in our line broke away in a panic and ran through the gates on his own; the camp guards shot him. He was outside and free for about half a second.

Then they loaded the rest of us into the trucks and drove out of Zelenets.

Seventy-two

The village Neven had named for their meeting point was the emptiest Alexandra had seen. There was no one on the pitted roads, no one sitting in the rusted chairs outside a single small grocery store. Storks stretched and flapped in their nests on the rooftops of abandoned houses—the biggest nest sat above a municipal building that looked deserted now, but had perhaps once been a school. Dogs slept right in the dust of the road. At the end of a shabby block, Bobby stopped the car and they got out, keeping Stoycho on his leash, and looked around. The café sat between two low houses, its door open. Darkness stared out of it and flies buzzed in the dirt yard around two tables.

"This must be our place," Bobby said, but he moved cautiously. Alexandra tied Stoycho to a tree, well away from the other dogs, and followed Bobby as he pushed through the plastic ribbons in the doorway.

The interior of the café was dark, after the brilliant light outside. It was as much a bar as anything—maybe in a village this deserted, one business served both needs, Alexandra thought. There was a wooden counter; behind it a woman with streaky pale hair sat hunched over a crossword puzzle. The air was sharp with a smell of singed coffee; a tray of cheese pastries wilted under glass. No customers.

Then a man unfolded himself in one corner, where he'd been sitting behind a table. His head seemed to brush the beams of the ceiling. Alexandra could not see his expression in the gloom, but he was so tall and real that she felt he might suddenly spread huge wings. Her heart seemed to be choking her. He stepped forward to shake Bobby's hand and then he turned and looked directly at her.

She could see his face now, the broad cheekbones and short, thick hair, the almond-shaped golden eyes, the lines around mouth and nose. This time she could also see in him his mother's beauty. He was even taller than she remembered, his broad shoulders a little stooped, his arms and hands graceful. He wore the white shirt she'd observed on him before, or one like it, with the sleeves rolled up. He had slung a black windbreaker and the strap of a small leather bag over his chair. He said nothing. After a step toward her, which he checked, he stood still.

Alexandra forced herself to look him in the eye. For a moment, she imagined falling to the ground at his feet, wordless, prostrating herself in apology. But that had been only a dream. Instead, as firmly as she could, she put out her hand.

"Neven," she said, "I'm Alexandra Boyd."

"I know who you are," said Neven, taking her

hand. She remembered his voice now—the slow clarity, the heavy accent.

Alexandra looked up at him. "I have something that belongs to you."

"I know," he said.

She tried to drop his hand, but he held onto hers. She drew an unsteady breath. "I want to tell you how sorry I am. That was your most treasured—" She almost said "possession," and then stopped. "The urn is safely in Morsko with your mother. And I'm truly sorry."

He stood looking down at her. "It *is* my treasure." He shook her hand again, as if he hadn't already. "That is why I gave it to you."

She stared at him. "Gave it to me?"

"Yes," he said. "We were—" He dropped her hand then and spoke to Bobby; his English was failing him. Bobby helped him, surprise lighting his own face: "They were being followed. He was afraid for his mother's life, and Milen Radev's, and he knew that he must hide the urn immediately." He paused and listened to Neven again. "He says he saw that you had it already mixed with your own bags, and he thought it would be hidden in that way. It—broke his heart to let it go." Neven gestured toward Alexandra. "What he did not know was, you are not a regular traveler, not a tourist kind of a person. He did not guess that you would look and look for them, to give it back. There was another problem, also.

In his hurry, he did not stop to think that you might go to the police."

Alexandra stood silent.

Bobby said sharply to Neven, "What do you know about Irina and Lenka? Are they safe?"

Neven shook his head. "I know nothing. I am waiting for a phone call that will tell where we can find them—a man called me during the night to say this, that he will telephone at noon and give us the place."

Alexandra's stomach tightened. The place where they would find—what?

"That is forty-five minutes, still," said Neven. "We cannot do anything before. First, let's go out, quickly." He gestured to the waitress on her stool, who looked up at them. Neven put a couple of bills under his coffee cup. "I would like to tell you something, not here. Can we go?"

Alexandra looked at Bobby. He nodded, and they went outside. The light was blinding and there were flies everywhere. Stoycho was watching the dogs in the road, who stood up now and then to bark at him. Out here, Neven looked even larger, tall but also wide-shouldered, hair dark in the sun, the gray at his temples silvered.

Suddenly Stoycho leapt on his leash, strangling, whining.

"What?" Neven stared at the dog.

Alexandra murmured, "I guess you know him."

But Neven had already knelt in front of Stoycho

and was looking into his eyes, rubbing the sides of his neck. "Antonio," he said. "This is our Antonio. You know? Like Vivaldi."

"That's Stoycho's real name?" Alexandra began to laugh, in spite of everything, and Neven turned and smiled at her. He pointed across the road, to where a path ran between the trees into a meadow.

"We can sit down and talk there," he said to Alexandra. "I want to tell you something that was important to my father."

Bobby said, sharply, "After, will you tell us more about why this is important to the police?"

Neven nodded. "Yes, I will. As much as I know. I think that no one will look for us here, and we have at least a little time."

Alexandra hesitated. "Bobby can translate for you, if you like."

"I certainly will," Bobby said severely. "You are not going out of my sight."

The path took them between scrubby pines, where someone had dropped several white plastic cups, an empty Coke bottle, a shriveled condom. But when they came into an open meadow, Alexandra saw that it was pristine—long grasses warmed by sun. Ahead lay a glinting gray-green river, narrow enough so that she could have crossed it in a few strides, with reeds and stones stretching out into it.

At the edge of the river, Neven spread his jacket on the ground and motioned for Alexandra to sit down. He set his leather bag beside him. Stoycho strained toward Neven, but Alexandra made him stay quiet. Bobby lay back on the grass next to them and lit a cigarette, smoking tensely, and Alexandra wondered if the gun was now in his jacket.

Seventy-three
1953

The trucks we'd been loaded into rolled through the village of Zelenets but did not stop. I saw people outside their houses, staring at us. We went on to a larger town, then called Yugovo but later known by some other name. There we were put on a train, in the same type of bare boxcar but this time with fewer prisoners per car and a stop every five hours to relieve ourselves outside, in open fields—the men guarded us with guns in plain view. They gave us water, too. By the first stop, we could see that the mountains were already distant; by the second, we were in another region, and the next morning when we stopped we could see the peaks around Sofia. Some of the prisoners cried; others lay muttering on the floor of the train car, unable to grasp what was happening. I thought a man in one corner was probably not alive. I tried not to allow my hope to become stronger; there was always the chance, still, that this was either a ruse or a dream, or that I was already dead like the man who didn't get out at our stops.

The train halted suddenly at the edge of Sofia and we were loaded onto trucks again, which made my heart plunge until I realized that it was natural they would not bring us into the main station and let us walk out in daylight among the crowds. The trucks took us to a building I had never seen before, on the outskirts of the city, where we were cleaned all over with strong disinfectant that burned our eyes and lips and private areas. Then, for the better part of a week, we slept on mats on the floors of large cells and ate three reasonable meals a day. I had not seen ordinary food for so long that I almost collapsed at the sight and smell of it. Some of the men ate too quickly and were sick all night, or sat on the latrines for hours. I was careful to eat sparingly, at first, and to rest whenever I could.

I watched my hands with curiosity; without a wheelbarrow to lift or rocks to break, they had begun to heal just a little, from the inside, although they looked almost as bad as ever and continued to hurt. During the day, we were presented individually with questions about how our rehabilitation had gone, to which the answer, which we were also given, was that we believed it was complete but would work in the future to prove that. We were not beaten, but the administrator who questioned me—a heavy man with pockmarks on his nose who looked too old to serve except behind the big table where he sat—told me in a deliberate voice that anyone who had been a criminal must be watched for the rest of his life, so that society could be kept safe. I would sign a statement agreeing to this. Did I under-stand?

I did. Or I thought I did. I said yes, I did.

Mainly I thought about Vera, now only a few miles away, and about my suffering parents—I could not even be sure that they and Vera's parents were all still living.

During the first night there, a man in one of the other group cells passed away, peacefully, in his sleep, for no reason that anyone could see, like the man on the train. The guards took his body in the morning, and asked us all if we knew anything about his death. As there were no wounds on the body, no one was interrogated further about him. I pondered that he might have died of happiness, or just as easily of a broken heart, and I resolved to keep my own emotions quiet so that they would not betray my body at the last minute. I thought again of Nasko Angelov and the years of friendship we could have had. I didn't know then that he had survived the infirmary at Zelenets and was already in Sofia at a different jail, where he would serve another three years.

The next day, they released my group one by one into the city, with only the clothes we were wearing.

Seventy-four

She could see the river through the tall fringe of reeds, could hear and smell it more than she could see it. Beyond flowers that looked like the Queen Anne's lace at home, she could just make out sunlight touching a green surface. She let her hands dangle between her knees.

Neven drew his hand over his hair. A scent something like the river, but more pleasant, came from him; she sensed that if she touched his shirt with her hand, which of course she would never do, he would be even warmer under it than the baking earth and grasses. She felt as if their hands were interlaced on the grass, although of course they weren't. When she glanced at him again, she saw his head drooping, the sides of his dark hair. She almost wished he wasn't going to speak. Then she would never have to know the next terrible thing.

Without looking at her, he said, "My English is not very good."

"It's fine," she told him quickly.

"Not fine. It is rough. Not—organized. I am ashamed to say—I wanted to go to English-language high school, but they would not let me in. Because of my father. I studied a lot with my friends who went to there, and a lot of the movies. And music." He frowned down at her, dissatisfied with his own efforts.

"I don't mind," Alexandra said. "And we can ask Bobby for help if we need it." For the first time since shaking his hand in the café, she did touch him, surreptitiously—the cuff of his warm smooth shirtsleeve.

"My father," he said, and stopped again. "He was a very good man who thought he was a very bad man. That is a—difficult combination. Of ideas. You see?"

He leaned forward, as if listening to the river, and then pulled a blade of grass expertly from its sheath. "Sometimes—sometimes we know a person who is a very bad man but who thinks he is a good man. Maybe that is even more bad. Even *worse*. Worse, because the bad man who thinks he is good thinks that he can do anything to anybody. But sometimes a man who is very good thinks, *I am very bad,* and it—destructs his life, every-thing. Because he does not believe that he has any right to do something, so he does less and less. This has happened with my father. He was always thinking, *Je n'ai pas le droit.*"

A strange reality was whispering in her head: *I am far from home, sitting by a river listening to French—but in Bulgaria, the place Jack always wanted to go.* It was as if she could hear music, where there was no music.

Neven shook his head and brushed the stem of

grass over the toe of his polished shoe. "After the first—*katastrofa*—it happened very slowly, the destruct of my father's life. And he was brave and quiet. So, nobody noticed it very much until he was dead."

Neven turned his head away. He reminded her of the way male lions look sad, as if their nobility is a terrible weight. She tried to think of something to comfort him.

"Your father had *you*." She wondered when they should give him what they had found behind Stoyan's calendar: *June 2006.*

"Oh, me." He shrugged. "Yes, he had me." He sat fiddling with the grass, dropped it, and worked to pluck another stem: long fingers, surprisingly fine, but with thick knuckles, as if he'd worked more than most people she'd known at home. No rings.

"I want to tell you what he said to me, because I believe that you have the right. To know." He looked to Bobby for help, to fill in some of his words. "I was working in Burgas, before he died. He telephoned me when he became sick. He asked for me to come to stay with him and with my mother for a week, or two weeks. He said that he wanted me to be there for my mother. But the truth was that every day he wanted me to be near to *him*. He was often lying on his bed. He was too sick to stand, on many days. Then he was better and he was sitting in a chair outside. It was in

635

Bovech, at their house. He asked Milen Radev to come live with them, already months before I went there, to help my mother."

Neven was silent a minute, and then seemed to collect himself. "My mother was very worried that my father would become too sick to go down the stairs, but I said to her that he wanted to be in his bedroom. I thought, *They will carry him out of here dead—he will not have to try to walk down the stairs.* And I was right. My father hated hospitals, and we could not afford a good one. I thought I might give him a lot of—pills, instead, if he wanted to end quick. Sometimes we went to the doctor and the doctor only—"

Neven shook his head, as if trying to convey the doctor's gesture. Alexandra understood that much, she thought—the doctor had dismissed Stoyan Lazarov, a case too far gone, too old, too insignificant, the cancer infinitely more vigorous than the shell that housed it. She wondered how they had been able to pay any of the bills.

Neven brushed invisible dirt from his sleeve. "He told me often that he wanted to talk to me, tell me things about his life. But then when I went to him, he simply looked at me, for hours, and said nothing. He had wonderful dark eyes. Wonderful even when he was sick. One time he asked me to bring him his violin, and he sat up in a chair and played it, the last time, Bach and some Brahms and of course Vivaldi."

"Oh," Alexandra said softly.

But Neven was clearly not listening to anything now except the music in his own head. "Finally, my father told me to make my mother to take a rest for herself, to go away and make a change. She went on the bus for an entire day to see her sister in Plovdiv. She was very worried to leave my father, but I told her that the worst was if he would die while she was gone, and she dried up her eyes, to be brave for him. She kisses him goodbye like, deep—on the mouth," he said, almost apologetically. "In the case she could not see him again alive."

Alexandra felt her own eyes beginning to sting, and she shook her head to thwart the tears. Long days, long journey, little sleep. It was his past, not hers.

"While my mother was gone, I went to my father's bed and I brought him some water, then some soup, and he try to eat a little. He say to me that he will sleep and then he will tell me a story. I sat next to him while he slept. His breathing was loud and sharp. I watched him all the time because I was afraid he would stop breathing before he could wake up and tell me the story. But when he woke he looked for me, saw me there, and immediately he started to talk. He said, 'Neven, I want you to know about something.'

"I wanted to hear, but his face was—terrible, so

I also did not want to hear. I asked him to rest instead."

Neven reached out and took Alexandra's hand. She didn't know how he knew where her hand was at that moment, and she had a feeling that he was simply reproducing a gesture in his memory, almost absently. Perhaps his father had reached out for him in the same way. But her hand was filled with the feeling of his; she thought she should pull away but no part of her wanted to. She looked down at the neat square fingernails, so much larger than her own. Their fingers lay entwined on the warm grass. She wondered if Bobby would disapprove; when she looked up, she saw him watching—listening hard, she knew, but tactful, ready at any minute to translate for her, or to rescue her. She imagined Stoyan Lazarov's face against a pillow, the dried lips forming a story, whispering his secret into the earth.

"My father said, *I want you to know*." Neven looked away from her, toward the river.

"Wait, please," said Alexandra. "I think we should give you something first. We haven't opened it."

She turned to Bobby, who drew an envelope from inside his jacket and handed it to Neven. *The last part.*

Neven held the envelope in both hands for a moment, looking at the handwriting, then took out the pages it contained. He read them through in silence. When he had finished, he looked up; amber tears stood in his eyes.

"You may read this to Alexandra," he told Bobby.

Seventy-five

1953

The last part. Never for publication.

With scabbed, red hands that were twice the size of my old hands, clean clothes that did not fit but had no holes in them, and a new stubble of hair on my head and chin, I stepped out into the streets of Sofia, trying to understand that I was free. I had no money in my pockets, no possessions except the curls of dirty bandages I had saved, and one other item, which I had hidden in my old clothes and then my new ones. I began to walk toward the city center, then toward our neighborhood. Every ten minutes, I stopped and rested anywhere I could, so that my heart would not give out.

Suddenly, I was more afraid than ever—what if my fears were true? She had forgotten about me, or given up on my returning, assumed I was dead. She no longer loved me. She was dead herself. What if they had had a memorial service for me while I was gone, and then moved on with their lives, because that was all they could do? Or what if this was all a test, and the guards from the station outside Sofia were following me even now, letting me lead them to Vera, to my parents, to arrest them in their turn? What if they had already been arrested, and Vera was far away, in some camp for women?

I began for the first time to observe the people around me—up to that moment, they had looked like ghosts, but now I saw that they were well and whole, or at least only normally worried and harried. The young girls were dressed in their spring clothes, the women were shopping for food, the young men had someplace to go, the elderly men in their elderly jackets paused to talk with each other. None of them knew about us, a camp full of skeletons. Or did they know, somehow? A sailor in uniform, far from the sea, was telling another man a joke and they had both stopped dead on the sidewalk to enjoy the full effect of it. I was the ghost; I saw myself, with huge empty eyes, in the plate glass of a restaurant window. I saw people glance at me, curious or sympathetic: a very sick man, poor, tottering, prematurely hairless, who shuffled forward in ridiculously large shoes.

Now I was on familiar streets, a beautiful plaza I knew in every detail, the yellow-cobbled streets of the center, the old palace covered with blooming wisteria, the domes of the churches glowing over the treetops, the mausoleum of the Great Leader shining in the sun. I sat down to rest at the edge of a park, on a bench. I had known not only the street and the park but even the bench, from my earliest childhood. I squeezed the edge of it with my aching hand.

When I could stand again, I made my way into our neighborhood, thinking that here, at any moment, I might see someone I knew, although perhaps no one would recognize me in turn. But I saw nobody. The trees were beautiful—the lindens lifting their blooms over everything, the fresh bright leaves of the maples and oaks and the candelabra of horse chestnuts lit by midmorning sun. It was nearly time for the holiday of Kiril and Metodii; we had discovered the exact date while we'd been in the cells outside Sofia. Houses at the end of one block that had been bombed into submission in the war and left there had finally been repaired while I was away. I marveled at the unreality of the smells of cooking that came from doorways and windows, the placidity of an old woman crocheting something white in a chair on her second-floor balcony. The sweetness of the air, after the exhaust of the buses on the main street. The wind in the leaves above my head. I had not realized before that I lived in a paradise. I could see our building now, the wrought-iron grilles on the windows. There was a new little tree, shorter than a person, planted next to the front step, and I wondered for a weird moment if it was a memorial to me. Everything else about the building looked the same as it always had.

My heart throbbed terribly, but I made myself try the front door. It was unlocked—yes, it frequently was, I remembered, during the day, with people going in and out on errands. I found the strength to walk up the first flight of stairs. Someone was having an argument with someone who was not arguing back, behind a door on the first floor—not a voice I remembered, so perhaps there were new neighbors. I rested for a few minutes, hoping no doors would open. Then I crept up the next flight, and the next. I hovered there in front of our door, hoping it would not open, either, until I had the strength to knock. Sweat trickled under my shirt and my heart pounded jaggedly. I wondered if I might have heart failure from climbing the stairs. But where else would I ever want to go? I raised my hand and rapped, which made my huge knuckles hurt.

A woman opened the door. She was smiling, apparently at something that somebody in the room behind her had just said. Her hair was dark and coiled up on the top of her head, and her eyes were like dark flowers. She wore a dress of well-washed cotton with blue stripes, a brown belt. She was a little less trim than I remembered, curving and womanly instead, with strong arms where the sleeves were folded back.

Her smile vanished and her mouth dropped open. A frantic pleasure, almost a terror, rose in her eyes. Then her head fell backward and her legs went out from under her.

I reached out and caught at her, but I was too feeble; I went down into the room almost on top of her, almost fainting with her. Fortunately, there was no furniture near the door and she did not hurt herself. Lying there, I kissed her face once, weakly, and then managed to clamber off her. She opened her eyes and stared at me. I could see now that her sister had risen from the table, a spoon from her coffee in one hand. Beyond that, next to the stove, stood a pram, angled away from the sun of the one window; and in it a baby woke and began to cry.

Seventy-six

Irina dropped her spoon and hurried forward to help Vera up, brought water for her to sip. I sat in a chair and watched, looking from her to the baby's flailing arms. It cried on. Then Vera got to her feet, with her sister's arm around her, and stood gazing at me. She didn't seem to hear the baby. She was as lovely as ever, more tired, trembling, a little older, but unvanquished.

I looked at Irina. "Is this baby yours?" I said in a shaking voice.

"No, he's mine," Vera said. She did not make a move toward me. "We thought you were dead."

Saying this seemed to unloose her and she suddenly burst into a wild sobbing, bending over as if she might vomit. I stood bewildered. I remembered how frightening I must look to her, a corpse. And this baby, who was Vera's but could not be mine. I stood up, my hands made a movement, and I thought it was to grab something from the table and hurl it at the wall—Irina's coffee cup, perhaps. But instead my arms threw themselves around Vera and she wrapped her sobs around my neck. She was tremendously alive, much stronger than I, and she was embracing a skeleton. She looked at my face, stroked my stubbly head, picked up my twisted hands and stared at them. She cried and cried. I couldn't speak; I only wanted to feel her touch and stare at her in return.

Irina stood frozen, watching us. After a couple of seconds she went over and picked up the baby, who stopped crying at once and turned a streaked red face toward us. He wore a shirt and knitted pants. He seemed about six months old, although I wasn't good at estimating such things, and he had Vera's remarkable eyes. He reached out for her and she took him from Irina. Irina shrank back into the corner of the kitchen, the only time I'd ever seen her cowed. Vera gazed at me over the baby's head, and then he swiveled and stared at me, too.

"I'm sorry," she said, her mouth quivering. Next to her, the baby looked more like himself, less like his mother. "We believed that you were dead."

"Are you married again?" I kept one hand on the edge of the table, for balance. Irina slipped quietly out, past us. I knew her—we would meet later, and say our greetings then. Her leaving me alone with Vera meant she trusted me not to hurt her sister; the knowledge of that steadied me further.

"No," she told me, in the same low voice.

I thought about asking the man's name, but at last I said, "Do you love his father?"

Her head drooped toward the baby's. He was watching me with those beautiful eyes. "No. But he helped me very much after they told me you were dead and that I should forget you. He was kind and good, and in love with me. He's not here anymore. He went to work in another city. He wanted to marry me, and to take me and the baby with him, but I said no."

"Who told you I was dead?"

"The police, eight months after you left. They said they had discovered that you were a criminal and that you had come to a bad end somewhere. They said they could not give me your body, but to forget about you as soon as possible. After a while I believed you really must be dead, or you would have come back to us." She began to weep again. "I never believed you were a criminal."

I stood shaking, on my unreliable feet. "And why did you stay here?"

She raised her head, and that was the proud, contained Vera, the schoolgirl. "Later, when I knew I was pregnant—after I knew that, I had a dream that you were coming back to see the baby. So I told everyone you were alive and that I had gone to visit you secretly, out in the country where you were working—that you had been sent to work far away—to make them think the child was—" She drew back again, confused, her hand stroking the baby's little shoulders.

Suddenly the baby leaned toward me, so far that I was afraid he would fall out of his mother's arms. He stretched out his hands and I came closer and bowed my head in front of him. He touched my rough scalp and leaned even closer, until I reached forward and took him.

I hadn't known I knew how to hold a baby. His limbs were warm even through the clothes. His shirt rode up to show his rounded belly and Vera automatically put a hand out to pull the hem back down and tuck it in. He gazed at me, somber but interested. He put his hand on my shoulder and left it there. His nose was small and flat, his cheeks broad and smooth. When he looked up at me, I could see the narrow wet paths where his tears had traveled. Even his tears must have been very small, each of them. It was strange to see the glow of his face up close, after my many months of looking into the faces of the dead, or the living dead. His body fitted mine, the hollows of my ribs and shoulders. I thought I must be mad, holding another man's child against my heart. I did not even want to know; the camp had emptied me of all questions except one, and that was about how to live. And one other.

"What do you call him?"

She smiled for the first time and wiped her face. "He has your father's name, but I could not use that, so I call him Neven."

Seventy-seven

I was a dearly loved child, Neven told Alexandra. I knew only that my father went away for a while before I was born, and then again two times when I was in school, and that my mother worried and cried sometimes. I remember the second time he was away, although I didn't see him leave. But my mother was kind and lively, younger than my father, a very strong person, and all four of my grandparents were alive and helped us. Once, when I was about eight, my father came home in the middle of his time away; he visited us in Burgas for three days and told me that he had to work in a village for a while longer because he was needed there, and that I must take care of my mother when he left again.

647

Each time, he returned to us with his hands terribly bruised from work; he was a fin musician but he often had trouble with his fingers—arthritis, he said. After every absence, he began very slowly to practice again until he could play in any orchestra that would have him, first in Sofia, and then, once Uncle Milen had helped us move to the sea, in Burgas. There my father got a job in a food-processing factory. I knew that when he went away he couldn't be working as a musician, because his violin always stayed behind and my mother would put it deep in our wardrobe under some extra blankets. I overheard him tell my mother that he was allowed to return sometimes to the orchestra only because they knew how good he was, and they needed him—the bitterness in his voice shocked me. He never spoke that way if he knew I was listening.

Sometimes, when my father was ill and tired and had a few days of vacation, my mother sent him to visit his friend Nasko Angelov, a painter she said my father had known during his work out in the country before I was born. Nasko had lived in Sofia for a while, and then moved back to his old village in the Rhodopes after he was married. He worked in a small factory near the village. My parents did not have many friends, but these two men, Nasko and Uncle Milen, were devoted to us.

My father wanted me to learn to play the violin. Our lessons were not a success. Even when my father was not away, he was tired and sickly—for years I thought he must be much older than he said he was—and he could be very quiet, even withdrawn. His attempts to teach me were interrupted for such long periods by his absences that I could not make the progress he wanted me to. I actually don't believe I would have been much good, anyway, although maybe it helped him to think I had unfulfilled talent.

Instead, I excelled in mathematics and at sports; I ran track—I was fast, although I never managed to win any big medals. I was a well-behaved child, too. I don't think I did anything wrong in my childhood, except that I sometimes put nails in the street near car tires when no one was looking—all the boys did that—and once I stole a map out of a library book, a big map of Europe from an old book I thought no one would ever want, and hung it on the wall in my little bedroom. It filled the room. My favorite part of it was Bulgaria, which was pale green; the rest always looked alien to me. I told my father I'd bought the map at a bookstore for a few *stotinki*, but he said nothing; he stared at it in silence and then went out of the room. So I was allowed to keep it.

When I was ten or eleven, my father called me to him and showed me a book, a rare book in Russian he had saved for and bought from the *antikvarna* in central Burgas. It was an illustrated history of the architecture of Italy, and he explained to me that when he was young he had been to Rome to play a concert, and had visited briefly in Florence, and he showed me the pictures. I knew better—and had known all my childhood—than to discuss with other people the fact that my father had studied music in the decadent West. Because of this, it was thrilling for me to listen to him talk about it, and a little frightening. This was the Colosseum, where men fought wild beasts—I had learned about that at school. This was something called a *duomo*, which Brunelleschi had designed for Florence. My father had seen these things with his own eyes.

And this, my father said, turning a leaf over very carefully, was Venice, the Queen of the Adriatic, *La Serenissima,* a great city he had not managed to visit in his youth. It was very special, he said, because it was built on islands and marshes, almost on water. I looked at the illustration, a painting reproduced in color. It showed high buildings all around a square, and the domes of a big church, and drawn up at the edge of the square was a fleet of little boats. Farther out on the water were sailing ships. The people walking around on the square, looking very small, wore cloaks and triangular hats, or long dresses with very wide hips. For years after, I thought of Venice as a place where the streets were made of water and, even more strangely, the people wore outlandish, outdated clothing.

Then my father said that I must never tell anyone, but that someday he and I would go to Venice together. He said he would finally see where his favorite composer, Vivaldi, had lived and worked, and he would take me with him, because together Vivaldi and I had saved his life. I must have looked puzzled; he pulled me to his side and kissed my cheek and ruffled my hair. He asked me to bring him his violin and he played me a piece from memory, a piece as beautiful and big and brilliant as the cathedral in the middle of Sofia.

"That is our friend Vivaldi," he said, when he'd finished. "When I'm long gone, this piece will be yours." His face was full of joy, which puzzled me again, because he was talking about his death—besides, he was still young, even if he looked older. I did not want him to die, ever.

By the time I was thirteen, I understood that my father was not like other people, and not only because he had been to the West and practiced the violin all the time and had vanished like a magician several times during my childhood. When he was living at home with us he had to check in at the police station in Burgas once a month—"official business," he always said. Sometimes he was called there suddenly, and he never went without kissing my mother goodbye, passionately, which always surprised and embarrassed me. My mother would pace the kitchen until he came home an hour later, except the times when he didn't come home for months.

He told me once that if he ever had to go again to work in another part of the country, I must call Milen Radev to help my mother and me, that Uncle Milen was absolutely loyal to us and would always help. That was their arrangement, he said. At least once a year my father took out his book and showed me Venice, and told me that someday we would see it, he and I.

I left home at nineteen and went into the army, as we all did, and my mother sent me socks she knitted and pieces of cloth to wrap my feet, to keep them drier inside my boots. I got blisters and funguses and lost my toenails anyway. The army was terrible, the food was terrible, we were always cold in the barracks. But I was young and it didn't matter so very much, in the end. I made some good friends there. After the army, I wanted to go to Sofia University in mathematics—not to the Conservatory, as my father had hoped I might. I could not get a good enough reference from my high school, although I had done well there. I settled instead for a place at the Institute of Chemical Technology in Burgas, where I studied petrochemical engineering. I lived at home, in our apartment in the new housing complexes near the stadium, and I did my work at the kitchen table. Then I went to work in the refinery, like everyone else, and later in a smaller plant.

Through all this, from my childhood on, my father loved me indulgently, although I know it must have been a disappointment to him—*I* must have been a disappointment to him. He smiled if I came into a room, kissed and hugged me almost every time he saw me. He loved my mother, too, watching her with bright eyes, but was silent and reserved with her even in front of me. Whenever he was at home, she was cheerful, although with a crease of anxiety across her forehead that looked older than she was, as if she had borrowed it from my father's worn-out face. I think they didn't talk much with each other about where he had been. I have often thought that the terrible thing in communism was not just that we turned against each other. It was that we turned away from each other.

After the changes, the plant where I worked was shut down. I began taking jobs in construction, often as a mason, lifting rocks and mixing cement; it upset my father, to see my hands bruised and injured, but there was no choice. I think young people now don't know much about those times, or don't understand—they think it's always been as it is now, the mobile phones and friends on the Internet and lots of people going to other countries to work. Soon we had even less money. The orchestra shrank when the government changed, because no one would pay for it—my father had retired before that, anyway. He wanted to give music lessons, but few could afford them, especially outside Sofia. My parents left the sea and a cousin of my mother shared her house in Bovech with them until she died and left it to them. It was much cheaper for them to live there. Sometimes they visited Gorno, of course. I went back to Sofia with a little money saved and did a course in bookkeeping, so I could get a job online. I almost got married, too, but it didn't work out. That was especially sad for my mother, because she has no grandchildren.

My father disliked Bovech, I am sure, although he said very little about it. He practiced his violin every day and read his books, and just before he got sick he found that dog, who loved him. He read a great deal, as I said—I think he reread his whole library. And I believe that Milen Radev helped with some money whenever he could, and he came to see them often, and to live with them once he retired.

When my father got sick, he told no one, even me, until it was very late. We could not have saved him anyway, the doctor said. That was why my father called me to be with him. And that day when he sent my mother to Plovdiv to have a rest, he told me about Zelenets, where Vivaldi and I had saved him because the thought of each of us was more powerful than anything they could do to him there. He told me why he had been arrested and how he had tried to do his own penance. I wept when he told me what he had lived through. And I was confused, because I knew he must have been in the camp when I was conceived and born. But he said he had looked forward to having a son and had known he would love him as he loved me. That was what he said, and suddenly I understood what his story meant. My mother had given him the son he wanted, and Stoyan Lazarov had become my father. For me he was truly my father, even if I guessed who in turn must have given me to him.

Then he told me that he still knew two people from Zelenets. I remember he was getting very weak from talking. He lay still for a while and his face was white on his pillow, and sweating. I brought him water and some of the pills for pain, but he said he did not want to take too many because they made him sleepy and he needed his mind clear to tell me the rest. It was early summer, like now, but already June, and I opened the window in his bedroom so he could feel the warm air. He smiled and said that it was good that he had turned over the page of the calendar ahead of time, so it would be on the right month when he died.

I sat down next to him and he put his hand out. That was a new thing for him, that he liked to have me hold his hand. His body had always been thin, and now it had grown even thinner in his bed. I sat with him and felt how soon he would not be there anymore, and I could hardly believe it.

Then he stirred and said, "I want to tell you about the two people from Zelenets I still know about. One is a saint, and the other is a devil. The saint, of course—" He lifted a hand as if pointing in someone's direction. "That is Nasko Angelov. You know now how we met. He is stronger than I am, and he will be your friend for as long as he lives. When I found him again in Sofia—alive—it was one of the happiest days of my life."

He licked his lips and I brought him water again and watched while he closed his eyes. "Please rest, Tatko," I said. "We can talk tomorrow."

"No," he said, and his eyes flew open. "Not when your mother is here. She has suffered enough. I will go out of here as quietly as I can, to make it easier for her. She knows where I was. I do not want her to know all the rest of it."

He kept his eyes on me. They had stayed brighter than the rest of his face—I loved those deep, dark eyes, always turned on me with affection. "There is something more I must tell you. Two years ago I was at Gorno, with your mother, the last time I ever went there. It was very early in the morning—a beautiful morning in spring." He clenched my hand, as if in a spasm of pain, and I thought again of reaching for the pills on the bureau. "I was walking on the hill road by myself, as you know I liked to do. I stepped off the road among some trees to see the flowers that hide there in spring. As I stood looking for them, a car came by on the road, a big expensive car I had never seen up there before, and I knew it must belong to the businessman who had built the huge house around the mountain—or perhaps this was one of his friends, visiting.

"Suddenly the car stopped and someone in the back seat opened the door and leaned out to adjust something—a seat belt or something that had become caught on the outside. I saw the man's face clearly, although I don't think he noticed me standing still among the trees in my work clothes and hat. If he did, he ignored me— of course I was just another villager. He was only five or six meters away from me. His face was covered with a heavy beard, the cheeks above it scarred and puckered as if by an old accident, the eyes yellowed. His hair was very strange— stiff and neat but long, almost to his shoulders, and dyed brown. To me, it looked like a wig.

"Then I heard the driver call from inside the car—'*Gospodin* Kurilkov!' and something else after that. Whatever the driver said made the man smile, so I could see his eyes lighting up pale blue and the gap showing between his top front teeth, and the wide bones of the face. It was the devil Momo I told you about, much older and well disguised, but the same. That is not a face you forget. A second later he closed the car door and they drove off. I hadn't moved. I did not move from my spot for a long time.

"I remembered that the newspapers said that as a young man this Kurilkov had become a guard at the Politburo, first a guard and then somehow the assistant to an important member, many years before the changes. After the changes, he made a lot of money, buying old mines—how, I will never know. He must have done this in secret, through other people. He was away from politics for a long time after that, probably waiting. Then he became a deputy minister and began to form a party—*Bez Koruptsiya*."

My father began to cough, and he took a long pause, while I gave him water.

"That's enough," he said after one sip. He spoke with his eyes closed. "There had never been any mention of Zelenets in the newspaper stories about him, no report of the murders they committed there. I had not even known he was alive until then—or any of the guards. But he was very much alive, and famous, and rich, and powerful—and he owned a mansion right in our village, the place in Bulgaria I loved most. I remembered reading an editor's opinion that this man might become prime minister someday, or possibly president, that he was elderly for a politician but very smart and with a clean past, unlike many other politicians. He would under-stand older people and their needs, and at the same time he would build a great future for Bulgaria."

My father moved his feet stiffly under the sheets. "I did not go outside again after that walk, and a couple of days later we returned here, to Bovech. The next time your mother wanted to visit Gorno I told her that I wasn't well enough to travel, which was soon true anyway. I have never gone back. I could not stop thinking about him. Finally, I wrote a letter to the newspaper in Sofia where I first read about his career. I described what I had seen in Zelenets. Other people had come forward and told about these things, you know, when the changes first happened—perhaps I should have been braver then, but I was afraid for you and your mother. My effort came too late, I suppose—it was not published."

He stopped and caught his breath. His face looked grayer than ever and his forehead glistened. "In fact, I never heard back from the newspaper—I received only silence, even when I tried again."

He paused again. "Momo is dead, but the person he has become is not. This Kurilkov, he calls himself the Bear."

He gripped my hand with some of his old strength, and I bent over him. I told him to rest. I told him to stop worrying about the past—it had been terrible, but it was over and there was no reason for him to worry more now. He kept his eyes on my face and his hand in my hand.

"Please," he said. "Please do not let anyone know whose son you are."

I bent to him and kissed his forehead, feeling the sweat on it. "Times have changed," I said. "And I am proud to be your son. I would always let anyone know that."

He smiled for a moment and I heard his breath whistling through his nose. "I did not try to send anything to the newspapers again, but I have written it all down. I have put it somewhere safe." He looked too weak now to move much, and I thought his mind might be wandering a little. "I must remember where that is. Nasko found a place for me to hide it. And I put part of it somewhere else, not to be published. Where did I put that part?"

"Don't worry, Tatko," I said. "Wherever it is, we will find it together. Just rest."

His head moved back and forth on the pillow. "The last time I read about him in the papers, he was proposing a plan to the Ministry of the Interior. For more prisons, for the prisoners to contribute to society by their hard work. He knows what to do with us, with prisoners. Is he over there, by the calendar?" His eyes were roving around the room.

"Tatko, it's only me," I said. "I'm right here. We won't let that happen, I promise."

He subsided, his face growing slack, and suddenly fell asleep. The sun was getting low;

my mother would be arriving soon on the Plovdiv bus, and I knew I should put out some dinner for her and try to get my father to eat something as well. Milen Radev was coming to spend the weekend with us. I knew Milen was afraid, each time he said goodbye, that he would not see my father alive again. Soon Milen Radev would be the only father left to me.

"One other thing," my father said, struggling awake again. "Forgive me—I did not take you to Venice. I never took you. I said I would, and then after they opened the borders there was no money. But I could have gotten you a passport, at least. I could have tried to save some more money."

"Please, Tatko, rest," I said. "You saved all you could. And we have enjoyed our books and our dreams."

"There is something valuable, but it is not with my other music. It is on the shelf of the *garderob*."

He made a movement with his hand, trying to point. "It has a special signature on the last page, which must be Vivaldi's. I bought it in Prague, before I came back to Bulgaria. If you sell it, maybe you can go. Take me with you—cremate me and take my ashes and bury me there." He smiled again, faintly. "You know, if Vivaldi was buried a pauper in Vienna, I can be buried a pauper in Venice."

Soon after this I gave him the pills for pain and made him sleep, and my mother arrived, and then

Milen. That evening he asked me very weakly to let his dog come inside to lie on the floor of the room. Then he told me to bring him his violin and put it beside him on the bed, touching his arm. "But don't take it out of the case," he whispered. Even then, he didn't want it to be injured. I understand now that he must have spent his life fearing it would be confiscated by the state—because it was beautiful and valuable and he had bought it before the war.

The next day my father died, just at sunset, with the violin beside him. It was devastating for my mother, but we could all see the quiet in his face. I was glad for him, even as I began to miss him; never again would he live with such memories.

I told my mother and Milen—not about Zelenets—I think each of them knew, in their different ways—but about the Vivaldi manuscript, and about his wish to be cremated and buried in Venice. My mother did not want to have him cremated, but she did it, because it had been his last plea. Nasko Angelov gave us an urn he had made at my father's request, carved with faces from the story of the Wolf and the Bear. When he brought it to us, I told him in private that I knew about Zelenets and asked him if he remembered something my father had written, but he shook his head without speaking. My mother kept the urn, in case we could somehow take it to Venice. We looked on the shelf of the clothes cabinet in their room and found several printed scores of Vivaldi, which I remembered his playing from sometimes. Inside one of them was a handwritten manuscript, very old and initialed the way he had described to me. I am no musician, but even to me it seemed remarkable looking.

We took the Vivaldi manuscript to Sofia, to a rare books dealer, and the man held it for a couple of days to examine. When we returned, he told us that he couldn't prove it had been written by Vivaldi. Vivaldi, he said, usually signed his pieces with a very different mark. He was sorry. But it was certainly an original manuscript, and from the eighteenth century, and he could put it up for sale on the Internet.

What he gave us for it in the end was enough to buy my mother and Milen ten months of heat, electricity, and food. Their pensions cover food or heat, but not both. The next month, we sold my father's violin, but I knew that this would see them through only another couple of years, especially if there were hospital bills, which there soon were—for Milen Radev. I was already using any extra money I could make to support the two of them. Milen aged badly after my father died. Then he had a heart attack and we thought he would die, too, and my mother was frantic. Instead he lived, but is much weaker. The last of the money from the violin paid for his wheelchair. This year my mother put the Bovech house up for sale and they moved to Gorno to save money, but no one is buying houses in Bovech. Then I felt consumed by anger and I looked everywhere for the document my father had told me about, thinking I would publish it at any cost. I wished I had asked my father more about it, but I could not find it—or maybe, I thought, he had only imagined that he'd written it all down.

It had been two years since his death, and we felt we shouldn't wait longer—we would never be able to go to Venice, or pay for a burial there— so we decided to take my father's ashes to Velin Monastery, where one of my mother's remaining cousins knew the priest and got permission. My father loved that monastery—the peace there, the old trees. And my mother thought that would be a worthy place for my father, in the cemetery outside the monastery. We took a train to Sofia to see her cousin and thank her. Also, the cousin had told us that her son drove a taxi and he could take us to Velin Monastery for free when we were ready.

But as I was sitting on the train, with the urn beside me, I thought of what my father had said about a place Nasko Angelov had found for him. When we got to Sofia, I opened the urn in private and discovered that it had a cavity built into a separate box, at the bottom. I read what I found in it and I knew I could never leave it unpublished.

The next day I made a copy of my father's

confession and put the original back inside, out of respect for him. I called a newspaper—not the one that had rejected my father's letter—and arranged to speak with one of the editors, hinting at the story I had. He wanted me to meet him at Hotel Forest. I thought that my mother and Milen should be there to speak with them, too, if it came to that, and they sat waiting in the lobby nearby, with our bags safely between them on the floor. When this editor arrived, I told him about my father's experience at Zelenets and gave him a copy of the document. I explained that my father had felt so deeply about it that he'd tried to publish his story once before and then had wanted it buried with his ashes. I said that I would rather publish it than bury it, but that I hoped to do both.

To my fury, the editor was contemptuous and said I had no real proof of this information and that I would probably be arrested if I spoke publicly about Kurilkov, who had done so much good for the country already. I was attacking a respected elder statesman with a story that might be considered slander. The editor said he would be reporting me to people who would want to make sure I never talked again. I shouted at him that he had no right to threaten those who had already suffered, but he told me my mother would suffer much more if I ever spoke about this matter in public. He left in a rage, taking my copy of the document away in his briefcase and threatening to call the police at once. I saw him push quickly out the doors at the back of the hotel.

I realized immediately that I might be followed —that he might intend to circle back around to the front of the building. I might be followed, my family might even be killed, and we must not be found with the urn in our hands. I went as quickly as I could to the front door of the hotel, taking my mother and Milen to meet her cousin's son and his taxi. I knew we had to bury my father's ashes at once, and that I must probably leave his grave at Velin unmarked, if I could.

Just then the cousin called me to say that her son could not come for us after all, and there was some confusion while we tried to get down the steps and take another taxi. I could not risk going to wait for a bus. As we were struggling with this, someone tried for the first time to help us. And then I let my father go, into the hands of a young woman he would have loved. I saw that you were holding the urn, Alexandra, without knowing it. What the urn contained had already endangered my mother and Milen—the last thing my father would have wanted—and I simply let him go.

But after he was gone, I realized that you might take the urn to the police. We had to disappear. I could only hope that you would not get in trouble, too. It never occurred to me that you would be kind enough, and persistent enough, to look for us everywhere.

Seventy-eight

The sun had moved to the middle of the sky and lay warm on Alexandra's hair. Neven stirred, shook his head as if rising from a dream, took his hand away from hers. Tears still pooled under her eyes and she was suddenly aware of them. He pulled a crumpled paper napkin from his pants pocket and dabbed her cheekbones for her; he said nothing, but his touch was careful. Bobby stirred, but didn't stop him.

"Where did you go, then?" she said. "We did look everywhere for you."

He nodded, gestured for Bobby to translate. "Of course, I could not tell my mother that I had given away the urn. We started off toward Velin in another cab, although I knew this would be expensive. When she realized the urn was gone, we went back to the hotel, where of course we found nothing—I was relieved to see no sign of the editor, either. Then I took her and Milen to Nasko Angelov's house in the mountains for a few days. It was before you visited, apparently." Neven's jaw tightened. "You know he is dead now."

"Yes," Alexandra said. "When he was killed, his son called Irina right away, and she called us."

"Nasko promised not to tell anyone we had been there—not even Irina. While we were with him, I told him in private that I had found my father's confession. I also told him what had happened with the editor in Sofia. He looked very serious and said that some things were meant to be secret unless the right time came for them and that perhaps my father had meant to keep them secret, in the end. He must have known I had put him in danger, since his name was in that confession. I will never forgive myself for what happened to him." Neven clenched his hands together. "Then Nasko said he would give me something else, in case I ever needed it. I think he did not want to be found with it in his possession. He said that Stoyan had given it to Milen Radev, and Milen had given it to him."

He opened his leather bag and took out an envelope, and from the envelope he drew a black-and-white photograph. It was printed on fine-grained paper, now yellowing, and the figures in it had the clarity of life. Neven held it out in the sunlight and Bobby sat closer to peer over Alexandra's shoulder. It showed three men standing together under an arched gateway, smiling, their arms slung around one another's shoulders. Two of them were in uniform, with military caps; one, much younger, wore a loose shirt and dark vest. The older men were black-haired and the younger had a light, thick mane of curls; his smile was broad, with a gap between his two front teeth. The photographer had been careful to catch the words on the arch above them. Bobby translated, automatically, but Alexandra knew almost before he read them: GLORIOUSLY FORWARD TO THE FUTURE.

Neven turned it over. On the back were words in a neat, faded handwriting, and he traced them with his finger. "*Zelenets facility, S. Nedyalkov, Vasko Hristov, Momo Kurilkov, 1952.* You remember my father wrote that Kurilkov—Momo—came to see him in the infirmary, at the camp. Momo dropped it by accident while he was visiting. He must have been carrying it around—and my father kept it and hid it. He told Nasko this."

"And he brought it home with him. I see." Bobby shook his head; he looked pale. "This kind of photograph is very rare," he said. "Also, we could probably all be killed for seeing it."

"Yes," Neven said. "I think someone knew that Nasko had this photo before. His son told me that Nasko got a phone call suddenly that he would not talk about, after you were there. He must have tried somehow to protect you."

But he could not protect himself, Alexandra thought.

Neven looked out at the river. "He had the same idea that I had with my father's confession—he gave me this photograph to keep safe. And to publish when he was gone, like my father."

"Your father's story, with the photograph," Bobby said. "It would be enough."

Suddenly, Neven's phone rang.

"Irina," cried Alexandra, but Bobby put a finger to his lips. Neven answered slowly and listened for a few seconds, and then they could hear whoever had spoken on the other end hang up. Neven's eyes were hard.

"This is the second time a man I do not know calls me. As I said, the first time he promised he will tell me at noon where Irina and Lenka are. Now he has told me."

Alexandra clutched Bobby's arm. "Where?"

"He says they are at Zelenets."

Seventy-nine

They all got quickly to their feet, Stoycho beside Alexandra.

"Who would take Irina and Lenka to Zelenets?" Alexandra was trying not to think about Nasko Angelov. "And we don't even know where that is."

Neven stood in front of them, hands on his hips. "There is something I would like to say. You have seen the plan of Kurilkov, on television? Many people talk about it, either for it or against it. He will help to open the mine at Chopek, near Novlievo, which will give jobs and is still full of important metals. It will be for a new economy, but along the route he will make another fortune to himself, because he owns some of the land of the mines. He is also telling that he will use prisoners to work there, so there will actually not be so many jobs, or so many people to pay."

"And if he becomes prime minister," Bobby said, "the prisoners will be anyone he doesn't like."

"Yes," Neven said. "But no one has really seen this place. The people who protested were not allowed to go near the mine, only in roads outside it."

"They protest mainly in Sofia." Bobby ran his fingers through his hair. "And—they are almost always arrested."

Alexandra said, "You think the mine is at Zelenets."

They both turned to look at her, Neven with a quick nod.

"There is some opposition still in the government," Bobby said thoughtfully. "I think that if the protesters could show that the mine at Chopek was a labor camp location, the opposition might grow much bigger."

"Yes," Alexandra said, "but especially if someone could prove that Kurilkov was a murderer there."

"As you know, his party stands on a campaign of purity," said Neven. "The Bear—'without corruption.' "

Bobby had driven his hands into his pockets. "If Kurilkov wants to reopen the mines at

Zelenets, and to run them with prison labor, it might as well be a new camp. One new camp will mean others. And he will do it all legally, starting with his purity campaign."

"I think the same," said Neven. "Little by little, we could have a Bulgaria like my father's. You and I will be the first in any new camp, my friend."

Alexandra put her hand into Neven's again. She felt that her previous life had never happened; it was as if she really had fallen off a bridge into white water and been pulled under. "What would your father have wanted us to do?" she said.

Neven glanced down at her hand and his, together.

Bobby was checking his pockets, rapidly, as if taking inventory of what he carried there. "I've already looked at maps," he said to Neven. "There is no photograph on television of this place yet—only machines that dig outside somewhere and a very general image of Bulgaria."

"And there is no Zelenets, not on any map I have seen," said Neven, "but names are often changed. I found on the Internet a couple of remarks about a camp at Zelenets, in a website about the communist time in Bulgaria. There was no exact location, but I read that Zelenets was in the mountains in central Stara Planina, near Chopek and Novlievo."

"Let's go," Bobby said. "We can at least start driving."

"No." Neven had dropped Alexandra's hand and was walking toward the road; they followed him. "You have had enough trouble, because of my family. You must go back to Sofia. I will call you when I find them."

"Irina is our friend now, too," she said stubbornly.

"I could be very helpful to you," Bobby told him.

"No," said Neven. "Thank you."

Bobby did not slow his pace.

"Bobby," Alexandra said. "Please don't go out of my sight."

Stoycho hurried after Neven. "Chopek is four hours from here," Neven said. "Maybe more, with the mountain roads. We can talk while we drive. But Alexandra must stay in the car, when we arrive."

Bobby signed to Alexandra not to protest.

Chopck, on Bobby's map, was north and west, into the mountains. They left Neven's car in a grove of trees just outside the village, where it could not be seen from any road, and crowded into the Ford. Neven sat beside Bobby in the front. Alexandra, in the back with Stoycho, watched the edge of Neven's shoulder and profile. It was strange, she thought; Stoyan Lazarov's blood didn't run in his veins, through those long, quiet limbs; and yet, as much as anything in the world, he was Stoyan's legacy. Stoyan Lazarov had made no recordings, played for no heads of state, done no world tours. He had had, instead, his violin, his Vivaldi, his love for one woman. He had also had this dignified son who could not inherit his musical genius or even learn his musical skill but had loved him unstintingly. Like Radev, Neven had been good with numbers and good with hearts. She left her hand on Stoycho's back and fell asleep, in spite of herself, cradled by the road.

When she woke they were in the mountains. The steepness of the road had shaken her; they were climbing a long pass into forests, up toward what looked like fog. The immense flat plain of Thrace was already behind them, stretching out to a haze that might be other mountains. The road was empty except for wisps of cloud that hung in their path or moved silently across it and into the forest. The sky was gone, as if the day—the bright morning on the sea, the vast sun over the plains —had never happened. It must be midafternoon already, but to Alexandra it felt like a void with no time to measure, no sun or even twilight to mark a normal passage. She pulled her sweater on, shivering with dread: *Irina, Lenka. Zelenets*. Stoycho stretched, too, stiffly, and swiveled his head to look up at her.

At the top of the pass, Bobby said they would make a quick stop and pulled in to a parking lot just off the road. The clouds filled everything around them and wind whipped at their clothes as they climbed out. It seemed to Alexandra that this was the highest peak she'd ever been on. The wind pulled them toward the public restrooms, and she noticed a few knots of people in warm jackets and hats or scarves, looking out over the valley as it reappeared.

Suddenly, the fog cleared itself, revealing an enormous monument. It rested on concrete platforms just beyond the parking lot—a gargantuan rocket ship, patterned in stone and bronze, poised for takeoff from the mountain. There was a door near the bottom, but it was bolted and held fast with a rusted padlock, as if no one had gone inside in many years. The tip of the rocket eight stories above them vanished into the fast-blown clouds, already traveling toward space. Someone had put a flag and a wreath, both now wilted by weather, against the door.

"What is this?" she asked Bobby.

Bobby was tugging on his jacket, too. "It is a memorial—TO THE FORTIETH ANNIVERSARY OF THE REVOLUTION, 1984. Schoolchildren all over Bulgaria were organized to raise the money to build it—I was too young to help, but I knew kids in our neighborhood who were collecting scrap metal and donations of *stotinki*. And all the workers were buying postage stamps to support it." He adjusted the collar of his jacket. "There was a big celebration on TV, for the dedication."

675

Neven stood with his head tipped back, his throat exposed, looking up at the rocket. "I remember that day," he said. "My father would not watch the television." He rubbed his arms and Alexandra thought he was shivering with anger, not cold. "Now he is dead, but Kurilkov has whatever he wants." Then he said something in Bulgarian and walked swiftly back toward the car.

"What?" Alexandra gripped Bobby's elbow.

Bobby turned, too. "He said, *What is the meaning of such suffering?* Hurry, Bird."

On the other side of the mountain, they drove as steeply down as they had driven up, and then into a new range where the road curved into denser spruce forest, with few villages and only a little chalet hotel here and there. Bobby had spread a map on the dashboard and was looking at it closely; he and Neven ignored a sign for Chopek and instead turned left into a valley and up a road that became gravel, then dirt.

"Here is the train line," Bobby said, and they saw the rails beside the road, and the narrow river beyond. "I think this will be the back way in toward the mines—Chopek is up at the main entrance to them, behind us. I hope the road we need is still there."

The road and the railway left the river after a few kilometers and climbed together to the first village they had seen in half an hour. Some of the houses had fallen in, and only a few looked inhabited. In the forest beyond, out of sight of the village, they found a wooden barricade set across the road. Bobby got out by himself, glancing sharply around. Neven joined him and they managed together to move the barricade, although it was heavy. Stoycho had sat up in the back seat, snuffing the air with his black nose raised; and Alexandra had to hold his collar to keep him from jumping out after the men. Bobby drove through and stopped, and they replaced the barrier behind the car. Farther up the road, there was another, but Bobby was able to drive around it. Alexandra sent a small prayer out to her parents, to forgive her if anything happened to her.

The road rejoined the river through dense forest that soon opened out into a scrubby flat area. Alexandra saw a pile of timber and a crushed building with a square roof lying among the trees. A bulldozer was parked beside it, and a front loader, both silent. No other sign of life. Bobby parked thc car behind a stand of bushes, and they got out with Stoycho on his leash. This time nobody spoke, and when they moved, it was quietly. To Alexandra's relief, Neven did not ask her to get back in the car. They crossed a cracked cement yard, Bobby and Neven walking ahead. Bobby stopped a couple of times to look at the ground; muddy footprints marked the open stretches of cement. Alexandra noted that the mud was fresh.

Coming around a curve through more trees, they saw a cluster of one- and two-story wooden buildings rotting at the edge of a large weedy square. There was still a semblance of order here: the structures faced the square at exact right angles, on three sides. A tower on weathered stilts guarded the entrance to the yard. Most of these buildings had little or no roof remaining, but the walls had been solidly made. Doorways gaped darkly open to the weather, and vines climbed into some of them from the ground and hung out of upper windows. At the far end was a mound of dirt like a landfill, caving in at the front around a low wooden frame. Alexandra felt the hair rising along her arms, and Stoycho backed away before he would go forward. She could see no one at work here, let alone Irina and Lenka or whoever had taken them.

Neven was gazing at the buildings, hands in his pockets. "What do you think?"

"Yes, this might be it." But Bobby spoke doubtfully. He would need proof, Alexandra thought. He was looking around, tense, listening.

They moved forward and stood in the yard, surrounded by the empty eyes of the barracks, or whatever they had been. Alexandra went toward one and looked in. There were no wooden bunks inside, although through the window hole she could see a couple of ancient sinks bolted to a wall. The steps up to the doorways had rotted away; she would be able to get in only if she climbed through a window. The whole place was sinking gradually into the ground. A push or two from a bulldozer would certainly finish it.

Then she saw that Neven had wandered away from them. He was standing inside the building opposite, staring out of the empty doorway. His hands hung by his sides. He had needed to climb up there, she thought—he had wanted to be on the inside for a minute, looking out. He stood straight, still; he seemed to be looking at something as far away as vision could reach. She had the urge to hurry over to him, to be sure he still exuded warmth. But this moment belonged to a world she had no part in. She tightened Stoycho's rope and made him sit quietly next to her.

After a few minutes, Bobby waved them back to the car. "Your father's story said that they marched about two kilometers to a quarry. Since no one is here in the camp, we should look up there."

He drove them along a wide path that might once have been a road. It led around the buildings and climbed gradually up through the woods. The face of the mountain was very close here. To their left, they saw the railroad, this spur of it abandoned and spiked with saplings of pine and birch. They went forward in silence and Bobby turned back once to glance at Alexandra, reassuring. Her heart was clenched tight and she wanted more than anything to reverse the car, to see all of them already driving back down the mountain, with Irina and Lenka safely among them. Neven was peering through the windshield; suddenly he motioned for Bobby to stop. They parked and got out, cautiously, Neven going ahead, his arm raised in a warning.

Only twenty feet in front of them, young trees hung in air—a huge pit, open to the woods, with several square blocks still lying unclaimed around the rim of it. Alexandra remembered the Roman theater in Plovdiv, the ancient quarried stones. She looked over the edge; beneath her the abyss fell very far, lined with shrubs and rock. The floor below was filled with trees and underbrush, more giant blocks half-choked among them.

Bobby had already begun to snap pictures with his phone; she remembered that her camera was in her sweater pocket and pulled it out. There was no sign of Irina or Lenka. A road curved around the edge of the quarry, along the overgrown rail line, and vanished climbing into the woods. In that direction, she thought, would be the mines. Her stomach tightened. Had someone taken Irina and Lenka up there?

She was just turning to speak to Bobby when everything happened at once. From behind them she heard the sound of a vehicle she knew must have gone past or even through the camp, lurching toward the quarry. For a moment Alexandra couldn't register this; she thought instead of some crazed movie scene, a car driving right over the edge into midair. But it stopped with a yelp of brakes—a gray sedan, only twenty feet away.

That car was followed by a black BMW with tinted windows, grotesquely shiny above its skirt of road-dust. Two men leapt out of the first car and went around to open the back doors. From the back seat they pulled a woman with braided dark hair who struggled against them—Lenka—and then an old woman who also struggled but looked about to faint. Alexandra started forward, but Bobby caught her arm in a painfully strong grip. Neven stepped to her side, so that she felt suddenly small. Lenka had apparently seen them; blood trickled from her nose, but she called something to Irina, who looked around. One of the men supported Irina so she could stand against the car and then put a knife to her throat, a long knife with a black handle. Lenka thrashed in the grasp of the other man and he swiped at her nose, as if they had been through this routine before.

Suddenly the driver's door of the BMW opened and a burly man ran toward them, covering them with a gun—the term flashed through Alexandra's head, that he was *covering* them, although of course he must really be threatening them. Neven and Alexandra put their hands up, but she saw Bobby reach swiftly inside his jacket, pull something out, and fire. The man running toward them jumped backward and fell, just as suddenly, and lay looking up among the trees and stones. He was large, intensely muscled, with a holster over his black shirt. Then Alexandra saw that he was alive and clutching his shoulder. How had she not known this about Bobby—that he was a perfect shot, that he would not hesitate but would never shoot to kill?

But now the back doors of the BMW opened and two figures stepped out. Alexandra felt she had stopped breathing. She knew both these men—one was the Wizard, his head gleaming in the pewter afternoon light. The other was stiffer, more dignified, filled with composure in his well-cut clothes—Kurilkov, the Bear. She saw the shining ankle of his boot, the stiff mane of dyed hair, the unnaturally brown beard, the pale eyes. He did not glance at the wounded man on the rocks, or at Bobby's gun.

Instead, the Bear looked at Neven, and held out an open hand—*Give it to me.* Then he turned and observed Irina, white and limp, with the knife leveled across her throat. Alexandra could see the glint of the brooch below the blade. *He really will do it,* she thought. *If Kurilkov tells him to, that man, that stranger, will kill Irina right here in front of us.* She felt suddenly the nearness of the quarry, just at their backs, the long drop into trees and rock. The Bear stepped closer, so that she felt she could smell him. Alexandra wondered if Bobby would dare to fire again. Stoycho had begun to bark, not wildly, but with an elemental warning snarl she had never heard from a dog. She felt his leash slip away from her upraised hand and wondered fleetingly if she had let it go.

The Wizard took a step toward them, too—she remembered his face at the police station, at their lunch, his secretive smile, but now he was not smiling. Now he was shouting something, and in that moment of distraction, the Bear drew a gun of his own, a neat little gun, and fired at Bobby. Alexandra screamed without feeling any sound leave her throat. There was the thud of a body in the leaves, but no answering scream, no writhing. The Bear was standing among them now and Alexandra looked up in time to see the Wizard with a gun in his hand, too, and to understand that he was aiming it at the Bear. She didn't know whether it had gone off, because just then Stoycho gathered himself beside her and leapt toward the Bear's throat. Brindled muscle uncoiled in midair, the throat tore open, naked red and white, and they both went over the edge of the quarry.

There must have been a noise far below, the shattering of bodies, a human shriek or a canine one, but Alexandra heard nothing. She was faintly aware of the Wizard, who stood facing them, his gun lowered. Then she was aware only of herself lying across Bobby's body, in time to hear him breathe and stop, breathe and not breathe again, and then of fumbling with Bobby's shirt and mouth in some half-forgotten ritual. And then of Neven lying on the ground beside her, holding Bobby's head.

Eighty

Suddenly Bobby drew a quick breath, just under her mouth, and she felt his chest inflate. Fresh color rushed into his face; she tore off her sweater and tied it around his thigh, clumsily but tightly, where the bleeding was. Looking up again, she realized that Neven had gotten to his feet and was running toward the gray sedan. The man guarding Irina had let go of her. Alexandra saw her sway toward the ground and saw Neven catch her up, holding her fast. The other man pushed Lenka away. The two men leapt into their car; it backed up into the woods, turned hard onto the road, and sped out of sight. The Wizard turned, fired once after them, and shook his head. Neven lifted Irina into the back seat of Bobby's car. Alexandra left Bobby for a moment to go to them; Lenka, streaked with mud, was already bending over the old lady.

"I am all right," Irina said faintly. "Asparuh?"

Alexandra ran back to Bobby. His eyes were open, alert, although he didn't speak. From time to time he winced. She gave him her hand and watched the Wizard bind his leg with a real tourniquet, then a bandage, then give him an injection. This last made her panic, but the Wizard nodded to her. "Just a painkiller. He has not lost too much blood. I think you saved his life, young woman. But you must take him to the hospital. There is one in Novlievo. Give him a minute before we try to move him." They stood looking down into the quarry, but there was nothing to see, only the rocks and forest on its distant floor.

"What about the Bear?" Alexandra said to him. He seemed more like a man now, and less like a wizard, in his white undershirt with Bobby's blood on it.

"Perhaps it is better this way," said the Wizard. "He would not have survived what was coming for him when you published his story."

"You knew," cried Alexandra. She was surprised to hear herself shrieking. She knelt and kissed Bobby's forehead, his face. His eyes were closed, but his chest rose and fell. Neven stood beside them again, looking at the Wizard.

"Yes," the Wizard said. "Wait for a minute." He went to the man Bobby had shot in the shoulder and tended to him, then returned just as quickly. "Kurilkov asked me to watch for certain names and we marked them in our system. Stoyan Lazarov's name was marked in this way, when I searched it for you. I told Kurilkov, although I did not think it was important until he became even more interested. He told me to follow you and frighten you, but he did not want to tell me why. Then I asked myself what he was hiding even from me."

The Wizard wiped his hands on his pants. He gestured to Bobby. "Here, help me to lift him, on that side. I am sure Kurilkov would have turned this on me, and on the police. Probably he planned to tell the press that I had invented this story about him. I learned two days ago that he was going to kill me, once he had killed you. His men have gotten away, of course, but I will find them later."

"We will never give you what you want," Alexandra said. Her voice trembled, but she made herself say it. Neven had hoisted Bobby up and she put Bobby's other arm around her shoulders, but the Wizard moved her aside and took her place.

"Young lady," he said. "You will not have to give me anything. I worked with Asparuh Iliev for several years, and I have no doubt that a copy of Stoyan Lazarov's story—whatever form it took— is already with the right newspaper. Also, I feel sure that Kurilkov's death will be determined a suicide."

Alexandra, standing by Bobby as they moved him, reached out to touch his hair. His eyes had opened and they seemed to see her. He had given the story to the papers, as surely as he'd been able to call a friend to bring him a car when he needed it. He must have mailed a copy from the hotel where they'd stayed with Stoycho, she thought, or somewhere else on their journey. That was Bobby. They had a photograph now, too, to complete the story.

Then she understood that Stoycho was really gone, and why.

The Wizard put a hand on Bobby's forehead, as if checking for fever. "I must go back to Sofia to speak with the press. I will call the hospital in Novlievo before you arrive there. We have not lost our best taxi driver, yet."

Neven put Bobby gently in the back seat of the Ford. Irina and Lenka braced him between them and Alexandra climbed into the front with Neven.

"Go fast," she said.

Afterward, she remembered only one moment of the ride down through the woods, and felt she might have dreamed it: a brindled flank and tail among the trees, a creature slipping back into the wild.

Eighty-one

The next evening, the television news in Baba Vanka's kitchen showed the Sofia Chief of Police, his big head toward the camera. He was reading his statement about Kurilkov, Minister of Roads, killed in a startling accident—probably suicide— at the quarry near a former labor camp called Zelenets. An investigation in process had already determined that Kurilkov had once been a guard there; he had apparently gone back to view the site. It seemed, too, that he had bought all the land on which the quarry and the mines had stood, years before. If Kurilkov had not taken his own life first, the Wizard said somberly to the camera, he might have been prosecuted for his crimes there, crimes that would soon be documented in the newspapers through the testimony of a deceased musician, Stoyan Lazarov. The mining project would be halted for further inquiry. A television anchor followed this statement with a report on the discovery of mass graves in the woods near the quarry. Now, at last, there were journalists everywhere, pushing with their cameras through the brush, striding past the buildings where Neven had looked silently out of a doorway.

Alexandra, sitting between Bobby and Neven,

kept her hand on Bobby's sound leg. She knew she would be writing again soon; she could already feel that same hand moving across the page, and later touching the keys of her laptop. This time, her stories and poems would be about a new world. Perhaps they would become essays, too, she thought—articles, the activism of the pen.

The following morning, Alexandra went to say goodbye to Irina and Lenka where they were staying outside Morsko. Baba Vanka's son had offered to drive the two women back to Plovdiv. They didn't talk about Stoyan Lazarov's story, but as she sat with them, Irina said, "He would have loved you, my dear. You are brave, and he valued courage and had to use it himself, all his life." When she kissed Irina goodbye, Alexandra saw the old woman's brooch glinting in the shadows. In the center of it, among vines and flowers, there was a pale image like the face of an apostle.

At Bovech, on their return for dinner with the Lazarovi, the house looked almost the way it had the first time they had visited—except, as Bobby pointed out with a faint smile, the curtains were now open. They knocked at the door and Neven answered it, the way Alexandra had dreamed so many times he might. He kissed her on each cheek, then helped Bobby navigate with his crutches through the doorway. She had wanted to see Neven since he'd left Morsko with his parents a couple of days before—she supposed she could call them his parents, now—but he was formal, quiet; it was Vera who hurried forward to embrace Alexandra and stroke her hair. Milen Radev, in his wheelchair, squeezed her proffered hand. Vera put Bobby on the bed in the kitchen, so he could keep his leg up.

They sat down to dinner; Neven poured *rakiya* and toasted Bobby and Alexandra and the memory of Stoyan Lazarov. Alexandra watched him—his beauty, his old-fashioned reserve. What, she thought, would the rest of his life be like, in this world of little work, much poverty, vulgar riches for a few? Despite Stoyan Lazarov's talents, his courage and his revelation, people like the Lazarovi had only their dignity, in which they would fade away. When they had all begun to eat, Neven told her that he had returned to his work in Burgas but could not concentrate, and then, finally, allowed his golden eyes to meet hers across the table.

After they'd finished dinner, and Vera had put out slices of cake, Alexandra collected herself to speak. "I have been thinking," she said, but for a moment she found it hard to go on. The image of Jack came to her. He was sitting at one corner of the table, his face full of mischief.

She turned to Vera and Neven. "I have some money left, what I saved to travel this year." She

690

stopped again, struggled to speak frankly. "If you would like, I could help send you to Venice with *gospodin* Lazarov's ashes. I don't know how you get permission to have a burial in a place like that, but there must be a way."

Bobby stared at her—she had not told him what she'd been pondering—and then he translated for Vera and Milen. Vera's gaze grew enormous, dark. Neven made a slight gesture and shook his head, although his eyes shone.

Alexandra said, "I don't think there is enough money for you all to go, but two of you could."

There was a rustle of talk in Bulgarian, Vera raising a hand to her face, Milen patting his wheelchair, resigned.

Neven nodded. "My parents can't travel so far," he said softly. "They know that they cannot manage this. But I am thinking about it—I mean to say, I could go. If you would not mind to come with me."

Eighty-two

A shop in Prague, sometime in 1937 or 1938, an ANTIKVARNA, *one that specializes in music. The man opening the door is in his early twenties, a foreigner with a violin case in his hand. He is tall and dark-haired and walks with an energy in his step that makes the shop owner look up*

*from cataloging. The owner knows this type:
they're usually poor students, but occasionally
they have money tucked away, and the passion
to spend it on a treasure. He leans over his
books to glance at the young man's violin case,
which is good quality, and then at his shoes,
which have been worn a while but are also
excellent. And highly polished.*

*The young man tips his hat, then takes it off.
"I saw your sign about antique music," he says
in French.*

*Well, if they have no other language in
common, this one will do.*

*"Yes," says the shop owner. "What are you
looking for?"*

*"Nothing in particular." The young man's eyes
gleam.*

"Violinist, I see?"

"Yes."

"Collector?"

*The young man laughs. "Of melodies, yes.
Expensive scores—I'm sorry, no."*

*His smile is so charming, his air of unbeatable
energy and unbreakable good spirits so
winning, that the shop owner smiles, too, and
shuts the catalog. "I have some things that are
very fine, but not necessarily expensive," he
says cautiously. "And for the violin."*

*The young man sets his case on the counter,
but with a courteous gesture, where it is not in*

the way. "Thank you," he says. "That would be interesting."

The shop owner is still finding out about him, however. "Are you here from Vienna, by chance?" He knows from the boy's accent that he isn't Viennese, of course.

Stoyan Lazarov laughs again. "Yes," he says.

The shop owner whistles. "I was there last night, for your concert. I wouldn't have missed it, no matter how much it cost. Well, you got a serious reception, I'd say."

Stoyan grins. The Philharmonic had played Tchaikovsky's Serenade for Strings, and at the end of it the students in the upper tiers had cheered and stamped for five whole minutes. Then, daringly, Stoyan's string quartet had played Dvořák's American Quartet right here in the composer's city, and the students of Prague had gone wild, tossed their hats and even their coats into the air. In fact, everyone had gone wild. Afterward, an old man who had known Dvořák personally had presented their conductor with a volume of memoirs, and women had thrown flowers at them as they left the concert hall. Tonight they will play Dvořák's Symphony No. 3, their final appearance.

"I've got something that would interest you," the shop owner says. "I don't show this to everyone, but you are a violinist and this will one day be even more valuable." He goes to a *cabinet behind the counter and unlocks it, looks through several piles of brittle scores. What he wants is wrapped in brown paper and tied with string, a special treatment. He unties it and opens it up on the counter in front of the young man. "This is very old, you know."*

Stoyan Lazarov leans over to see the score lying exposed before him. The paper is discolored and yet looks strong, and it is faintly ruled for music. To his astonishment, the score on it is handwritten, a manuscript. The hand in which it's written makes something lurch inside him— it races across the staff, scratched rapidly onto it in spidery, resounding flourishes. He knows from his training in Bach and Handel that this is a page from the Baroque, but it is also unlike anything he's ever seen. A virtuosic work, whatever it is, and only a virtuoso would be able to play it, especially at the pace he imagines it deserves.

He looks up at the shop owner, who is watching him closely. "What is it?"

The owner opens the next page—the piece seems to consist of just three pages, but they offer plenty of opportunity for repetition and perhaps further embellishment. They are crudely stitched together at one edge. Stoyan has begun to hear some of the lines of the melody, off the page; it races, yes, but glows with emotion, too. This is something quite different from his beloved Bach.

The shop owner turns over the last sheet and points to a couple of small letters: PV, 1715 it says, in a neat hand completely unlike the taut wildness of the notation.

"I believe," says the shop owner, "that this symbol here stands for Vivaldi, Antonio Vivaldi, the Venetian composer. You see. It is the right style, in the music, and Vivaldi was a priest, so the P could mean Prete."

Stoyan touches the lower edge of the last page, but carefully. "Yes, I know his name, and a piece or two, for chamber orchestra." He thinks for a moment. He has long been aware of the concerti Bach had based on Vivaldi's. Also a piece the great Fritz Kreisler had claimed was Vivaldi's and then had revealed just a few years earlier as his own composition. Stoyan has always vaguely associated the name with something quaint and tinkling, not with the passionate impatience he sees on the page before him.

"My colleague in Rome has helped to examine other scores, but I have never been able to show him this one. He left Prague before I received this. He wrote me that they have found much more of Vivaldi's music in Italy, these last years, but it is all in libraries and private collections."

"Where did you get this, then?" Stoyan can't take his eyes off the manuscript. The sheer energy of it looks alive on the page, as if the ink has not yet dried. Only the two initials at the end stand still—perhaps the composer had penned them later, in a calmer state.

"I found it inside a book—a portfolio of engravings of Venice—that I sold some years ago. For a good price, in fact. But I removed this because the buyer did not care about music."

"I think," Stoyan says thoughtfully, "that it is a cadenza."

The shopkeeper stands listening.

"Yes," says Stoyan. "You see, it has no title or number at the top, and as I look at the melody, I think that it belongs to a larger piece of music. This would have been a special addition to a work that the composer had already written, a solo—perhaps a spectacular way to end the piece. A challenge."

"Would you like to play it?" the shopkeeper says suddenly. There is no one in the shop.

"It will be quite difficult, the first time. Do you have a music stand?"

He does—a stand nearly as old and elegant as the score. They arrange it together and Stoyan tunes his violin.

It is indeed difficult. It taunts him—the hand of the master, racing ahead of his across the page. This Venetian priest had been able to compose *like an angel, but also to play like a devil, apparently. The melody makes his heart pound. There is still no one in the shop, so he tries again. The piece is very short, written with a great range, some of it so high on the finger-board that he has to strain his carefully trained ear for the pitches. It is elaborate beyond its own logic, and yet a strange sweetness rises off the notes. It will take weeks for him to make his hands do this, and months to memorize properly. It is, he thinks, the kind of gem a great violinist might make his own, his signature, his encore. And he has never heard it before— possibly no one living in the last two centuries ever heard it.*

He might have to eat bread and water for a long time, of course. He turns to the shopkeeper, who is nodding.

"How much?" says Stoyan Lazarov.

Eighty-three

The train trip from Milan into the Santa Lucia station, and then the *vaporetto* ride along the Grand Canal, had the effect of putting Alexandra into a stupor. Despite—or maybe because of— her exhaustion, it was a stupor of beauty. Neven settled next to her at the front of the boat, where they could see together the beige and slate-blue buildings rising up on densely laden islands. Between his shoes sat a travel bag heavy with a polished wooden urn, and all too light with human ashes. It was late afternoon, late May, 2008. Neven had placed his suitcase, which looked forty years old and like the ones Alexandra's grandparents owned, next to him on the ferry seats.

Alexandra had with her everything she'd brought to Bulgaria, except a few garments she felt she didn't need anymore; those she'd left folded on a park bench outside her hostel in Sofia. She wore Bobby's necklace of brass and carnelian over her blouse, worrying it with one hand from time to time; it would be years, and several repairs—and a whole future life of writing and motherhood and teaching—before she stopped wearing it every day. In the pocket of her sweater she carried a poem, folded into a thick square, Bobby's most recent gift.

"This is the first time I've written one in English," he'd said. "Written in English from the beginning. Not translated."

The poem was entitled "A Bird," and she had already memorized the opening, the way the startling first words merged into an equally sharp second and third line, the restrained flow of grief as it was transmuted into history, the beautiful and unexpected verb he'd chosen to imagine Jack's last moments.

Now there are spires in sight, churches that fill entire islands, ornaments curled like the shells of snails. Water splashing and shining in place of land. She rubs her tired face and looks at Neven, and he takes her hand, as Bobby might have. They sit there comfortably, her heart beating only a little harder than usual. The *vaporetto* passes gondolas the way a bus passes pedestrians. Now they are staring at palaces, which seem to bob at the water's edge.

Suddenly Neven laughs. He points to the sidewalks, the people walking over the little bridges, the edge of the piazzas. "Look," he says.

"What?" Alexandra cranes, without letting go of his hand.

"The people," Neven says. "They are dressed modern."

At a wharf for Piazza di San Marco, they cross onto Venetian soil, onto ancient pavement, and stand collecting themselves and their baggage. Alexandra has booked them into a small hotel six blocks from the Piazza, whatever six blocks means in Venice. First they wander for a few minutes, staring at the pink cliff of the Doge's Palace and frequently setting down their suitcases. The Piazza is very much larger than she'd imagined, and the flocks of pigeons settling in it are vast, like birds on an Antarctic shore. She recognizes the Campanile and the long, long colonnades. Presiding over all of it, the Cathedral of San Marco, where Vivaldi's father played in an orchestra even before his son was born. Alexandra remembers walking into the church at Velinski *manastir* with Bobby. She wants to go inside San Marco, once they've found their hotel, to see it for him, and for Stoyan. She tries to remember whether there are candles to buy and light, in Catholic churches. She tries to picture Jack's face, and finds it has faded a little.

Neven is silent, and when she asks him what he's thinking he says soberly, "I just realized that I have not ever been anywhere."

Their hotel is indeed small, little wider than its own front door. An orange tree in a pot stands to one side of the door, filling half the alley, so that passersby have to skirt it. Just beyond, a covered bridge joins two buildings; Alexandra wishes the bridge were part of the hotel, but maybe they will be able to see it from their room. Room, singular—she's reserved only one at an already heart-stopping rate, four nights. Then, with some meals and their plane tickets, her savings from the last three years will be gone.

But their view, when the hotelkeeper shows it to them, is better than she'd expected: they look from the third floor across to ornate windows and down into a canal as narrow as an afterthought, a byway that only the tiniest motorboats can traverse, their engines cut to walking. An aroma of sewage and fish and mildew drifts up from it, sharply different from the fresh air of Morsko; she can hear the slap of little waves catching the wakes of bigger boats on bigger canals nearby. In spite of the smell, Alexandra draws a long breath. The room is correspondingly small, and dominated not by the twin beds she had requested but by a canopied monster—a palanquin with gold velvet curtains, the worse for wear like the rest of the city. At home, it would look impossible, she thinks, and in Bulgaria peculiar. Here, it is perfect, but for her a disaster. She tries to ask the hotel-keeper for another option; there is none, *signora* —she notes that word, for a married lady. He goes out smiling, not even apologetic.

Neven sets Stoyan Lazarov's urn on the floor, next to the falsely painted bureau. She hangs up her sweater, then takes it down again. She washes her hands in the sink near the tiny closet and doesn't look at Neven. He has opened his suitcase and is unpacking into the bottom of the bureau, politely leaving the top drawers for her, as if they will be staying for weeks. He looks taller than ever in the close room—broader, his arms longer; he seems to brush the ceiling.

"Let's go find some dinner," she says. The bed is awkward enough, and the dimensions of the room, but the main problem now is the exquisite air of lassitude, the drowsy beauty outside the window, the damask hangings, the warm air.

Out in the alleys and squares, it strikes her as even worse: a romantic twilight has fallen, and the hotels and restaurants have turned on soft lights above their doors. The slop of water in the dark is gorgeous, rougher now; a breeze has come up. Alexandra pauses before a window heaped with *frutti di mare*, their legs and tentacles and sharp-edged shells displayed in a rosy mound. She and Neven smile at each other, embarrassed by the abundance and the question of price. In the end, they find a busy outdoor restaurant and sit eating spaghetti and long sticks of bread. They order some wine, and then a whole bottle of wine; Alexandra finds it's like drinking a ruby.

"You are as hungry as wolves," Neven tells her. "Do you say that in English?"

They wander into the vast Piazza again, to view it in its cloak of lights, a dazzle that reaches out across the water. Alexandra has never seen so many beautiful people in one city—tourists, yes, but also Italian women in high heels and narrow skirts, and Italian men in their slim suits, shirts open at the throat. The doors of the cathedral stand open, shedding light into the dark end of the square, and they enter under the prancing bronze horses Alexandra has always wanted to photograph.

Inside, there is more light than in Bulgarian churches—candles and electric chandeliers that make the gold ceiling glitter—but like those churches it is filled with Byzantine faces. Neven takes her hand again; she finds she has been waiting, and this time her stomach drops inside her. They amble the length and breadth of the church, trying to guess where the orchestra sat in Vivaldi's time. The cathedral's ceiling billows in her head with the wine, and she pauses to look straight up into one of the domes. Neven comes to stand beside her, putting an arm quietly around her shoulders. After they leave the cathedral, they drift along the alleys, getting lost for a long while. When they find their hotel door, Alexandra walks in first, up the narrow spiraling stairs.

In their room, she turns on the lamp and Neven draws the curtains and takes off his shoes, lining them up side by side just under the bureau. Alexandra goes into the bathroom for a few minutes, and spends them washing her face and trying to arrange her thoughts. When she comes out again, he's standing still fully dressed beside the bed, tall and serious, his amber eyes fixed on her. She knows only a little about him, but because she knows so much about where he has come from, it doesn't seem to matter. He strokes her hair back on each side of her head and tucks it behind her ears. That soft hum has returned to the room, but she can't tell whether it comes from the city outside or the urn in its shadowed corner.

The next day, she thinks, they will see the door of the church where the Red Priest was baptized. A trembling has set up shop just below her rib-cage. They will walk for hours, visit the *palazzi* and museums Stoyan Lazarov longed for, and rest in the shade of buildings where Vivaldi might have sat to cool himself. They will step into the acoustics of the big church of the Ospedale della Pietà, built two decades after Vivaldi died, where Stoyan Lazarov would have played his violin if the borders of Europe had been drawn differently. They will walk for miles, the way people are supposed to in Venice, drawn on by every turn, and by ghosts.

Author's Note

I first visited Bulgaria, a country of spectacular natural beauty, in 1989; in fact, I arrived a week after the fall of the Berlin Wall, which was quickly followed by the collapse of forty-five years of Bulgarian communist dictatorship. The morning my train entered this mysterious country, hidden for so long behind the Iron Curtain, I woke early to see fields, villages, and forested mountains under a gray sky. Arriving in Sofia, the capital, I found it both elegantly historic and bleakly East-Bloc-communist. Like the young protagonist of *The Shadow Land*, I felt I had somehow come home.

Bulgaria, currently a nation of about seven million people, is an ancient place—the first version of a Bulgarian state on this territory was established in A.D. 681—whose history has also been characterized by centuries of occupation and cultural blending, especially under the Byzantine and Ottoman empires. The Bulgarian lands are some of the most archaeologically rich in Europe, with sites that were among the first settled by Homo sapiens—and on up through the Thracian, ancient Greek, Roman, Byzantine, medieval Bulgarian, and Ottoman periods. As a modern nation, however, Bulgaria is relatively young, dating from 1878 and its liberation from the Ottoman Empire.

During twenty-plus years of returning to a post-communist landscape there, I married a Bulgarian man and acquired a family, friends, and colleagues in my new country. Along the way, I dreamed of writing a novel set entirely in Bulgaria—one that would draw on aspects of its communist experi-ence, which has already become remote for younger generations. However, it was not until I found myself standing in the closed-off ruins of a forced-labor camp that I discovered the heart of my story.

Between 1944 and 1989, and especially up to 1962, as many as a hundred camps (by some estimates) served the needs of the communist regime, brutalizing a spectrum of citizens who ranged from Nazi collaborators to loyal communists, political dissidents to young people targeted for small cultural infringements—and others rounded up on false charges. Many were held without trial or sentencing. These camps were based on and imposed by the Soviet system. Their existence—partly unknown to the population, partly known and feared—provided an important way for the regime to maintain control. An ultimate count of the incarcerated has never been established; most historians agree that they numbered at least in the tens of thousands.

Most of the sites of the camps are now lost to remote rural landscapes, and their victims are overwhelmingly un-memorialized. What, I wondered, looking around at the desolate ruins of barracks and guardhouses, would have given anyone a chance of survival in such a place? And how could I contribute in some small way to a growing movement to examine the recent history of my beloved adoptive country? I knew as I stood there that my characters and I would have to reckon with this past.

The resulting book is very much a work of fiction—and all its characters are fictional figures. In it, I've written about imaginary places based on real Bulgarian villages, towns, rivers, and mountains. And I've tried to stay sharply true to history—especially to the realities that camp survivors and their families later reported—without trespassing too closely on the sacredness of individual experiences. I'm indebted in my effort to Tzvetan Todorov's work *Voices from the Gulag: Life and Death in Communist Bulgaria* (translated by Robert Zaretsky; Penn State Press, 1999), to those individuals who granted me personal interviews, and to the organizations, journalists, artists, and writers in Bulgaria who are courageously exploring a difficult legacy. I offer them my sincere respect and gratitude.

Acknowledgments

I'd like to thank the many people in Bulgaria and the U.S.—family, friends, colleagues—who made this book possible. Those who read and reread it or conversed with me about it are too numerous for me to name without risk of omission, and details of the assistance they've rendered me during years of writing and editing would not fit on this page. The same is true of the many writers, historians, journalists, and musicians whose own work has informed this novel. However, I would like to thank personally a few people who provided extraordinary help with research, travel, and fact checking: Dimana Trankova, Boris Deliradev, Anthony Georgieff, Jeremiah Chamberlin, Lily Honigberg, Corina Kesler, Georgi Gospodinov, and Vanya Tomova. Thanks also to my peerless agent, Amy Williams.

Finally, and above all, profound gratitude to my editor at Ballantine, Jennifer Hershey, mentor and guardian angel of this story.

I have composed my work of fiction in a spirit of respectful grief for those whose lives were touched by the real history on which it is based.

About the Author

ELIZABETH KOSTOVA is the author of the best-selling novels *The Historian* and *The Swan Thieves*. She graduated from Yale and holds an MFA from the University of Michigan, where she won a Hopwood Award for Novel-in-Progress. She is co-founder in Bulgaria of the Elizabeth Kostova Foundation for Creative Writing, which brings together writers in English and Bulgarian for workshops and other programs, and fosters the translation and publication of Bulgarian writers in the English-speaking world. To learn more about Bulgarian literature or apply to EKF's programs, see:

www.ekf.bg

and

www.contemporarybulgarianwriters.com.

elizabethkostova.com

Center Point Large Print
600 Brooks Road / PO Box 1
Thorndike, ME 04986-0001 USA

(207) 568-3717

US & Canada:
1 800 929-9108
www.centerpointlargeprint.com